KNOWLEDGE
A VISUAL COMPENDIUM
MAKING SENSE OF OUR WORLD

KNOWLEDGE
A VISUAL COMPENDIUM
MAKING SENSE OF OUR WORLD

Senior Editors Dr. Virien Chopra, Rebecca Fry, Rupa Rao
Project Editors Kathakali Banerjee, Bipasha Roy
Senior Art Editors Ragini Rawat, Jessica Tapolcai
Project Art Editors Revati Anand, Heena Sharma
Senior US Editor Megan Douglass
Editorial Team Zarak Rais, Suchismita Banerjee,
Agnibesh Das, Deeksha Micek, Neha Ruth Samuel
Design Team Anastasia Baliyan, Aparajita Sen, Vidit Vashisht
Senior Picture Researcher Nishwan Rasool
Picture Research Team Geetam Biswas, Geetika Bhandari
Deputy Managing Art Editor Shreya Anand
Managing Editors Kingshuk Ghoshal, Carine Tracanelli
Managing Art Editors Govind Mittal, Anna Hall
DTP Designers Vikram Singh, Pawan Kumar,
Rakesh Kumar, Mohammad Rizwan, Syed Md Farhan
Hi-Res Coordinator Jagtar Singh

Production Editor Anita Yadav
Pre-Production Manager Balwant Singh
Production Manager Pankaj Sharma
Production Controller Jack Matts
Jacket Designer Rhea Menon
Senior Jackets Coordinator Priyanka Sharma Saddi
Jacket Design Development Manager Sophia MTT
DK India Creative Head Malavika Talukder

Illustrator Mark Clifton

Lead contributors Lizzie Munsey, Scarlett O'Hara
Contributors Riley Black, Chris Clennett, Prof. Adam Hart,
Derek Harvey, Cathriona Hickey, Jayne Miller,
Prof. Obert Bernard Mlambo, Giles Sparrow, Chris Woodford

Fact Checker Steve Hoffman
Sensitivity Reader Sarosh Arif

Consultants Jon Astbury, Riley Black, Dr. Nemata A Blyden, Roger Bridgman, Peter Chrisp, Chris Clennett, Gareth Dawson, Cynthia Fisher, Clive Gifford, Dr. Sama Haq, Derek Harvey, Prof. Adam Hart, Cathriona Hickey, Jayne Miller, Prof. Obert Bernard Mlambo, Jessica Mooney, Douglas Palmer, Ian Ridpath, Kristina Routh, Giles Sparrow, David Stuttard, Chris Woodford

First American Edition, 2024
Published in the United States by DK Publishing,
a division of Penguin Random House LLC
1745 Broadway, 20th Floor, New York, NY 10019

Copyright © 2024 Dorling Kindersley Limited
24 25 26 27 28 10 9 8 7 6 5 4 3 2 1
001–337263–Oct/2024

A catalog record for this book is available from the Library of Congress.
ISBN 978-0-5938-4377-2

DK books are available at special discounts when purchased in bulk for sales promotions, premiums, fund-raising, or educational use. For details, contact:
DK Publishing Special Markets,
1745 Broadway, 20th Floor, New York, NY 10019
SpecialSales@dk.com

Printed and bound in China

www.dk.com

MIX
Paper | Supporting
responsible forestry
FSC™ C018179

This book was made with Forest Stewardship Council™ certified paper—one small step in DK's commitment to a sustainable future. Learn more at **www.dk.com/uk/information/sustainability**

CONTENTS

MAKING SENSE OF OUR WORLD

This book is a celebration of the many different and amazing ways that humans have ordered and made sense of the world around them—organizing, naming, and listing everything from animals to space missions.

Patterns in nature

Throughout history, people have noticed patterns in areas of life, or in collections of certain things. More than 2,000 years ago, the ancient Greeks were masters of classification—the process of organizing things into groups based on their similarities. The philosopher Aristotle studied nature and divided living things into two "kingdoms"—animals and plants. The animals were then split into further groups based on how they moved: "Did they walk, fly, or swim?"

Geographer-historian Herodotus created one of the earliest maps of the world, based on his research into historical and geographical accounts from travelers. Hippocrates studied human illness and medicine, while Pythagoras taught that the universe follows mathematical rules.

Tracking the stars

It wasn't just the Greeks who were intrigued by the natural world. Wherever people settled, they began creating systems that attempted to explain and categorize things. The night skies were often one of the first things people began to study, because they realized the importance of tracking the sun, the moon, and stars in their everyday lives.

▲ **Plotting the stars**
Invented by the ancient Greeks, astrolabes were refined by Islamic astronomers and used worldwide to measure the position of the stars and to navigate.

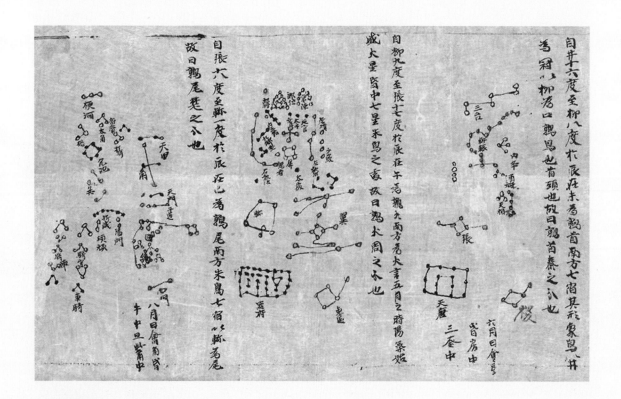

◀ **Cave treasure**
The *Dunhuang Star Chart*, which shows 157 star clusters, was discovered in a cave in China. It dates from the 7th century, making it the earliest star chart ever found.

The ancient Greek astronomers divided the stars into patterns we call constellations. But they weren't the only ones to do this—people in China, Assyria, Egypt, Polynesia, Australia, India, and North America were also noticing patterns in the stars.

The constellations don't stay in fixed positions. They shift across the year, moving in patterns that people learned to predict and to connect with the timing of important events in the farming year. So, star charts and atlases were carefully drawn up to track the movement of the constellations, stars, and other bodies around the night sky.

Looking to the East

During the middle ages, there were centers of learning all over the world, where early scientists investigated what they did and didn't know. For example, the city of Baghdad in the Persian Empire contained a library and center of learning called the "House of Wisdom." Here, in the 9th century, the mathematician Al Khwarizmi wrote books about math that changed how the world understood and used numbers. His ideas were translated into Latin, and inspired mathematicians everywhere. They are the basis of the modern algebra we use today.

▲ Turning around
This illustration shows Nicolaus Copernicus's model of the solar system, with the sun in the middle. Until the 16th century, it was widely thought that Earth was at the center of the universe.

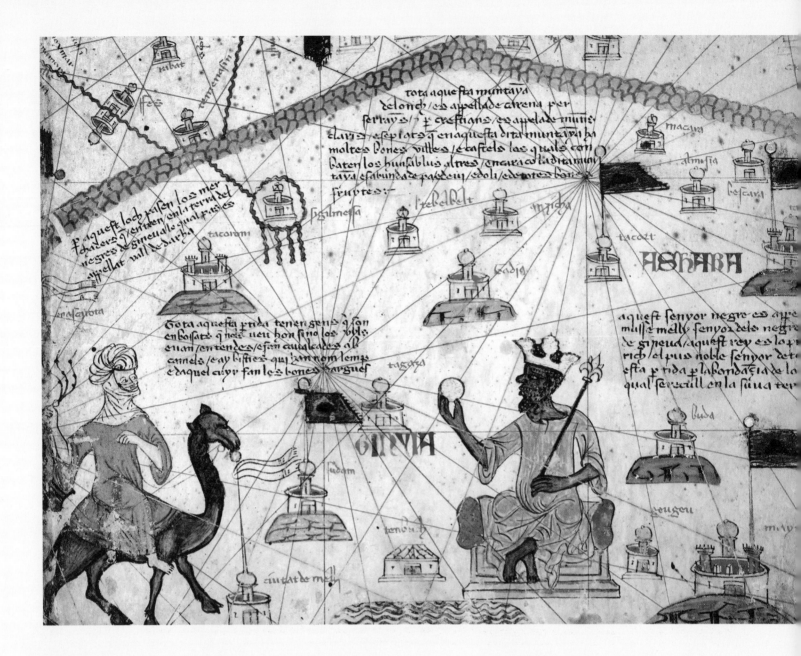

▲ Mapping the world
The *Catalan Atlas*, drawn in 1375, is a detailed map of the world based on accounts by sailors and explorers. Here, Mansa Musa, the ruler of the Empire of Mali in Africa, is shown on his throne, as well as one of the Tuareg people on a camel.

China was home to similar centers of academic excellence. In the 11th century, scientist and engineer Su Song studied and plotted the stars and designed a mechanical, water-driven astronomical clock. He also studied the ingredients that could be used as medicine, collecting samples of more than a thousand different types of plants, and compiling entries about each of them in a book called the *Bencao Tujing*. His book covered a range of other related scientific subjects, such as botany, zoology, and the study of minerals and metals. In the 16th century, another Chinese scientist, Li Shizhen, compiled a more extensive list.

New old ideas

In the 15th and 16th centuries, countries across Europe experienced a literary and cultural revolution, which has become known as the Renaissance. People studied ideas from ancient Greece and Rome, and built on them to create new ideas and make scientific discoveries. For example, Polish astronomer Nicolaus Copernicus was able to show that Earth travels around the sun—before this time, people had thought it was the other way around. The Renaissance was also a time of incredible artistic creation, with talented artists such as Michelangelo and da Vinci studying and portraying the human form.

A scientific revolution

In the 17th and 18th centuries, a European "Age of Enlightenment" followed the Renaissance. There was an explosion in scientific study, and a huge number of classification systems were invented to help scientists explain the world around them. This was the beginning of the modern era of science in Europe, with scientists applying more rigorous methods to their investigations, and using their own logic to make discoveries, rather than following older teachings.

Many of the European Enlightenment scientists were financially supported by royal families or extremely wealthy people. Science was now popular, so having a famous scientist on call became fashionable. For the scientists, it meant they could focus on their research, without having financial worries. Many wealthy men, and even some monarchs, became interested in science too, and studied it almost like a hobby.

Incredible inventions

New inventions helped change people's ideas about the world. For example, Italian scientist Galileo Galilei invented a new type of telescope, which could magnify objects by 20 times. This new telescope allowed him to look more closely at space objects such as the moon, Venus, and Jupiter, observing them in more detail than ever before. He drew detailed sketches of the phases of the moon, which included drawings of the craters on its surface.

Mendeleev's table

As the Enlightenment progressed, science, literature, and art exploded into different strands. Scientists, thinkers, writers, and artists all studied the world, and used their different methods to organize and depict it. They continued to develop new theories, as well as refining those that already existed.

One pioneering scientist, Russian chemist Dmitri Mendeleev, studied the properties of elements—the basic building blocks of the universe. He arranged them in order of their atomic mass (the weight of an atom of an element), and noticed that there were patterns in the properties that the elements shared. He even left gaps in his new "periodic table," which

he correctly predicted would be filled with elements that were yet to be discovered. We still use his table today, and new elements have indeed been discovered and added to it. The modern table uses atomic number (the number of protons in an atom) instead of atomic mass.

The Father of Classification

The Enlightenment was also a time when many Europeans set off in ships to explore new continents, taking with them scientists, naturalists, and artists to study and record the plants and wildlife they found in these new lands. The naturalists returned with

▼ **Perfect form**
The Vitruvian Man, drawn by artist and scientist Leonardo da Vinci in 1490, depicts his study of the proportions of the human body by applying geometry and mathematics.

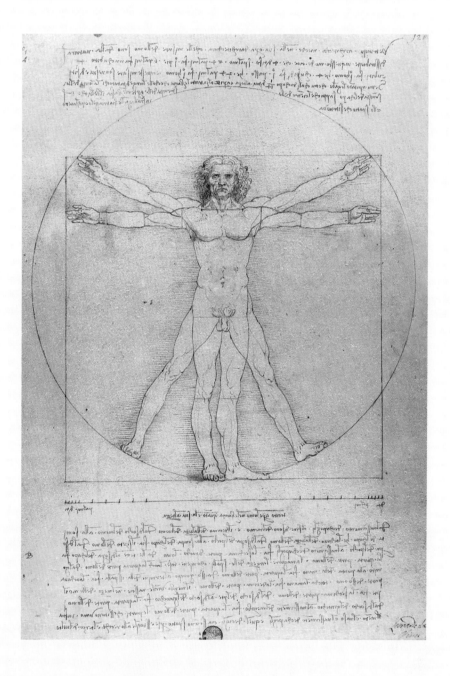

drawings and specimens of exotic species, but didn't know how they were related to the ones that they already knew.

Luckily, back in Europe, a Swedish biologist called Carl Linnaeus had been working on a way of classifying all living things, which we call taxonomy. He was a botanist at heart, so Linnaeus's quest for organization began with the many plants he found in his home land of Sweden, but soon expanded to include animals. Linnaeus's classification system allowed naturalists to look at the features of any plant or animal they found and compare it with his descriptions, to learn what it was and

how it fitted into the rest of the natural world. His amazing taxonomic system is still in use today. It divides living things into groups, based on their shared features. These groups are then further subdivided, getting more and more specific. Each life form is given a scientific name in two parts. The first part shows which group it belongs to, and the second pinpoints its unique species.

Darwin's finches

One famous example of a naturalist who set off to explore the world is British biologist Charles Darwin. His journey aboard the HMS *Beagle* began in 1831 and would take five years—traveling in a loop around the globe, with a particular focus on South America. He studied the different types of life that occurred in different places, and collected samples of them to take back to Britain. While he was in the Galápagos Islands, Darwin observed that there were different species of finches (a type of bird) on each island, and that each species had a beak that helped it to collect the type of food that was available on that island. This observation led Darwin to develop his theory of evolution: the idea that over time animal species change and adapt to suit their environments.

The quest for understanding

The human quest for understanding took off centuries ago, but it continues to this day. Modern technology has allowed us to look at things in more detail and travel farther than ever before. We have sent spacecraft to the planets and moons. We have created telescopes that are so powerful we can look beyond our solar system, and see a whole range of new space bodies to classify. We have created microscopes powerful enough to look inside our cells to find DNA, and then studied the tiny chemicals that make up the DNA in order to learn what each of them does for us.

Evidence-based science is now used to classify, catalog, and categorize everything in our lives, whether that's the muscles in our bodies, the languages we speak, or the types of cheese we eat. Humans continue to study the world and its contents, and find new ways to bring order to their discoveries.

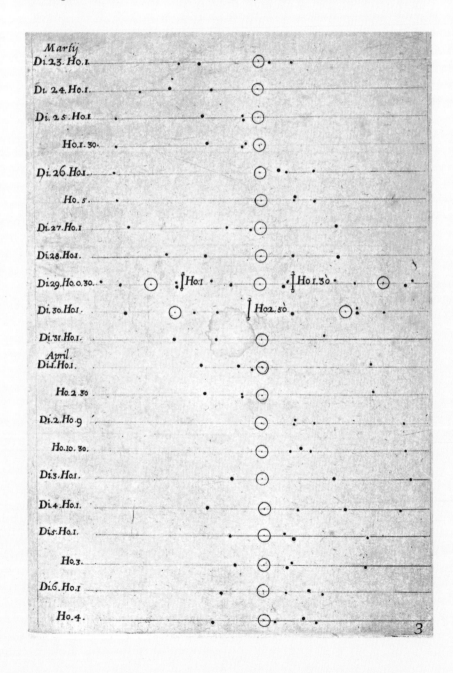

▼ **Jupiter's moons**
Italian scientist, Galileo Galilei, turned his new telescope on the stars and planets. Below are his notes from March and April, 1612, showing the movement of Jupiter's four largest moons.

CHRYSOMELA, CICADA, AND CICINDELA.

N.º 1 to 18, Different Species of Chrysomelæ, 19 to 26 Cicadæ, 27 to 30 Cicindelæ.

London Published as the Act directs Feb.ᵉ 10 1800 by J. Wilkes

◀ **Insects in order**
This page showing beetle species is from an early 19th-century illustrated dictionary of arts, sciences, and literature. It shows just how quickly the Linnaean system of classification became general knowledge.

EARTH
and our
UNIVERSE

TYPES OF GALAXY

SPIRAL

Pinwheel Galaxy (M101)

Milky Way (artist's impression)

Bode's Galaxy (M81)

NGC 1365

Condor Galaxy (NGC 6872)

Andromeda Galaxy

Whirlpool Galaxy

Triangulum Galaxy

Sunflower Galaxy (M63)

Sombrero Galaxy (M104)

NGC 1300

NGC 1512

ELLIPTICAL

M60

Virgo A (M87)

M49 (NGC 4472)

NGC 4697

Centaurus A (NGC 5128)

NGC 2865

NGC 4150

NGC 2768

Hercules A

LENTICULAR

Spindle Galaxy (NGC 3115)

NGC 4866

NGC 2787

Cartwheel Galaxy

NGC 4111

NGC 5866

Large Magellanic Cloud

Cigar Galaxy (M82)

NGC 1427A

Hoag's Object Ring Galaxy

UGC 8091

A selection of galaxies of the four types

Types of
GALAXY

The universe contains large collections of stars, planets, gas, and dust called galaxies. They can be grouped into types based on their shape.

Astronomers think that the universe is larger than we can imagine. We can only see a certain part of it—the "observable universe," which is the area of space surveyed by telescopes. This region contains all the galaxies we know of. Based on their shape, these galaxies can be divided into four types—spiral, elliptical, lenticular, and irregular.

Galaxies such as the Pinwheel Galaxy and the Whirlpool Galaxy are spiral in shape—their arms wind through space like a Catherine wheel. Our galaxy, the Milky Way, is also a spiral galaxy, but it appears as a band of light in the sky because Earth is inside its plane and we see its edge.

Other galaxies are elliptical, shaped like an oval made of stars. Then there are lenticular galaxies such as the Cartwheel Galaxy. These look like a glowing disk in space. The fourth type are the irregular galaxies with no regular shape—examples include the Large Magellanic Cloud.

The biggest galaxies contain trillions of stars, the smallest have only a few thousand stars. Galaxies are held together by gravity and can be more than a million light years across or have a diameter of only a few hundred light years. A light year is the distance traveled by light in one year.

> **At around 2.5 million light years away, Andromeda is our nearest galaxy.**

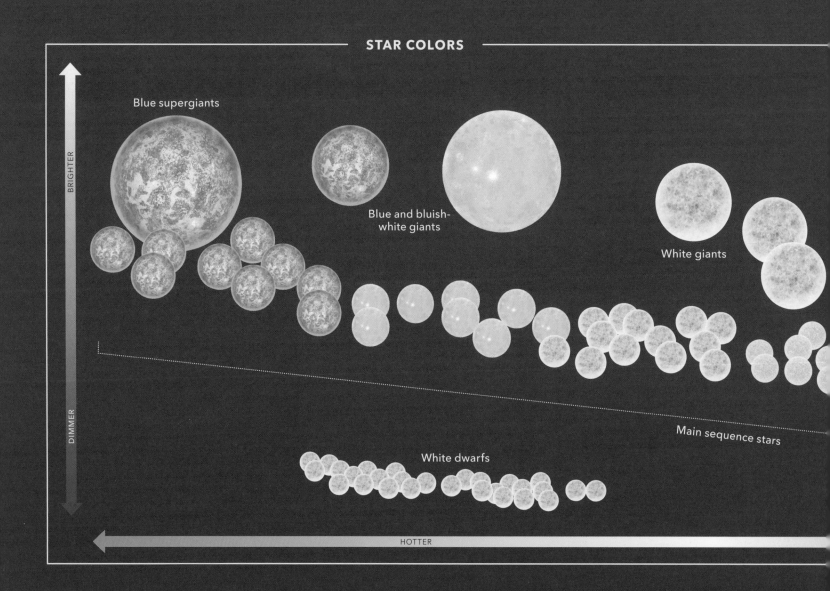

BRIGHTER

DIMMER

Blue supergiants

Blue and bluish-white giants

White giants

Main sequence stars

White dwarfs

HOTTER

STAR
colors

When people look up at the night sky from Earth, the stars all look pretty much the same—like tiny white dots in the sky. In reality, they are different colors, ranging from blue to orange-red. The star colors occur due to the temperature and brightness of each of the stars.

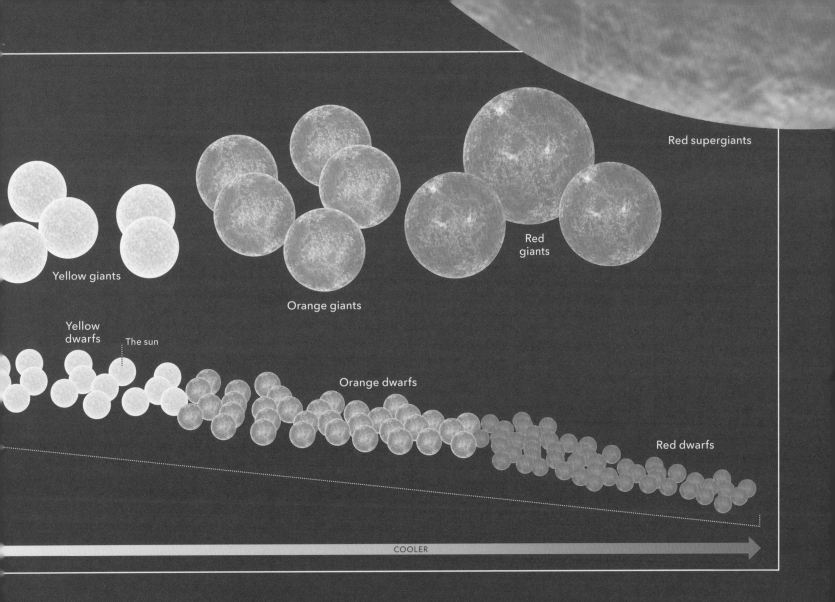

Red supergiants

Red giants

Yellow giants

Orange giants

Yellow dwarfs

The sun

Orange dwarfs

Red dwarfs

COOLER

Astronomers Ejnar Hertzsprung and Henry Russell created a chart called the Hertzsprung-Russell diagram (above), which classifies stars into types and allows us to see the stage a star has reached in its life cycle. This chart plots how bright a star is (its light output or luminosity) up the side and how hot it is (its surface temperature) along the bottom. The sizes of each circle show how big a star is, and its color on the chart shows how hot it is—red stars are the coolest, while the blue ones are the hottest.

> **White dwarfs are the remnants of giants, which have lost their outer layers.**

Most stars are placed in a diagonal band across the middle of the diagram, in an area that is called the main sequence. Stars in this band fuse (burn) hydrogen into helium in their core (central part). Our sun is a main sequence star.

Stars stay in the main sequence for most of their lives. Away from this sequence are the giants and white dwarfs. These are older stars, which would once have been part of the main sequence, but have changed over their life cycle. Stars become giants when they have used up all the hydrogen in their cores. This makes them swell, and they become bigger and brighter, but their surfaces become cooler and redder. Giants are thousands of times brighter than the sun, while supergiants can be up to a billion times brighter than it. As a star grows hotter, the light that it emits changes from red to orange, then yellow, white, and blue. While a red supergiant can burn at up to 6,500°F (3,500°C), a blue supergiant may have a temperature of about 80,000°F (45,000°C).

Dwarf stars are dimmer. They range in size from five times as massive as the sun (a yellow dwarf) to smaller ones called red dwarfs or white dwarfs.

Types of
NEBULA

Scattered across space are swirling clouds of gas and dust called nebulae. Some are brightly colored and look like giant mountains of foam, others appear as dark shapes against brighter backgrounds.

The space between stars is called the interstellar medium. Over many millions of years, the gas and dust in this space come together to form a nebula (cloud). The gas is mainly hydrogen and some helium. If the gas becomes dense enough, the cloud can begin to collapse, creating an even denser area. This increases the gravitational pull of the gas, causing it to draw in more and more gas. Eventually, the cloud becomes hot enough that hydrogen atoms begin to fuse together and release vast amounts of energy—forming a star. This is why some nebulae are also called "star nurseries." One of the most famous regions of the Eagle Nebula is three giant pillars of interstellar gas and dust where stars are being formed. These have been nicknamed the "Pillars of Creation."

But other nebulae are formed in an opposite manner—after a star dies. These are clouds of gas and material left behind after the death of a star. A very large star dies in an explosion called a supernova—the nebula left behind after this event is called a supernova remnant. The Crab Nebula is the remnant of a star that went supernova around 1054 CE, while Cassiopeia A was formed 340 years ago. A smaller star dies by gently shedding off its outer layers, which results in a planetary nebula—so called because it looks like a planet, although it is not one. Famous examples include the Ring Nebula and the Owl Nebula.

Planetary nebulae and supernova remnants are examples of bright nebulae, which look as though they glow in the dark sky. Some nebulae, such as the Orion Nebula, are bright because their gas glows from radiation of the stars within them. These are known as emission nebulae. Other nebulae, such as the Witch Head Nebula, are illuminated by light reflected from nearby stars, and are known as reflection nebulae.

Dark nebulae do not glow—they are so dense that they absorb light, appearing as dark silhouettes against light emitted or reflected from elsewhere, such as stars around or behind them. They also contain large amounts of thick dust. The Horsehead Nebula is a dark nebula in the constellation of Orion that looks like a horse's head or a knight chess piece. The dark Cone Nebula is a tower of gas and dust in a star-forming area of space.

At −460°F (−272°C), the Boomerang Nebula is the coldest place in the universe.

A nebula the size of Earth would only weigh a few pounds.

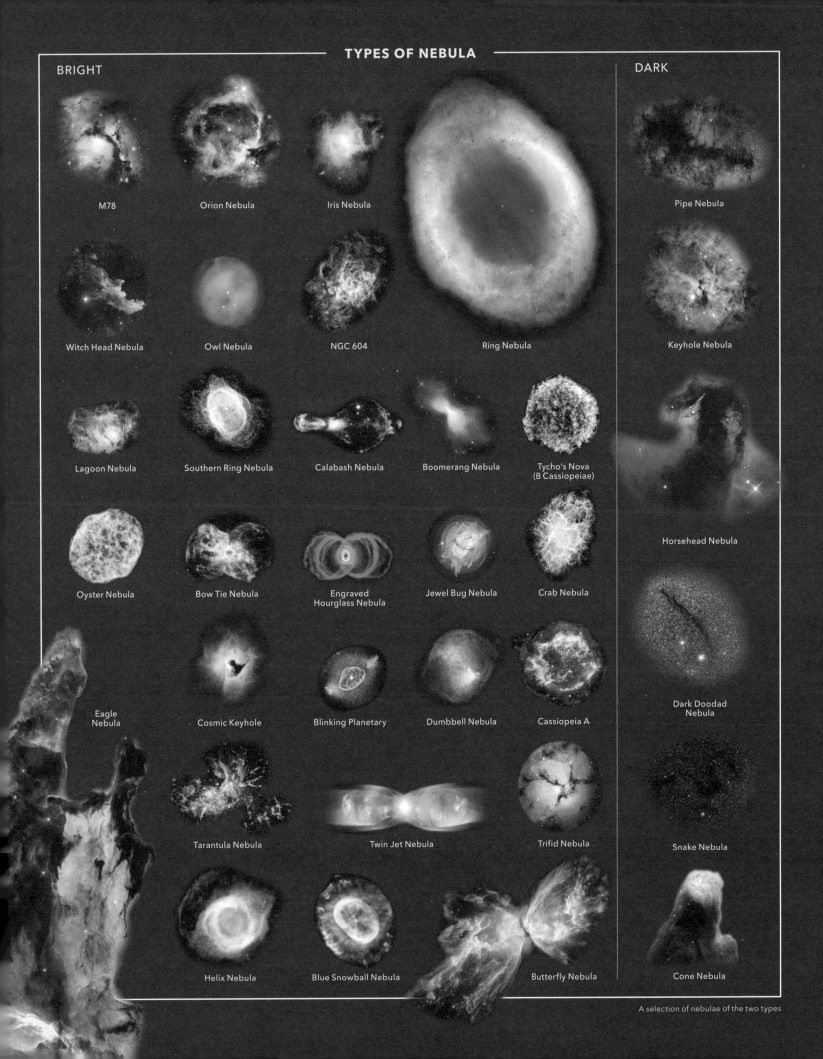

TYPES OF NEBULA

BRIGHT

M78

Orion Nebula

Iris Nebula

Witch Head Nebula

Owl Nebula

NGC 604

Ring Nebula

Lagoon Nebula

Southern Ring Nebula

Calabash Nebula

Boomerang Nebula

Tycho's Nova
(B Cassiopeiae)

Oyster Nebula

Bow Tie Nebula

Engraved
Hourglass Nebula

Jewel Bug Nebula

Crab Nebula

Eagle
Nebula

Cosmic Keyhole

Blinking Planetary

Dumbbell Nebula

Cassiopeia A

Tarantula Nebula

Twin Jet Nebula

Trifid Nebula

Helix Nebula

Blue Snowball Nebula

Butterfly Nebula

DARK

Pipe Nebula

Keyhole Nebula

Horsehead Nebula

Dark Doodad
Nebula

Snake Nebula

Cone Nebula

A selection of nebulae of the two types

CONSTELLATIONS
in the night sky

When our ancestors looked up at the night sky, they realized they could make shapes by drawing imaginary lines between the stars. The groups of stars in these shapes are called constellations.

CONSTELLATIONS IN THE NORTHERN HEMISPHERE

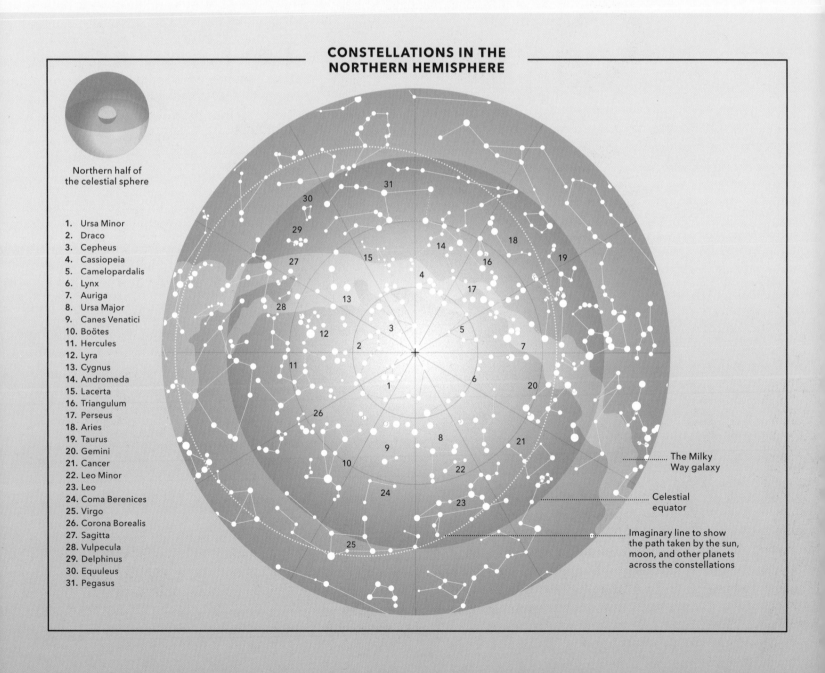

Northern half of the celestial sphere

1. Ursa Minor
2. Draco
3. Cepheus
4. Cassiopeia
5. Camelopardalis
6. Lynx
7. Auriga
8. Ursa Major
9. Canes Venatici
10. Boötes
11. Hercules
12. Lyra
13. Cygnus
14. Andromeda
15. Lacerta
16. Triangulum
17. Perseus
18. Aries
19. Taurus
20. Gemini
21. Cancer
22. Leo Minor
23. Leo
24. Coma Berenices
25. Virgo
26. Corona Borealis
27. Sagitta
28. Vulpecula
29. Delphinus
30. Equuleus
31. Pegasus

The Milky Way galaxy

Celestial equator

Imaginary line to show the path taken by the sun, moon, and other planets across the constellations

People in the northern and southern hemispheres of Earth see different sets of constellations in their skies, as shown in the flat celestial maps below. If we look up at the night sky from Earth, the constellations will appear to move during the night because of our planet's rotation. But they also move in the night sky with the seasons because of Earth moving around the sun.

Around 150 CE, the Greek astronomer Ptolemy described 48 constellations. Another 40 were added in the 17th and 18th centuries, making a total of 88 recognized today. They include Orion (a hunter) and Draco (a dragon), as well as the 12 signs of the Western zodiac.

The celestial hemisphere (half of the sky) that lies around Earth's northern hemisphere contains 31 constellations, visible from Europe, North America, and northern Asia. There are 57 constellations that people in the southern hemisphere (Australasia, most of South America, and parts of Asia) can see. Up to 15 constellations can be seen in both hemispheres by people who live near Earth's equator.

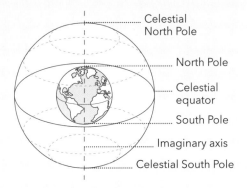

▲ CELESTIAL SPHERE
Astronomers use an imaginary shell around Earth, called the celestial sphere, to plot the position of all the stars in the night sky.

CONSTELLATIONS IN THE SOUTHERN HEMISPHERE

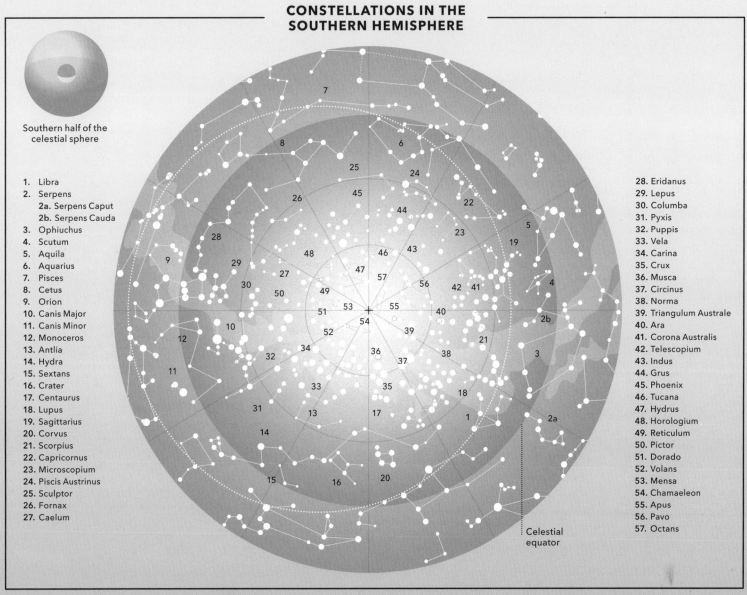

Southern half of the celestial sphere

1. Libra
2. Serpens
  2a. Serpens Caput
  2b. Serpens Cauda
3. Ophiuchus
4. Scutum
5. Aquila
6. Aquarius
7. Pisces
8. Cetus
9. Orion
10. Canis Major
11. Canis Minor
12. Monoceros
13. Antlia
14. Hydra
15. Sextans
16. Crater
17. Centaurus
18. Lupus
19. Sagittarius
20. Corvus
21. Scorpius
22. Capricornus
23. Microscopium
24. Piscis Austrinus
25. Sculptor
26. Fornax
27. Caelum

28. Eridanus
29. Lepus
30. Columba
31. Pyxis
32. Puppis
33. Vela
34. Carina
35. Crux
36. Musca
37. Circinus
38. Norma
39. Triangulum Australe
40. Ara
41. Corona Australis
42. Telescopium
43. Indus
44. Grus
45. Phoenix
46. Tucana
47. Hydrus
48. Horologium
49. Reticulum
50. Pictor
51. Dorado
52. Volans
53. Mensa
54. Chamaeleon
55. Apus
56. Pavo
57. Octans

Celestial equator

Serpens (the serpent constellation) is divided in two—Serpens Caput (its head) and Serpens Cauda (its tail)—on either side of Ophiuchus, "the serpent bearer."

CONSTELLATIONS

NORTHERN SKY

Ursa Minor

Draco

Cepheus

Cassiopeia

Camelopardalis

Lynx

Andromeda

Lacerta

Triangulum

Aries

Cancer

Leo Minor

Coma Berenices

CELESTIAL EQUATOR

Taurus

Leo

Virgo

Serpens Caput

Serpens Cauda

Ophiuchus

Aquila

Aquarius

SOUTHERN SKY

Libra

Scutum

Canis Major

Antlia

Caelum

Crater

Centaurus

Piscis Austrinus

Sculptor

Fornax

Lepus

Norma

Triangulum Australe

Ara

Corona Australis

Telescopium

Indus

Circinus

Reticulum

Pictor

Dorado

Chamaeleon

Mensa

Ursa Major

Canes
Venatici

Hercules

Lyra

Cygnus

Auriga

Boötes

Perseus

Corona Borealis

Vulpecula

Pegasus

Gemini

Sagitta

Delphinus

Equuleus

Pisces

Orion

Sextans

Cetus

Canis Minor

Monoceros

Hydra

Eridanus

Lupus

Corvus

Microscopium

Scorpius

Capricornus

Sagittarius

Columba

Carina

Musca

Puppis

Vela

Crux

Pyxis

Grus

Hydrus

Phoenix

Pavo

Tucana

Volans

Apus

Horologium

Octans

Objects in the
SOLAR SYSTEM

At the center of our solar system lies a star—our sun. Traveling around it in elliptical orbits are eight planets and five dwarf planets (many with their own moons), thousands of comets, and millions of asteroids.

Over time, astronomers have identified and classified objects in our solar system into different groups. Planets are the largest objects and have enough gravity to pull them together equally from all sides, giving them a spherical shape. Their strong gravity draws in or deflects other objects in their orbit (the path in which they revolve around the sun), clearing it.

The four planets nearest to the sun are formed of rock, while the next four are giants, with a solid core surrounded by swirling gases—Jupiter and Saturn are gas giants, and Uranus and Neptune are ice giants. Mercury and Venus do not have moons orbiting them, but all the other planets do. Earth is orbited by one moon, while Jupiter has 95—including Ganymede, which is the largest moon in the solar system.

At first, astronomers thought Pluto was also a planet, but it was reclassified as a dwarf planet in 2006. Dwarf planets are smaller than planets and usually spherical, and they may share their orbits with smaller bodies. Pluto and Eris are some of the dwarf planets in the Kuiper Belt, an area beyond Neptune that contains many icy, rocky objects. A few of the dwarf planets have their own moons.

Comets come from the Kuiper Belt or a region beyond it called the Oort Cloud. They are made of ice, dust, and rock, but when they get closer to the sun, they melt and the ice turns into glowing gases. Some travel near Earth on a regular basis.

Other small bodies in our solar system are asteroids, which are formed of rock, metal, or ice, but are smaller than dwarf planets. Most are found in a ring between Mars and Jupiter called the Asteroid Belt.

> **The sun makes up 99.8 percent of all the mass in the solar system.**

The sun   Venus   Mars   Saturn   Uranus

Mercury   Earth   Jupiter   Neptune

◀ ORDER OF PLANETS
Closest to the sun is Mercury. The next three rocky planets are Venus, Earth, and Mars. Farther out are the four giants—Jupiter, Saturn, Uranus, and Neptune. The sun and planets are shown beside each other here. In reality, they are millions of miles apart in space.

ROCKY PLANETS

The sun

Mercury

Venus

Earth

Mars

GIANT PLANETS

Jupiter

Uranus

Neptune

Saturn

DWARF PLANETS

Eris

Makemake

Ceres

Pluto

Haumea

MOONS
14 OF 290 KNOWN MOONS IN THE SOLAR SYSTEM

The moon
EARTH

Phobos
MARS

Callisto
JUPITER

Miranda
URANUS

Proteus
NEPTUNE

Triton
NEPTUNE

Europa
JUPITER

Io
JUPITER

Ganymede
JUPITER

Enceladus
SATURN

Iapetus
SATURN

Titania
URANUS

Titan
SATURN

Hyperion
SATURN

COMETS
FIVE OF NEARLY 4,000 KNOWN COMETS IN THE SOLAR SYSTEM

Comet
McNaught

Comet
Hale-Bopp

Comet
Halley

Comet
Hyakutake

Comet C/2020 F3
(NEOWISE)

ASTEROIDS
SEVEN OF THE MILLIONS OF ASTEROIDS IN THE SOLAR SYSTEM

433 Eros

21 Lutetia

4 Vesta

243 Ida

16 Psyche

101955 Bennu

2 Pallas

PHASES OF THE MOON

Full moon · Waning gibbous · Last quarter · Waxing gibbous · New moon · Waxing crescent · First quarter · Waning crescent

January
1 2 3 4 5 6 7 8 9 10 11 12 13 14 15 16 17 18 19 20 21 22

February
1 2 3 4 5 6 7 8 9 10 11 12 13 14 15 16 17 18 19 20 21 22

March
1 2 3 4 5 6 7 8 9 10 11 12 13 14 15 16 17 18 19 20 21 22

April
1 2 3 4 5 6 7 8 9 10 11 12 13 14 15 16 17 18 19 20 21 22

May
1 2 3 4 5 6 7 8 9 10 11 12 13 14 15 16 17 18 19 20 21 22

June
1 2 3 4 5 6 7 8 9 10 11 12 13 14 15 16 17 18 19 20 21 22

July
1 2 3 4 5 6 7 8 9 10 11 12 13 14 15 16 17 18 19 20 21 22

August
1 2 3 4 5 6 7 8 9 10 11 12 13 14 15 16 17 18 19 20 21 22

September
1 2 3 4 5 6 7 8 9 10 11 12 13 14 15 16 17 18 19 20 21 22

October
1 2 3 4 5 6 7 8 9 10 11 12 13 14 15 16 17 18 19 20 21 22

November
1 2 3 4 5 6 7 8 9 10 11 12 13 14 15 16 17 18 19 20 21 22

December
1 2 3 4 5 6 7 8 9 10 11 12 13 14 15 16 17 18 19 20 21 22

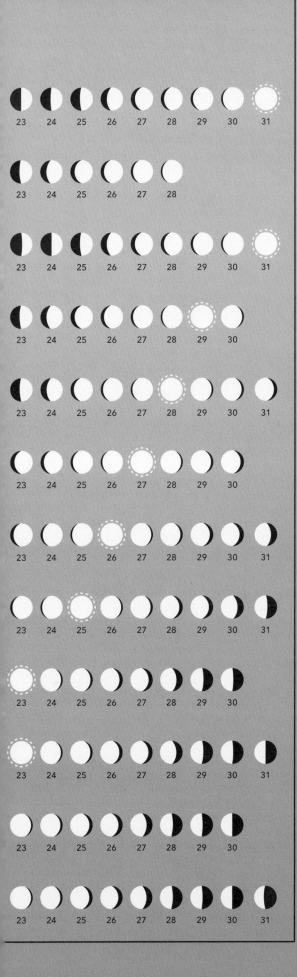

Phases of
THE MOON

Our view of the moon changes every night. We can see a sliver, a crescent, a full circle, or sometimes nothing at all.

Our planet's only natural satellite is the moon. It is the largest and brightest object in the night sky. The different shapes of the moon that we see throughout the month are known as the phases of the moon. The moon itself does not change. It moves around Earth, spinning so the same side of it is always facing us.

As the moon moves around Earth, the sun's light falls upon different parts of the moon—this is what causes the phases. And these phases change periodically, as seen on the left in this lunar calendar. It shows when the different phases of the moon would appear across the year if the first of January was a full moon (when we see the moon's full disk). When the moon is between Earth and the sun, it is not lit up at all, and there is a new moon (when the moon's disk is not visible). The moon then moves away from the sun, and a crescent of light becomes visible on one side.

Each month's full moon has a name, such as January's "Wolf Moon."

Once the moon is a quarter of the way around its orbit, half of its face is lit up—this is called a first quarter. Halfway around its orbit, the whole face is lit, in a perfectly circular full moon. The sunlit area then shrinks again, with the opposite side being lit in a last quarter, once the moon is three-fourths of the way around its orbit.

PAYLOAD

- □ Satellite
- ■ Uncrewed spacecraft
- ▨ Crewed spacecraft

Sputnik RUSSIA, 1957–1958

Vanguard USA, 1957–1959

Juno I USA, 1958

Thor-Able USA, 1958–1960

Redstone USA, 1960–1961

Atlas LV-3B USA, 1960–1963

Atlas Agena USA, 1960–1978

Vostok RUSSIA, 1960–1991

Voskhod RUSSIA, 1963–1976

Titan II USA, 1964–1966

Soyuz RUSSIA, 1966–PRESENT DAY

Saturn V USA, 1967–1973

Kosmos-3M RUSSIA, 1967–2010

Black Arrow UK, 1969–1971

N1 RUSSIA, 1969–1972

N-I JAPAN, 1975–1982

Tsyklon-3 RUSSIA, 1977–2009

Ariane I ESA, 1979–1986

STS USA, 1981–2011

Zenit RUSSIA/UKRAINE, 1985–2017

Energia RUSSIA, 1987–1988

Atlas II USA, 1991–2004

Long March 2D CHINA, 1992–PRESENT DAY

PSLV INDIA, 1993–PRESENT DAY

H-II JAPAN, 1994–1999

Ariane V ESA, 1996–2023

Long March 3B CHINA, 1996–PRESENT DAY

Long March 4B CHINA, 1999–PRESENT DAY

Long March 2F CHINA, 1999–PRESENT DAY

Atlas III USA, 2000–2005

Minotaur I USA, 2000–PRESENT DAY

GSLV INDIA, 2001–PRESENT DAY

Delta IV Heavy USA, 2004–2024

Falcon 1 USA, 2006–2009

Falcon 9 v1.0 USA, 2010–2013

Minotaur IV USA, 2010–PRESENT DAY

Vega ESA, 2012–PRESENT DAY

Falcon 9 v1.1 USA, 2013–2016

Antares USA, 2013–PRESENT DAY

Angara 5 RUSSIA, 2014–PRESENT DAY

Falcon 9 v1.2 USA, 2015–PRESENT DAY

Long March 5 CHINA, 2016–PRESENT DAY

Long March 6 CHINA, 2016–PRESENT DAY

Long March 7 CHINA, 2016–PRESENT DAY

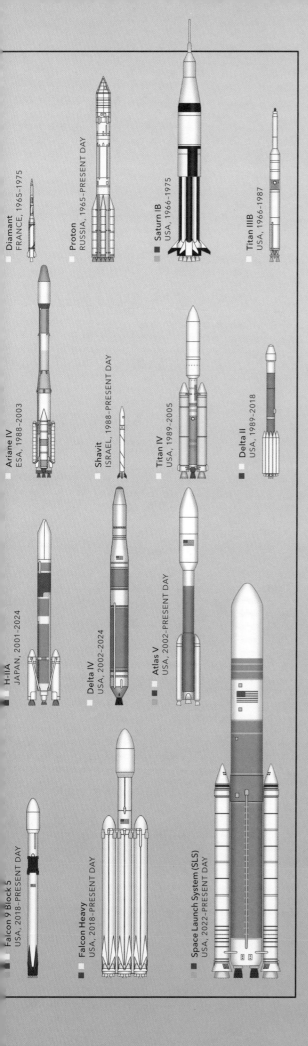

Diamant
FRANCE, 1965–1975

Proton
RUSSIA, 1965–PRESENT DAY

Saturn IB
USA, 1966–1975

Titan IIIB
USA, 1966–1987

Ariane IV
ESA, 1988–2003

Shavit
ISRAEL, 1988–PRESENT DAY

Titan IV
USA, 1989–2005

Delta II
USA, 1989–2018

H-IIA
JAPAN, 2001–2024

Delta IV
USA, 2002–2024

Atlas V
USA, 2002–PRESENT DAY

Falcon 9 Block 5
USA, 2018–PRESENT DAY

Falcon Heavy
USA, 2018–PRESENT DAY

Space Launch System (SLS)
USA, 2022–PRESENT DAY

Space
ROCKETS

Since the 1950s, rockets have placed satellites in Earth orbit, taken humans to the moon, and sent space probes to the very edge of the solar system.

R ockets are projectiles that send out a burning mixture of hot gas at one end, which generates the force needed to push them in the opposite direction. This allows a rocket to take off and fly against Earth's gravity, carrying satellites and other cargo (its "payload") into space.

Originally made as military weapons, rockets had been transformed into machines for space exploration by the mid-20th century. Over the next 70 years, larger and more powerful rockets were developed, capable of ferrying satellites into orbit around Earth and sending space probes to the moon and planets.

Sputnik 1, the world's first artificial satellite, was launched on the Sputnik rocket by the USSR (the Soviet Union) in 1957. It was followed by the Vostok 1 in 1961 that took the first human into space—Yuri Gagarin. In 1969, the US-built Saturn V rocket carried the Apollo 11 spacecraft to Earth orbit, from where it then voyaged to the moon and put the first humans on the lunar surface. Rockets such as the Saturn V and the Soyuz were developed to take crew and cargo into space. More recently, private companies have developed reusable rockets, such as the Falcon Heavy.

The next big step in space exploration is NASA's Artemis program, which has developed the Space Launch System (SLS), a super heavy rocket that will take humans back to the moon and beyond.

Types of uncrewed
SPACECRAFT

Uncrewed spacecraft are robots that are launched into space without anyone on board. They perform a variety of roles, such as traveling to distant planets, observing space, and allowing communication on Earth.

Uncrewed spacecraft are sent into space to carry out many different functions. Some land on the objects they are studying, while others study objects from orbit or when flying past them.

The orbiter Cassini studied Saturn for nearly two decades, traveling in loops around the planet 294 times, sending photos and data about Saturn, its rings, and moons back to Earth. Flyby craft, such as New Horizons, fly past an object, without stopping or orbiting it. They make observations and take photos, and usually visit multiple objects in space during their mission. Atmospheric spacecraft such as Galileo gather information about a planet's atmosphere. They are often dropped off in the atmosphere by another craft.

Landers, such as Vikram—which landed on the moon—are spacecraft that touch down on the surface of a space object. They carry scientific instruments, or even other spacecraft such as rovers. Landers do not move once they have landed. Rovers are remote-controlled space cars. They explore the surface of an object, driving across it while taking photos, mapping the terrain, and undertaking scientific experiments. So far, rovers have been sent only to the moon and the planet Mars.

The penetrator type of spacecraft act as probes. They may be carried by other craft. They visit the surface of their target, often penetrating the ground, and send information and collected materials back to Earth. The penetrator carried by Deep Impact probed beneath the surface of a comet.

Observatories are space-based telescopes. They take images using a range of different types of light, which helps us to look further into and learn more about space. Communications and navigation satellites relay information to and from Earth, helping us find our way around or communicate with each other.

> Voyager 1 has traveled farther away from Earth than any other craft.

▶ SCANNING A MOON
Uncrewed spacecraft can investigate space objects without a human being present. Cassini used a radar beam to scan the surface of Titan, Saturn's largest moon.

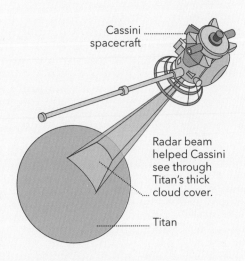

Cassini spacecraft

Radar beam helped Cassini see through Titan's thick cloud cover.

Titan

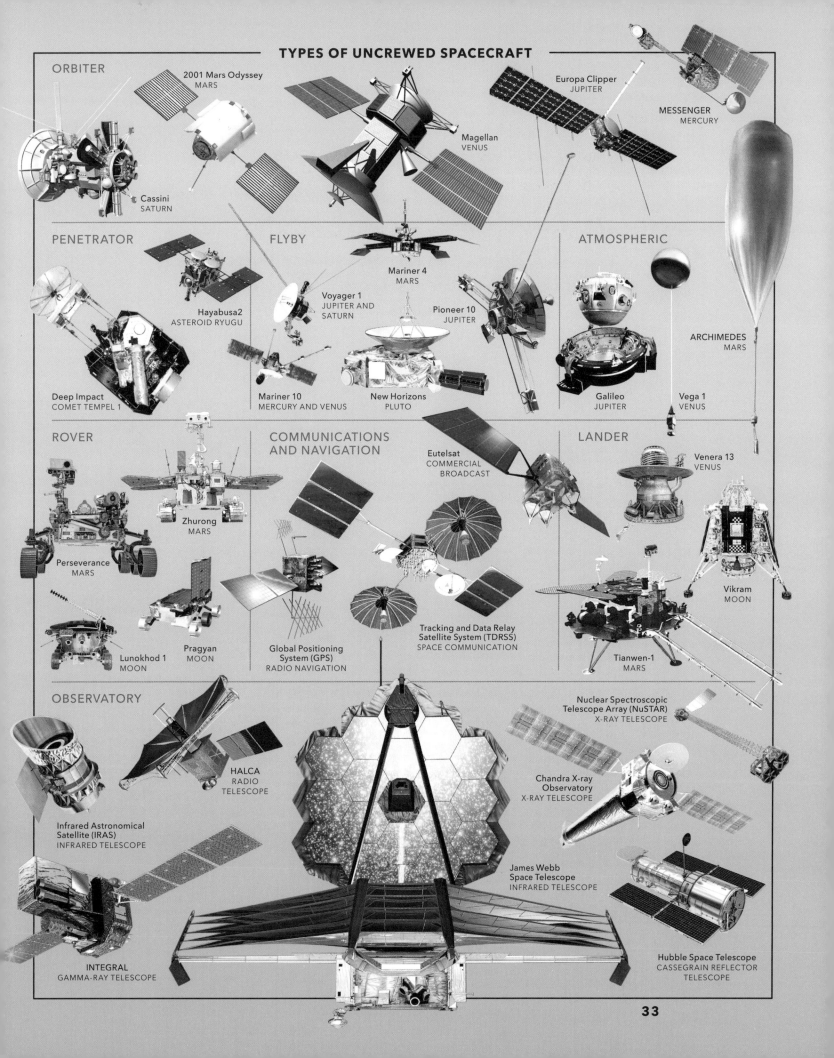

TYPES OF UNCREWED SPACECRAFT

ORBITER

2001 Mars Odyssey
MARS

Cassini
SATURN

Magellan
VENUS

Europa Clipper
JUPITER

MESSENGER
MERCURY

PENETRATOR

Hayabusa2
ASTEROID RYUGU

Deep Impact
COMET TEMPEL 1

FLYBY

Mariner 4
MARS

Voyager 1
JUPITER AND SATURN

Pioneer 10
JUPITER

Mariner 10
MERCURY AND VENUS

New Horizons
PLUTO

ATMOSPHERIC

ARCHIMEDES
MARS

Galileo
JUPITER

Vega 1
VENUS

ROVER

Zhurong
MARS

Perseverance
MARS

Lunokhod 1
MOON

Pragyan
MOON

COMMUNICATIONS AND NAVIGATION

Eutelsat
COMMERCIAL BROADCAST

Global Positioning System (GPS)
RADIO NAVIGATION

Tracking and Data Relay Satellite System (TDRSS)
SPACE COMMUNICATION

LANDER

Venera 13
VENUS

Vikram
MOON

Tianwen-1
MARS

OBSERVATORY

HALCA
RADIO TELESCOPE

Infrared Astronomical Satellite (IRAS)
INFRARED TELESCOPE

James Webb Space Telescope
INFRARED TELESCOPE

Nuclear Spectroscopic Telescope Array (NuSTAR)
X-RAY TELESCOPE

Chandra X-ray Observatory
X-RAY TELESCOPE

Hubble Space Telescope
CASSEGRAIN REFLECTOR TELESCOPE

INTEGRAL
GAMMA-RAY TELESCOPE

Missions to
THE MOON

Earth's moon is a natural destination for space explorers. Missions can test new technologies, uncover secrets of the solar system, and pave the way for trips to more distant worlds.

Luna 3 took the first images of the moon's far side, which always faces away from Earth.

Our planet's only natural satellite, the moon, orbits Earth at an average distance of around 238,855 miles (384,400 km). This relative closeness made it the ideal target in the early days of space exploration. Although it was a thousand times farther away than where artificial satellites orbited Earth, the moon was still close enough to reach in a few days.

In the late 1950s, the two most powerful nations, the United States and the Soviet Union, raced to outdo each other in conquering space, and so exploring the moon became the prime goal of this "Space Race." The Soviet Union's Luna mission was the first to reach the moon, but the US space agency NASA soon sent its own uncrewed missions to orbit the moon or land on it. Beginning in the early 1960s, both countries also made competing plans to land humans on the moon. While Soviet plans faltered, engineers at NASA developed Apollo—a complex spacecraft built to carry three astronauts to lunar orbit and put two of them on the surface. The US won the race with two successful crewed flights around the moon, followed by six human landings between 1969 and 1972. A technical problem prevented

NASA's Apollo 13 Mission from successfully landing humans on the moon. Apart from being a huge technical achievement, rock samples from Apollo landing sites also offered insights into the solar system's history.

After the Apollo missions, interest in lunar exploration waned until the 1990s, when new technologies allowed for new types of exploration. Upgraded spacecraft carried advanced instruments to map the moon's surface, hunting for minerals and ice that might be used to set up a permanent human outpost. Many countries have now sent spacecraft to orbit the moon or make landings, such as China's Chang'e craft. Meanwhile, NASA has begun its Artemis program, aimed at putting humans back on the moon, and establishing a space station in lunar orbit that could act as a starting point for missions to Mars.

▼ JOURNEY TO THE MOON
Each Apollo spacecraft was made of a three-seat Command Module (CM), a Service Module (SM), and a two-person Lunar Module (LM).

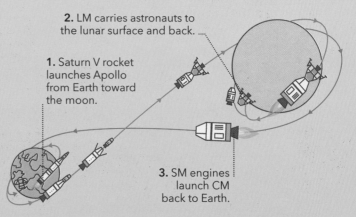

2. LM carries astronauts to the lunar surface and back.

1. Saturn V rocket launches Apollo from Earth toward the moon.

3. SM engines launch CM back to Earth.

MOON LANDINGS BY CREWED MISSIONS

Apollo 15 landed at Hadley Rille.

Apollo 17 landed in the Taurus-Littrow Valley.

Apollo 11 landed in the Sea of Tranquility.

Apollo 12 landed in the Ocean of Storms.

Apollo 14 landed at Fra Mauro.

Apollo 16 landed at the Descartes Highlands.

Apollo 11
JULY 16-24, 1969
Neil Armstrong, Buzz Aldrin, and Michael Collins

Apollo 12
NOVEMBER 14-24, 1969
Charles Conrad, Alan Bean, and Richard F. Gordon

Apollo 14
JANUARY 31-FEBRUARY 9, 1971
Alan B. Shepard Jr., Edgar D. Mitchell, and Stuart A. Roosa

Apollo 15
JULY 26-AUGUST 7, 1971
David R. Scott, James B. Irwin, and Alfred M. Worden

Apollo 16
APRIL 16-27, 1972
John W. Young, Charles M. Duke Jr., and Thomas K. Mattingly II

Apollo 17
DECEMBER 7-19, 1972
Eugene Cernan, Harrison Hagan Schmitt, and Ronald Evans

SUCCESSFUL UNCREWED MOON MISSIONS

Luna 2 LAUNCH: SEPT 12, 1959 *USSR*	**Luna 12** OCT 22, 1966 *USSR*	**Luna 14** APR 7 ,1968 *USSR*	**Apollo 14** JAN 31, 1971 *USA*	**Lunar Prospector** JAN 7, 1998 *USA*	**Chang'e 5-T1** OCT 23, 2014 *China*
Luna 3 OCT 4, 1959 *USSR*	**Lunar Orbiter 2** NOV 6, 1966 *USA*	**Zond 5** SEPT 14, 1968 *USSR*	**Apollo 15** JUL 26, 1971 *USA*	**SMART-1** SEPT 27, 2003 *Europe*	**Queqiao/ Longjiang-2** MAY 20, 2018 *China*
Ranger 7 JUL 28, 1964 *USA*	**Luna 13** DEC 21, 1966 *USSR*	**Apollo 8** DEC 21, 1968 *USA*	**Luna 19** SEPT 28, 1971 *USSR*	**SELENE** SEPT 14, 2007 *Japan*	**Chang'e 4/ Yutu-2** DEC 7, 2018 *China*
Ranger 8 FEB 17, 1965 *USA*	**Lunar Orbiter 3** FEB 5, 1967 *USA*	**Apollo 10** MAY 18, 1969 *USA*	**Luna 20** FEB 14, 1972 *USSR*	**Chang'e 1** OCT 24, 2007 *China*	**Chandrayaan-2** JUL 22, 2019 *India*
Ranger 9 MAR 21, 1965 *USA*	**Surveyor 3** APR 17, 1967 *USA*	**Luna 15** JUL 13, 1969 *USSR*	**Apollo 16** APR 16, 1972 *USA*	**Chandrayaan-1** OCT 22, 2008 *India*	**Chang'e 5** NOV 23, 2020 *China*
Zond 3 JUL 18, 1965 *USSR*	**Lunar Orbiter 4** MAY 4, 1967 *USA*	**Apollo 11** JUL 16, 1969 *USA*	**Apollo 17** DEC 7, 1972 *USA*	**ARTEMIS-P1 and P2** JAN 1, 2009 *USA*	**CAPSTONE** JUN 28, 2022 *USA*
Luna 9 JAN 31, 1966 *USSR*	**Explorer 35** JUL 19, 1967 *USA*	**Zond 7** AUG 7, 1969 *USSR*	**Luna 21/ Lunokhod 2** JAN 8, 1973 *USSR*	**Lunar Reconnaissance Orbiter (LRO)/ LCROSS** JUN 18, 2009 *USA*	**Danuri** AUG 4, 2022 *South Korea*
Luna 10 MAR 31, 1966 *USSR*	**Lunar Orbiter 5** AUG 1, 1967 *USA*	**Apollo 12** NOV 14, 1969 *USA*	**Luna 22** MAY 29, 1974 *USSR*	**Chang'e 2** OCT 1, 2010 *China*	**Artemis I** NOV 16, 2022 *USA*
Surveyor 1 MAY 30, 1966 *USA*	**Surveyor 5** SEPT 8, 1967 *USA*	**Luna 16** SEPT 12, 1970 *USSR*	**Luna 24** AUG 9, 1976 *USSR*	**GRAIL** SEPT 10, 2011 *USA*	**Chandrayaan-3/ Vikram** JUL 14, 2023 *India*
Lunar Orbiter 1 AUG 10, 1966 *USA*	**Surveyor 6** NOV 7, 1967 *USA*	**Zond 8** OCT 20, 1970 *USSR*	**Hiten** JAN 24, 1990 *Japan*	**LADEE** SEPT 7, 2013 *USA*	**SLIM** SEPT 6, 2023 *Japan*
Luna 11 AUG 21, 1966 *USSR*	**Surveyor 7** JAN 7, 1968 *USA*	**Luna 17/ Lunokhod 1** NOV 10, 1970 *USSR*	**Clementine** JAN 25, 1994 *USA*	**Chang'e 3/ Yutu** DEC 1, 2013 *China*	**IM-1** FEB 15, 2024 *USA*

Timeline of
EARTH'S HISTORY

Our planet is 4.6 billion years old. To help make sense of such a vast timescale, scientists have broken down Earth's incredibly long history into smaller sections of time known as eras, periods, and epochs.

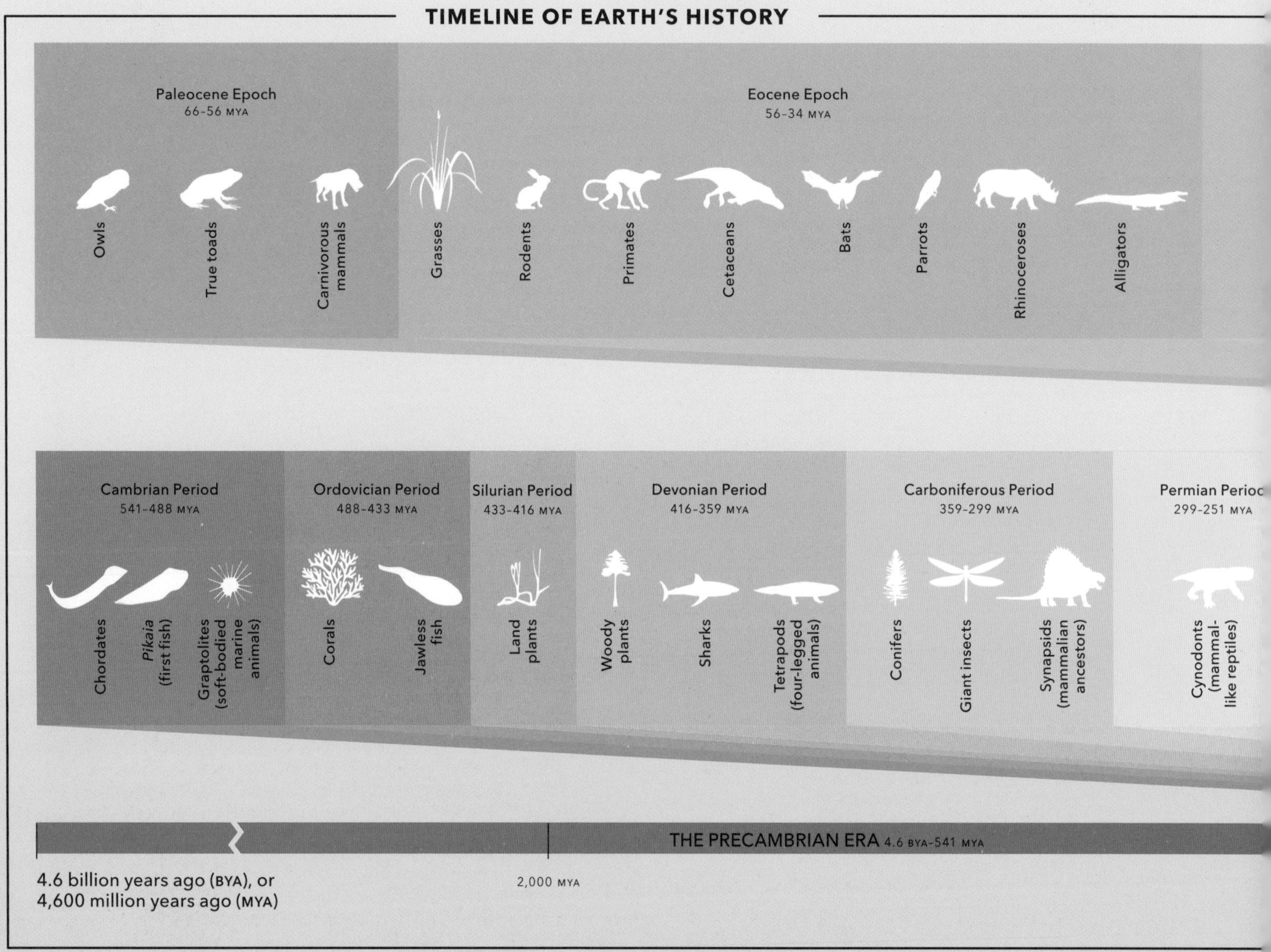

TIMELINE OF EARTH'S HISTORY

Paleocene Epoch
66–56 MYA

- Owls
- True toads
- Carnivorous mammals

Eocene Epoch
56–34 MYA

- Grasses
- Rodents
- Primates
- Cetaceans
- Bats
- Parrots
- Rhinoceroses
- Alligators

Cambrian Period
541–488 MYA

- Chordates
- Pikaia (first fish)
- Graptolites (soft-bodied marine animals)

Ordovician Period
488–433 MYA

- Corals
- Jawless fish

Silurian Period
433–416 MYA

- Land plants

Devonian Period
416–359 MYA

- Woody plants
- Sharks
- Tetrapods (four-legged animals)

Carboniferous Period
359–299 MYA

- Conifers
- Giant insects
- Synapsids (mammalian ancestors)

Permian Period
299–251 MYA

- Cynodonts (mammal-like reptiles)

THE PRECAMBRIAN ERA 4.6 BYA–541 MYA

4.6 billion years ago (BYA), or 4,600 million years ago (MYA)

2,000 MYA

The age of our planet is hard to conceive when measured against the much shorter timescales we use in our daily lives. Therefore, scientists have devised a way of organizing it into increasingly smaller chunks of time. The largest chunks are eras. The longest era, before life flourished on Earth, is called the Precambrian. Then, there are the Paleozoic, Mesozoic, and Cenozoic Eras. These are divided into periods (12 in total), then subdivided again, into epochs. We live in the newest epoch—the Holocene. Humans talk about their own history in even smaller units of time, such as millennia, centuries, years, months, and days.

The first life forms on Earth were single cells that appeared 3.7 billion years ago. Then, during the Cambrian Period, multicellular marine creatures, such as corals, appeared. From the Ordovician onward, more types of complex life existed on Earth— some, such as conifers and snakes, are still around today, while others, such as the dinosaurs, lived for 165 million years, then became extinct. Placental mammals (which give birth to fully developed young) first appeared in the Cretaceous Period, but over the following periods mammals evolved into a range of body sizes and shapes, and moved into nearly every habitat on Earth. Modern humans—one of the more recent mammal species— emerged around 300,000 years ago, in the Pleistocene Epoch and, by the Holocene, had established civilizations.

> **Modern humans have existed for less than 0.01 percent of Earth's history.**

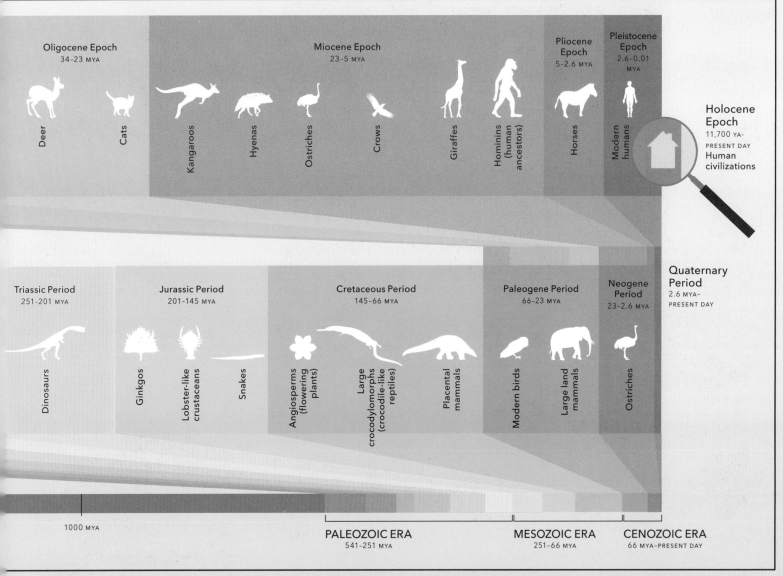

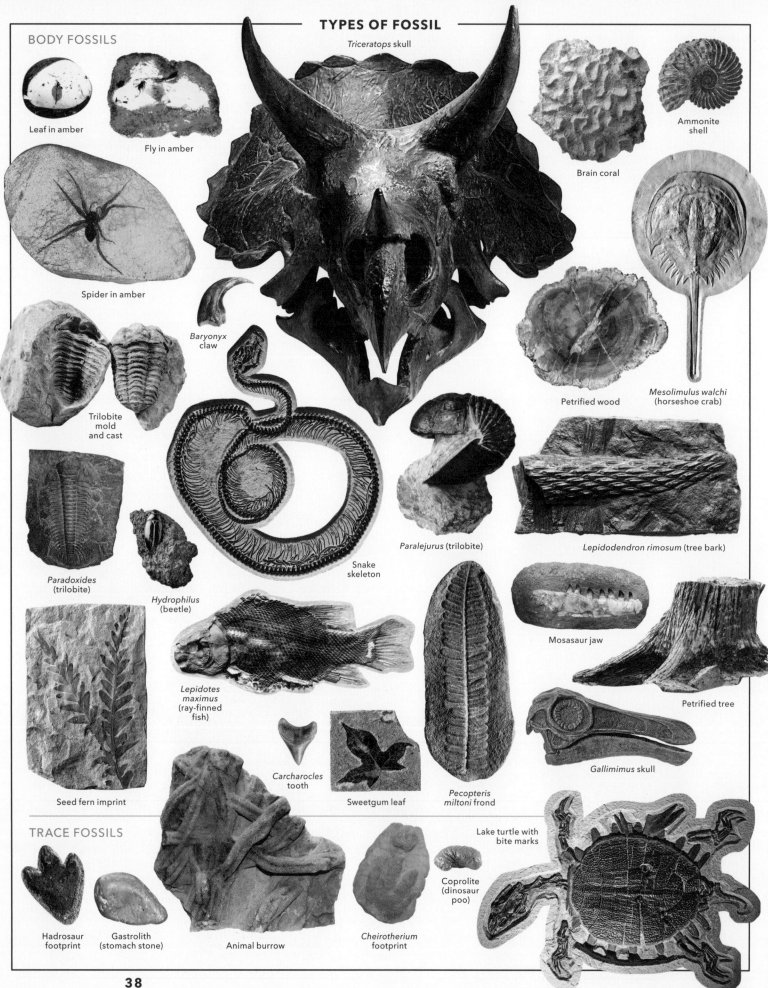

TYPES OF FOSSIL

BODY FOSSILS

Leaf in amber

Fly in amber

Spider in amber

Triceratops skull

Brain coral

Ammonite shell

Baryonyx claw

Petrified wood

Mesolimulus walchi (horseshoe crab)

Trilobite mold and cast

Paradoxides (trilobite)

Hydrophilus (beetle)

Snake skeleton

Paralejurus (trilobite)

Lepidodendron rimosum (tree bark)

Mosasaur jaw

Petrified tree

Seed fern imprint

Lepidotes maximus (ray-finned fish)

Carcharocles tooth

Sweetgum leaf

Pecopteris miltoni frond

Gallimimus skull

TRACE FOSSILS

Hadrosaur footprint

Gastrolith (stomach stone)

Animal burrow

Cheirotherium footprint

Coprolite (dinosaur poo)

Lake turtle with bite marks

Types of
FOSSIL

When a large fossil dinosaur bone was found in 1677, people thought it was from a giant human. We know better now, thanks in part to the countless fossils, large and small, discovered since then.

Fossils show us what plants and animals from many thousands and millions of years ago looked like. More than that, as the remains of once-living organisms, some contain chemicals such as proteins, fats, and DNA, which can be extracted from a fossil before it degrades. These chemicals can then be analyzed to give us information about how those organisms lived and died.

> A fossil is defined as any evidence of life more than 10,000 years old.

The scientists who study fossils are called paleontologists—*palaeo* is a Latin word meaning "ancient" or "old"—and they divide fossils into two main types. As their name suggests, body fossils are preserved physical remains. A *T. rex* jaw and a *Diplodocus* thigh bone are body fossils, for example, and so is a woolly mammoth tusk, or a spider, mosquito, or tree leaf trapped in amber.

Trace fossils are the marks left behind by long-vanished life forms. A dinosaur footprint stamped into ancient mud is a trace fossil, and so are the etchings formed by the roots of prehistoric trees and the furrows left by fish fins in a riverbed. The information that trace fossils leave behind can be invaluable: the dimensions and depth of a footprint can tell paleontologists a lot about the size and weight of the animal that made it; trilobite tracks on the seafloor can show where and how far those extinct invertebrates walked.

A bone, leaf, insect, tree, or even a piece of dinosaur poop (a coprolite) transforms into a fossil when it becomes completely covered, sometimes in amber, but mostly in sediment—when a river floods, for example. When this happens, it becomes "petrified," which means "turned to stone." Over thousands of years, it absorbs minerals in the sediment, such as quartz and silica, which alter and replace its hard parts. Most of its organic material decomposes slowly.

Trace fossils form in a similar way, when a footprint or a trilobite track is filled with mineral-rich sediment that dries and is covered in mud and soil until it is found by a paleontologist millions of years later.

▶ **FOSSIL ORIGINS**
The word "fossil" comes from the Latin *fossilis*, meaning "dug up." Experts classify fossils of ancient life forms as trace or body fossils.

Body fossils are a mix of organic and mineral matter.

Trace fossils are ancient imprints.

Types of
ROCK

Rocks are natural combinations of minerals. Three types of rock–igneous, sedimentary, and metamorphic–are found on Earth. These rocks have formed over millions of years.

The rocks all around us are mostly made up of minerals, which are themselves made of combinations of elements. Minerals bind with each other naturally or are pressed together by an outside force. Things in the natural world that act on rocks include heat, pressure, wind, rain, waves, rivers, and even animals. They cause rocks to change from one type to another. Movements in Earth's crust and underground volcanic activity spew molten rock or magma onto the surface of the planet. This magma cools down to form igneous rocks, such as granite, basalt, leucogabbro, and pumice. Rocks that begin to cool while still underground have coarser grains and are called intrusive igneous rocks. Those that cool after they reach the surface develop fine grains and are called extrusive igneous rocks.

Over time, igneous rocks are worn down by weathering and erosion by wind and water. They break down into smaller pieces and are transported by rivers, settling on riverbeds. As the layers build up, they compress the ones beneath to form compact layers of sedimentary rock. This type of rock includes shale, sandstone, limestone, and siltstone.

As time passes, sedimentary rocks sink down into Earth's crust, where heat and pressure change them into metamorphic rock, such as marble, slate, gneiss, and schist. Metamorphic rocks tend to be the hardest types of rock because of the effect of intense heat and pressure.

Underground rocks are melted by the heat from volcanic activity. In time, they are returned to the planet's surface as magma, continuing the rock cycle.

> **The rocks in Earth's crust are mainly made up of silicon and oxygen.**

> **The term igneous comes from the Latin word for "fire."**

▶ **THE ROCK CYCLE**
This is a never-ending process in which one type of rock changes into another.

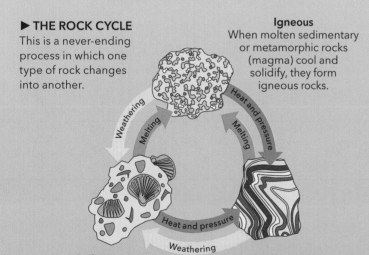

Igneous
When molten sedimentary or metamorphic rocks (magma) cool and solidify, they form igneous rocks.

Sedimentary
Grains (sediments) of rocks are squeezed together to form sedimentary rocks.

Metamorphic
These rocks are formed when older rocks are heated and squeezed in Earth's crust.

Weathering
Melting
Heat and pressure
Melting
Heat and pressure
Weathering

TYPES OF ROCK

IGNEOUS

Rhyolite

Andesite

Pumice

Peridotite

Feldspar pegmatite

Leucogabbro

Obsidian

Granite

Dolerite

Basalt

METAMORPHIC

Fulgurite

Slate

Eclogite

Skarn

Schist

Serpentinite

Amphibolite

Hornfels

Quartzite

Gneiss

Marble

SEDIMENTARY

Shale

Sandstone

Peat

Limestone

Siltstone

Tufa

Anthracite

Dolomite

Banded iron

Conglomerate

Travertine

A selection of rocks from among the major named igneous, metamorphic, and sedimentary rocks

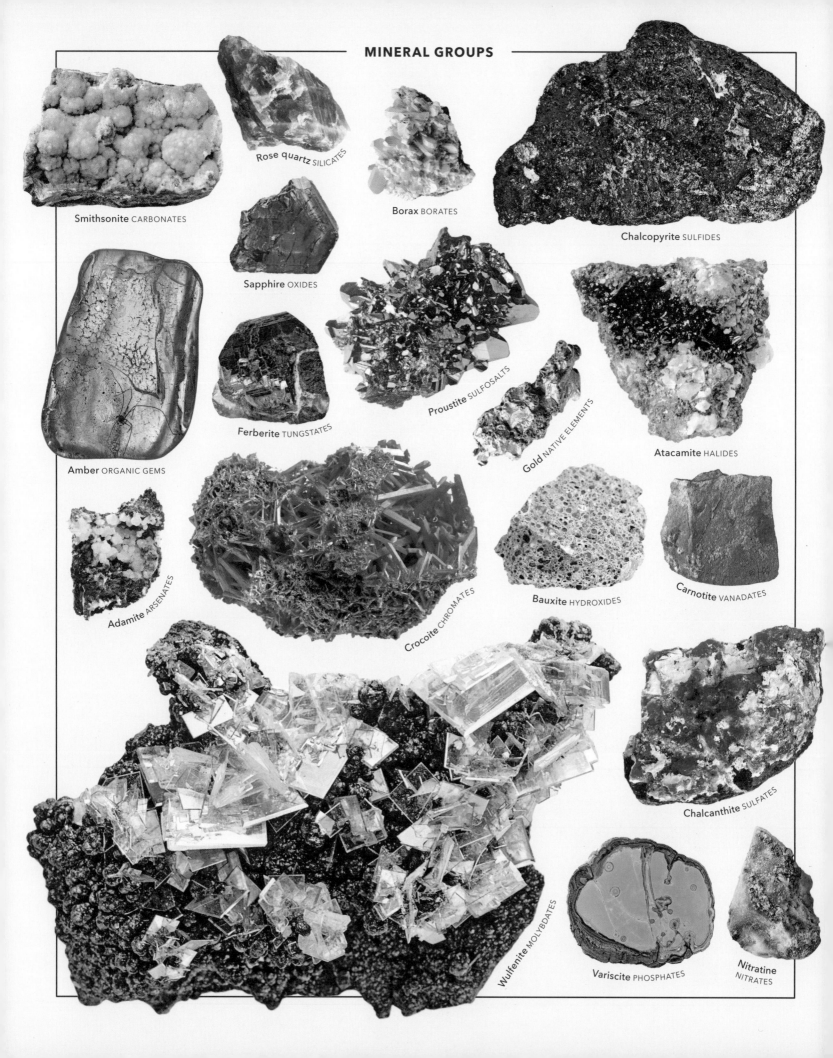

MINERAL GROUPS

Smithsonite CARBONATES

Rose quartz SILICATES

Borax BORATES

Chalcopyrite SULFIDES

Sapphire OXIDES

Amber ORGANIC GEMS

Ferberite TUNGSTATES

Proustite SULFOSALTS

Gold NATIVE ELEMENTS

Atacamite HALIDES

Adamite ARSENATES

Crocoite CHROMATES

Bauxite HYDROXIDES

Carnotite VANADATES

Wulfenite MOLYBDATES

Chalcanthite SULFATES

Variscite PHOSPHATES

Nitratine NITRATES

MINERAL
groups

All the rocks on Earth, as well as in space, are made up of minerals. They are natural solids with definite chemical compositions, according to which they are classified into different groups.

Minerals are solids found in rocks. They can consist of elements (substances that cannot be broken down any further) or compounds (mixtures of elements). Geologists (scientists who study rocks) organize minerals into 18 groups according to the elements they contain and the shapes of the crystals they make. Every mineral belongs to one of these groups.

Oxides include oxygen, sulfates include sulfur, carbonates include carbon and oxygen, nitrates include nitrogen and oxygen, and silicates include silicon. The silicates form the largest group and make up more than 90 percent of Earth's crust.

Minerals form naturally but are generally not made from plant or animal remains. The only exception is the group called organic gems in which organic remains have been replaced by minerals over time. The mineral group called "native elements" includes pure, uncombined elements such as gold. But, minerals in rocks are rarely in their pure state—they are found combined with sand, clay, and other impurities.

Almost all minerals form crystals. This is because they are made up of tiny building blocks called atoms. These atoms are arranged in precise patterns to form crystal structures. In some rocks, the crystals of different minerals are easily visible, while in other rocks, the mineral crystals can only be seen under a microscope.

There are many ways to identify minerals—by observing their color, the shape of their crystals, their hardness, the mark they leave when scratched on a tile, their luster (the way they reflect light), and their cleavage (the way the mineral splits or breaks).

Many minerals contain metals, such as iron, manganese, and lead. The rocks in which these minerals are found are also known as ores. An ore must be processed to extract the metal within.

> **There are around 5,000 known minerals on Earth.**

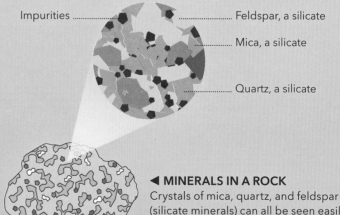

Impurities .... Feldspar, a silicate

.... Mica, a silicate

.... Quartz, a silicate

Pink granite

◀ MINERALS IN A ROCK
Crystals of mica, quartz, and feldspar (silicate minerals) can all be seen easily in the rock called pink granite. While this type of rock includes multiple minerals, there are some rocks that only include one mineral.

PRECIOUS AND SEMIPRECIOUS GEMSTONES

SEMIPRECIOUS

Cubic zirconia

Citrine

Indicolite

Hauyne

Chrysocolla

Sinhalite

Heliodor

Carnelian

Topaz

Moonstone

Jade

Bloodstone

Amber

Sardonyx

Opal

Turquoise

Sapphire

Peridot

Agate

Sunstone

Aquamarine

Ruby

PRECIOUS

Emerald

Jet

Malachite

Lapis lazuli

Diamond

Rhodonite

Obsidian

Garnet

Kyanite

Rose quartz

Amethyst

Mother of pearl

Pearl

Watermelon tourmaline

Jasper

33 semiprecious gemstones of more than 300 found on Earth

Precious and semiprecious
GEMSTONES

Brightly colored, sparkling gemstones have been prized by people all over the world for tens of thousands of years. These are mostly minerals, and can be divided into precious and semiprecious ones.

Gemstones are minerals that are valued for their rarity, hardness, color, and beauty. The best gemstones are chosen, then shaped and polished to make them shine for use in jewelery.

Gemstones are divided into two main categories: precious and semiprecious. Precious stones are those that were historically the most rare, and therefore the most valuable. Semiprecious stones were more common and less expensive than precious stones. These categories are still used today, but it is now a gem's popularity that makes it valuable, and some semiprecious gems can be more expensive than precious ones.

There are only four types of precious gem: emerald, ruby, sapphire, and diamond. Sapphire and ruby are both made of the same hard mineral: corundum. Emeralds are a part of the beryl mineral group, which also includes semiprecious stones such as aquamarine and heliodor.

Semiprecious stones come in a much wider variety. For instance, amethyst, citrine, and rose quartz are all part of the quartz group, formed by intense heat under the ground. Some semiprecious gems, such as pearls and

Peridots have been found in meteorites that fell from space.

amber, are organic (made of animal or plant materials). A pearl forms around grains of sand caught inside an oyster, and amber is tree resin that has become fossilized over time. Rather than being found in nature, some semiprecious gems are created synthetically (in a laboratory) and polished up. For example, cubic zirconia, which looks like diamonds, is made in laboratories.

Most gems can be shaped to further enhance their beauty. In the jewelery industry, shaping a gem is known as "cutting" it, although the process is actually more like sanding. The stone is first ground into a rough shape following its crystal form. Then a series of flat faces called "facets" are added, before the gem is polished. A finished gemstone can be used to add sparkle to jewelery such as necklaces, rings, earrings, or even crowns.

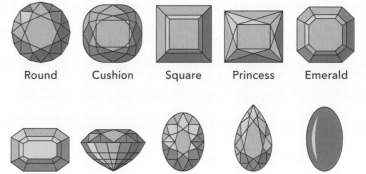

Round · Cushion · Square · Princess · Emerald

Octagon · Brilliant · Oval · Pear · Cabochon

▲ GEM CUTS
Gemstones are carefully shaped, or "cut," to allow more light to reflect around inside them, making the gem appear even sparklier. There are many different types of cut.

HABITATS
of Earth

The natural home of a plant or animal is called its habitat. There are lots of different habitats on Earth, which can be classified into 18 main types based on geography, climate, and vegetation.

Animals and plants live in an incredible range of places on Earth, from tiny tropical ponds to vast sheets of ice. These places are broadly grouped into the 18 main habitats that are shown on the right. Each one has environmental conditions that suit the wildlife and vegetation that thrive there.

The coldest and driest habitats on Earth are the polar deserts, which exist at the North and South Poles. Here, the land and parts of the sea are covered in permanent ice, and any animals that make this habitat their home live in or near the water. Moving farther south, away from the North Pole, is the Arctic tundra, which is still cold, but a thin layer of soil lies over the land. This allows grasses, mosses, and hardy plants to grow. Animals living here often have thick coats or layers of fat to keep warm, and hibernate or migrate during the long, harsh winters. Next to the Arctic tundra is Earth's northernmost forest habitat, called the boreal forest, which extends from Canada to Russia. Here, the winters are also harsh and trees grow in a short, cool summer.

Moving still closer to the equator, are the "temperate" habitats, where the weather is much milder, but with distinct warmer and cooler seasons throughout the year. Habitats here include temperate grasslands and two types of temperate forest: temperate broadleaf, with trees that lose their leaves in the cooler months; and temperate coniferous, where the trees have needle-shaped leaves that they keep all year round.

Tropical habitats occur on either side of Earth's equator, where the climate is hot all year round. The hot and rainy tropical rainforests are the richest habitats on Earth in terms of animal and plant life. Tropical grasslands and tropical dry forests have distinct wet and dry seasons, where plants and animals must survive with very little rainfall for much of the year. Deserts are the driest habitats on Earth.

The planet's watery habitats include freshwater places, such as rivers, lakes, and ponds. Wetlands include swamps and marshes inland, and mangrove forests along tropical coastlines. The shallow, wave-pounded coastal seas make for a turbulent habitat for their residents, while the largest habitat on Earth is the vast expanse of the open ocean, where the animal life varies greatly depending on the depth.

Some life forms live in a smaller part of a habitat called a microhabitat.

Rainforests are home to more than half of all animal and plant species living on Earth.

HABITATS OF EARTH

Polar desert

Arctic tundra

Boreal forest

Temperate grassland

Temperate broadleaf forest

Temperate coniferous forest

Tropical coniferous forest

Freshwater habitats

Tropical rainforest

Tropical dry forest

Tropical grassland

Mountain habitats

Desert and dry shrubland

Mediterranean-style shrubland

Wetlands

Coral reef

Coastal sea

Open ocean

RIVERS
of the world

Many people live near rivers, using them to get from place to place and as a source of freshwater and food. There are more than 150,000 rivers in the world and the top 20 longest are shown below.

RIVER BASINS OF THE 20 LONGEST RIVERS

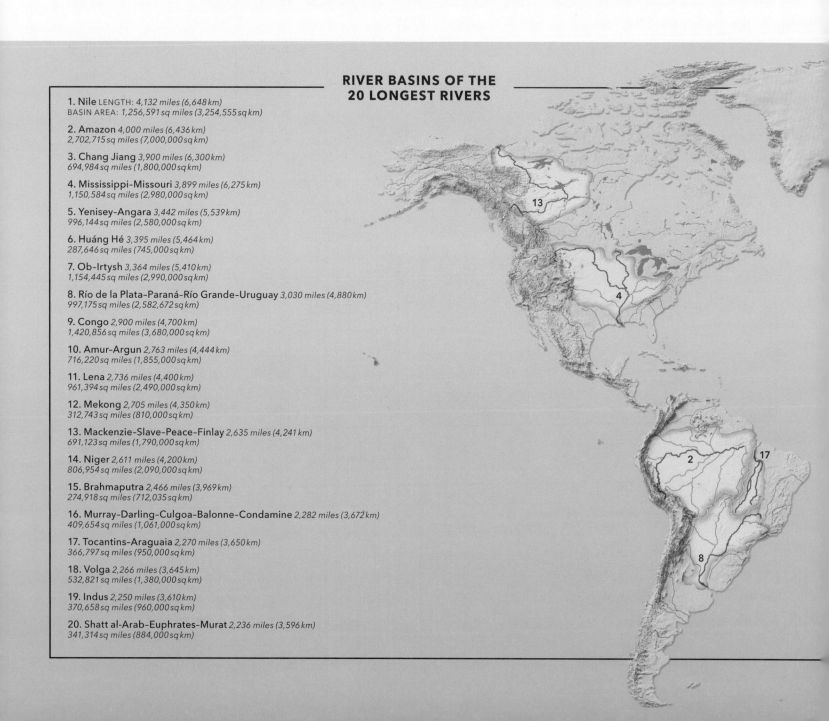

1. Nile LENGTH: *4,132 miles (6,648 km)*
BASIN AREA: *1,256,591 sq miles (3,254,555 sq km)*

2. Amazon *4,000 miles (6,436 km)*
2,702,715 sq miles (7,000,000 sq km)

3. Chang Jiang *3,900 miles (6,300 km)*
694,984 sq miles (1,800,000 sq km)

4. Mississippi-Missouri *3,899 miles (6,275 km)*
1,150,584 sq miles (2,980,000 sq km)

5. Yenisey-Angara *3,442 miles (5,539 km)*
996,144 sq miles (2,580,000 sq km)

6. Huáng Hé *3,395 miles (5,464 km)*
287,646 sq miles (745,000 sq km)

7. Ob-Irtysh *3,364 miles (5,410 km)*
1,154,445 sq miles (2,990,000 sq km)

8. Río de la Plata-Paraná-Río Grande-Uruguay *3,030 miles (4,880 km)*
997,175 sq miles (2,582,672 sq km)

9. Congo *2,900 miles (4,700 km)*
1,420,856 sq miles (3,680,000 sq km)

10. Amur-Argun *2,763 miles (4,444 km)*
716,220 sq miles (1,855,000 sq km)

11. Lena *2,736 miles (4,400 km)*
961,394 sq miles (2,490,000 sq km)

12. Mekong *2,705 miles (4,350 km)*
312,743 sq miles (810,000 sq km)

13. Mackenzie-Slave-Peace-Finlay *2,635 miles (4,241 km)*
691,123 sq miles (1,790,000 sq km)

14. Niger *2,611 miles (4,200 km)*
806,954 sq miles (2,090,000 sq km)

15. Brahmaputra *2,466 miles (3,969 km)*
274,918 sq miles (712,035 sq km)

16. Murray-Darling-Culgoa-Balonne-Condamine *2,282 miles (3,672 km)*
409,654 sq miles (1,061,000 sq km)

17. Tocantins-Araguaia *2,270 miles (3,650 km)*
366,797 sq miles (950,000 sq km)

18. Volga *2,266 miles (3,645 km)*
532,821 sq miles (1,380,000 sq km)

19. Indus *2,250 miles (3,610 km)*
370,658 sq miles (960,000 sq km)

20. Shatt al-Arab-Euphrates-Murat *2,236 miles (3,596 km)*
341,314 sq miles (884,000 sq km)

Most rivers begin in the mountains, where melting ice and glaciers create streams that run down the mountainside, gathering more water as they go. Sometimes the water comes up from an underground spring or flows out from a lake. When the streams reach flatter land, they become wider rivers, slowing down, and beginning to move in curves across the land. Smaller rivers, called tributaries, join big rivers, and this network of waterways is called a river basin. As rivers near the coast, they widen into estuaries or deltas with many channels pouring into the sea.

There are rivers on every continent, but the longest is the Nile River in Africa, which flows from central Africa to the Mediterranean Sea. The Amazon River in South America is also very long. It runs from western South America to the Atlantic Ocean and its river basin is home to the world's largest rainforest.

As rivers flow, they carry rocks, sand, mud, and salts, and deposit them around their banks, making the soil fertile and allowing plant and animal life to thrive. This, along with an abundant supply of freshwater, is why most of the earliest human settlements grew up around river systems. This includes the ancient civilizations of Mesopotamia around the Tigris–Euphrates river system, ancient Egypt on the Nile, ancient China in the Huang He Valley, and ancient India in the Indus river valley.

The Amazon and its tributaries carry more water than any other river.

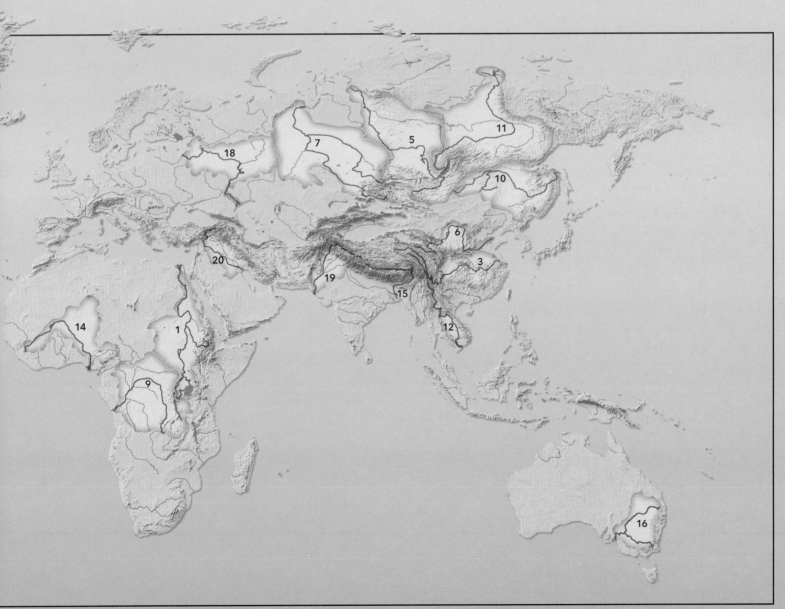

SEAS
and oceans

Earth is covered in one great, continuous body of water. People have named and divided different parts of it into seas and oceans.

Seas are smaller than oceans and always next to land—sometimes surrounded by it. The largest sea is the Mediterranean, between southern Europe and North Africa. It is around a quarter of the size of the whole of the US. Next comes the Caribbean Sea, north of South America and east of Central America. It contains lots of islands, including Jamaica and Saint Lucia. Its average depth is 7,217 ft (2,200 m), almost twice that of the Mediterranean. The Baltic Sea in northern Europe is quite shallow. Its average depth is 180 ft (55 m)—as tall as 12 double-decker buses piled on top of each other.

Some seas are known as bays or gulfs. Bays and gulfs are mostly surrounded by land, but a gulf has a narrower mouth than a bay.

Oceans are much bigger and mostly deeper than seas. The Pacific is the largest (and deepest) ocean, and is more than twice the size of the second biggest, the Atlantic. The next largest is the Indian Ocean, which borders Africa, Asia, and Australia, followed by the Southern Ocean, which flows around Antarctica. At the other end of the planet is the Arctic Ocean. This body of water is mostly covered by sea ice, although climate change is now making the ice melt and sea and ocean levels rise.

The Pacific Ocean contains just over 50 percent of all of the planet's open water.

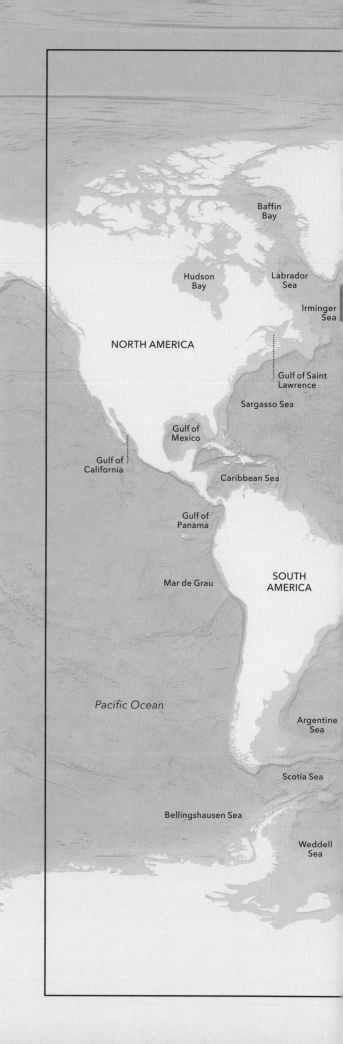

Baffin Bay

Hudson Bay

Labrador Sea

Irminger Sea

NORTH AMERICA

Gulf of Saint Lawrence

Sargasso Sea

Gulf of Mexico

Gulf of California

Caribbean Sea

Gulf of Panama

Mar de Grau

SOUTH AMERICA

Pacific Ocean

Argentine Sea

Scotia Sea

Bellingshausen Sea

Weddell Sea

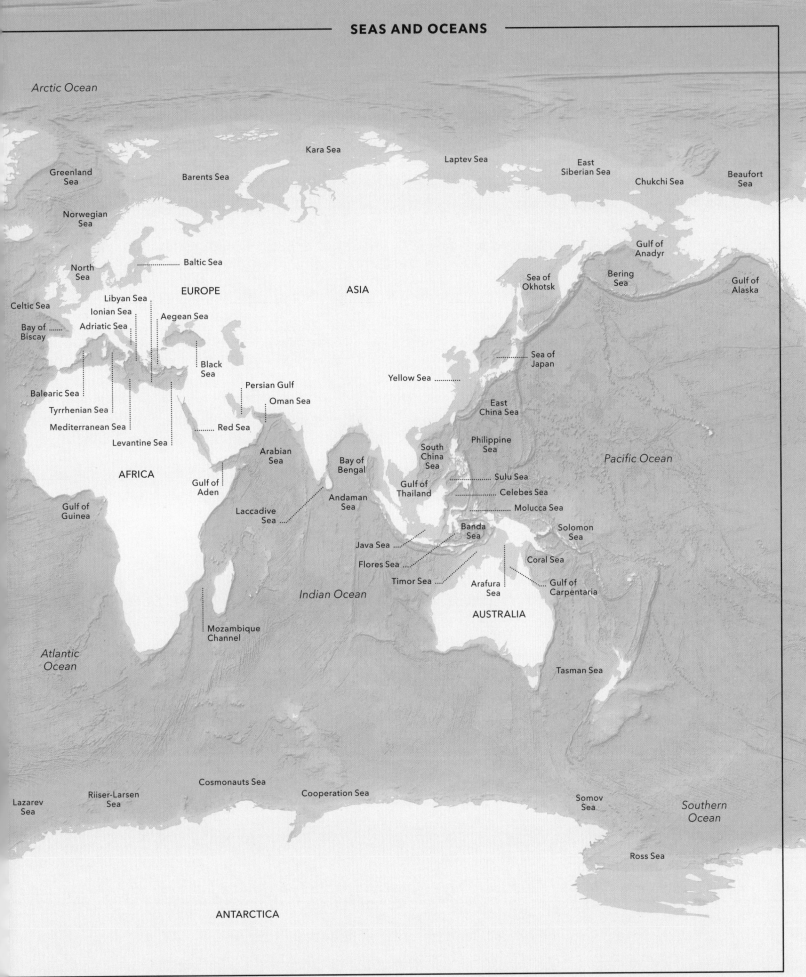

Arctic Ocean

Greenland Sea

Kara Sea

Laptev Sea

East Siberian Sea

Chukchi Sea

Beaufort Sea

Barents Sea

Norwegian Sea

Gulf of Anadyr

Sea of Okhotsk

Bering Sea

Gulf of Alaska

North Sea

Baltic Sea

EUROPE

ASIA

Celtic Sea

Libyan Sea

Ionian Sea

Aegean Sea

Sea of Japan

Adriatic Sea

Bay of Biscay

Black Sea

Yellow Sea

East China Sea

Balearic Sea

Persian Gulf

Oman Sea

Philippine Sea

Pacific Ocean

Tyrrhenian Sea

Mediterranean Sea

Red Sea

Arabian Sea

Bay of Bengal

South China Sea

Levantine Sea

AFRICA

Gulf of Aden

Andaman Sea

Gulf of Thailand

Sulu Sea

Celebes Sea

Molucca Sea

Gulf of Guinea

Laccadive Sea

Banda Sea

Solomon Sea

Java Sea

Coral Sea

Flores Sea

Timor Sea

Arafura Sea

Gulf of Carpentaria

Indian Ocean

AUSTRALIA

Atlantic Ocean

Mozambique Channel

Tasman Sea

Cosmonauts Sea

Cooperation Sea

Somov Sea

Southern Ocean

Lazarev Sea

Riiser-Larsen Sea

Ross Sea

ANTARCTICA

LARGEST LAKES

Caspian Sea
ASIA
149,200 sq miles
(386,400 sq km)

Lake Superior
NORTH AMERICA
31,700 sq miles
(82,100 sq km)

Lake Victoria
AFRICA
26,828 sq miles
(69,484 sq km)

Lake Huron
NORTH AMERICA
23,000 sq miles
(59,570 sq km)

Lake Baikal
ASIA
12,200 sq miles
(31,500 sq km)

Great Bear Lake
NORTH AMERICA
12,096 sq miles
(31,328 sq km)

Lake Malawi
AFRICA
11,430 sq miles
(29,604 sq km)

Great Slave Lake
NORTH AMERICA
11,030 sq miles
(28,568 sq km)

Lake Ontario
NORTH AMERICA
7,340 sq miles
(19,011 sq km)

Lake Ladoga
EUROPE
6,800 sq miles
(17,600 sq km)

Lake Balkhash
ASIA
6,000 sq miles
(15,500 sq km)

Lake Vostok
ANTARCTICA
4,633 sq miles
(12,000 sq km)

Lake Nicaragua
NORTH AMERICA
3,149 sq miles
(8,157 sq km)

Lake Athabasca
NORTH AMERICA
3,064 sq miles
(7,936 sq km)

Lake Turkana
AFRICA
2,472 sq miles
(6,405 sq km)

Reindeer Lake
NORTH AMERICA
2,444 sq miles
(6,330 sq km)

Lake Urmia
ASIA
2,316 sq miles
(6,001 sq km)

Lake Torrens
AUSTRALIA
2,200 sq miles
(5,698 sq km)

Lake Vänern
EUROPE
2,140 sq miles
(5,545 sq km)

Lake Winnipegosis
NORTH AMERICA
2,086 sq miles
(5,403 sq km)

DEEPEST LAKES

Lake Baikal ASIA
5,315 ft (1,620 m)

Lake Tanganyika AFRICA
4,711 ft (1,436 m)

Caspian Sea ASIA
3,362 ft (1,025 m)

Lake Viedma SOUTH AMERICA
2,953 ft (900 m)

Lake Vostok ANTARCTICA
2,953 ft (900 m)

O'Higgins / San Martín Lake SOUTH AMERICA
2,743 ft (836 m)

Lake Malawi AFRICA
2,316 ft (706 m)

Lake Issyk-Kul ASIA
2,191 ft (668 m)

Great Slave Lake NORTH AMERICA
2,014 ft (614 m)

Crater Lake NORTH AMERICA
1,942 ft (592 m)

Lake Matano ASIA
1,935 ft (590 m)

General Carrera Lake SOUTH AMERICA
1,922 ft (586 m)

Hornindalsvatn Lake EUROPE
1,686 ft (514 m)

Quesnel Lake NORTH AMERICA
1,676 ft (511 m)

Lake Toba ASIA
1,656 ft (505 m)

Sarez Lake ASIA
1,656 ft (505 m)

Lake Tahoe NORTH AMERICA
1,643 ft (501 m)

Argentino Lake SOUTH AMERICA
1,640 ft (500 m)

Lake Kivu AFRICA
1,574 ft (480 m)

Lake Salvatnet EUROPE
1,522 ft (464 m)

Lake Nahuel Huapí SOUTH AMERICA
1,522 ft (464 m)

Lake Hauroko AUSTRALASIA AND OCEANIA

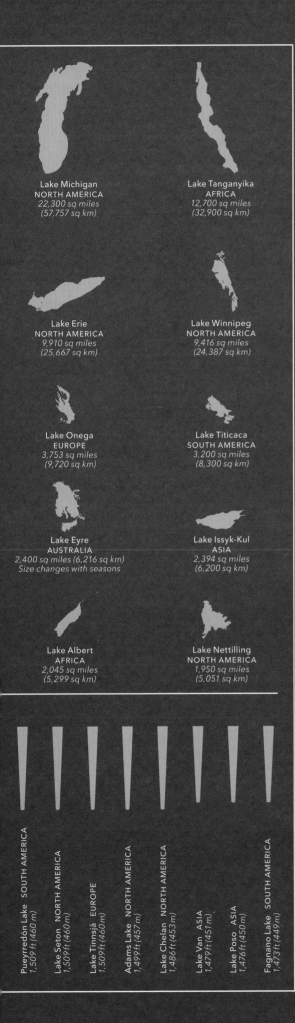

Lake Michigan
NORTH AMERICA
22,300 sq miles
(57,757 sq km)

Lake Tanganyika
AFRICA
12,700 sq miles
(32,900 sq km)

Lake Erie
NORTH AMERICA
9,910 sq miles
(25,667 sq km)

Lake Winnipeg
NORTH AMERICA
9,416 sq miles
(24,387 sq km)

Lake Onega
EUROPE
3,753 sq miles
(9,720 sq km)

Lake Titicaca
SOUTH AMERICA
3,200 sq miles
(8,300 sq km)

Lake Eyre
AUSTRALIA
2,400 sq miles (6,216 sq km)
Size changes with seasons

Lake Issyk-Kul
ASIA
2,394 sq miles
(6,200 sq km)

Lake Albert
AFRICA
2,045 sq miles
(5,299 sq km)

Lake Nettilling
NORTH AMERICA
1,950 sq miles
(5,051 sq km)

Pueyrredón Lake SOUTH AMERICA
1,509 ft (460 m)

Lake Seton NORTH AMERICA
1,509 ft (460 m)

Lake Tinnsjä EUROPE
1,509 ft (460 m)

Adams Lake NORTH AMERICA
1,499 ft (457 m)

Lake Chelan NORTH AMERICA
1,486 ft (453 m)

Lake Van ASIA
1,479 ft (451 m)

Lake Poso ASIA
1,476 ft (450 m)

Fagnano Lake SOUTH AMERICA
1,473 ft (449 m)

Largest and deepest
LAKES

Every continent has its lakes, including some with record-setting sizes and depths. Lakes are bodies of water surrounded by land.

Lakes can be very large and deep, and hold a huge amount of water, which can be fresh or salty. Lake Tanganyika in Africa, for example, holds about 16 percent of all the world's fresh water. The world's 30 largest lakes and 30 deepest lakes are shown on the left.

The world's largest lake is the Caspian Sea. Despite it being called a sea by many people, it is actually a lake. It is surrounded by Russia, Kazakhstan, Turkmenistan, Iran, and Azerbaijan. This lake covers an area larger than the whole of Japan, and stores about a third of all the planet's inland water. Although it is now landlocked, meaning that it has no outlet to the ocean, it used to have one millions of years ago.

The Great Lakes of North America (Superior, Huron, Michigan, Erie, and Ontario) are some of the largest—they are interconnected via rivers, and hold around 20 percent of the world's fresh water. Astonishingly, the water in all five of the Great Lakes is equivalent to the water held by one single lake—Lake Baikal in Siberia. This is the world's deepest lake. It holds about 22 percent of all our fresh water. It is so deep that the heights of the Burj Khalifa (Dubai), the Empire State Building (New York City), and the Eiffel Tower (Paris) together are about equal to its depth.

> **Lake Vostok lies hidden beneath the Antarctic ice.**

Types of
CLOUD

Knowing how to identify a cloud is a great skill to have, because its size, shape, and color will reveal lots about what's going on in the atmosphere—and what the weather's going to be like.

Clouds form when water vapor high in the air cools and becomes tiny droplets of water or ice crystals in a process called condensation. When enough droplets join together they become a cloud. There are three main types: cirrus, cumulus, and stratus. Cirrus clouds are thin and wispy and float in the sky at heights greater than 20,000 ft (6,000 m). Cumulus clouds are puffy and look like cotton. They float 1,000–6,500 ft (300–2,000 m) above the ground. Stratus clouds are flat, are found low in the sky, and don't move much. They can cover the whole sky like a blanket. If they are just above the ground, they are called fog. When these last two types of cloud look dark and gray, they may be bringing rain or snow and are called cumulonimbus or nimbostratus. When a cumulonimbus rises to become tall and puffy, it can produce storms and tornadoes.

Sometimes, when the weight of moisture in clouds causes them to descend or air pressure from below forces them to rise, different cloud types can collide. This is how we get combinations of clouds such as stratocumulus, cirrostratus, and cirrocumulus. If a cloud is called "alto" cumulus or stratus, this means it is higher in the sky than a normal cumulus or stratus cloud.

There are lots of other cloud shapes: lenticular clouds are saucer-shaped, while mammatus clouds have bulges along their base. Hole-punch clouds have circles called fallstreaks "cut out" of them and fractus are ragged pieces of cloud that break off from stratus or cumulus clouds.

Clouds reflect some of the sunlight falling on Earth during the day, keeping our planet from getting too warm. They also trap some of the heat given off by Earth's surface, radiating it back to keep our planet just warm enough.

About 67 percent of Earth is covered by clouds at any one time.

Exosphere
*370–6,200 miles
(600–10,000 km)*

Thermosphere
53–370 miles (85–600 km)

Mesosphere
30–53 miles (50–85 km)

Stratosphere
7.5–30 miles (12–50 km)
Troposphere
0–7.5 miles (0–12 km)

◀ **LAYERS OF ATMOSPHERE**
Earth's atmosphere has five layers. Clouds form and weather happens in the troposphere. A particularly tall cumulonimbus may just reach as high as the stratosphere.

Cirrostratus

Cirrocumulus

Cirrus

Mammatus cloud

Altocumulus

Hole-punch cloud

Altostratus

Lenticular cloud

Stratocumulus

Fractus cloud

Cumulus

Stratus

Nimbostratus

Shelf cloud

Funnel cloud

Wall cloud

Cumulonimbus

A selection of 17 cloud types

Types of
SNOWFLAKE

No two snowflakes are exactly the same, but each one is made of frozen ice crystals. A snowflake can have one of many shapes, and based on the shape, snowflakes can be classified into 35 types.

On a snowy day, the layers of snow that cover the ground are made up of uncountable numbers of individual flakes of fluffy white snow. All snowflakes form in the same way—when water inside clouds condenses on dust or other particles and freezes to form ice crystals. As these crystals fall to the ground, they stick to one another and get bigger as snowflakes, arranging themselves into the shapes shown on the right. If we were to look at a snowflake under a microscope, we would be able to see its ice crystal pattern.

Each ice crystal starts as a hexagon (a shape with six sides). This is because it is formed from frozen water, and water molecules are made up of two hydrogen atoms and one oxygen atom. The most efficient way for these molecules to fit together is in a hexagon shape.

No two snowflakes look alike. Each snowflake takes its own path down to the ground. The conditions it encounters on its way affect how the ice crystals form and stick together, and this makes each snowflake different. There are two factors that affect the formation of the shapes: the temperature of the clouds

that the ice crystals fall through and the amount of water in the air. Any tiny variation in these two things will change the shape of the snowflake. Colder temperatures cause smaller, more pointed ice crystals. Warmer temperatures produce larger crystals. When there is more moisture in the air, more complex shapes tend to form. The shapes taken by the snowflakes can range from flat hollow plates and arrowhead twins to simple crossed needles and fernlike stellar dendrites.

Dendrite snowflakes, which have many branches, form high up inside clouds that are very cold. Snowflakes without these branches are called thin plate snowflakes and these form because there isn't enough water in the air to form the branches.

> The biggest snowflake ever recorded was 15 in (38 cm) in diameter.

▼ SNOWFLAKE SHAPE AND SIZE
The shape and size of snowflakes depend on the moisture in the air and how warm or cold it is.

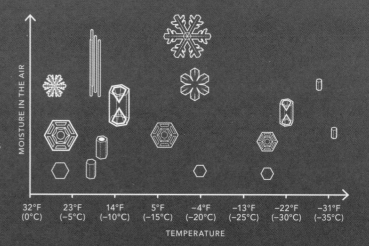

MOISTURE IN THE AIR

| 32°F (0°C) | 23°F (−5°C) | 14°F (−10°C) | 5°F (−15°C) | −4°F (−20°C) | −13°F (−25°C) | −22°F (−30°C) | −31°F (−35°C) |

TEMPERATURE

TYPES OF SNOWFLAKE

Simple prisms

Solid columns

Sheaths

Scrolls on plates

Triangular forms

Hexagonal plates

Hollow columns

Cups

Multiply capped columns

12-branched stars

Crossed plates

Bullet rosettes

Capped columns

Split plates and stars

Radiating plates

Columns on plates

Skeletal forms

Capped bullets

Radiating dendrites

Simple stars

Twin columns

Isolated bullets

Arrowhead twins

Hollow plates

Double plates

Irregulars

Stellar dendrites

Fernlike stellar dendrites

Crossed needles

Rimed

Stellar plates

Sectored plates

Needle clusters

Simple needles

Graupel

Measuring
NATURAL DISASTERS

Volcanic eruptions, earthquakes, and hurricanes are some of the natural disasters that cause immense damage to life and property. Scientists use scales that measure the intensity of these disasters.

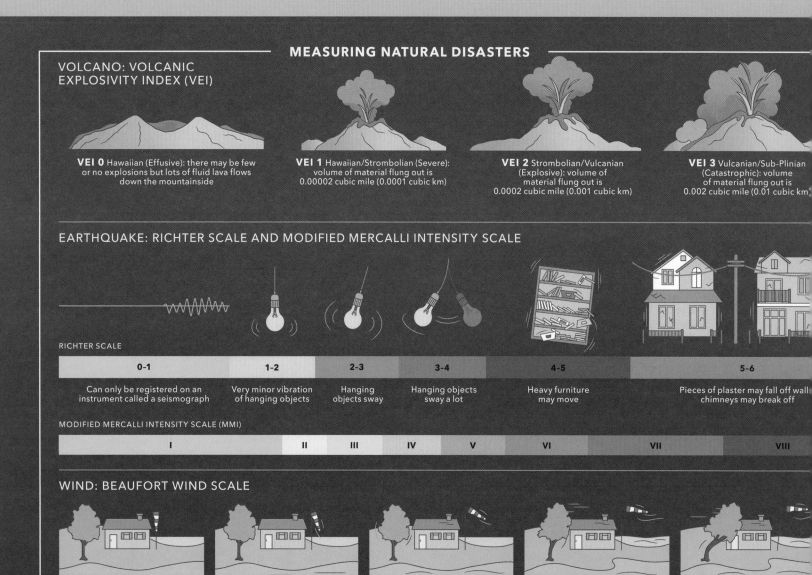

MEASURING NATURAL DISASTERS

VOLCANO: VOLCANIC EXPLOSIVITY INDEX (VEI)

VEI 0 Hawaiian (Effusive): there may be few or no explosions but lots of fluid lava flows down the mountainside

VEI 1 Hawaiian/Strombolian (Severe): volume of material flung out is 0.00002 cubic mile (0.0001 cubic km)

VEI 2 Strombolian/Vulcanian (Explosive): volume of material flung out is 0.0002 cubic mile (0.001 cubic km)

VEI 3 Vulcanian/Sub-Plinian (Catastrophic): volume of material flung out is 0.002 cubic mile (0.01 cubic km)

EARTHQUAKE: RICHTER SCALE AND MODIFIED MERCALLI INTENSITY SCALE

RICHTER SCALE

0-1	1-2	2-3	3-4	4-5	5-6
Can only be registered on an instrument called a seismograph	Very minor vibration of hanging objects	Hanging objects sway	Hanging objects sway a lot	Heavy furniture may move	Pieces of plaster may fall off walls; chimneys may break off

MODIFIED MERCALLI INTENSITY SCALE (MMI)

I	II	III	IV	V	VI	VII	VIII

WIND: BEAUFORT WIND SCALE

0 Calm: windsock hangs straight down

1-2 Light air to light breeze: windsock flutters

3-5 Gentle to fresh breeze: leaves sway and water has waves

6 Strong breeze: branches move and large waves form

7 Near gale: tree moves violently and sea heaps up

There are different methods for measuring natural disasters. The Volcanic Explosivity Index (VEI) measures the intensity of volcanic eruptions. A score of 0 does not mean that the eruption is small— it means the intensity of the explosion is very low and not a lot of volcanic rock, ash, and cinders are flung into the air. For example, Hawai'i has some of the largest volcanoes in the world, but they score a 0 on the VEI as their eruptions usually produce constantly flowing lava, not explosions.

The first widely used scale for measuring earthquakes was the Richter scale, which measures the energy released by the shock waves of an earthquake. This scale measures the strength of an earthquake at its epicenter (source). While it is still the most well-known scale, scientists have developed more useful scales. These include the Modified Mercalli Intensity scale (MMI), which measures the intensity of earthquakes and how much damage is caused at a particular location. It is based mainly on observations by people.

Wind levels on land and at sea are measured using the Beaufort wind scale. It begins at a score of 0 with calm blue skies, then builds up to cover increasingly windy conditions, ending at 12 with a full hurricane. Wind speeds during hurricanes can reach up to 215 mph (346 kph).

VEI 4-5 Sub-Plinian–Plinian (Cataclysmic to Paroxysmal): volume of material flung out is 0.02-0.2 cubic mile (0.1-1 cubic km)

VEI 6 Plinian/Ultra-Plinian (Colossal): volume of material flung out is 2.4 cubic miles (10 cubic km)

VEI 7-8 Ultra-Plinian (Mega-colossal to Apocalyptic): volume of material flung out is 24-240 cubic miles (100-1,000 cubic km)

| 6-7 | 7-8 | 8-9 |

Sturdy buildings start breaking and may shift off their foundations

Few structures remain and the ground breaks open in fissures

Total destruction of buildings and roads

| IX | X | XI | XII |

8 Gale: twigs break off and moderately high waves form

9 Severe gale: high waves form and roof shingles fly off

10 Storm: trees are uprooted and high waves with white crests form

11 Violent storm: sea becomes completely white with foam

12 Hurricane: air is hazy with foam and hurricanes form

NATURE

Kingdoms of
LIFE

Biologists have devised a simple system of naming and organizing all the millions of living things on our planet in order to understand the relationships between them and figure out how they evolved.

In the mid 1700s, Swedish scientist Carl Linnaeus came up with a way of classifying all life on Earth, known as "taxonomy." He started by sorting living things into large groups called "kingdoms" and then divided them further, into smaller and smaller groups, based on shared characteristics—a bit like folders in a giant filing cabinet.

The six kingdoms—animals, plants, fungi, bacteria, archaea, and protists—are shown opposite. Animals, plants, and fungi are living things made up of many cells, whereas protists, bacteria, and archaea are living things that consist of just a single cell.

Each kingdom has its own special features. Animals move around, and eat other things. Plants make their food through photosynthesis (using the sun's rays). Many fungi, like bread mold, feed on dead animals and plants, and produce tiny spores. Protists are microscopic, but their single cell is complex, whereas bacteria and archaea are even smaller and have much simpler cells.

Within each kingdom, the living things are subdivided into increasingly smaller groups based on common features. The first group is called phylum (or "division" in the plant kingdom), then class, followed by order. Next comes family, followed by genus, and finally, species. So, if we use humans as an example, we belong to the animal kingdom because we are animals. Then, we are in the chordates phylum because we have a backbone. From there, we are in the mammal class because we produce milk for our babies, we are in the primate order because of features of our limbs and hands, and the hominid family, because we have features such as a large brain and upright body posture. Finally, our genus is *Homo*, and our species is *sapiens*.

Scientists estimate there are 8.7 million plant and animal species on Earth.

▶ **TOP TO BOTTOM**
Carl Linnaeus's system for organizing nature into seven biological levels, based on more and more specific features, works for all living things. The classification for humans is shown here.

KINGDOM	Animals
PHYLUM	Chordates
CLASS	Mammals
ORDER	Primates
FAMILY	Hominids
GENUS	*Homo*
SPECIES	*sapiens*

KINGDOMS OF LIFE

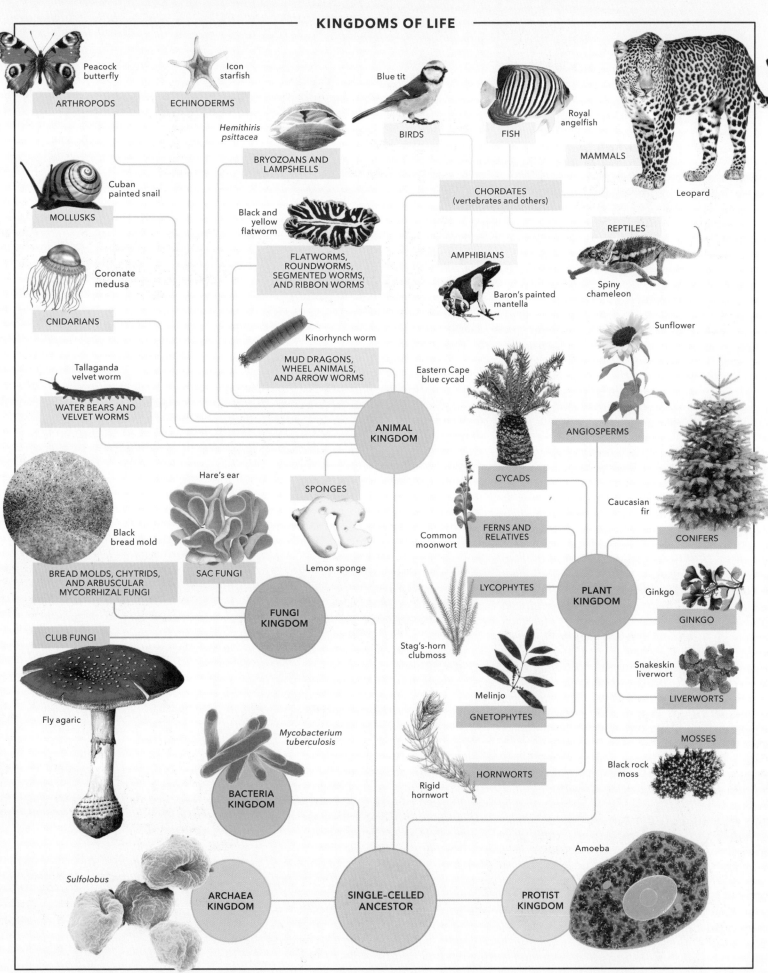

Peacock butterfly
ARTHROPODS

Icon starfish
ECHINODERMS

Blue tit
BIRDS

Royal angelfish
FISH

MAMMALS

Leopard

Hemithiris psittacea
BRYOZOANS AND LAMPSHELLS

Cuban painted snail
MOLLUSKS

Black and yellow flatworm
FLATWORMS, ROUNDWORMS, SEGMENTED WORMS, AND RIBBON WORMS

CHORDATES (vertebrates and others)

REPTILES

AMPHIBIANS

Baron's painted mantella

Spiny chameleon

Coronate medusa
CNIDARIANS

Kinorhynch worm
MUD DRAGONS, WHEEL ANIMALS, AND ARROW WORMS

Sunflower

Eastern Cape blue cycad

Tallaganda velvet worm
WATER BEARS AND VELVET WORMS

ANGIOSPERMS

Hare's ear
SPONGES

ANIMAL KINGDOM

CYCADS

Black bread mold
BREAD MOLDS, CHYTRIDS, AND ARBUSCULAR MYCORRHIZAL FUNGI

SAC FUNGI

Lemon sponge

Common moonwort
FERNS AND RELATIVES

Caucasian fir
CONIFERS

CLUB FUNGI

FUNGI KINGDOM

LYCOPHYTES

PLANT KINGDOM

Ginkgo
GINKGO

Stag's-horn clubmoss

Snakeskin liverwort
LIVERWORTS

Melinjo
GNETOPHYTES

Fly agaric

Mycobacterium tuberculosis

BACTERIA KINGDOM

Rigid hornwort
HORNWORTS

MOSSES

Black rock moss

Amoeba

Sulfolobus

ARCHAEA KINGDOM

SINGLE-CELLED ANCESTOR

PROTIST KINGDOM

This tree shows the six kingdoms (in colored circles) and the phyla or divisions for most of them.
The vertebrate classes under the chordates phylum are also given.

PLANT DIVISIONS

ANGIOSPERMS

London plane

Prickly water lily

King protea

Red silky oak

Bay laurel

Winter's bark

Ylang ylang

Blue plantain lily

Titan arum

Traveler's palm

GNETOPHYTES

Melinjo

Ma huang

Welwitschia

CYCADS

Eastern Cape blue cycad

Japanese sago palm

Burrawang

MOSSES

Ostrich plume feather moss

Black rock moss

Capillary thread moss

HORNWORTS

Field hornwort

Carolina hornwort

Smooth hornwort

LYCOPHYTES

Fan club moss

Stag's-horn club moss

Peacock fern

FERNS AND RELATIVES

Common moonwort

Common horsetail

Royal fern

Mosquito fern

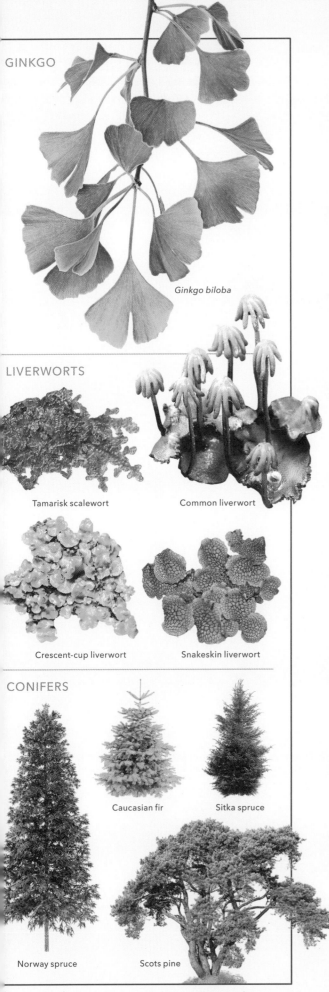

GINKGO

Ginkgo biloba

LIVERWORTS

Tamarisk scalewort

Common liverwort

Crescent-cup liverwort

Snakeskin liverwort

CONIFERS

Caucasian fir

Sitka spruce

Norway spruce

Scots pine

A selection of species from the 10 plant divisions

PLANT
divisions

Tiny mosses may look very different from towering conifer trees, but they are both plants—a group of organisms with a vast range of shapes and sizes.

KINGDOM
DIVISION
CLASS
ORDER
FAMILY
GENUS
SPECIES

To bring order to the amazing variety of plant life, botanists (scientists who study plants) classify all species in the plant kingdom into 10 divisions, based on their shape, structure, and how they reproduce.

Mosses, liverworts, and hornworts are some of the oldest and simplest plants. They live in damp places, have no roots or proper leaves, and reproduce by releasing spores into the water. Their spores travel to other similar plants for reproduction.

Lycophytes are also primitive plants that release spores, but they have very basic leaves and roots. Ferns have veined leaves and roots. Their windblown spores spread far but grow into tiny plants that need water to reproduce.

Pollen (dustlike substance containing male reproductive cells) and seeds evolved as some plants adapted to living on dry land—they no longer needed to rely on water to reproduce because pollen can be carried in many ways, including by the wind or insects. The first seed-bearing plants evolved around 380 million years ago. Pollen is carried from the male part of a flower to the female part of another flower. Seeds can also be scattered in many ways. Cycads, ginkgos, conifers, and gnetophytes have pollen and seeds. Conifer seeds are protected inside a woody cone.

Angiosperms, or flowering plants, bear seeds that have a protective seed coat and grow within a fruit. They evolved colored flowers to attract pollinators.

Parts of a PLANT

Plants are complex organisms and each part of their structure has a role in their life cycle. They cannot move to eat, but they can absorb water to drink and get food from the sun and the soil.

Almost all flowering plants have a similar set of structures that they use for survival and reproduction. Their roots have two main functions: to anchor the plant and to absorb water and nutrients from the soil. Where there is little water available, like in a desert, a plant's root system can be extensive because it needs to stretch far and wide in search of a drink.

The stem and leaves are the energy factories of the plant. The stem carries water absorbed through the roots up to the flowers, fruit, and leaves, keeping them healthy, while transporting sugars and other foods in the opposite direction, down to the roots to supply energy and for storage. The leaves are generally thin and wide, so more sunlight can be captured over a larger area. Special pores on their underside also allow gases such as carbon dioxide to be absorbed, transformed, and released as oxygen in a process known as photosynthesis. Any unused water, meanwhile, is expelled through the leaves, which keeps the plant cool.

As the plant grows, new shoots and leaves branch out from small bulges called nodes along the stem. Sections between these nodes are called "internodes." At the tips of the stems are the flowers and fruit. Flowers are a plant's reproductive parts. The male part, or stamen, of one plant makes pollen that is transferred (by bees or the wind, for example) to the female parts, or carpel, of another plant, inside which is an ovule. When it is fertilized by pollen, the ovule becomes a seed. Fruits develop rapidly after ovules are fertilized. For tomatoes, fleshy layers develop around the seeds. As the fruit ripens, it changes color from green to red. This attracts animals to eat it and spread its seeds (tomato seeds are resistant to stomach acid). Once deposited on bare soil, a seed will grow into a new plant.

> *On average, about a quarter of a plant's mass is under the ground, in its roots.*

> *There are almost 400,000 plant species; 2,000 new types are discovered each year.*

▶ MAKING FOOD

Plants use the green pigment in their leaves to create sugars from water and carbon dioxide, "cooked" by the sun's energy. Oxygen, a byproduct of this process (called photosynthesis), is used by animals and humans to breathe.

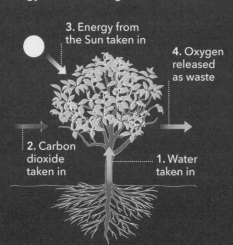

3. Energy from the Sun taken in

4. Oxygen released as waste

2. Carbon dioxide taken in

1. Water taken in

PARTS OF A PLANT

TOMATO PLANT

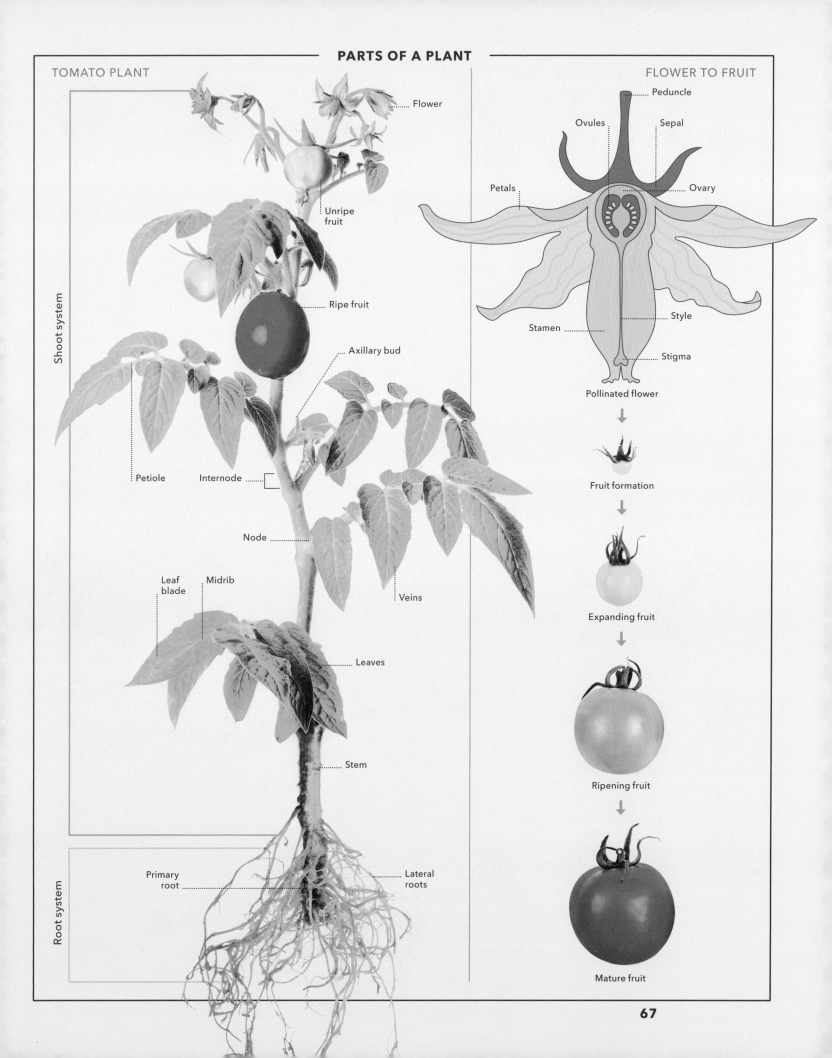

Flower

Unripe fruit

Ripe fruit

Axillary bud

Shoot system

Petiole

Internode

Node

Leaf blade

Midrib

Veins

Leaves

Stem

Root system

Primary root

Lateral roots

FLOWER TO FRUIT

Peduncle

Ovules

Sepal

Petals

Ovary

Stamen

Style

Stigma

Pollinated flower

Fruit formation

Expanding fruit

Ripening fruit

Mature fruit

LEAF SHAPES

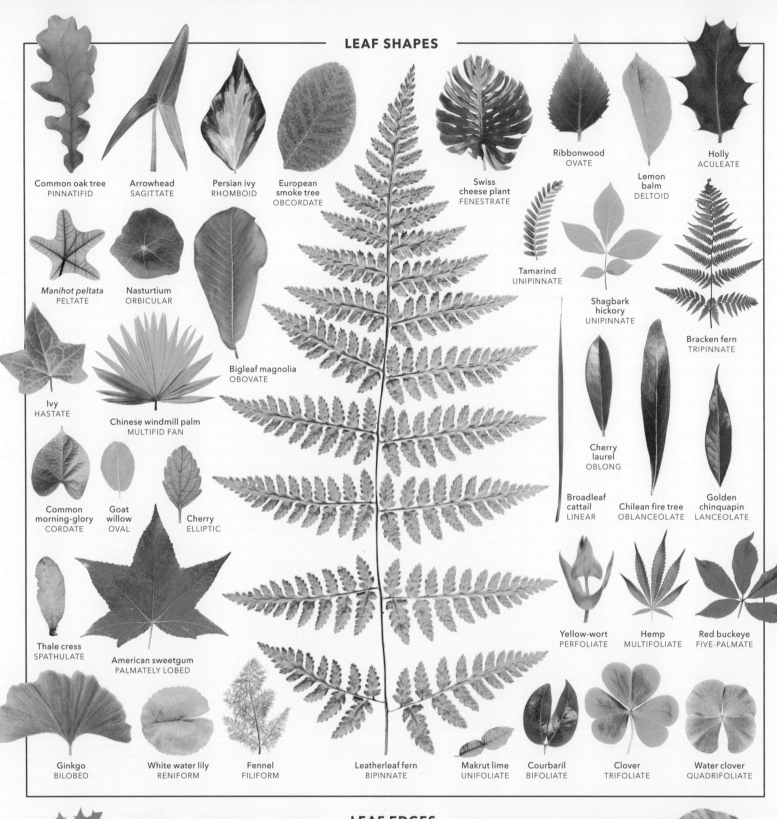

Common oak tree
PINNATIFID

Arrowhead
SAGITTATE

Persian ivy
RHOMBOID

European smoke tree
OBCORDATE

Swiss cheese plant
FENESTRATE

Ribbonwood
OVATE

Lemon balm
DELTOID

Holly
ACULEATE

Manihot peltata
PELTATE

Nasturtium
ORBICULAR

Tamarind
UNIPINNATE

Shagbark hickory
UNIPINNATE

Bracken fern
TRIPINNATE

Ivy
HASTATE

Chinese windmill palm
MULTIFID FAN

Bigleaf magnolia
OBOVATE

Cherry laurel
OBLONG

Common morning-glory
CORDATE

Goat willow
OVAL

Cherry
ELLIPTIC

Broadleaf cattail
LINEAR

Chilean fire tree
OBLANCEOLATE

Golden chinquapin
LANCEOLATE

Thale cress
SPATHULATE

American sweetgum
PALMATELY LOBED

Yellow-wort
PERFOLIATE

Hemp
MULTIFOLIATE

Red buckeye
FIVE-PALMATE

Ginkgo
BILOBED

White water lily
RENIFORM

Fennel
FILIFORM

Leatherleaf fern
BIPINNATE

Makrut lime
UNIFOLIATE

Courbaril
BIFOLIATE

Clover
TRIFOLIATE

Water clover
QUADRIFOLIATE

LEAF EDGES

Pin oak
CLEFT

Caucasian oak
SINUATE

Goldenrain tree
INCISED

Japanese maple
DOUBLE SERRATE

Mint
SERRATE

Balsam fir
PECTINATE

Higan cherry
SERRULATE

Philodendron
UNDULATE

Turkey oak
DENTATE

Red mulberry
DENTICULATE

Sessile oak
LOBATE

English holly
SPINOUS

Katsura
CRENULATE

Early dog-violet
CRENATE

Tree of heaven
CILIATE

Leatherwood
ENTIRE

LEAF SHAPES
and edges

Leaves are a plant's powerhouse and lungs. Over time, leaves of different plants have developed many shapes and sizes. They can be classified according to their shape or the shape of their edge, or margin.

Leaves are where most photosynthesis (the process through which plants produce energy) happens and where gases and water vapor are exchanged with the air. Water vapor is also lost through openings in the leaves.

Plants must balance this water loss with the rate at which they can create sugars to store energy. Leaves that grow in cold or dry climates tend to be smaller and narrower in order to minimize water loss. They are also often deciduous, which means they are shed by plants as the climate becomes too extreme for them.

In wet, tropical climates, leaves often have a glossy upper surface and a pointed, downward-facing tip (lanceolate shape). This directs water from the leaf toward the soil below. In some palms, with fan-shaped

> The unipinnate leaves of *Raphia regalis* are the world's longest leaves.

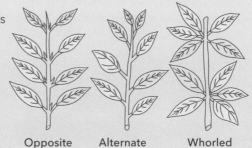

Opposite   Alternate   Whorled

leaves that are multifid (split into similar segments), rain runs inward toward the trunk, where it trickles down to the roots. Plants of the forest floor often need to have multi-part leaves (such as bipinnate). Although leaf shape may be affected by climate, the shape of a plant's leaves is a result of evolution. Species within each group of plants have similar leaves. This is used by botanists to classify plants and by gardeners to identify them.

The different edges of leaves are also important. In trees, all the leaves need light, so a pattern called a leaf mosaic develops, where leaves do not shade each other. Lobate, serrate, and cleft leaves allow more light to penetrate through the canopy to the leaves below. Spinous (spiny) edges deter grazers from eating lower leaves. Other plant defenses include sharp silica crystals in the leaf edges. Broken leaf edges, including serrate edges, make the leaves harder to pick out in dappled shade.

◀ LEAF ARRANGEMENT
Leaves grow from a stem in three patterns. Opposite leaves are paired, growing from the same node (point). Alternate leaves grow from separate nodes, while in a whorled pattern, several leaves grow from each node.

▶ SIMPLE AND COMPOUND
Leaves are also classified as simple and compound. Simple leaves have only a single leaf blade. Compound leaves are divided into leaflets, each on a small side stem.

Simple leaf

Compound leaf

TREE
orders

Many people think trees are different from plants, but they are actually tall, long-lived plants that evolved a woody stem.

Trees evolved strong, woody stems and grew tall so their canopy of leaves could have better access to sunlight. Trees can be found in 46 plant orders, and come in many different shapes and sizes. Shown on the right is an example of a tree from each order. These orders include nearly 64,000 species of tree in habitats around the world.

The ginkgo, which is the only member of the order ginkgoales, is an ancient plant whose relatives could be found on Earth more than 200 million years ago. Also ancient are the cycadales, such as queen sago, and conifers (trees whose seeds are contained in cones), such as the monkey puzzle tree. The Chinese tulip tree is in the magnoliales order, which includes some primitive flowering plants.

> The bark of the monkey puzzle tree is fire-resistant.

Most trees have trunks that broaden as the tree ages—growing to a huge width in long-lived trees such as oaks. The trunks of other trees, such as palms, stay narrow all their life.

Whether trees have leaves all year round or not depends on their habitat. In humid tropical rainforests, most trees are evergreen and keep their leaves all year round. In habitats with dry or cold seasons, many trees are deciduous (shed their leaves seasonally) to conserve energy in winter, when there isn't enough sunlight for the leaves to make food.

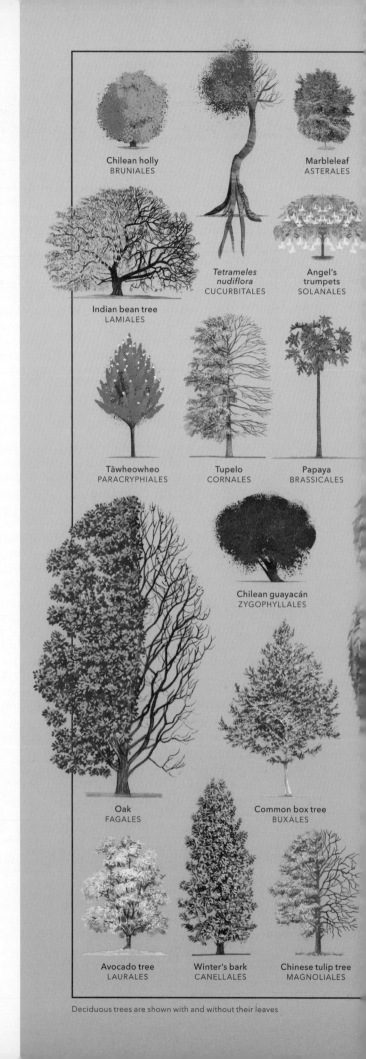

Chilean holly
BRUNIALES

Marbleleaf
ASTERALES

Indian bean tree
LAMIALES

Tetrameles nudiflora
CUCURBITALES

Angel's trumpets
SOLANALES

Tāwheowheo
PARACRYPHIALES

Tupelo
CORNALES

Papaya
BRASSICALES

Chilean guayacán
ZYGOPHYLLALES

Oak
FAGALES

Common box tree
BUXALES

Avocado tree
LAURALES

Winter's bark
CANELLALES

Chinese tulip tree
MAGNOLIALES

Deciduous trees are shown with and without their leaves

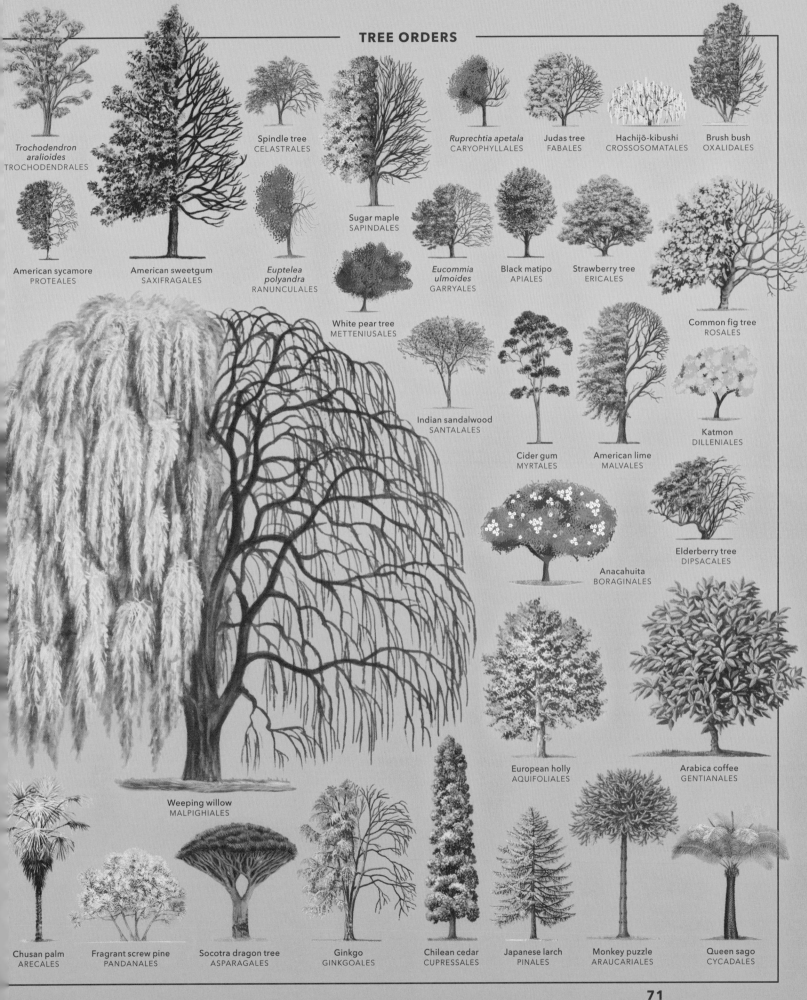

Trochodendron aralioides
TROCHODENDRALES

Spindle tree
CELASTRALES

Ruprechtia apetala
CARYOPHYLLALES

Judas tree
FABALES

Hachijō-kibushi
CROSSOSOMATALES

Brush bush
OXALIDALES

American sycamore
PROTEALES

American sweetgum
SAXIFRAGALES

Euptelea polyandra
RANUNCULALES

Sugar maple
SAPINDALES

Eucommia ulmoides
GARRYALES

Black matipo
APIALES

Strawberry tree
ERICALES

White pear tree
METTENIUSALES

Common fig tree
ROSALES

Indian sandalwood
SANTALALES

Cider gum
MYRTALES

American lime
MALVALES

Katmon
DILLENIALES

Anacahuita
BORAGINALES

Elderberry tree
DIPSACALES

European holly
AQUIFOLIALES

Arabica coffee
GENTIANALES

Weeping willow
MALPIGHIALES

Chusan palm
ARECALES

Fragrant screw pine
PANDANALES

Socotra dragon tree
ASPARAGALES

Ginkgo
GINKGOALES

Chilean cedar
CUPRESSALES

Japanese larch
PINALES

Monkey puzzle
ARAUCARIALES

Queen sago
CYCADALES

FLOWERING PLANT
orders

Nearly every plant on Earth is a flowering plant. To bring order to their incredible variety, botanists (scientists who study plants) group them into 65 orders.

Many types of plant had appeared on land before the age of the dinosaurs, but around 250 million years ago, brightly colored flowers began blooming around the planet. These flowers were the reproductive structures of the angiosperms, or flowering plants. The flowers attracted animals to help scatter pollen grains for reproduction. Different angiosperms developed flowers with unique shapes, colors, and scents suited to particular animals, which helped them spread around the world.

They evolved into many different forms, from tiny grasses to giant trees and aquatic plants. All flowering plants bear flowers and fruit, which have seeds with a hard outer casing. Botanists group them into different orders by how they are related to each other, and each one is represented by a plant on the right. This is based on our knowledge of plant DNA.

Each flowering plant order is further divided into families, which usually share more physical similarities. For example, the Asterales order includes the daisy family, members of which are characterized by flower heads made of many tiny florets (stalkless flowers). Some orders have families with very few species, while other orders have enormous numbers of species. The Asparagales, for example, includes more than 20,000 species of orchid.

| KINGDOM |
| DIVISION |
| CLASS |
| **ORDER** |
| FAMILY |
| GENUS |
| SPECIES |

Chilean holly
BRUNIALES

Mexican alvaradoa
PICRAMNIALES

Little wheel bush
PROTEALES

'le'ie
PANDANALES

Carnation
CARYOPHYLLALES

Mulan magnolia
MAGNOLIALES

Bristly hollyhock
MALVALES

Big-leaf hydrangea
CORNALES

Grape vine
VITALES

Big-leaf grass of Parnassus
CELASTRALES

Tuberous pea
FABALES

Tāwheowheo
PARACRYPHIALES

European bladdernut
CROSSOSOMATALES

Ceylon ironwood
MALPIGHIALES

Amborella
AMBORELLALES

Holly
AQUIFOLIALES

Redclaws
ESCALLONIALES

Wild carrot
APIALES

Flowering pepper
PIPERALES

Rigid hornwort
CERATOPHYLLALES

Sweet flag
ACORALES

Ghanera
ICACINALES

Japanese spurge
BUXALES

Neem
SAPINDALES

FLOWERING PLANT ORDERS

Pink wood sorrel
OXALIDALES

Blume
CARDIOPTERIDALES

Bolivian fuchsia
MYRTALES

Bahama whitewood
CANELLALES

Persian ironwood
SAXIFRAGALES

Olomea
HUERTEALES

Asiatic dayflower
COMMELINALES

Viper's bugloss
BORAGINALES

Giant rhubarb
GUNNERALES

Eastern sweetshrub
LAURALES

Marsh cranesbill
GERANIALES

Indian sandalwood
SANTALALES

Dragon arum
ALISMATALES

Pampas grass
POALES

Coconut
ARECALES

Chinese aconite
RANUNCULALES

Sweet briar
ROSALES

Double-spike bluethread
DIOSCOREALES

Bittersweet nightshade
SOLANALES

Italian honeysuckle
DIPSACALES

Willow gentian
GENTIANALES

Northern blue flag
ASPARAGALES

Kibi hitori-shizuka
CHLORANTHALES

Japanese star anise
AUSTROBAILEYALES

Spotted laurel
GARRYALES

Garden balsam
ERICALES

European beech
FAGALES

Tessmann's metteniusa
METTENIUSALES

Coral plant
BERBERIDOPSIDALES

Buffalo gourd
CUCURBITALES

Large-flowered hemp-nettle
LAMIALES

Sunflower
ASTERALES

Toiingbossie
VAHLIALES

Red ginger
ZINGIBERALES

Water lily
NYMPHAEALES

Wheel tree
TROCHODENDRALES

Creosote bush
ZYGOPHYLLALES

Sakurai's petrosavia
PETROSAVIALES

Peruvian lily
LILIALES

Star guinea flower
DILLENIALES

Winter cress
BRASSICALES

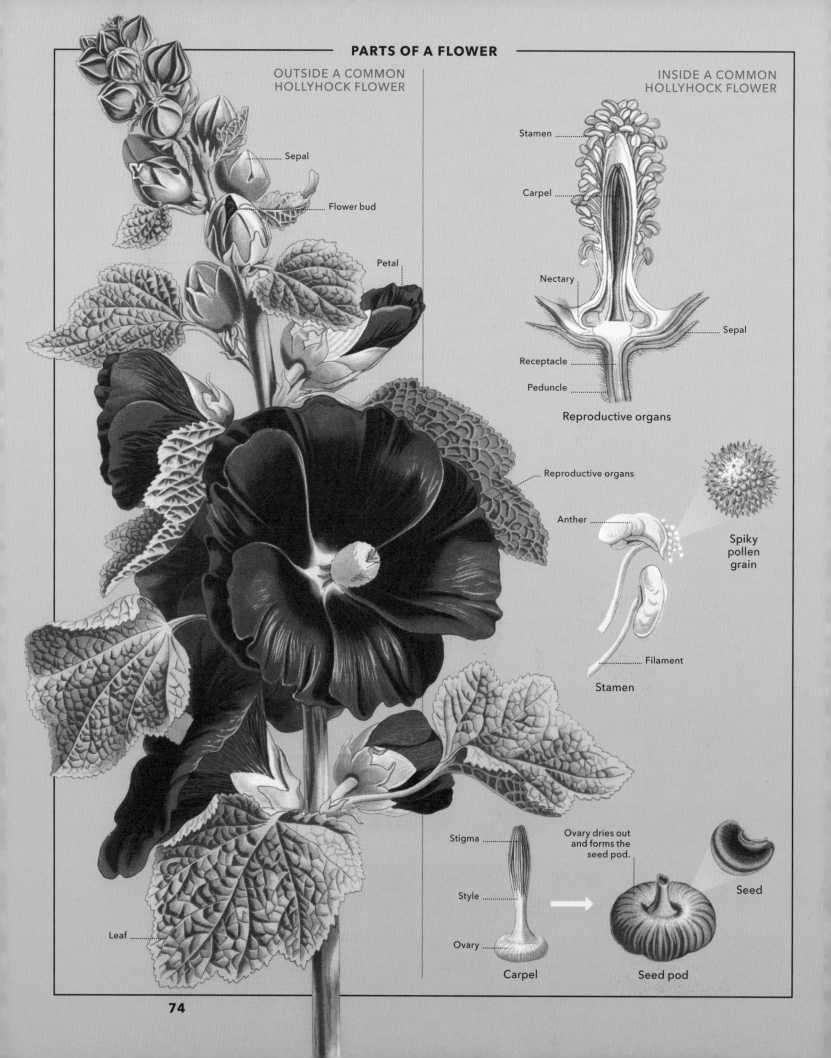

PARTS OF A FLOWER

OUTSIDE A COMMON HOLLYHOCK FLOWER

Sepal

Flower bud

Petal

Reproductive organs

Leaf

INSIDE A COMMON HOLLYHOCK FLOWER

Stamen

Carpel

Nectary

Sepal

Receptacle

Peduncle

Reproductive organs

Anther

Spiky pollen grain

Filament

Stamen

Stigma

Style

Ovary

Carpel

Ovary dries out and forms the seed pod.

Seed

Seed pod

Parts of a
FLOWER

Many plants produce seeds, but not all bear flowers. A flower is the reproductive structure of a flowering plant, or angiosperm. It gives rise to a fruit, which protects the plant's seeds.

Mature plants produce flowers. Each flower grows on a stem called a peduncle, on which are a series of structures in whorls (rings). Each part of a flower has a specific function. Sepals form the outermost whorl at the base of the flower. They are usually green, like leaves, and protect the delicate inner structures of the flower bud. Within the sepals are the petals. Plants that rely on insects for pollination, such as the common hollyhock shown on the left, have brightly colored petals. Initially packed inside the sepals, petals unfurl and grow rapidly as the flower opens. The nectaries are glands that produce nectar, which also attracts insects and birds to the flower.

Immediately inside the petals are the male parts of the flower—the stamens. Each of these is made up of a thin filament that supports an anther. Anthers contain pollen grains, which must be transported to the female parts of another flower to create seeds. This is the process of pollination. In plants where pollination is done by the wind, the pollen grains are smooth so they can blow away as soon as the anther opens. However, the pollen grains of

plants that rely on insects or birds for pollination are spiky so they can stick to the animals and be carried away.

The innermost whorl of flower parts are the female organs. Collectively called the carpel, these consist of a stigma that pollen sticks to, an ovary where the ovules are held, and a style that links the stigma to the ovary. When pollen lands on the stigma, fine tubes grow down the style to the ovules and fertilize them. The ovules then become seeds and the walls of the ovary (or sometimes the receptacle) swell or thicken to become a fruit or seed pod, while the petals, sepals, and stamens fall off.

> The flowers of the common hollyhock can be up to 5 in (13 cm) in diameter.

▼ LIFE CYCLE OF A PLANT
All flowering plants follow a similar life cycle from a seed to an adult plant.

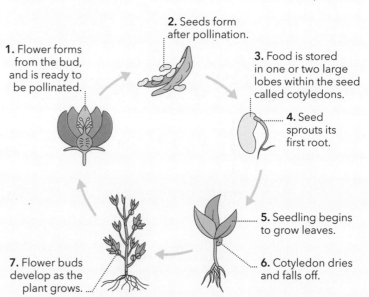

1. Flower forms from the bud, and is ready to be pollinated.

2. Seeds form after pollination.

3. Food is stored in one or two large lobes within the seed called cotyledons.

4. Seed sprouts its first root.

5. Seedling begins to grow leaves.

6. Cotyledon dries and falls off.

7. Flower buds develop as the plant grows.

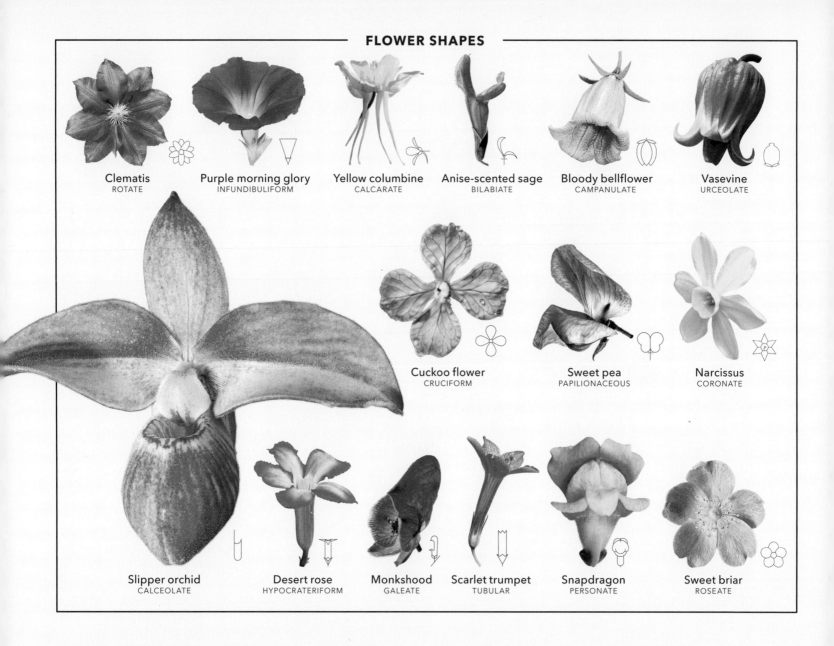

FLOWER SHAPES

Clematis
ROTATE

Purple morning glory
INFUNDIBULIFORM

Yellow columbine
CALCARATE

Anise-scented sage
BILABIATE

Bloody bellflower
CAMPANULATE

Vasevine
URCEOLATE

Cuckoo flower
CRUCIFORM

Sweet pea
PAPILIONACEOUS

Narcissus
CORONATE

Slipper orchid
CALCEOLATE

Desert rose
HYPOCRATERIFORM

Monkshood
GALEATE

Scarlet trumpet
TUBULAR

Snapdragon
PERSONATE

Sweet briar
ROSEATE

FLOWER SHAPES
and arrangements

Flowers help plants reproduce through pollination. Their shapes and arrangements have evolved with the single purpose of attracting the right animal, bird, or insect that can help pollinate them.

TYPES OF ARRANGEMENT

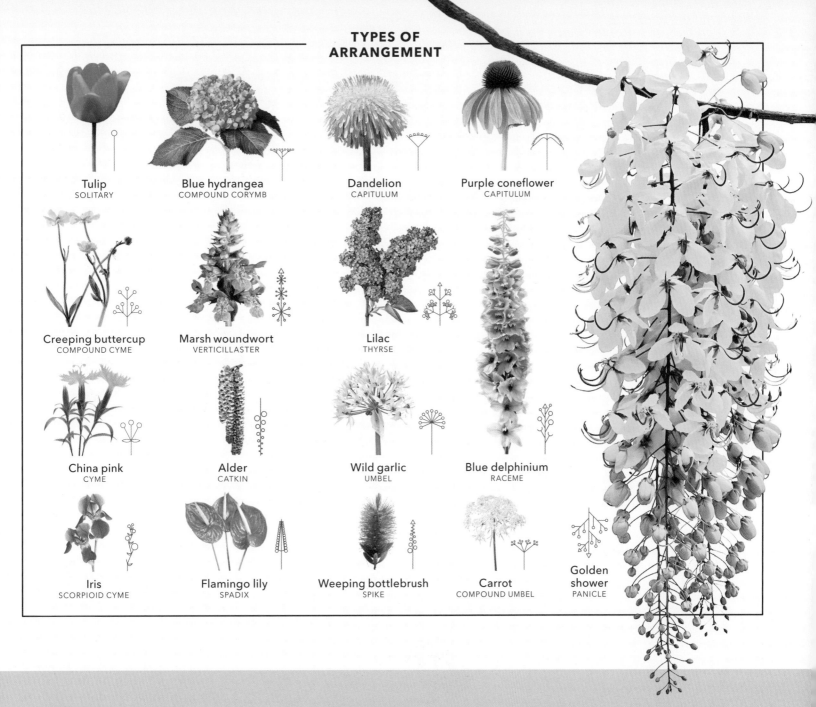

Tulip
SOLITARY

Blue hydrangea
COMPOUND CORYMB

Dandelion
CAPITULUM

Purple coneflower
CAPITULUM

Creeping buttercup
COMPOUND CYME

Marsh woundwort
VERTICILLASTER

Lilac
THYRSE

China pink
CYME

Alder
CATKIN

Wild garlic
UMBEL

Blue delphinium
RACEME

Iris
SCORPIOID CYME

Flamingo lily
SPADIX

Weeping bottlebrush
SPIKE

Carrot
COMPOUND UMBEL

Golden shower
PANICLE

Just by looking at a flower's shape, we can try and guess the creature that would help pollinate it.

Flowers with a roseate shape, such as sweet briar, have separate petals in a flat or cup shape that is easy for bees to sit on. Personate flowers, such as snapdragons, rely on bumblebees to open their liplike petals to reach the sweet nectar.

Tubular, urn-shaped (urceolate), and bell-shaped (campanulate) flowers are pollinated by insects and birds with long tongues. The long spurs of calcarate flowers such as the yellow columbine have nectar at the tips, where insects can feed. Orchids have a slipper-like (calceolate) structure. They have a fused petal, which acts like a landing platform for flying insects and makes them brush past the pollen to drink nectar.

The ways in which flowers are arranged on their stems have also evolved to attract pollinators. Single or solitary flowers such as tulips are large, but their size uses a lot of their energy. In a more energy-efficient arrangement, small flowers (florets) cluster together to form what looks like a large flower (inflorescence). This can be along the stem, as seen in blue delphiniums, or arranged in a flat top, such as in the China pink flower. In more complex arrangements such as thyrse in lilacs, more florets grow on side branches.

The daisy family has the most complex inflorescences, as seen in purple coneflowers. Here, florets cluster in a domed head called a capitulum. It has almost petalless disk florets in the middle. The florets on the edge have long ray petals.

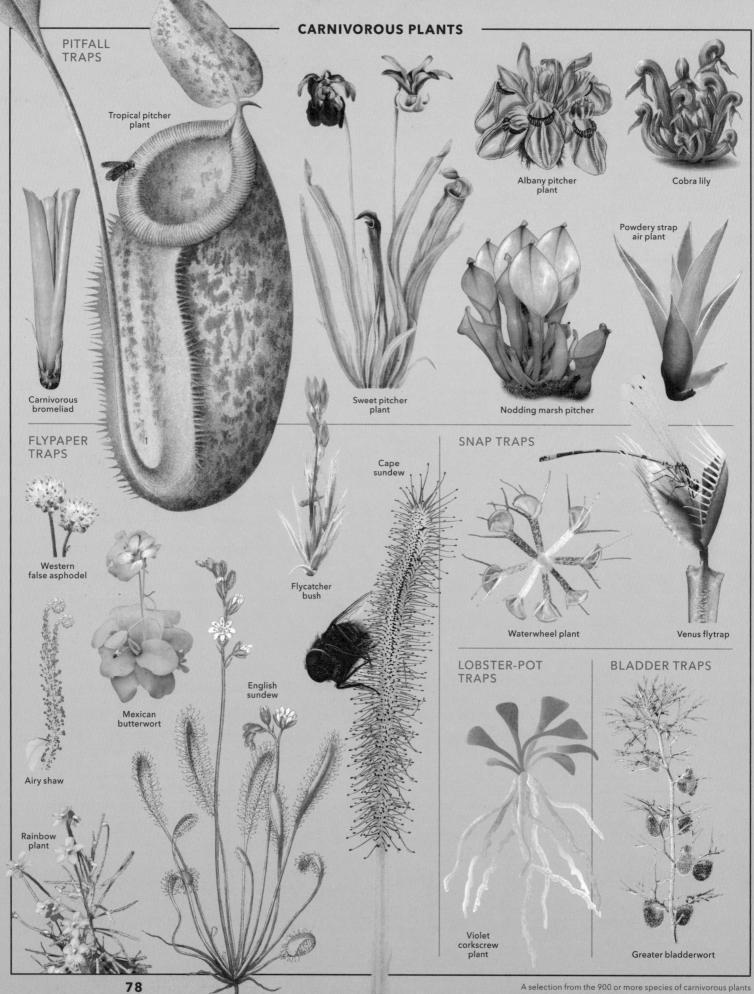

CARNIVOROUS PLANTS

PITFALL TRAPS

Tropical pitcher plant

Carnivorous bromeliad

Sweet pitcher plant

Albany pitcher plant

Cobra lily

Powdery strap air plant

Nodding marsh pitcher

FLYPAPER TRAPS

Western false asphodel

Airy shaw

Rainbow plant

Mexican butterwort

English sundew

Cape sundew

Flycatcher bush

SNAP TRAPS

Waterwheel plant

Venus flytrap

LOBSTER-POT TRAPS

Violet corkscrew plant

BLADDER TRAPS

Greater bladderwort

A selection from the 900 or more species of carnivorous plants

CARNIVOROUS
plants

Over millions of years, some plants have evolved into carnivores with fascinating ways to lure, trap, and digest some animals, mainly insects. These plants are classified by the type of trap they use.

There are more than 900 species of carnivorous, or meat-eating, plants on Earth. They are found in very poor soils, where their roots cannot obtain enough nutrients for them to grow.

This need to obtain nutrients, particularly nitrogen and phosphorus, has driven these plants to evolve ways to catch animals. Over time, some of their leaves have adapted to capture and digest prey. Carnivorous plants can be classified into five broad groups, based on the type of trap they use.

Most traps have bright colors, usually reds, to attract their prey. Pitfall traps in pitcher plants have patches of color and lines leading into the trap to guide insects to their fate. Their slippery surfaces make it hard for insects to avoid falling into the pitcher or to escape afterward. The pitcher contains a fluid that digests the prey slowly.

Flypaper traps have sticky surfaces or specialized hairs on their leaves or stems that ensnare prey and hold it still. In sundews, the leaf curls around the trapped prey to engulf it, making digestion faster.

Snap traps are found on the most advanced carnivorous plants. In Venus flytraps, the traps stay open, waiting to ensnare any insects attracted by their bright coloring. As soon as an insect triggers tiny hairs inside the trap, it snaps shut.

Lobster-pot traps have inward-facing hairs that force the prey deeper into the trap. Bladder traps are usually found in water. They act like a vacuum when the trap door on one side is triggered.

> A Venus flytrap catches prey in a tenth of a second.

▼ TYPES OF TRAP
Each type of trap is specialized to catch certain animals, usually small insects.

Pitcher-shaped leaf

Pitfall trap
Jug-like leaves contain digestive fluid.

Sticky hair

Flypaper trap
Sticky hairs trap prey.

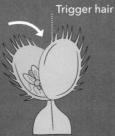

Trigger hair

Snap trap
Trigger hairs snap the trap shut when prey is detected.

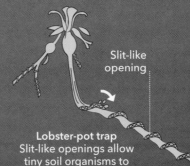

Slit-like opening

Lobster-pot trap
Slit-like openings allow tiny soil organisms to move inside.

Trap

Bladder trap
Trap sucks in insects when triggered.

Types of
FUNGI

Neither plant nor animal, fungi belong to a kingdom of their own, and are classified largely by how they reproduce. More than 150,000 fungal species have been identified, but there could be millions more.

Fungi are nature's recyclers. They find nourishment in food rejected by other living things, including tree stumps and dead leaves on the forest floor. And the fuzzy growth of a mold is key to this resourcefulness: a mesh of fine white threads growing over the source of nourishment is an efficient digestive system. Each thread, called a hypha, generates digestive juices and millions of hyphae soak up plenty of nutrients. By breaking down dead material in this way, fungi are vital decomposers.

Most fungi reproduce by releasing spores in the wind, which helps new fungi germinate on distant ground.

Because many unrelated fungi have similar lifestyles, scientists look to their reproductive structures to classify them into five phyla.

For bread molds, chytrids, and arbuscular mycorrhizae, these reproductive structures are tiny or microscopic. In other fungi, the hyphae bunch together to make large "fruiting" bodies in the form of mushrooms, which scatter the spores. In club fungi, which include the recognizable shapes of the stinkhorns, the spores bud from tiny club-like stalks, typically on the underside of their rounded caps. In sac fungi, including morels, the spores are made in tiny sacs, like peas in a pod.

Fungi have evolved ways to make the most of their unique way of feeding and how they interact with other living things. Forest fungi enmesh with plant roots to form partnerships called mycorrhizas: the fungus passes nutrients from decaying litter in return for some of the plant's sugar. In lichens, fungi bond with algae for a similar reason. Other fungi are parasitic on living tissue, but many more survive on waste—from single-celled yeast blooming on fruits, to enormous bracket fungi growing on dead and dying wood.

KINGDOM
PHYLUM
CLASS
ORDER
FAMILY
GENUS
SPECIES

Bloodlike red droplets ooze out of the devil's tooth fungus.

5. Spores are given off by the mushroom.

4. A new mushroom forms from the fused hypha.

1. Hyphae grow from spores on the ground.

3. Fused hypha has both parents' genes.

2. A pair of hyphae mate and fuse.

▲ LIFE CYCLE OF A FUNGUS
Fungal hyphae grow from single-celled spores. Hyphae fuse to mix genes as a form of sexual mating. They then develop into "fruiting" bodies—such as mushrooms—to produce more spores.

TYPES OF FUNGI

CLUB FUNGI

Fluted bird's nest

Anemone stinkhorn

Pink waxcap

Mallow rust

Hydnoporia tabacina

Anise mazegill

Black tooth

Fly agaric

Rosy brittlegill

Violet coral

Toothed jelly fungus

Turkey tail fungus

Golden chanterelle

Blue pinkgill

Amethyst deceiver

Pink oyster mushroom

Yellow stagshorn

Orange mosscap

Basket stinkhorn

Devil's tooth

Pepper pot

Woolly chanterelle

Porcini

SAC FUNGI

Nail fungus

Black truffle

Map lichen

Green elfcup

Orange peel

BREAD MOLDS, CHYTRIDS, AND ARBUSCULAR MYCORRHIZAS

Dead man's fingers

Candlesnuff fungus

Monk's hood lichen

Botrytis cinerea

Hare's ear

Black bread mold

Yellow morel

Yeast cells

Common sunburst lichen

Beech jellydisc

Eyelash fungus

Glutinous earth tongue

Yellow fairy cup

Penicillium digitatum

Spizellomyces acuminatus

Glomus sp.

Scarlet caterpillarclub

Scarlet cup

A selection of species from the five fungal phyla

81

INVERTEBRATE
phyla

A clam, a starfish, and a spider look very different, but they are all invertebrates. This group makes up around 90 percent of Earth's animals.

Invertebrates are animals without a backbone. Any animal that is not a fish, amphibian, reptile, bird, or mammal is an invertebrate. These animals are categorized into groups called phyla (singular: phylum) based on physical features. There are more than 30 phyla of invertebrates—the 16 major ones are shown on the right. The invertebrates have different shapes and sizes, ranging from microscopic roundworms to gigantic squid—these creatures are so varied that scientists studying their DNA often debate the number of phyla in which they can be classified.

KINGDOM
PHYLUM
CLASS
ORDER
FAMILY
GENUS
SPECIES

Animals in some phyla are soft-bodied, including the many types of worm, and the cnidarians, which include jellyfish and sea anemones. Many other invertebrates have hard parts—shells or exoskeletons (external skeletons). Mollusks such as snails have hard shells to protect themselves, while other mollusks, including cuttlefish, have a shell inside their body. Arthropods, such as scorpions, have hard exoskeletons and jointed legs. This is the largest group of invertebrates, and includes over three-quarters of all animals.

Echinoderms form a large phylum of marine animals, and include the starfish. These have five, or sometimes 10, arms, and hundreds of tiny "tube-feet" that allow them to move.

Some segmented worms can grow up to 66 ft (20 m).

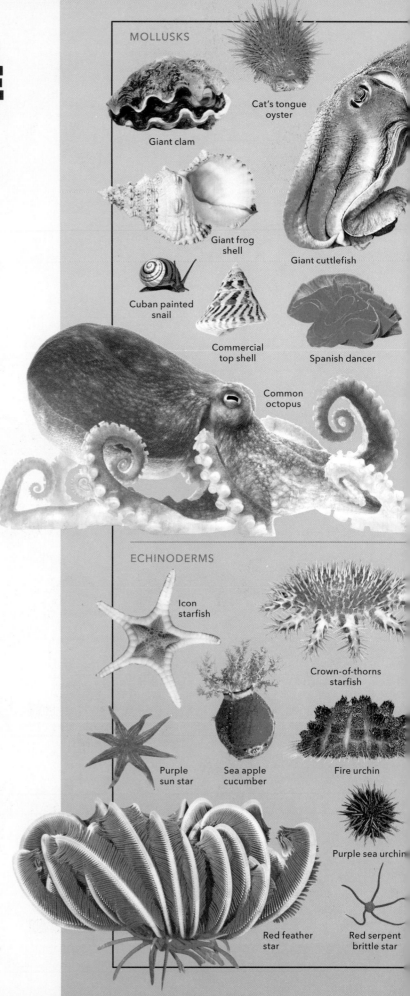

MOLLUSKS

Giant clam

Cat's tongue oyster

Giant frog shell

Giant cuttlefish

Cuban painted snail

Commercial top shell

Spanish dancer

Common octopus

ECHINODERMS

Icon starfish

Crown-of-thorns starfish

Purple sun star

Sea apple cucumber

Fire urchin

Purple sea urchin

Red feather star

Red serpent brittle star

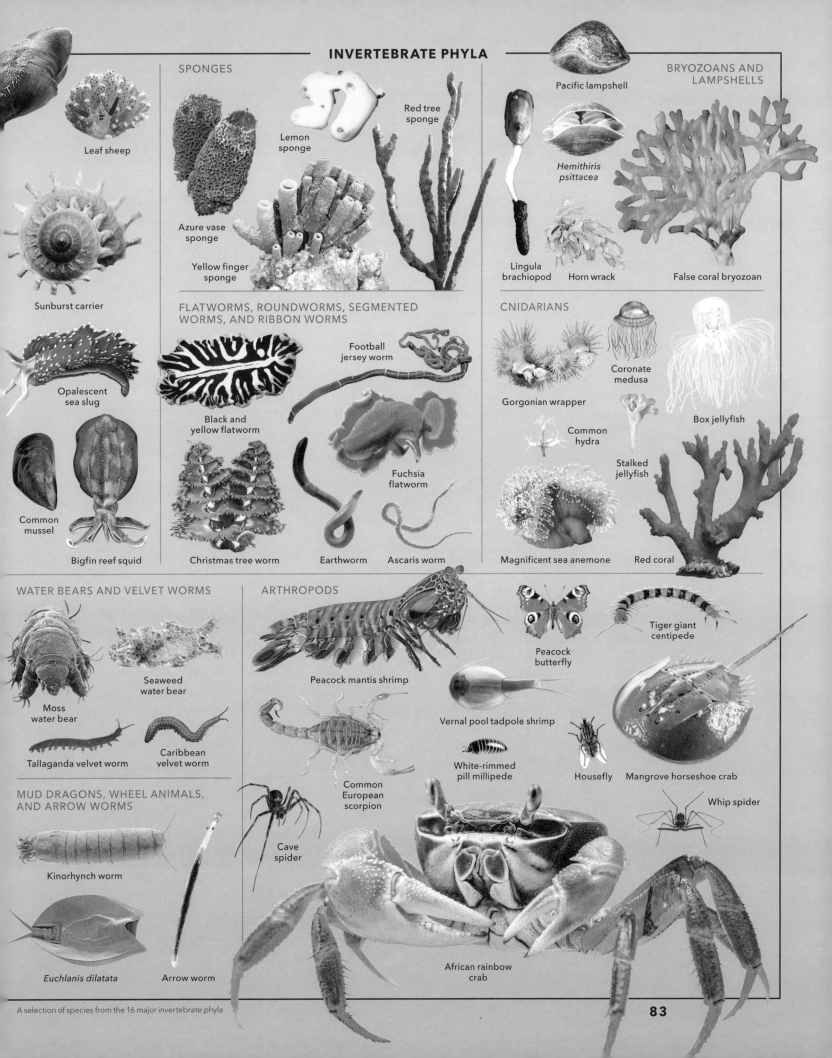

INVERTEBRATE PHYLA

SPONGES

Leaf sheep

Sunburst carrier

Lemon sponge

Azure vase sponge

Yellow finger sponge

Red tree sponge

BRYOZOANS AND LAMPSHELLS

Pacific lampshell

Hemithiris psittacea

Lingula brachiopod

Horn wrack

False coral bryozoan

FLATWORMS, ROUNDWORMS, SEGMENTED WORMS, AND RIBBON WORMS

Opalescent sea slug

Common mussel

Bigfin reef squid

Black and yellow flatworm

Christmas tree worm

Football jersey worm

Fuchsia flatworm

Earthworm

Ascaris worm

CNIDARIANS

Gorgonian wrapper

Common hydra

Coronate medusa

Box jellyfish

Stalked jellyfish

Magnificent sea anemone

Red coral

WATER BEARS AND VELVET WORMS

Moss water bear

Seaweed water bear

Tallaganda velvet worm

Caribbean velvet worm

ARTHROPODS

Peacock mantis shrimp

Common European scorpion

Vernal pool tadpole shrimp

White-rimmed pill millipede

Peacock butterfly

Housefly

Tiger giant centipede

Mangrove horseshoe crab

Cave spider

Whip spider

African rainbow crab

MUD DRAGONS, WHEEL ANIMALS, AND ARROW WORMS

Kinorhynch worm

Euchlanis dilatata

Arrow worm

A selection of species from the 16 major invertebrate phyla

Sea
SHELLS

Some animals that live in the sea or ocean have soft bodies that are protected by hard outer skeletons called shells. These come in many different shapes and sizes and often have vivid patterns and colors.

Among the invertebrates (animals without a backbone), there are those that grow shells to protect their soft bodies. These organisms belong to two phyla: brachiopods and mollusks. Within the mollusk phylum there are five classes of shelled animals: bivalves, chitons, tusk shells, cephalopods, and gastropods. Using chemicals from seawater, these animals make a mineral called calcium carbonate (the same mineral that makes up egg shells and chalk). They mix this calcium carbonate with a protein produced in their body to build layers of shell.

Shells come in a wide range of shapes and designs. Bivalves, such as scallops and oysters, have shells in two separate parts, which are joined by a hinge in the middle. Many of their shells have a smooth, shiny lining, known as mother of pearl, which can form pearls if sand grains make their way inside the shell. Invertebrates in the brachiopod phylum also have two shells joined by a hinge, but one shell is larger than the other. Chitons have shells that protect only the top part of their body, while the underside is protected by the rocks they cling to. The shell is made up of eight sections called plates, joined together by a muscular layer called the girdle. These plates allow a chiton to curl up into a ball if it is threatened.

Tusk shells are tube-shaped, resembling an elephant's tusk, with one end wider than the other. The head of the animal is at the wider end, with an opening for waste at the narrow end. Cephalopods include octopuses, squid, and nautiluses, but only nautiluses have external shells. They are spiral-shaped, with air chambers inside that help the nautilus sink and float. Gastropods have spiral-shaped shells as well, with the animal's head at the wide end where the shell opens out.

> **The shell of a giant clam can weigh up to 440 lb (200 kg).**

▼ SHELL DESIGN
Brachiopods and the five classes of mollusk have different types of shell.

Bivalves
Two shells, with a hinge

Chitons
Shell divided into eight plates

Tusk shells
Long, tubelike shell

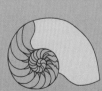

Cephalopods
Spiral with air chambers

Gastropods
Spiral-shaped shell

Brachiopods
Two shells, with a hinge

SEA SHELLS

BIVALVES

Australian brooch clam

Great scallop

Heart cockle

Regal thorny oyster

Penguin's wing oyster

Royal cloak scallop

Common mussel

Camp pitar venus

Giant clam

Razor shell

Pearl oyster

CHITONS

West Indian green chiton

Common chiton

Licorice sea cradle

Spiny chiton

Lined chiton

West Indian fuzzy chiton

TUSK SHELLS

European tusk

Common tusk shell

Fissidentalium vicdani

CEPHALOPODS

Common spirula

Chambered nautilus

White paper nautilus

BRACHIOPODS

Northern lamp shell

Lingula anatina

GASTROPODS

Broad Pacific conch

Channeled tun

Matchless cone

Powis's tibia

Japanese wonder

Triton's trumpet

Chocolate cowrie

West Indian fighting conch

Venus comb murex

Rose-branch murex

Silver conch

Glory of the sea

Philbert's peristernia

South African turban

Thorn latirus

Zigzag nerite

Broad-ribbed limpet

Purple drupe

Japanese Babylon

Tiger cowrie

Subulate auger

Shinbone tibia

Rumphius' slit shell

Sunburst star turban

Donkey's ear abalone

Waved goblet

Clear sundial

Spider conch

A selection of shells from the brachiopod and mollusk phyla

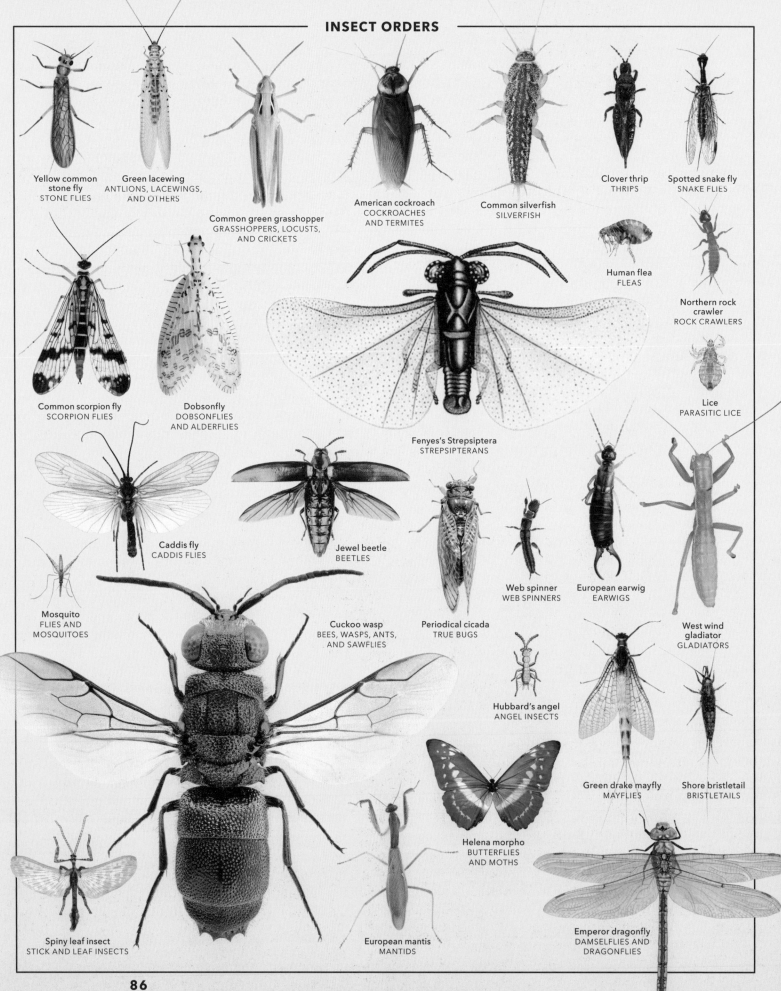

INSECT ORDERS

Yellow common stone fly
STONE FLIES

Green lacewing
ANTLIONS, LACEWINGS, AND OTHERS

Common green grasshopper
GRASSHOPPERS, LOCUSTS, AND CRICKETS

American cockroach
COCKROACHES AND TERMITES

Common silverfish
SILVERFISH

Clover thrip
THRIPS

Spotted snake fly
SNAKE FLIES

Human flea
FLEAS

Northern rock crawler
ROCK CRAWLERS

Lice
PARASITIC LICE

Common scorpion fly
SCORPION FLIES

Dobsonfly
DOBSONFLIES AND ALDERFLIES

Fenyes's Strepsiptera
STREPSIPTERANS

Caddis fly
CADDIS FLIES

Jewel beetle
BEETLES

Web spinner
WEB SPINNERS

European earwig
EARWIGS

Mosquito
FLIES AND MOSQUITOES

Cuckoo wasp
BEES, WASPS, ANTS, AND SAWFLIES

Periodical cicada
TRUE BUGS

West wind gladiator
GLADIATORS

Hubbard's angel
ANGEL INSECTS

Green drake mayfly
MAYFLIES

Shore bristletail
BRISTLETAILS

Spiny leaf insect
STICK AND LEAF INSECTS

European mantis
MANTIDS

Helena morpho
BUTTERFLIES AND MOTHS

Emperor dragonfly
DAMSELFLIES AND DRAGONFLIES

INSECT orders

Scientists have identified a million species of insect, but a mind-boggling 10 million may be living on our planet. To try and make sense of this incredible diversity, insects have been classified into orders.

KINGDOM
PHYLUM
CLASS
ORDER
FAMILY
GENUS
SPECIES

Insects have evolved to live almost everywhere, except in the seas and oceans. All insects are invertebrates with bodies that have three sections (head, thorax, and abdomen), with a tough exoskeleton (external skeleton) made from a hard substance called chitin. They have three pairs of jointed legs and usually two pairs of wings, although some have only one pair and others none. Almost all parts are used in classifying insects into the 28 orders. One species from each of these orders is shown on the left. Key features used to identify insects include the antennae; the arrangement of their mouthparts; and the shape and number of wings, legs, and features of the abdomen.

Female mosquitoes feed on human blood to nourish their eggs.

Beetles are the most diverse order, making up a third or more of all insect species. Their forewings have evolved into hardened wing cases called elytra that protect their delicate rear wings. The dragonflies and damselflies have elongated abdomens and two pairs of large, paddle-shaped wings. The flies—an order that includes mosquitoes, houseflies, and fruit flies—have one pair of wings, with the rear pair having evolved into small club-like organs used for balancing in flight.

The grasshoppers, locusts, and crickets have very long back legs for jumping, but many are also strong fliers with well-developed wings. The butterflies and moths have the most colorful of all insect wings and, despite their delicate appearance, some are able to migrate thousands of miles periodically.

Insects such as grasshoppers lead solitary lives. In contrast, the bees, wasps, and ants include thousands of highly social species. They have two pairs of see-through wings, and most of them have well-developed mouthparts for chewing food. Social insects live together in large groups, and individuals take on specific tasks such as egg-laying or food collection.

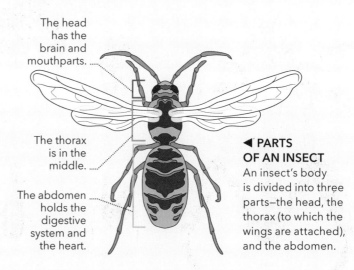

The head has the brain and mouthparts.

The thorax is in the middle.

The abdomen holds the digestive system and the heart.

◀ PARTS OF AN INSECT
An insect's body is divided into three parts—the head, the thorax (to which the wings are attached), and the abdomen.

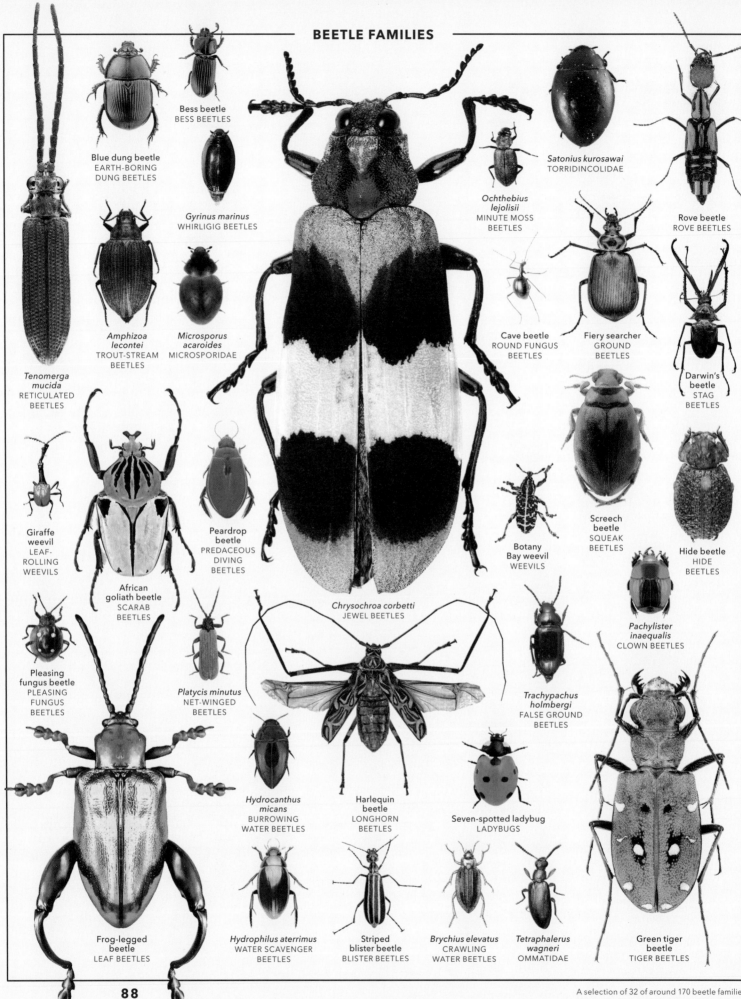

BEETLE FAMILIES

Blue dung beetle
EARTH-BORING
DUNG BEETLES

Bess beetle
BESS BEETLES

Gyrinus marinus
WHIRLIGIG BEETLES

*Amphizoa
lecontei*
TROUT-STREAM
BEETLES

*Microsporus
acaroides*
MICROSPORIDAE

Satonius kurosawai
TORRIDINCOLIDAE

*Ochthebius
lejolisii*
MINUTE MOSS
BEETLES

Rove beetle
ROVE BEETLES

Cave beetle
ROUND FUNGUS
BEETLES

Fiery searcher
GROUND
BEETLES

Darwin's
beetle
STAG
BEETLES

*Tenomerga
mucida*
RETICULATED
BEETLES

Giraffe
weevil
LEAF-
ROLLING
WEEVILS

African
goliath beetle
SCARAB
BEETLES

Peardrop
beetle
PREDACEOUS
DIVING
BEETLES

Botany
Bay weevil
WEEVILS

Screech
beetle
SQUEAK
BEETLES

Hide beetle
HIDE
BEETLES

Chrysochroa corbetti
JEWEL BEETLES

*Pachylister
inaequalis*
CLOWN BEETLES

Pleasing
fungus beetle
PLEASING
FUNGUS
BEETLES

Platycis minutus
NET-WINGED
BEETLES

*Trachypachus
holmbergi*
FALSE GROUND
BEETLES

*Hydrocanthus
micans*
BURROWING
WATER BEETLES

Harlequin
beetle
LONGHORN
BEETLES

Seven-spotted ladybug
LADYBUGS

Frog-legged
beetle
LEAF BEETLES

Hydrophilus aterrimus
WATER SCAVENGER
BEETLES

Striped
blister beetle
BLISTER BEETLES

Brychius elevatus
CRAWLING
WATER BEETLES

*Tetraphalerus
wagneri*
OMMATIDAE

Green tiger
beetle
TIGER BEETLES

88

A selection of 32 of around 170 beetle families

BEETLE
families

One in four animal species is a beetle, and scientists are still discovering more. They group these species into around 170 families. All beetles have a shiny, hard wing case that protects their delicate hindwings.

KINGDOM
PHYLUM
CLASS
ORDER
FAMILY
GENUS
SPECIES

Beetles are insects with six legs and small breathing holes (spiracles) on their bodies. Often brightly colored, their front wings have evolved into hardened cases called elytra that protect the soft hindwings used for flight. Beyond these features, as a group they are all very different—32 of nearly 170 beetle families are shown on the left. They have evolved to be superbly adapted, with a wide range of lifestyles and diets—including insects, plants, fungi, and even dung. This lets them thrive almost everywhere—they are found in most habitats on Earth, except in the sea or the polar regions. Their diversity and abundance make them a vital part of many ecosystems where they play different roles—from eating pests that affect crops to restoring minerals in soil.

There may be as many as 2 million beetle species.

One of the largest beetle families is the weevils (or "snout beetles"), which includes the Botany Bay weevil. The members of this family of mostly small beetles are known for their elongated mouthparts, used to bore into plant stems. Another large family is the scarab beetles. These robust insects are nature's recyclers—feeding on dead plants or animals, or dung. The family includes the goliath beetle—one of the world's largest beetles—which can grow to 4⅓ in (11 cm) in length.

Many beetle families have distinctive adaptations. The longhorn beetles are recognizable (and named) for their long antennae, which are covered in sensors to pick up the smell of food or a mate as they are flying. The diving beetles are known for their paddlelike back legs, which are perfect for swimming. Members of the tiger beetle family, on the other hand, are characterized by their incredible speed, serrated jaws, and predatory nature.

Probably the most well-known beetle family is the colorful ladybugs, which includes nearly 6,000 species worldwide. Often appearing in children's stories and nursery rhymes, they are also loved by gardeners for their habit of eating other plant-eating insects, such as aphids (greenfly).

Thin hindwings are used to fly.

Rigid elytra (wing cases) protect the hindwings.

◀ **BEETLE WINGS**
Beetles have four wings—two forewings and two hindwings. Their forewings have evolved to become hard cases that protect the soft, membranous flying wings when resting.

MOTH FAMILIES

Black-lined eggar
LAPPET MOTHS

Fire-grid burnet
BURNET MOTHS

White
plume moth
PLUME MOTHS

Privet hawk moth
HAWK MOTHS

Eyespot anthelid
**AUSTRALIAN
LAPPET MOTHS**

Garden tiger moth
TIGER MOTHS

Inquisitive monkey
MONKEY MOTHS

Indian silk moth
**SILKWORM
MOTHS**

Boisduval's autumn moth
OENOSANDRID MOTHS

Festoon
CUP MOTHS

Doherty's
longtail
**LONG-TAILED
BURNET MOTHS**

Eight-spotted
forester
OWLET MOTHS

Banksia
PROMINENT MOTHS

Hieroglyphic
moth
TUFT MOTHS

Common aenetus
GHOST MOTHS

Lettered
habrosyne
**HOOKTIP
MOTHS**

Leopard moth
**COSSID
MILLERS**

Hornet moth
CLEARWING MOTHS

Peacock moth
SATURNIIDS

Owl moth
**BRAHMIN
MOTHS**

Madagascan sunset
SWALLOWTAIL MOTHS

Orange-spotted castniid
CASTNIID MOTHS

False tiger moth
GEOMETER MOTHS

A selection of 23 of more than
120 moth families

MOTH
families

There are more than 120 families of moths, divided into 15,670 genera with more than 160,000 species. These insects appeared more than 250 million years ago, spreading to almost every habitat on Earth.

KINGDOM
PHYLUM
CLASS
ORDER
▶ **FAMILY** ◀
GENUS
SPECIES

The moth families belong to an order of insects called Lepidoptera, which also includes the families of butterflies—insects that evolved from moths. People often get confused between moths and butterflies, which share similar characteristics.

Classifying moths is challenging because of their incredible diversity. Scientists divide the moths into families based on their mouthparts, antennae, and wings, and especially the pattern of supporting veins on the wings. Some of the major moth families are shown on the left.

All moths typically have two pairs of large wings covered in small scales. Many moth species have feathery or comblike antennae, and males may have particularly well-developed antennae for detecting odors produced by females. Although many moths are active at night, there are numerous day-flying moths. Moths often appear "hairy" because their scales have hairlike structures that keep them warm while flying at night.

Among the moth families, the tiger moths are known for their bright colors, as are the hawk moths, which also have very large and colorful larvae. Although the larvae of some moths are crop pests, those of the silk moths make a cocoon that humans unravel to produce valuable silk. The spectacular swallowtail moths are so named because of long extensions to their hindwings.

The T-shaped bodies of the plume moths make them one of the most distinctive families. Their wings have evolved into spars with trailing bristles that allow them to fly. The clearwing moths are so named because they have transparent panels on their wings, and some even mimic hornets to protect themselves from predators.

> **The hawk moths are the fastest-flying moths in the world.**

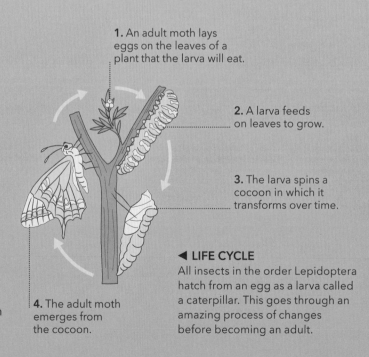

1. An adult moth lays eggs on the leaves of a plant that the larva will eat.

2. A larva feeds on leaves to grow.

3. The larva spins a cocoon in which it transforms over time.

4. The adult moth emerges from the cocoon.

◀ LIFE CYCLE
All insects in the order Lepidoptera hatch from an egg as a larva called a caterpillar. This goes through an amazing process of changes before becoming an adult.

BUTTERFLY
families

Butterflies are winged insects that evolved from moths during the Cretaceous Period (145–66 million years ago). Over time, they developed into six distinct families, each of which has unique characteristics.

The butterfly families belong to the insect order Lepidoptera—the same order as moths. These families are found all over the world, except Antarctica, and include more than 18,000 known species.

The diversity of butterflies can make identifying them difficult. The first step is to figure out which family they are in, and this is relatively straightforward. Butterflies are classified into six families based on characteristics that include antennal structure, wing vein pattern, and features of their legs. A selection from each family is shown on the right.

The brush-footed butterflies (Nymphalidae) are the largest and most diverse family, and include monarch and admiral butterflies. Their forelegs lack feet and instead have little brushes made of hair. The second-largest family is made up of the gossamer-winged butterflies (Lycaenidae), including the blues, coppers, and hairstreaks. They are small in size with subtle coloring. Most have reduced front legs, so they look like they only have four legs when at rest.

The swallowtail butterflies (Papilionidae) are often large in size and colorful. Many of them have distinctive "tails" on their hindwings. The skippers (Hesperiidae) are small to medium-size insects known for their rapid, darting flight and hooked antennae.

The metalmarks (Riodinidae) are found in the tropics and have metallic spots on their wings. Very common in gardens in North America and Europe are the whites and allies (Pieridae), which are mostly white or pale-yellow.

> **The world's largest butterfly is Queen Alexandra's birdwing.**

KINGDOM
PHYLUM
CLASS
ORDER
▶ FAMILY ◀
GENUS
SPECIES

Wings
Butterflies (left) sit with their wings folded, while moths (right) often sit with their wings open.

Bodies and antennae
Butterflies have smooth, slender bodies with thin antennae, while moths tend to have hairy and robust bodies with feathery antennae.

▶ BUTTERFLIES AND MOTHS
Although butterflies and moths are related to each other, and even look similar, there are some basic differences that can help tell them apart.

BUTTERFLY FAMILIES

BRUSH-FOOTED

Red admiral

Malachite

Comma

Eighty-eight

Peacock pansy

Iole's daggerwing

Monarch

GOSSAMER-WINGED

Green hairstreak

Mazarine blue

Adonis blue

Scarce copper

Purple-shot copper

Genoveva azure

Fiery jewel

SWALLOWTAILS

Tailed jay

Apollo

Yellow-bodied clubtail

Ludlow's Bhutan swallowtail

Queen Alexandra's birdwing

Ulysses

Old world swallowtail

SKIPPERS

Regent skipper

Large skipper

Guava skipper

Gold-spotted sylph

Euribates scarlet-eye

Bell's longtail

METALMARKS

Periander metalmark

Nais metalmark

Electron pixie

Jewelmark

Lampeto metalmark

Spangled cupid

Cramer's mesene

WHITES AND ALLIES

Common Jezebel

Cabbage white

Orange-tip

Eastern greenish black-tip

Orange-barred sulfur

Red-banded pereute

Orange albatross

A selection of species from the six butterfly families

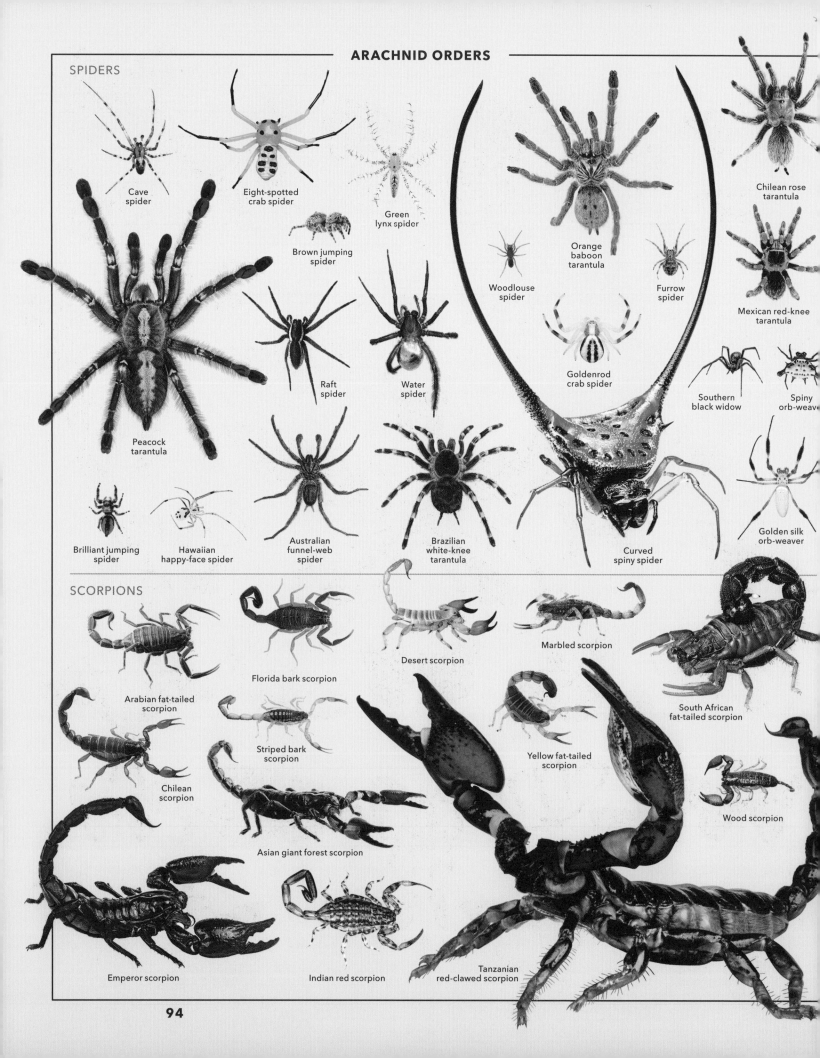

SPIDERS

Cave spider

Eight-spotted crab spider

Green lynx spider

Brown jumping spider

Chilean rose tarantula

Orange baboon tarantula

Woodlouse spider

Furrow spider

Mexican red-knee tarantula

Goldenrod crab spider

Peacock tarantula

Raft spider

Water spider

Southern black widow

Spiny orb-weaver

Brilliant jumping spider

Hawaiian happy-face spider

Australian funnel-web spider

Brazilian white-knee tarantula

Curved spiny spider

Golden silk orb-weaver

SCORPIONS

Arabian fat-tailed scorpion

Florida bark scorpion

Desert scorpion

Marbled scorpion

South African fat-tailed scorpion

Chilean scorpion

Striped bark scorpion

Yellow fat-tailed scorpion

Wood scorpion

Asian giant forest scorpion

Emperor scorpion

Indian red scorpion

Tanzanian red-clawed scorpion

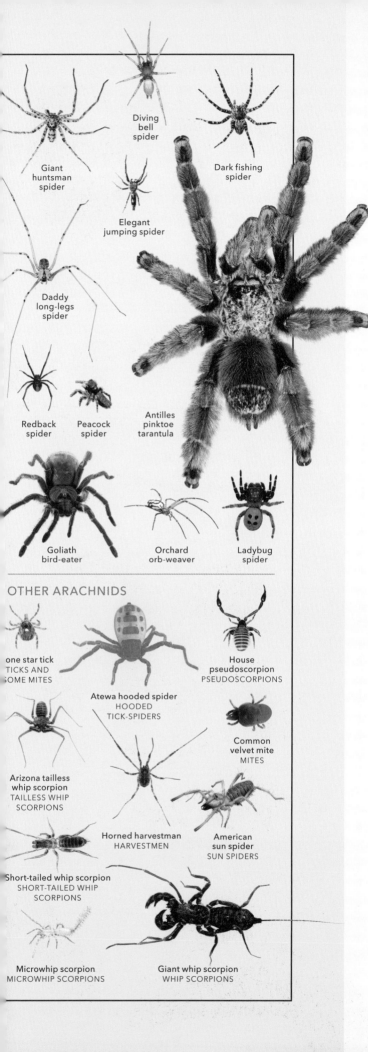

Diving bell spider

Giant huntsman spider

Dark fishing spider

Elegant jumping spider

Daddy long-legs spider

Redback spider

Peacock spider

Antilles pinktoe tarantula

Goliath bird-eater

Orchard orb-weaver

Ladybug spider

OTHER ARACHNIDS

one star tick
TICKS AND
SOME MITES

House pseudoscorpion
PSEUDOSCORPIONS

Atewa hooded spider
HOODED
TICK-SPIDERS

Common velvet mite
MITES

Arizona tailless whip scorpion
TAILLESS WHIP SCORPIONS

Horned harvestman
HARVESTMEN

American sun spider
SUN SPIDERS

Short-tailed whip scorpion
SHORT-TAILED WHIP SCORPIONS

Microwhip scorpion
MICROWHIP SCORPIONS

Giant whip scorpion
WHIP SCORPIONS

ARACHNID
orders

This class of eight-legged invertebrates are mostly predatory. They ensnare their prey in a variety of ways, and some are venomous.

| KINGDOM |
| PHYLUM |
| CLASS |
| ► ORDER ◄ |
| FAMILY |
| GENUS |
| SPECIES |

There are 12 orders of arachnids, which are distinguished from each other mainly by body shape, but also by specific adaptations such as silk production in spiders and a tail sting in scorpions. The most recognizable arachnids are spiders, which have around 50,000 species. Spiders come in a range of sizes: some are less than 0.04 in (1 mm) in length, while the goliath bird-eater can grow to around 4¾ in (12 cm) long. A spider's body is divided into two clear sections. The front has legs used for walking, capturing prey, and making webs. The back is often large and rounded, containing organs used for digestion and reproduction, as well as the spinnerets, which make the silk that spiders use to weave webs. Most spiders produce venom that is injected through hollow fangs to kill prey caught in their webs.

Scorpions form another well-known order. They hunt by grabbing their prey with large pincers and stabbing it with their distinctive long tail, which is tipped with a stinger that produces and stores venom.

The other 10 arachnid orders include the whip scorpions, short-tailed whip scorpions, microwhip scorpions, pseudoscorpions, harvestmen, tailless whip scorpions, sun spiders, hooded tick-spiders, mites, and ticks. Pseudoscorpions have pincers like scorpions but no stingers, while harvestmen resemble spiders but with only one body section. Mites and ticks are the smallest arachnids. Some cause diseases, but most are harmless.

VERTEBRATE
classes

Many of the animals we see every day, from sparrows and squirrels to humans, are vertebrates—creatures with a bony skeleton, and particularly a backbone.

The phylum chordates includes the vertebrates. Biologists classify vertebrates into 11 main classes—mammals, birds, reptiles, amphibians, and seven classes of fish—based on their shape and structure. These classes include the 70,000 or more vertebrate species on Earth.

Fish are adapted for a life in the water, breathing through gills and using fins to swim. The seven classes of fish make up around 60 percent of all vertebrate species.

Amphibians, such as frogs, toads, and salamanders, live both on land and in water during different stages of their lives. Their young live in water, but undergo a process called metamorphosis in which they change to become air-breathing, land-dwelling adults.

Reptiles have scaly skin and lay eggs. They include animals such as snakes, tortoises, lizards, and crocodiles. Birds have feathers and lay eggs with hard shells. Most of them can fly, although some, such as penguins, have become flightless.

Mammals are warm-blooded vertebrates with fur or hair. They give birth to live young, and nurse them with milk. Most mammals live on land, but some, such as bats, have evolved to fly. Other mammals, such as dolphins and whales, can live in the water.

KINGDOM
PHYLUM
▶ **CLASS** ◀
ORDER
FAMILY
GENUS
SPECIES

At 7 tons (6.3 metric tons) the African elephant is the heaviest land animal.

SEVEN CLASSES OF FISH

Guppy
RAY-FINNED FISH

Pacific hagfish
HAGFISH

Blacktip reef shark
SHARKS, RAYS, SKATES, AND SAWFISH

Spotted ratfish
CHIMERAS

West Indian Ocean coelacanth
COELACANTHS

African lungfish
LUNGFISH

Pacific lamprey
LAMPREYS

REPTILES

Radiated tortoise

Green sea turtle

Tuatara

Chinese water dragon

Siamese crocodile

American alligator

Rubber boa

Giant spiny chameleon

VERTEBRATE CLASSES

AMPHIBIANS

Tiger salamander

Axolotl

Northern spectacled salamander

Blue-spotted mole salamander

Mandarin salamander

Common toad

Blue poison dart frog

Baron's painted mantella

Tinker reed frog

Sumatran caecilian

Southern banded newt

BIRDS

Saddle-billed stork

Red-billed blue magpie

Bald eagle

Scarlet macaw

King eider

Kiwi

Caribbean flamingo

Ruby-topaz hummingbird

Barn owl

Southern crowned pigeon

American white pelican

MAMMALS

Fin whale

Giant anteater

Zebra

Red fox

Leopard

Common wombat

Striped hyena

Bongo

Greater bilby

Platypus

Red kangaroo

Long-eared bat

Mandrill

Bactrian camel

African elephant

A selection of species from the 11 vertebrate classes

FISH

classes

Fish are scaly, finned animals with gills, instead of lungs, for breathing underwater. They are divided into seven classes, including nearly 34,000 species, ranging from the goldfish to the whale shark.

The seven classes of fish are the ray-finned fish, two classes of cartilaginous fish (chimeras form one class and sharks, rays, skates, and sawfish the other), two classes of lobe-finned fish (coelacanths and lungfish), and two classes of jawless fish (lampreys and hagfish). All of these fish have adapted over millions of years to survive in our rivers, seas, and oceans.

Fish in each class have distinct identifying features. Ray-finned fish form the largest class of fish, and include more than 32,000 species. All fish in this class have fins that are supported by rays of bones coming out of a bony spine. They have an air bladder that allows them to remain still while taking in oxygen from their surroundings. Most have overlapping scales made of bone as well as a triangular bony flap that covers and protects the gills. The eggs of all ray-finned fish are fertilized outside the female's body. This sets them apart from cartilaginous fish, such as sharks and rays, whose eggs are fertilized internally.

Cartilaginous fish don't have bones. Instead, their skeletons, teeth, and scales are made of a strong flexible tissue called cartilage. They also lack a swim bladder, which means they must keep swimming to stay afloat. This class includes the world's biggest fish—the whale shark.

Jawless fish have sucker-like mouths with which they cling to prey or dead creatures while using rows of teeth to tear into their flesh. Some of the lampreys, though, prefer to suck the blood of other fish for food. Jawless fish also have their gills in pouches and not slits like the other classes.

Lobe-finned fish are an ancient pair of fish classes. These fish have muscular, fleshy fins attached by a single bone. Unusually for fish, their teeth are covered with enamel—the same hard substance that covers mammal teeth.

KINGDOM
PHYLUM
CLASS
ORDER
FAMILY
GENUS
SPECIES

The whale shark can grow up to an amazing 39 ft (12 m).

▼ PARTS OF A FISH

Fish are vertebrates (animals with a backbone). Features common to all fish include gills, fins, and a tail. Shown here is an example of a ray-finned fish.

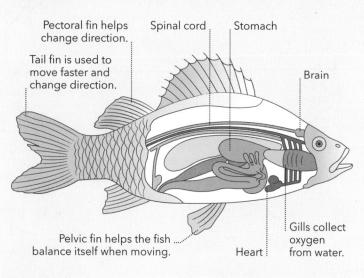

Pectoral fin helps change direction.

Tail fin is used to move faster and change direction.

Spinal cord

Stomach

Brain

Pelvic fin helps the fish balance itself when moving.

Heart

Gills collect oxygen from water.

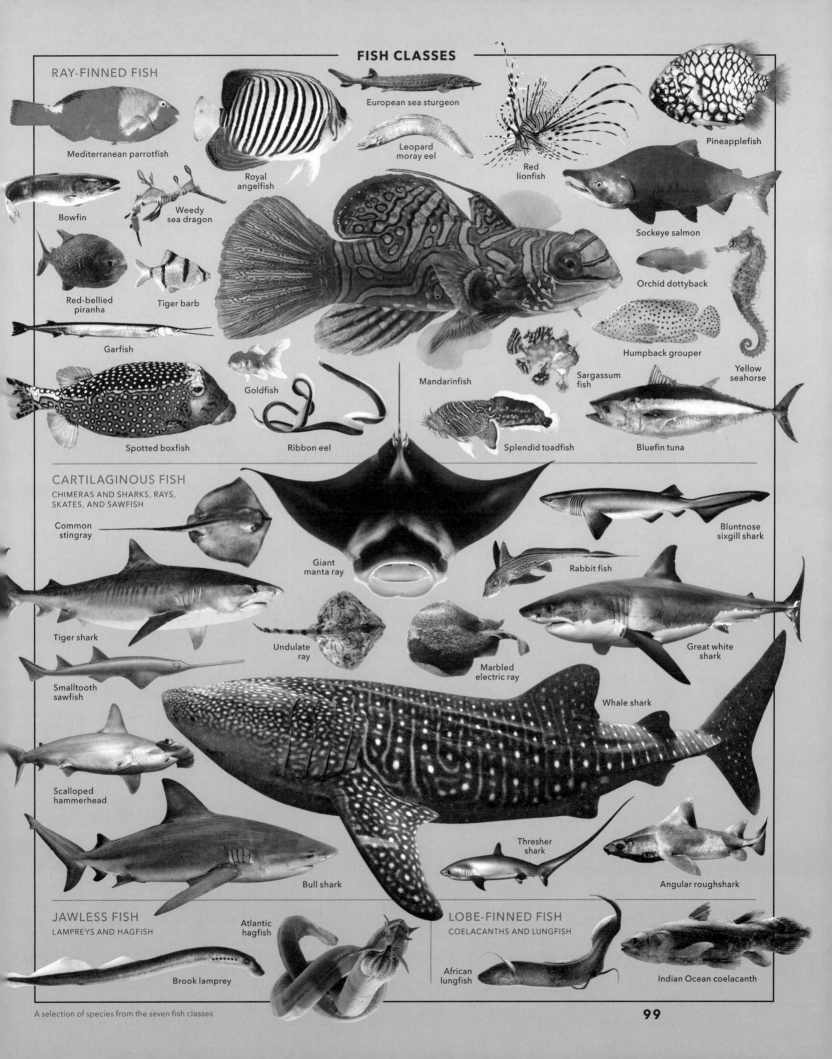

FISH CLASSES

RAY-FINNED FISH

Mediterranean parrotfish

Royal angelfish

European sea sturgeon

Leopard moray eel

Red lionfish

Pineapplefish

Bowfin

Weedy sea dragon

Sockeye salmon

Red-bellied piranha

Tiger barb

Orchid dottyback

Garfish

Mandarinfish

Humpback grouper

Yellow seahorse

Spotted boxfish

Goldfish

Ribbon eel

Sargassum fish

Splendid toadfish

Bluefin tuna

CARTILAGINOUS FISH
CHIMERAS AND SHARKS, RAYS, SKATES, AND SAWFISH

Common stingray

Giant manta ray

Rabbit fish

Bluntnose sixgill shark

Tiger shark

Undulate ray

Marbled electric ray

Great white shark

Smalltooth sawfish

Whale shark

Scalloped hammerhead

Thresher shark

Angular roughshark

Bull shark

JAWLESS FISH
LAMPREYS AND HAGFISH

Atlantic hagfish

LOBE-FINNED FISH
COELACANTHS AND LUNGFISH

Brook lamprey

African lungfish

Indian Ocean coelacanth

A selection of species from the seven fish classes

99

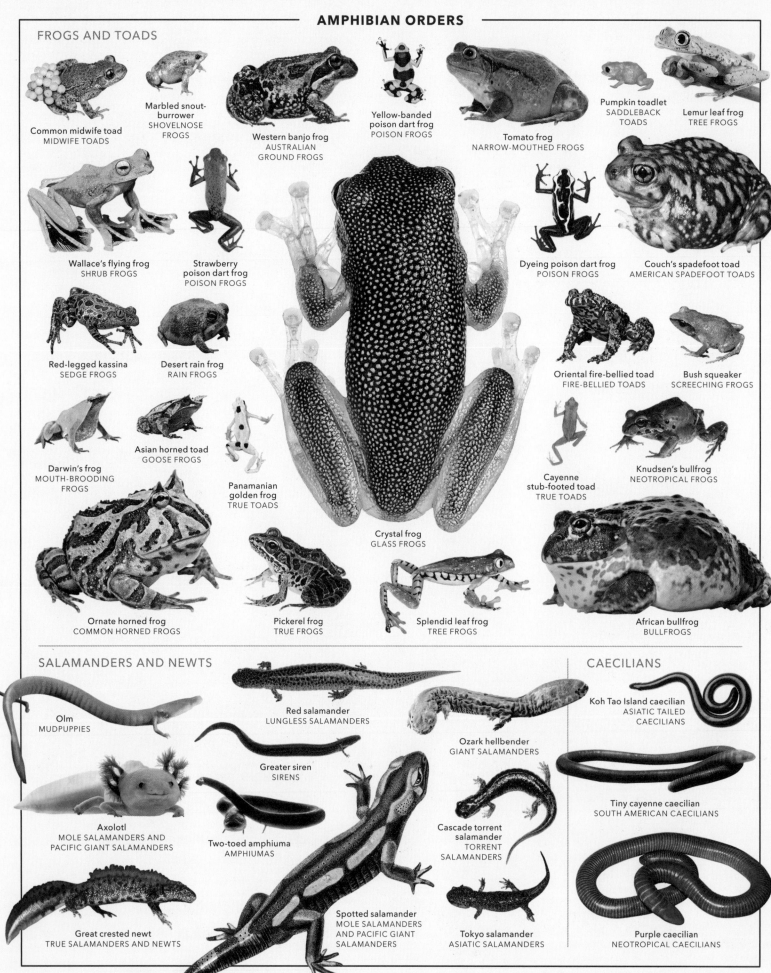

FROGS AND TOADS

Common midwife toad
MIDWIFE TOADS

Marbled snout-burrower
SHOVELNOSE FROGS

Western banjo frog
AUSTRALIAN GROUND FROGS

Yellow-banded poison dart frog
POISON FROGS

Tomato frog
NARROW-MOUTHED FROGS

Pumpkin toadlet
SADDLEBACK TOADS

Lemur leaf frog
TREE FROGS

Wallace's flying frog
SHRUB FROGS

Strawberry poison dart frog
POISON FROGS

Dyeing poison dart frog
POISON FROGS

Couch's spadefoot toad
AMERICAN SPADEFOOT TOADS

Red-legged kassina
SEDGE FROGS

Desert rain frog
RAIN FROGS

Oriental fire-bellied toad
FIRE-BELLIED TOADS

Bush squeaker
SCREECHING FROGS

Darwin's frog
MOUTH-BROODING FROGS

Asian horned toad
GOOSE FROGS

Panamanian golden frog
TRUE TOADS

Crystal frog
GLASS FROGS

Cayenne stub-footed toad
TRUE TOADS

Knudsen's bullfrog
NEOTROPICAL FROGS

Ornate horned frog
COMMON HORNED FROGS

Pickerel frog
TRUE FROGS

Splendid leaf frog
TREE FROGS

African bullfrog
BULLFROGS

SALAMANDERS AND NEWTS

Olm
MUDPUPPIES

Red salamander
LUNGLESS SALAMANDERS

Ozark hellbender
GIANT SALAMANDERS

Axolotl
MOLE SALAMANDERS AND PACIFIC GIANT SALAMANDERS

Greater siren
SIRENS

Two-toed amphiuma
AMPHIUMAS

Cascade torrent salamander
TORRENT SALAMANDERS

Great crested newt
TRUE SALAMANDERS AND NEWTS

Spotted salamander
MOLE SALAMANDERS AND PACIFIC GIANT SALAMANDERS

Tokyo salamander
ASIATIC SALAMANDERS

CAECILIANS

Koh Tao Island caecilian
ASIATIC TAILED CAECILIANS

Tiny cayenne caecilian
SOUTH AMERICAN CAECILIANS

Purple caecilian
NEOTROPICAL CAECILIANS

A selection of species from 33 of the 77 amphibian families

AMPHIBIAN
orders

Amphibians are cold-blooded vertebrates (animals with a backbone) that can live in water and on land. Scientists divide amphibians into three orders: frogs and toads, salamanders and newts, and caecilians.

KINGDOM
PHYLUM
CLASS
ORDER
FAMILY
GENUS
SPECIES

The word "amphibian" translates to "double life" in ancient Greek, and this neatly describes their life cycle. Most amphibians start life in water and move onto land as adults—although adults need to keep their skin moist, so they stay close to water in order to survive. These ancient animals were the first vertebrates to climb out of water onto land. Most amphibians undergo "complete metamorphosis"—the adults look very different from their young. Gills allow young amphibians to breathe underwater, but as they mature, the amphibians grow legs and gain the ability to breathe not just through gills or lungs but also through their skin.

> Amphibians evolved from lobe-finned fish more than 400 million years ago.

The three orders of amphibians contain 77 families. The largest amphibian order, the frogs and toads, accounts for around 88 percent of all amphibians. They are identified by the lack of a tail. Frogs have moist skin and long legs, while toads have dry skin and short legs. Frogs and toads come in all sizes. Some poison frogs measure no more than a centimeter, while the African bullfrog grows to 10 in (25 cm) long.

The salamander order is made up of salamanders, newts, and sirens, which all keep their tail into adulthood. The olm,

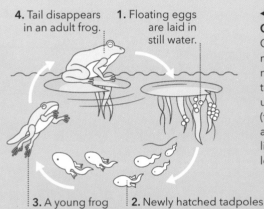

4. Tail disappears in an adult frog.

1. Floating eggs are laid in still water.

3. A young frog develops legs.

2. Newly hatched tadpoles have long tails for swimming.

◀ **LIFE CYCLE OF A FROG**
Complete metamorphosis means frogs and toads change from underwater young (tadpoles) with tails and gills to land-living adults with legs and lungs.

an ancient blind salamander, lives underwater in dark caves (for up to 100 years), going 10 years at a time without eating. Tiger salamanders lose their gills and form lungs as adults, spending all their time on land, and only returning to the water to lay eggs. The flat tail of newts, such as the great crested newt, separates them from other salamanders. Sirens, such as the greater siren, have lungs as well as gills, and never grow up—staying in the larval stage, with only two legs, unlike adult salamanders. Sirens, like axolotls, can also regenerate body parts.

The third order, the caecilians are often mistaken for snakes because of their lack of legs. Their folded skin is happiest underground in moist earth or in water. Their hard, pointed skulls help them move easily through the soil.

REPTILE
orders

There are around 12,000 species of reptile on our planet, which belong in four distinct orders—tortoises and turtles, lizards and snakes, crocodilians, and the tuatara.

Reptiles are cold-blooded animals that rely on their surroundings to control their body temperature. Most of them have scales made of keratin—the same material that makes up human hair and nails. Almost all reptiles lay eggs, but some give birth to live young. Based on their physical features, reptiles are classified into the four orders. These include 93 families—examples from 28 families are shown on the right.

Snakes, legless lizards, and lizards form the first order. Members of this diverse order are found on every continent except Antarctica. They have scales that do not grow with their bodies, which means they have to keep shedding their skin as they grow.

Turtles, terrapins, and tortoises have a hard shell on top (carapace) and a bottom part made of tough bone connected to their ribs. Their whole body is enclosed in their bony shell. Crocodiles, alligators, caimans, and gharials are crocodilians. These semiaquatic reptiles have a unique body shape that allows their eyes, ears, and nostrils to remain above the water while the rest of their body can remain hidden, making them perfect hunters. The final order has just one species—the tuatara. This reptile has a double row of teeth in its upper jaw, and a third eye on its head, which is covered up by scales in adults.

| KINGDOM |
| PHYLUM |
| CLASS |
| ► ORDER ◄ |
| FAMILY |
| GENUS |
| SPECIES |

Panther chameleon
CHAMELEONS

Children's python
PYTHONS

Gharial
GHARIALS

Cuban crocodile
CROCODILES

American alligator
ALLIGATORS AND CAIMANS

REPTILE ORDERS

SNAKES AND LIZARDS

Frilled lizard
AGAMID LIZARDS

Sungazer
GIRDLED LIZARDS

Green anole
ANOLES

Red tegu
TEGUS AND WHIPTAILS

Marine iguana
IGUANIDS

Milk snake
COLUBRIDS

Gila monster
BEADED LIZARDS

Boa constrictor
BOAS

arudny's worm lizard
WORM LIZARDS

Green basilisk
HELMETED LIZARDS

Madagascar day gecko
COMMON GECKOS

Komodo dragon
MONITOR LIZARDS

Fire skink
SKINKS

TURTLES AND TORTOISES

Ornate box turtle
POND TURTLES

Pig-nosed turtle
PIG-NOSED TURTLES

Golden coin turtle
LEAF TURTLES

Alligator snapping turtle
SNAPPING TURTLES

Loggerhead sea turtle
SEA TURTLES

Matamata
AUSTRO-AMERICAN
SIDE-NECKED TURTLES

Common musk turtle
MUD AND MUSK TURTLES

Indian star tortoise
TORTOISES

Asiatic softshell turtle
SOFTSHELL TURTLES

TUATARA

Tuatara
TUATARA

CROCODILIANS

Saltwater crocodile
CROCODILES

Black caiman
ALLIGATORS AND CAIMANS

Chinese alligator
ALLIGATORS AND CAIMANS

Cuvier's dwarf caiman
ALLIGATORS AND CAIMANS

Spectacled caiman
ALLIGATORS AND CAIMANS

African dwarf crocodile
CROCODILES

Nile crocodile
CROCODILES

A selection of species from 28 of the 93 reptile families

SNAKE families

All snakes, from tiny thread snakes to massive pythons, are slithering reptiles. These predators kill prey using different methods.

Snakes are found on every continent except Antarctica. Evolving from lizards, they became legless and elongated over millions of years. There are more than 4,100 species of snakes, which are divided into 31 families. A member of each family is shown here.

Scientists use the arrangement of teeth and the structure of the skull to classify snakes. Many snakes have a mobile skull, which lets them swallow prey killed with a venomous bite. Vipers and pit vipers have elongated, hollow fangs that can rotate into a biting position when the jaws open. The elapids, such as the king cobra, have shorter, downward-pointing fangs enclosing a hollow channel to deliver venom. The colubrids, which are the largest family, have a pair of large grooved teeth toward the back of the mouth that venom runs down. Many families lack specialized teeth for injecting venom, such as the pythons and boas. These are constrictors, which coil their muscular bodies around their prey to suffocate it to death.

The shape and arrangement of scales is also important in identifying snake families, like the highly modified scales that form the "rattle" at the tip of a rattlesnake's tail.

| KINGDOM |
| PHYLUM |
| CLASS |
| ORDER |
| ► FAMILY ◄ |
| GENUS |
| SPECIES |

Rattlesnakes can shake their rattle 90 times per second.

Reinhardt's lined snake
PHILIPPINE WATER AND BURROWING SNAKES

Malayan spinejaw
SPINE-JAWED SNAKES

Pale-headed blind snake
DAWN BLIND SNAKES

Spotted harlequin
MOLE VIPERS

Prairie rattlesnake
VIPERS AND PIT VIPERS

Striped house snake
AFRICAN HOUSE, FILE, AND GROUND SNAKES

King cobra
ELAPIDS

Lined blind snake
TYPICAL BLIND SNAKES

Bombay earth snake
SHIELD-TAIL SNAKES

Scarlet kingsnake
COLUBRIDS

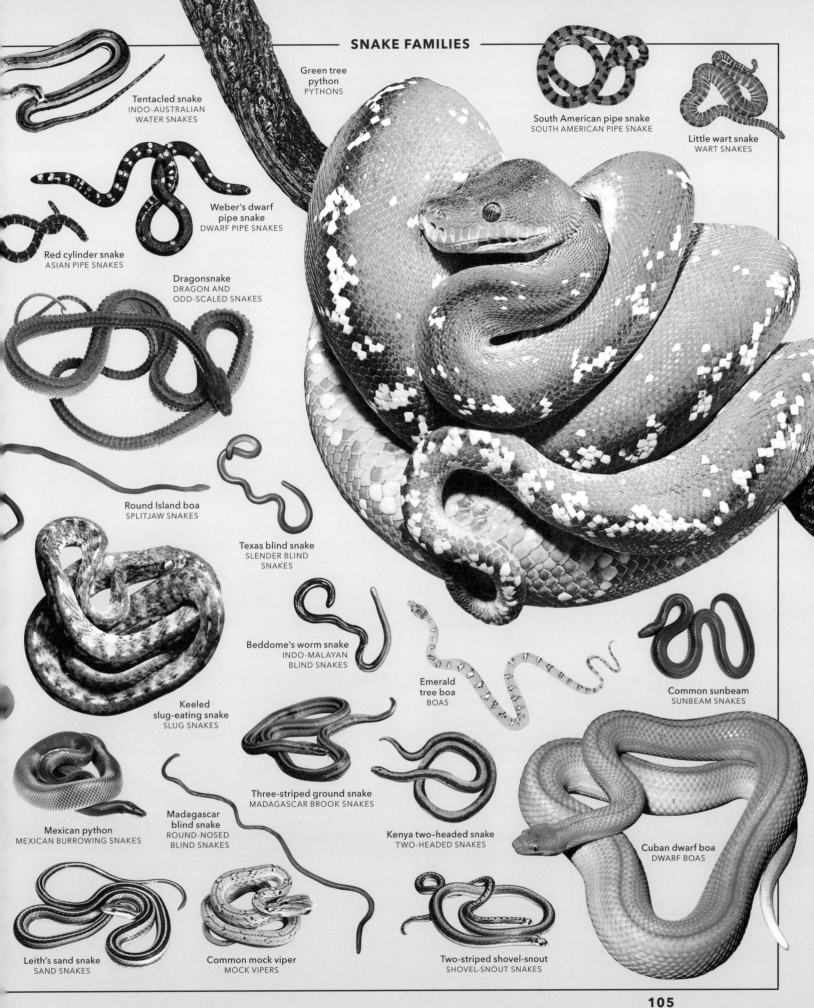

Tentacled snake
INDO-AUSTRALIAN
WATER SNAKES

Green tree
python
PYTHONS

South American pipe snake
SOUTH AMERICAN PIPE SNAKE

Little wart snake
WART SNAKES

Weber's dwarf
pipe snake
DWARF PIPE SNAKES

Red cylinder snake
ASIAN PIPE SNAKES

Dragonsnake
DRAGON AND
ODD-SCALED SNAKES

Round Island boa
SPLITJAW SNAKES

Texas blind snake
SLENDER BLIND
SNAKES

Beddome's worm snake
INDO-MALAYAN
BLIND SNAKES

Emerald
tree boa
BOAS

Common sunbeam
SUNBEAM SNAKES

Keeled
slug-eating snake
SLUG SNAKES

Three-striped ground snake
MADAGASCAR BROOK SNAKES

Madagascar
blind snake
ROUND-NOSED
BLIND SNAKES

Mexican python
MEXICAN BURROWING SNAKES

Kenya two-headed snake
TWO-HEADED SNAKES

Cuban dwarf boa
DWARF BOAS

Leith's sand snake
SAND SNAKES

Common mock viper
MOCK VIPERS

Two-striped shovel-snout
SHOVEL-SNOUT SNAKES

BIRD
orders

From the hummingbird to the condor, birds have evolved in different ways to adapt to their environment. This evolution has led to 40 unique groups of bird that we know as the bird orders.

Fossil evidence shows that birds are descendants of some feathered theropods, which were a kind of dinosaur. Birds are the only living animals with feathers, and their forelimbs have evolved over time to become wings. All birds have two legs and lay eggs, though they cannot all fly.

The busy, beautiful birds that live alongside us today are all part of the class Aves. This class is divided into the 40 orders shown opposite (with one example from each order). The birds in each of these orders have shared DNA, habits, and characteristics.

For instance, ducks, geese, and swans belong to one order of birds that all have waterproof feathers and webbed feet. Owls, on the other hand, have their own order and are classified by their upright stance; large, forward-facing eyes; and nighttime hunting habits.

Orders are then further divided into families and each family is then divided into many species. So far, scientists have identified and named thousands of bird species and organized them into orders according to how they are related.

Some orders contain few birds, such as the order of rheas, which includes two species—the greater rhea and the lesser rhea. Others are huge—the order of passerines, for example, contains 60 percent of all birds, with 6,000 species, ranging from the lesser bird of paradise to the barn swallow and the blue tit to the Andean cock-of-the-rock.

The classification of birds is still ongoing, and DNA evidence can produce surprises. For example, peregrine falcons turn out to be closely related to parrots, and owls to toucans.

> The word "Aves" is the Latin term for "birds."

> Hummingbirds are the only birds that can fly backward.

KINGDOM
PHYLUM
CLASS
ORDER
FAMILY
GENUS
SPECIES

▶ BIRD FEET
All birds in an order share physical features. One way to identify a bird order is by a bird's feet. Bird feet have evolved to suit their lifestyles.

Passerines have a back toe that helps them perch on branches.

Waterfowl have webbed feet for swimming.

Birds of prey have sharp talons to grip prey tightly.

Waders, gulls, and auks have wading feet with wide toe spans to avoid sinking in mud.

Ostriches have running feet with short, thick claws.

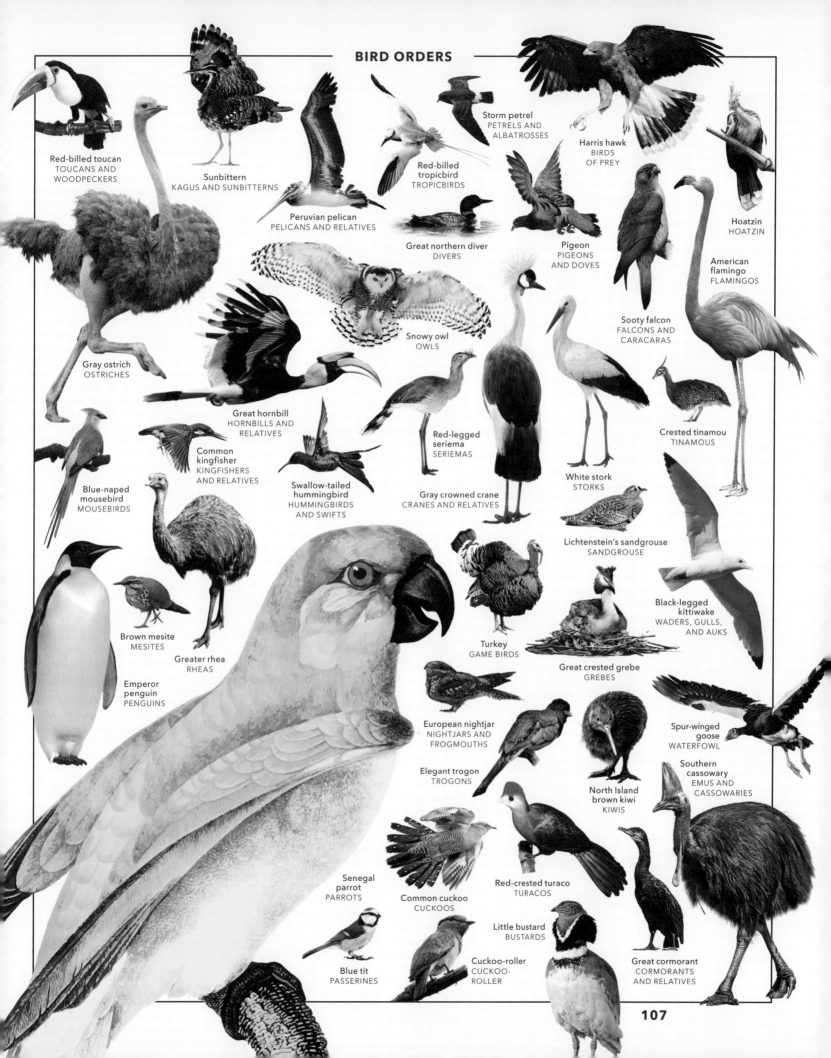

BIRD ORDERS

Red-billed toucan
TOUCANS AND
WOODPECKERS

Sunbittern
KAGUS AND SUNBITTERNS

Peruvian pelican
PELICANS AND RELATIVES

Red-billed
tropicbird
TROPICBIRDS

Storm petrel
PETRELS AND
ALBATROSSES

Harris hawk
BIRDS
OF PREY

Hoatzin
HOATZIN

Great northern diver
DIVERS

Pigeon
PIGEONS
AND DOVES

American
flamingo
FLAMINGOS

Gray ostrich
OSTRICHES

Snowy owl
OWLS

Sooty falcon
FALCONS AND
CARACARAS

Great hornbill
HORNBILLS AND
RELATIVES

Red-legged
seriema
SERIEMAS

Crested tinamou
TINAMOUS

Common
kingfisher
KINGFISHERS
AND RELATIVES

White stork
STORKS

Blue-naped
mousebird
MOUSEBIRDS

Swallow-tailed
hummingbird
HUMMINGBIRDS
AND SWIFTS

Gray crowned crane
CRANES AND RELATIVES

Lichtenstein's sandgrouse
SANDGROUSE

Black-legged
kittiwake
WADERS, GULLS,
AND AUKS

Brown mesite
MESITES

Greater rhea
RHEAS

Turkey
GAME BIRDS

Great crested grebe
GREBES

Emperor
penguin
PENGUINS

European nightjar
NIGHTJARS AND
FROGMOUTHS

Spur-winged
goose
WATERFOWL

Elegant trogon
TROGONS

Southern
cassowary
EMUS AND
CASSOWARIES

North Island
brown kiwi
KIWIS

Senegal
parrot
PARROTS

Common cuckoo
CUCKOOS

Red-crested turaco
TURACOS

Little bustard
BUSTARDS

Blue tit
PASSERINES

Cuckoo-roller
CUCKOO-
ROLLER

Great cormorant
CORMORANTS
AND RELATIVES

Types of
FEATHER

Whether colorful or dull, feathers are what set birds apart from other animals. Birds have four main types of feather, which help them in various ways to fly, keep warm, or find a mate.

Feathers are flat structures that grow from a bird's skin. These are made of keratin—the same substance that forms the hair and nails in humans. Every feather has a strong central shaft, with smaller strands called barbules arranged around it. On most types of feather, the barbules hook around each other, keeping the feather in shape even when the bird flies through strong winds. Feathers grow almost all over a bird's body and are of four types—flight, contour, down, and tail.

Flight feathers are long and very stiff. Their job is to power the bird through the air—pushing it along in a similar way to oars in a row boat pushing against the water. The outermost part of a bird's wing is fringed with a layer of long, strong flight feathers. Smaller flight feathers are attached further along on the top of the wing.

Contour feathers form an overlapping layer around the bird's body. They create a smooth, streamlined surface that allows the bird to move easily through the air when it is in flight. Contour feathers are also waterproof—water rolls off them, so the bird can stay dry.

Down feathers do not have hooks on their barbules, which makes them look soft and fluffy rather than smooth and sleek. Down feathers grow close to the bird's skin, underneath its other body feathers. They trap a layer of air closely around the bird, keeping it warm. Some birds pull out their down feathers to line their nests, which helps keep their eggs and chicks warm.

The tail feathers allow the bird to steer from side to side while it is in the air, balance when it is perched on a branch, and brake when it's ready to stop flying. They are often more brightly colored or elaborate than body feathers, and can be used as a form of display to attract a mate.

> **A bird's feathers often weigh more than its skeleton.**

Flight feathers push the bird along as it flies.

Down feathers trap body heat.

Contour feathers repel water.

Tail feathers help maintain balance.

▶ FEATHERY BODY
Down feathers occur all over a bird's body, with contour feathers on top of them. Flight feathers sprout from the bird's wings, while tail feathers form the fan shape of the tail.

TYPES OF FEATHER

KEY
- ● Flight
- ● Contour
- ● Down
- ● Tail

Japanese green woodpecker
Blue jay
Flamingo
Eagle owl
Ring-necked parakeet
Budgerigar
Parakeet
Hoatzin
Indian roller
Green woodpecker
African gray parrot
Red-winged blackbird
Ocellated turkey
Nicobar pigeon
Macaw
Pheasant
Magpie
Pink cockatoo
Peacock
Blue macaw
Resplendent quetzal
Lady Amherst's pheasant
Kingfisher
Goose
Long-eared owl
Bird of paradise
European turtle dove
Great argus pheasant
Scarlet macaw
Curlew
Northern flicker
Greater racket-tailed drongo
Guinea fowl
Mandarin duck
Glossy black cockatoo
European bee-eater
Macaw

BIRD EGGS FROM AROUND THE WORLD

Chicken

Southern masked weaver

Golden plover

Jungle babbler

Cetti's warbler

Gray catbird

American crow

Egyptian nightjar

Northern mockingbird

Eurasian oystercatcher

Peregrine falcon

Kākāpō

Atlantic puffin

Northern lapwing

Mallard

Common eider

Albatross

Rock bunting

Cormorant

Eastern screech owl

American robin

Common murre

Common cuckoo

Hoatzin

African spoonbill

Great spotted woodpecker

House finch

Hummingbird

Golden eagle

House wren

Goose

Southern cassowary

Emu

Northern gannet

Emperor penguin

Common blackbird

Black guillemot

Ostrich

Quail

Common tern

Kiwi

BIRD EGGS
from around the world

Eggs provide the perfect place for baby chicks to develop before hatching. Bird eggs come in a variety of shapes, sizes, and colors that mirror the diversity of the birds that lay them.

Bird eggs are wonders of evolution. Laid by female birds, an egg provides a safe place for a young chick to develop before hatching. The chick is well protected inside the shell, which is made of a mineral called calcium carbonate. Eggshells are strong and hard, and are able to bear the weight of the parent bird when they sit on them to keep them warm. But the shell is also porous (has lots of tiny holes)—allowing air to move in and out of the egg so the chick can breathe.

Most eggs are oval, with a pointed end and a blunt end. The oval shape of an egg is also what gives it strength. Any force that pushes on the dome-shaped ends gets spread out on the curved surface, reducing its effect. The unique shape also makes them roll in a circular path, which helps prevent eggs from rolling out of the nest. This is why species that nest on cliffs, such as the guillemot, tend to have longer and more pointed eggs.

Eggs vary greatly in size but, in general, egg size is related to the body size of the species laying it. For example, the largest egg is laid by the ostrich, the largest bird. But there are always exceptions. The brown kiwi—around the size of a chicken—lays the largest eggs relative to its body size. Kiwi eggs can be six times bigger than a chicken egg and weigh around a fifth of the weight of the adult bird.

As well as size and shape, color and pattern can vary greatly between species. All eggs start off white when inside the mother, but pigments (natural substances that give color to things) are deposited onto the shells before the eggs are laid. There are two pigments that determine the color of a bird's egg: one is red-brown, the other green-blue. Different combinations of these pigments added in differing amounts across the shell give the tremendous diversity of egg colors and patterns across bird species, from the almost-black emu egg to the rich red of the Cetti's warbler egg.

> *An ostrich egg is 20 times heavier than a chicken egg.*

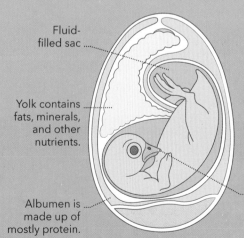

Fluid-filled sac

Yolk contains fats, minerals, and other nutrients.

Albumen is made up of mostly protein.

◄ INSIDE AN EGG
Inside the egg, the embryo, or baby bird, develops within a fluid-filled sac that, together with the albumen, protects it. The yolk provides nutrients for the embryo to grow.

Egg tooth is used to break out of the shell and disappears afterward.

Takahē

Invisible rail

White-throated rail

Henderson crake

Woodford's rail

Tasmanian native hen

North Island brown kiwi

Gough moorhen

Giant coot

Inaccessible Island rail

Weka

Domestic duck

Campbell teal

Snoring rail

New Guinea flightless rail

Domestic chicken

Magellanic flightless steamer duck

Kākāpō

Domestic turkey

Titicaca grebe

Royal penguin

Gentoo penguin

Yellow-eyed penguin

Junín grebe

Galápagos penguin

Greater rhea

Emperor penguin

Little penguin

Southern cassowary

Common ostrich

Common emu

Brown mesite

Galápagos cormorant

One species from each of the 33 genera that include flightless birds

FLIGHTLESS
birds

Not all birds fly. Some of them have lost the ability to fly over time because they had enough to eat on the ground and no predators to fear in their habitat. Flightless birds belong to many different bird genera.

Most birds can fly. Many are capable of incredible feats of aerobatics, while others can only cover short distances near the ground. But some birds cannot fly at all. There are 33 genera of birds with more than 60 living species that are flightless. Each genus is represented by a flightless bird on the left.

Probably the best-known flightless birds are the ostriches, cassowaries, emus, and rheas—genera of large birds, with long necks, an upright stance, and powerful legs for running and defense. Ostriches live in open grasslands. Few predators will take on such big birds, and being tall allows them to spot danger in long grass and to run away. These birds can run at astonishing speeds of up to 37 mph (60 kph).

All birds in the six genera of penguins are flightless, but they have evolved to "fly" underwater, with their wings acting as flippers. Many other flightless species have evolved adaptations for a life in or on water. All flightless steamer ducks have wings that propel them over the surface of the water, acting like paddles.

Much smaller than most flightless birds are the kiwis of New Zealand, where they have no natural predators. In their case, neither flying nor being large were benefits, so they evolved to be small and flightless. With no natural defenses, they were unprepared for the cats that were introduced to their home by humans. There has been a great decline in kiwi numbers since the introduction of cats. Like the kiwi, the flightless rails, the Gough moorhen, and the takahē have all evolved to be flightless in areas where the lack of natural predators makes flight unnecessary.

> The kākāpō is the world's only flightless parrot.

▶ FLYING VS FLIGHTLESS

Unlike birds that can fly, most flightless birds have a short breastbone, and wings that are too small for flight. These wings have either become useless, or adapted for other uses—an ostrich uses its wings for display, and penguin wings are flippers used for swimming.

The keel is a big anchor for powerful flight muscles that help the wings flap.

Long, stiff wing feathers support the body during flight.

The keel is too small to support flight muscles.

Long tail feathers maintain balance during flight.

Bird that can fly

Small wing feathers are unsuitable for flight.

Short tail feathers

Flightless bird

PENGUIN
species

With their comical waddling walk, penguins are immediately recognizable. The 19 species of these remarkable flightless birds are well adapted to a life in the cold Southern Ocean.

There is only one family of penguins, which is further divided into six genera. These genera include 19 species (shown on the right), all found in the southern hemisphere.

Penguins are suited to a life in the ocean, typically spending at least half their lives in water. A thick layer of insulating feathers keeps them warm in the cold waters of the ocean. All penguins have a streamlined shape and flipper-like wings that they use for swimming. They can appear clumsy on land but are graceful swimmers, able to reach speeds of up to 23 mph (36 kph). They appear to "fly" in the water and can dive to great depths in search of small fish, krill, and squid. Emperor penguins have been recorded at depths of more than 1,640 ft (500 m).

While most people imagine the king or emperor penguins when they picture these flightless birds, penguins come in many shapes and sizes. The emperor penguin is larger than the king penguin, but they are otherwise quite similar. Humboldt, Magellanic, Galápagos, and African penguins have banded patterns on their fronts, while Adélie, chinstrap,

> **Penguins can jump 7–10 ft (2–3 m) out of the water using their flippers.**

and gentoo penguins have a tail that brushes across the ground as they walk. Other species have distinctive crests on their heads.

Only emperor and Adélie penguins live and breed in Antarctica, while the other species live across the Southern Ocean. Some, such as the chinstrap, gentoo, and macaroni penguins, occasionally visit Antarctica, but most penguin species are generally found in southern Africa, Australia, South America, and southern oceanic islands. Galápagos penguins are the most northerly species, living in the Galápagos Islands, which straddle the equator.

KINGDOM
PHYLUM
CLASS
ORDER
FAMILY
GENUS
SPECIES

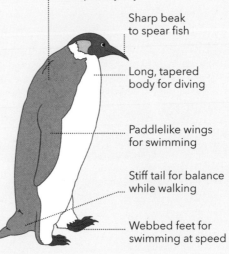

Waterproof plumage (feathers) to keep body dry

Sharp beak to spear fish

Long, tapered body for diving

Paddlelike wings for swimming

Stiff tail for balance while walking

Webbed feet for swimming at speed

◀ PENGUIN FEATURES
Many penguin species live in cold environments with icy seas. Their rounded bodies reduce heat loss, and layers of feathers, including a thick fluffy down, protect them from the cold.

PENGUIN SPECIES

Chinstrap penguin

Northern rockhopper penguin

Little penguin

Australian little penguin

Galápagos penguin

Southern rockhopper penguin

Macaroni penguin

Erect-crested penguin

Royal penguin

Humboldt penguin

Snares penguin

Fiordland penguin

Adélie penguin

African penguin

King penguin

Yellow-eyed penguin

Emperor penguin

Magellanic penguin

Gentoo penguin

MAMMAL ORDERS

PLACENTALS

Three-toed sloth
SLOTHS AND ANTEATERS

Indian flying fox
BATS

Cape golden mole
TENRECS AND GOLDEN MOLES

European rabbit
RABBITS, HARES, AND PIKAS

Indian rhinoceros
ODD-TOED UNGULATES

Sunda flying lemur
COLUGOS

Indian elephant
ELEPHANTS

Western tree hyrax
HYRAXES

Rufous sengi
SENGIS

Large tree shrew
TREE SHREWS

Giraffe
EVEN-TOED UNGULATES

Mandrill
PRIMATES

California sea lion
CARNIVORES

Long-eared hedgehog
HEDGEHOGS, MOLES, AND RELATIVES

Aardvark
AARDVARK

Nine-banded armadillo
ARMADILLOS

Crested porcupine
RODENTS

Amazonian manatee
DUGONGS AND MANATEES

Commerson's dolphin
WHALES, PORPOISES, AND DOLPHINS

Long-tailed pangolin
PANGOLINS

MARSUPIALS

MONOTREMES

Virginia opossum
AMERICAN OPOSSUMS

Tiger quoll
AUSTRALASIAN CARNIVOROUS MARSUPIALS

Dusky shrew opossum
SHREW OPOSSUMS

Koala
AUSTRALASIAN MARSUPIALS

Long-nosed bandicoot
BANDICOOTS AND BILBIES

Monito del monte
MONITO DEL MONTE

Southern marsupial mole
MARSUPIAL MOLES

Short-beaked echidna
MONOTREMES

MAMMAL
orders

Many of the most familiar animals in the world are mammals. This diverse set of animals is divided into 28 orders, which belong in three groups according to how they give birth.

KINGDOM
PHYLUM
CLASS
ORDER
FAMILY
GENUS
SPECIES

Mammals are warm-blooded vertebrates (animals with a backbone). They are covered in hair or fur, and their babies are fed on milk from the mother. Over time, mammals evolved characteristics and ways in which they survived and thrived in different habitats, leading to the 28 orders of mammals we see today. An example of each is shown on the left.

Scientists have classified mammals into different orders based on common features of their skeleton and teeth as well as other similarities in body parts, diet, or behavior. The orders can be grouped together into three types—placental mammals, marsupials, and monotremes—based on how their young are born.

Placental mammals are the largest group, accounting for 20 out of the 28 orders. These mammals give birth to fully developed young. Among the placentals, rodents form the largest order, with 40 percent of mammal species, including rats, mice, squirrels, and beavers. Bats make up the second-largest order. They have well-developed wings, and are the only mammals that are truly able to fly. Some mammal orders, such as primates (which includes monkeys and apes), live on land. Whales, dolphins, and porpoises form a very different order—they are nearly hairless and live and breed in water.

Marsupials give birth to young that finish growing in a pouch on the mother's body. The seven orders of marsupial include species such as the kangaroos. Unusually for mammals, monotremes lay eggs from which their young hatch. The five species of monotremes, including the short-beaked echidna and duck-billed platypus, belong to a single order.

> There are nearly 6,400 species of mammal.

Placental mammal
A rabbit is a placental mammal—these mammals give birth to young that are fully developed at birth.

Marsupial
In a marsupial, such as a kangaroo, the young finish developing in a pouch on the mother's body.

Monotreme
The young of a monotreme, such as a platypus, hatch from eggs.

◀ **GROUPS OF MAMMAL**
Mammals are divided into three groups based on how their young are born.

PRIMATE
families

Primates are the order of mammals that humans belong to. The order includes 16 families—from tiny bush babies to great apes. All primates have large brains for their size and eyes that see in 3D.

Most primates (other than humans) live only in South America, Africa, and Asia. All mammals give birth to live young and feed them on milk. They rely mainly on sight rather than smell to gather information about their environment. Most primates are social animals and live in small groups. Each of the 16 primate families is shown with one example on the right. Scientists organize primates into families by their size, diet, and where they live.

Many primates, such as lorises, pottos, tarsiers, three-striped night monkeys, bush babies, and several different lemur families live in forests or woodlands. These nocturnal animals have large eyes and an acute sense of smell that comes in handy in the dark. Lemurs and aye-ayes live mainly on the island of Madagascar. Sportive lemurs are a separate family with a low-energy diet, which means they are not very active. There are also families of small monkeys that include marmosets, tamarins, and capuchins. The strange-looking bald uakari, with its hairless face and head, is part of the titi, saki, and uakari monkey family. Monkeys and apes live in trees and have long arms and legs and a prehensile (grasping) tail that helps them leap from branch to branch. They are able to use tools because their thumbs are opposable (able to touch the other fingers on the same hand in order to hold things).

Larger howler monkeys belong to the family of howler and spider monkeys. They have a loud call that can be heard several miles away. Proboscis monkeys live in mangrove forests. The males have long, hanging noses.

Orangutans, chimpanzees, gorillas, and bonobos are the great apes—a family that includes humans. Gibbons are classified as lesser apes because of their smaller size. Their extra-long arms help them swing through the trees.

> *Tarsiers have the largest eyes of any mammal in relation to their body size.*

| KINGDOM |
| PHYLUM |
| CLASS |
| ORDER |
| ▶ **FAMILY** ◀ |
| GENUS |
| SPECIES |

Forward-facing eyes

Flexible shoulders

Opposable thumb on hand

Flat nail on the big toe

◀ PRIMATE FEATURES
Primates have evolved for life in the trees. They have forward-facing eyes to judge distances between branches, flexible shoulders for swinging, opposable thumbs for holding on, and flat digits with nails, instead of claws, for balancing.

PRIMATE FAMILIES

Proboscis monkey
OLD WORLD MONKEYS

Verreaux's sifaka
WOOLLY LEMURS

Black-and-gold howler monkey
HOWLER AND SPIDER MONKEYS

White-footed sportive lemur
SPORTIVE LEMURS

Colombian white-faced capuchin
CAPUCHINS AND SQUIRREL MONKEYS

Sunda slow loris
LORISES AND POTTOS

Bald uakari
SAKIS, TITIS, AND UAKARIS

Cotton-top tamarin
MARMOSETS AND TAMARINS

Aye-aye
AYE-AYE

Philippine tarsier
TARSIERS

Three-striped night monkey
NIGHT MONKEYS

Senegal bush baby
BUSH BABIES

Fat-tailed dwarf lemur
DWARF AND MOUSE LEMURS

Lar gibbon
LESSER APES

Orangutan
GREAT APES

Ring-tailed lemur
RING-TAILED LEMURS AND ALLIES

119

CETACEAN
genera

Cetaceans are a group of water-dwelling mammals, commonly known as whales, dolphins, and porpoises.

Whales, dolphins, and porpoises can be found in seas and rivers around the world, and scientists have divided them into 40 genera, based on traits such as size or diet. With their tapered and streamlined bodies and forelimbs modified into flippers, these animals are superbly adapted for life in the water. Some cetaceans can dive very deep in search of food, while others feed closer to the surface. One species from each of the cetacean genera is shown on the right.

Around 34 genera of cetaceans are known as toothed whales. They have conical teeth adapted for feeding on fish and other prey. This group includes all the dolphins and porpoises, as well as some whales such as the sperm whale, deep-diving beaked whales, beluga (the "white whale"), orca, and the narwhal, with its distinctive "unicorn" tusk. The other six genera of cetaceans are known

KINGDOM	
PHYLUM	
CLASS	
ORDER	
FAMILY	
► **GENUS** ◄	
SPECIES	

All cetaceans are related to hippopotamuses.

---

as baleen whales. They lack teeth and feed using sievelike baleen plates made from a hard substance called keratin. The baleen whales fill their mouths with water and expel it through the plates, leaving plankton (microscopic organisms) behind to eat. This group contains the blue whale—the largest animal ever.

Ganges river dolphin
PLATANISTA

Dusky dolphin
LAGENORHYNCHUS

Dall's porpoise
PHOCOENOIDES

Yangtze finless porpoise
NEOPHOCAENA

Tucuxi
SOTALIA

Common dolphin
DELPHINUS

La Plata dolphin
PONTOPORIA

Bowhead whale
BALAENA

Blue whale
BALAENOPTERA

Cuvier's beaked whale
ZIPHIUS

Narwhal
MONODON

CETACEAN GENERA

Gray whale
ESCHRICHTIUS

Atlantic humpback dolphin
SOUSA

Amazon River dolphin
INIA

Commerson's dolphin
CEPHALORHYNCHUS

Orca
ORCINUS

Harbor porpoise
PHOCOENA

Baiji
LIPOTES

Melon-headed whale
PEPONOCEPHALA

Southern right whale
EUBALAENA

Northern right whale dolphin
LISSODELPHIS

Fraser's dolphin
LAGENODELPHIS

Long-finned pilot whale
GLOBICEPHALA

Pygmy right whale
CAPEREA

Irrawaddy dolphin
ORCAELLA

Rough-toothed dolphin
STENO

Striped dolphin
STENELLA

Dwarf sperm whale
KOGIA

Risso's dolphin
GRAMPUS

Common bottlenose dolphin
TURSIOPS

Tropical bottlenose whale
INDOPACETUS

Pygmy beaked whale
MESOPLODON

Beluga whale
DELPHINAPTERUS

Humpback whale
MEGAPTERA

False killer whale
PSEUDORCA

Arnoux's beaked whale
BERARDIUS

Pygmy killer whale
FERESA

Northern bottlenose whale
HYPEROODON

Shepherd's beaked whale
TASMACETUS

Sperm whale
PHYSETER

BEAR

species

Most bears are solitary creatures that eat both plants and meat. There are eight species of bear in the world, but many of them have subspecies that look different from the main species and one another.

KINGDOM
PHYLUM
CLASS
ORDER
FAMILY
GENUS
SPECIES

EIGHT BEAR SPECIES

American black bear
Ursus americanus

Asiatic black bear
Ursus thibetanus

Spectacled bear
Tremarctos ornatus

Polar bear
Ursus maritimus

Sloth bear
Tremarctos ornatus

Brown bear
Ursus arctos

Sun bear
Ursus malayanus

Giant panda
Ailuropoda melanoleuca

The Ursidae family consists of the eight species of bear: brown bears, which live in Asia, northern Europe, and North America; American black bears, which live in North America; Asiatic black bears, which inhabit the tropical forests of Asia; South American spectacled bears; polar bears, whose home is the Arctic sea ice; sun bears, which live in the forests of Southeast Asia; sloth bears, which live in and around India; and finally, giant pandas, which live in the bamboo forests of central China. Giant pandas are the only herbivorous bear species—they eat mostly bamboo.

All other bear species are omnivores, eating plants as well as meat. The polar bear is one of the largest land predators at 9 ft (2.8 m) long, and the most carnivorous bear, mainly eating seals, whose fat provides it with lots of energy. Brown bears catch salmon during the spawning season, and eat berries at other times of the year. The sun bear likes honey, as well as insects, fruit, and plant shoots, while the sloth bear has extra-long claws to probe termite mounds and catch the insects. Spectacled bears, which live in scrubland, even eat snails and cacti.

Most bears live solitary lives, except for female bears when they are raising their young. Many bears in northern climates spend the winter in a state of "torpor" (a type of sleep) in a den or pit in the snow, to save energy.

Some bears also have subspecies, which are populations of bears with features that make them different to the rest of the species. The brown bear has the most subspecies, some of which are shown below. For example, grizzlies are a brown bear with a humped back and white-tipped fur, and Kodiak bears are a larger brown bear that live in Alaska.

SUBSPECIES OF BROWN BEARS

Kamchatka brown bear
Ursus arctos beringianus

Grizzly bear
Ursus arctos horribilis

Gobi bear
Ursus arctos gobiensis

Eurasian brown bear
Ursus arctos arctos

Himalayan brown bear
Ursus arctos isabellinus

Alaska Peninsula brown bear
Ursus arctos gyas

Cantabrian brown bear
Ursus arctos pyrenaicus

Syrian brown bear
Ursus arctos syriacus

Marsican brown bear
Ursus arctos marsicanus

Kodiak bear
Ursus arctos middendorffi

Amur brown bear
Ursus arctos lasiotus

Himalayan blue bear
Ursus arctos pruinosus

WILD CAT
species

The cat family includes 40 species of wild cat seen here. Some of these are big cats, while others are smaller in size. A few of the big cats can roar, while most smaller cats can only purr.

Wild cats are members of the cat family, which is known as Felidae. They are further classified into two groups—big cats (which belong to the subfamily Pantherinae) and small cats (which belong to the subfamily Felinae). There are only seven species of big cat: the tiger, the lion, the jaguar, the leopard, the snow leopard, and the two clouded leopards. These are all carnivorous mammals with strong jaws and teeth to tear the flesh of their prey. The first four of these big cats have the ability to roar because of a special tissue in their throat. The snow leopard and other, smaller, cats cannot roar, though most are able to purr.

Tigers are the largest of the big cats, with many subspecies (variants). Lions have two subspecies, the African lion and the Asiatic lion. While there is only one type of jaguar, there are nine subspecies of leopard. The snow leopard is a separate species from the leopard, and shares more characteristics with the tiger. In 2006, scientists found the Sunda clouded leopard to be a separate species from the Indochinese clouded leopard.

The small cats include 33 species, including the cheetah, which lacks retractable claws and is the fastest animal on land. This group has cats that are found in many habitats—pumas live on mountains, while ocelots and margays live in steamy rainforests. Unlike many others, the fishing cat spends a lot of time swimming. It has partially webbed front paws and a thick coat of fur to keep warm in the water. Though they are all carnivores and predators, smaller cats are also prey for larger animals, including the big cats.

> *Lions are the only cats to live in groups, called prides.*

KINGDOM
PHYLUM
CLASS
ORDER
FAMILY
GENUS
▶ SPECIES ◀

▶ **MANY MARKINGS**
Many wild cats have patterned coats. A tiger's stripes break up its shape making it harder to see. A cheetah's rosettes and leopard's spots help them hide in the undergrowth. The smaller ocelots have heavier markings.

Tiger

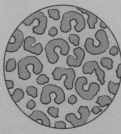
Leopard

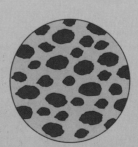
Cheetah

American ocelot

WILD CAT SPECIES

BIG CATS

Lion

Leopard

Snow leopard

Indochinese clouded leopard

Sunda clouded leopard

Tiger

Jaguar

SMALL CATS

Jungle cat

European wildcat

Jaguarundi

Iberian lynx

Pampas cat

Geoffroy's cat

Andean mountain cat

Margay

Oncilla

Rusty-spotted cat

Fishing cat

Puma

Eurasian lynx

Ocelot

Leopard cat

Black-footed cat

Asian golden cat

African wildcat

Serval

Chinese mountain cat

Canadian lynx

Flat-headed cat

Marbled cat

Cheetah

Bay cat

Kodkod

Sand cat

Caracal

Bob cat

Pallas's cat

Sunda leopard cat

African golden cat

Southern tiger cat

125

CAT BREEDS

SHORTHAIR

Manx

Bombay

American shorthair

Siamese

Scottish fold

British shorthair

Australian mist

Japanese bobtail

Arabian mau

Egyptian mau

Korat

Russian blue

Snowshoe

Oriental shorthair

Munchkin

Ceylon

Abyssinian

Lykoi

LONGHAIR

Aphrodite giant

Ragdoll

Somali

Chantilly/Tiffany

Siberian forest cat

Maine coon

Persian

Ragamuffin

Norwegian forest cat

Turkish van

Turkish angora

Nebelung

American bobtail

York chocolate

Balinese

Highlander

A selection of 49 out of more than 70 cat breeds

REX

Selkirk rex

German rex

Skookum

Devon rex

LaPerm

Cornish rex

HAIRLESS

Ukrainian Levkoy

Sphynx

Bambino

Donskoy

Peterbald

Elf cat

HYBRID

Savannah

Bengal

Chausie

CAT
breeds

People and cats have lived together for thousands of years. Cat lovers have created different "breeds" of cats, focusing on specific features.

When humans began farming, they domesticated cats to hunt rodents that were eating their crops. Over time people created cat breeds—types of domesticated cat that all have the same appearance or attributes. Within each breed there may be a range of colors and patterns. Each breed is made by selecting a cat with the desired characteristics and breeding it over many generations. There are more than 70 different cat breeds, which are generally split into five groups, based on the length of their fur. However, many pet cats don't have a breed at all and are called domestic shorthair or domestic longhair.

Short-haired cats are the most common type. They have short hair, and any markings on their coats are clear to see. Long-haired cats have longer coats, which can be "shaggy" (thick and rough), "silky" smooth, or "fluffy." Some of them also have a second layer of thick undercoat. Rex cats have curly hairs, which create waves of fur across their bodies. Hairless breeds have no hair at all. For some, that includes having no whiskers or eyelashes.

Crosses between pet cats and wild cats give rise to "hybrid" cat breeds. For example, savannah cats were created by mixing pet cats with wild cats known as servals.

> **Hairless cats need to live indoors—they get cold easily.**

DOG
breeds

Dogs, which evolved from wolves, have lived alongside humans for thousands of years. Over the centuries, people began breeding dogs with particular features, creating the dog breeds we know today.

DOG BREEDS

PRIMITIVE DOGS
OLDEST BREEDS OF DOGS

Peruvian Inca orchid

Ibizan hound

New Guinea singing dog

Basenji

SIGHT HOUNDS
KEEN EYESIGHT FOR HUNTING

Saluki

Greyhound

Afghan hound

Borzoi

COMPANION DOGS
HOUSE PETS

Havanese

Pug

Poodle

Pekingese

Shih Tzu

Chihuah

WORKING DOGS
GUARD PROPERTY AND ANIMALS

Australian cattle dog

German shepherd

Boxer

Border collie

Pyrenean sheepdog

Great Dane

Pembroke Welsh corgi

A selection of 47 out of more than 340 dog breeds

The first dogs that lived with people were wolves, which learned they could get food and warmth near our campfires. They became hunting companions and, eventually, pet dogs. Over time, dogs were bred for specific purposes. Each dog breed today has its own look, skills, and temperament. There are around 340 breeds, organized into groups that are mostly based on the purpose for which they were bred.

Primitive dogs are closest to wolves—some are still partly wild. Sight hounds are hunting dogs, which use their keen eyesight to spot prey, unlike scent hounds, which use their keen sense of smell to sniff out prey. Spitz breeds come from cold places—they have two layers of thick fur, and furry feet. Many of them hunt game or pull sleds, although they've also become popular pet breeds. Gun dogs work alongside hunters. They wait until their owner shoots a bird or another animal before fetching it.

Working dogs guard property and flocks of animals, while terriers hunt vermin, such as rats. Some terriers are small enough to chase prey down burrows and catch them. Companion dogs have been bred to be pets and are often small. Toy breeds are even smaller.

Crossbreeds are the result of planned mixing of different breeds. One example is the labradoodle—a mix of Labrador retriever and poodle.

> **Dogs have lived with people for more than 12,000 years.**

SCENT HOUNDS
KEEN SENSE OF SMELL FOR HUNTING

Beagle

Basset hound

Mountain cur

Schiller hound

Bloodhound

GUN DOGS
HUNTING COMPANIONS

Labrador retriever

American cocker spaniel

Golden retriever

English setter

Standard poodle

Nova Scotia duck tolling retriever

TERRIERS
HUNT SMALL PREY

Scottish terrier

Australian terrier

Boston terrier

Dutch Smoushond

Jack Russell terrier

TOY BREEDS
BRED TO BE SMALL

Toy fox terrier

Russian toy terrier

Chinese crested

SPITZ DOGS
LIVE IN THE COLD

Samoyed

Siberian husky

Chow chow

Pomeranian

CROSSBREEDS
MIX OF DIFFERENT BREEDS

Bichon Yorkie

Labradoodle

Puggle

PARTS OF A HORSE

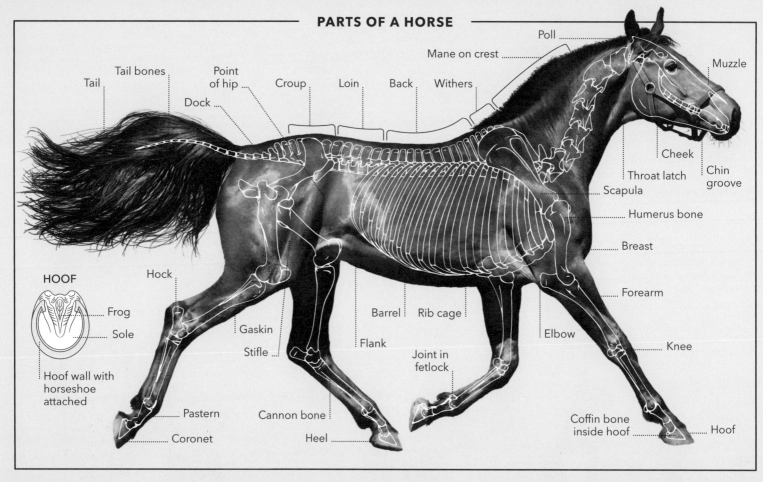

Poll
Mane on crest
Muzzle
Tail bones
Point of hip
Croup
Loin
Back
Withers
Tail
Dock
Cheek
Chin groove
Throat latch
Scapula
Humerus bone
Breast
Forearm
Hock
Gaskin
Stifle
Barrel
Rib cage
Flank
Joint in fetlock
Elbow
Knee

HOOF

Frog
Sole
Hoof wall with horseshoe attached
Pastern
Coronet
Cannon bone
Heel
Coffin bone inside hoof
Hoof

HORSE BREEDS

LIGHT HORSE

Haflinger Selle Français Andalusian Appaloosa Barb Kathiawari

HEAVY HORSE

Clydesdale Irish Draught Brabant Shire Percheron

PONY

Hokkaido Pony Connemara Pony of the Americas Falabella Shetland Welsh Mountain Pony

A selection of 17 out of more than 350 horse breeds

HORSE
breeds

Horses are grazing animals that can run at high speeds. Humans began taming them around 5,500 years ago, and over time, took the one species and created many breeds—all different from one another.

Modern horses evolved in Central Asia and gradually replaced their wild ancestors. Horses are powerful, four-legged animals with a strong back, big lungs, and a long neck. Once domesticated (tamed), they made a valuable addition to the farm and a powerful aid for warriors in battle. People selected horses with specific desired traits—for example, speed, size, or color—and bred them over many generations to develop the different horse breeds.

Horses are ungulates, which means their legs end with a hoof that is covered with a material called keratin (the material in human fingernails). Most domesticated horses have a piece of metal called a horseshoe fitted to each hoof to help protect it. Modern-day breeds can be divided into heavy horses, light horses, and ponies. These breeds are measured in "hands." One hand typically equals 4 in (10.16 cm).

Light horses, which are usually more than 14.2 hands in size, have narrow bodies and slender legs. These agile breeds—such as the Andalusian and the Appaloosa—make excellent race horses. The Selle Français, with its long, muscular neck and powerfully built body, is a show jumper known for its athletic moves.

Heavy horses are larger—measuring over 16.2 hands—and stronger than light horses. In the past, breeds such as the Shire were commonly used to pull carriages or haul loads on farms. The Clydesdale was bred to have durable hooves, and can be seen pulling loads on city streets. Ponies are smaller than horses—usually 14.2 hands or smaller. They have shorter legs, are stockier, and are extremely strong for their size. They include the Argentinian Falabella, which grows to no more than 8 hands high and can live more than 40 years.

The only truly wild horses left in the world are the takhi, or Przewalski's horses, which live in protected areas in Mongolia or in zoos or reserves around the world.

> A Clydesdale can pull an incredible 5,950 lb (2,700 kg).

Shetland is up to 10.2 hands

Selle Français is 15.2–16.2 hands

◄ **HORSE HEIGHTS**
Horses are measured in units called "hands." A horse's height is measured from the ground to its withers.

TYPES OF TEETH

KEY ■ Incisor ■ Canine ■ Carnassial ■ Molar ■ Premolar

TEETH OF A HERBIVORE

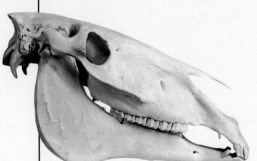

Horse skull
42 TEETH

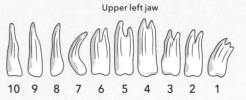

Upper right jaw — Upper left jaw

20 19 18 17 16 15 14 13 12 11   10 9 8 7 6 5 4 3 2 1

21 22 23 24 25 26 27 28 29 30 31   32 33 34 35 36 37 38 39 40 41 42

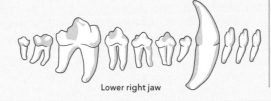

Lower right jaw — Lower left jaw

TEETH OF A CARNIVORE

Wolf skull
42 TEETH

Upper right jaw — Upper left jaw

20 19 18 17 16 15 14 13 12 11   10 9 8 7 6 5 4 3 2 1

21 22 23 24 25 26 27 28 29 30 31   32 33 34 35 36 37 38 39 40 41 42

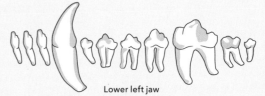

Lower right jaw — Lower left jaw

TEETH OF AN OMNIVORE

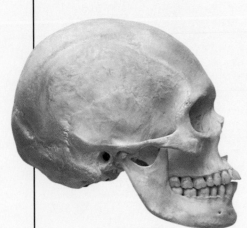

Human skull
32 TEETH

Upper right jaw — Upper left jaw

16 15 14 13 12 11 10 9   8 7 6 5 4 3 2 1

17 18 19 20 21 22 23 24   25 26 27 28 29 30 31 32

Lower right jaw — Lower left jaw

Types of
TEETH

Almost all animals have teeth, but mammal teeth have evolved into different shapes based on the kind of food eaten by the animal. There are four main types—incisors, canines, premolars, and molars.

Teeth are like a little tool kit inside a mammal's mouth. These tools are perfectly designed for cutting, slicing, tearing, and chewing food. Each type of tooth is shaped according to its specific job. Most mammals have a mixture of incisors, canines, premolars, and molars arranged neatly in rows in their jaws.

> *Tooth covering, or enamel, is the hardest substance of an animal's body.*

At the front of the mouth, mammals have 8-12 incisors. These thin, flat, sharp teeth (perfect for biting) cut and slice food. Next are the sharp canines that grab, pierce, and tear tough meat. Behind these are the premolars, which grip, grind, and crush food. These are flat with two ridges on top. They break food up before passing it to the wide molars at the back of the mouth. The molars are flat with four ridges on top. They crush, grind, and mash food with the full power of the jaw.

The size, shape, and layout of teeth in a mammal varies depending on what it eats. Herbivores primarily eat plants and tough vegetation. They use their incisors to snip off grass and leaves. Then their strong molars provide a wide, flat surface for squashing and grinding—helping them chew the tough food for a long time.

Carnivores (animals that eat only meat) have long, pointed canines, which they use to stab and grip their prey, as well as slice and rip the meat they eat. Some carnivores, such as wolves and sea lions, also have carnassial teeth—large cutting teeth on either jaw that work together like a pair of scissors to shear through meat and bone.

Humans, bears, and foxes are all omnivores, who eat both plants and animals. They have a mixture of sharp incisors and canines for cutting through flesh, and flat premolars and molars for breaking down plant material.

▶ **TEETH SHAPES AND POSITIONS**
The wide and thin incisors are at the front of the mouth. Next to them are the pointed canines, behind which are the flat premolars. The broader molars at the back have the largest surface area for chewing and grinding food.

Incisors
Flat and sharp for biting or clipping food

Canine
Pointed tip for sinking into flesh or meat

Premolar
Broad head for tearing and crushing food

Molar
Thick and wide for crushing and grinding

Animals under
THREAT

Many species across the world are in danger, mainly because of human activities, such as deforestation, agriculture, and pollution. Understanding the threats they face can help us protect them.

ANIMALS UNDER THREAT

NEAR THREATENED
LIKELY TO BE IN DANGER IN THE FUTURE

Plains zebra

Blue ground beetle

Spiny-headed tree frog

Jaguar

Green salamander

Ball python

Longsnout seahorse

Pacific bluefin tuna

VULNERABLE
LOW ENOUGH NUMBERS IN THE WILD TO BE OF CONCERN

Blyth's tragopan

Freycinet's frog

Lion

Loggerhead turtle

Giant panda

Common yabby

Dugong

ENDANGERED
COULD GO EXTINCT IN THE WILD IF THREATS CONTINUE

Saker falcon

Asian elephant

A selection of threatened species from the 2022 IUCN Red List

Whenever humans grow food, build houses, or cut down forests, they can cause harm to the wildlife that live in the areas they take over. The International Union for Conservation of Nature (IUCN) uses experts to figure out what threats different species face. The information is gathered in a database known as the "IUCN Red List." The IUCN classifies species in different categories. If a species is not under threat of extinction (dying out), it is "Least Concern." But about 42,000 species (28 percent of all species studied) are under threat as per the 2022 Red List data.

There are four levels of threat, each more serious than the last. "Near Threatened" species aren't currently endangered, but they are close to becoming "Vulnerable." The declining numbers of "Vulnerable" species are of concern, and if these numbers keep falling, the species may become "Endangered." A species may be classified as "Endangered" based on several factors, including a population declining by more than half over a period of 10 years. "Critically Endangered" species face a very high risk of becoming extinct and include animals such as the Javan rhinoceros and the slender-snouted crocodile.

Some species have already become "Extinct in the Wild," although they exist in captivity. If their numbers continue to dwindle in captivity, the species may go extinct.

Around the world, 4,008 animals are critically endangered.

CRITICALLY ENDANGERED
VERY HIGH RISK OF GOING EXTINCT IN THE WILD

Whooping crane

Scissor-tailed hummingbird

Queen Alexandra's bird-wing

Galápagos penguin

African spurred tortoise

Jeweled gecko

Minkley's cichlid

Irrawaddy dolphin

Rusty patched bumble bee

California condor

Javan rhinoceros

Peacock tarantula

American burying beetle

Slender-snouted crocodile

Lemur leaf frog

Malaysian giant turtle

Great hammerhead shark

EXTINCT IN THE WILD
ONLY EXISTS IN CAPTIVITY

Hawaiian crow

Spix's macaw

Blue-tailed shinning-skink

Père David's deer

Kihansi spray toad

Golden skiffia

Yangtze sturgeon

EXTINCT
animals

A species is considered extinct when there are no more living members. While animal species may die out naturally, human activities have caused some animal species to die out much faster.

Human impact on the planet has increased enormously since the Industrial Revolution began in Europe around 1750. We need more energy, more resources, and more space than ever before. In many cases, our activities have upset the balance of nature, driving birds, mammals, reptiles, amphibians, fish, mollusks, insects, and other animals, such as some worms, to extinction. As many as 779 animal species have gone extinct since the year 1500, many because of human activities.

Extinctions occur naturally, but sometimes the rate at which species go extinct dramatically increases. The best known "mass extinction" event was caused by an asteroid collision about 66 million years ago that wiped out all non-flying dinosaurs. Right now, though, it is our actions that are causing a similar extinction event.

Some species die out because we deliberately kill them. People hunted the Tasmanian tiger because it was a threat to farm animals. Many animals have died out because of large-scale poaching (illegal hunting and trading of animals).

Species that only live in one small place are particularly vulnerable to extinction, especially if we change their habitat. The po'o-uli was a bird that lived only on one Hawaiian island. Human activity there killed off the bird in 2004.

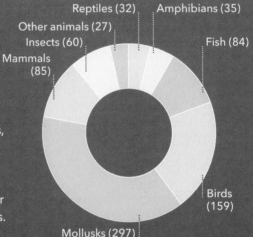

Reptiles (32)
Amphibians (35)
Other animals (27)
Insects (60)
Fish (84)
Mammals (85)
Birds (159)
Mollusks (297)

◄ RECORDED EXTINCTIONS
This pie chart shows the number of animal species that have gone extinct since the year 1500. The data has been taken from the 2022 version of the Red List (a growing list of threatened and extinct species created by an organization called IUCN).

We also cause extinctions by introducing invasive species. Domestic cats, for example, have been transported around the world, causing more than 60 species of birds, mammals, and reptiles to die out.

Larger animals attract attention if they go extinct. Sometimes though, we don't even know what we are losing. Scientists believe that many mollusk and insect species are going extinct before we are able to discover them.

It would be far better if we could save species before they get close to the brink of extinction, perhaps through captive breeding programs. An even better approach is to change how we exploit the planet, finding ways that allow us to live alongside nature.

EXTINCT ANIMALS

Tasmanian tiger
1936

Sampson's naiad
2000

Bramble Cay mosaic-tailed rat
2015

Dodo
1662

Passenger pigeon
1914

Round Island burrowing boa
1975

Great auk
1852

Saddle-backed Rodrigues giant tortoise
AROUND 1800

White swamphen
1834

Kaua'i 'ō'ō
1987

Choiseul pigeon
1904

Xerces blue
1940s

Steller's sea cow
1768

Bluebuck
AROUND 1799–1800

Chinese paddlefish
2003

Rocky Mountain locust
1902

Golden toad
1989

Splendid poison frog
2018

Carelia dolei
1996

Labrador duck
1878

Falkland Islands wolf
1876

Tahiti rail
1930s

Desert-rat kangaroo
1935

Toolache wallaby
1939

Japanese sea lion
1970s

Yunnan Lake newt
1979

Silver trout
1930

Caribbean monk seal
1952

New Zealand grayling
1927

A selection of animals that have gone extinct due to human activities

PREHISTORIC REPTILES

IN THE AIR

Hatzegopteryx

Pterodactylus

Pterodaustro

Tupandactylus

Pteranodon

Rhamphorhynchus

Peteinosaurus

Eudimorphodon

Tupuxuara

Quetzalcoatlus

Dimorphodon

Tropeognathus

ON LAND

Postosuchus

Desmatosuchus

Smilosuchus

Proganochelys

Kaprosuchus

Erythrosuchus

Sarcosuchus

IN THE WATER

Nothosaurus

Archelon

Placodus

Psephoderma

Mosasaurus

Stenopterygius

Dakosaurus

Elasmosaurus

Shonisaurus

Plesiosaurus

Temnodontosaurus

Ophthalmosaurus

Liopleurodon

Atopodentatus

PREHISTORIC
reptiles

Dinosaurs are so popular that people often assume all ancient reptiles were dinosaurs. But dinosaurs shared their world with many other reptiles who flew in the air, crawled on land, or swam in the water.

Reptiles evolved around 320 million years ago, and over the millennia, they evolved into many different shapes and sizes. By the Mesozoic Era (251–66 million years ago), they had spread across our planet, and many had evolved into gigantic predators.

The seas and oceans were filled with giant reptiles that preyed on marine life and on each other. Plesiosaurs were enormous carnivores with four powerful fins to push them through the water. They came in two types—one with long, snakelike necks and small heads, such as *Plesiosaurus*, and another with shorter necks and large heads, bristling with sharp teeth, such as *Liopleurodon*. Ichthyosaurs, such as *Temnodontosaurus*, were reptiles that looked a little like dolphins. They had to travel up to the water's surface to breathe. Some ichthyosaurs were among the largest marine reptiles to ever swim in Earth's oceans. Mosasaurs, such as *Mosasaurus*, were colossal hunters, with lizard-like bodies adapted for swimming, and large jaws for crushing prey. Some of their prey were creatures that look more familiar to us, such as the prehistoric marine turtles *Archelon* and *Psephoderma*.

Mosasaurus was longer than a city bus.

Pterosaurs were reptiles that ruled the skies. They had wings made of a thin layer of skin, which was attached to the arms and legs, and ran along the side of the body. Early pterosaurs were small, and probably glided through the air instead of flying by flapping their wings. Later species of pterosaur, such as *Quetzalcoatlus*, were enormous, and probably flapped their wings to fly. When not in the air, they are likely to have folded their wings and walked along the ground on all fours, perhaps on the hunt for smaller prey.

On land, some of the largest reptiles were the pseudosuchians, which included the prehistoric ancestors of crocodiles and their relatives, such as *Sarcosuchus*. Other reptiles included land-based turtles, such as *Proganochelys*, which had a row of spikes around its head.

The pterosaurs and the pseudosuchians belonged to the reptile group called archosaurs, which also included dinosaurs. Early pseudosuchians were larger than dinosaurs, and even preyed on them, but by the middle of the Mesozoic Era, most pseudosuchians had died out. Dinosaurs grew larger in size, becoming the prominent group on land, and ushering in an age of dinosaurs.

The skull of *Hatzegopteryx* was nearly 8 ft (2.5 m) long.

Types of
DINOSAUR

Prehistoric reptiles called dinosaurs flourished on Earth between 243 and 66 million years ago. They all looked very different, but studying their hip bones has revealed there were two main types.

Paleontologists (scientists who study ancient life) came up with a way to classify dinosaurs—and it's all in the hips. In 1887, British paleontologist Harry Seeley split dinosaurs into two groups based on the shape of their hip bones. Ornithischians, or "bird-hipped" dinosaurs, had hip bones that looked like those of birds. The "lizard-hipped" dinosaurs, also called saurischians, were named for hips resembling those of lizards. Paleontologists eventually realized that modern birds actually evolved from theropods, which were lizard-hipped dinosaurs. This means that birds are the only living dinosaurs, as all other types died out around 66 million years ago when an asteroid struck our planet.

Dinosaurs had already split into the saurischian and ornithischian groups by around 233 million years ago. The ornithischians were all plant eaters. They evolved into a stunning variety of shapes and sizes, but can be sorted into three main kinds. *Triceratops* was one of the marginocephalians, most of which had horns. The ornithopods were "duck-billed," and included

Parasaurolophus and *Edmontosaurus*. More armored than these two kinds were the thyreophorans, which included spike-tailed giants such as *Stegosaurus* and smaller armored ankylosaurs such as *Euoplocephalus*.

The saurischians were of two kinds. One group of saurischians evolved longer necks, smaller heads, and leaflike teeth—becoming specialized in eating plants. These were the sauropodomorphs, which included giants such as *Mamenchisaurus* and *Argentinosaurus*, as well as smaller herbivores such as *Anchisaurus*.

The second type of saurischian was the group called the theropods. They started as carnivores, but evolved a more varied diet over time. *Allosaurus* was a giant meat eater, *Baryonyx* ate only fish, and some others became herbivorous, such as the small, beaked *Caudipteryx*.

The term "dinosaur" comes from the Greek for "terrible lizard."

▼ **DINOSAUR HIP BONES**
The hip bones of lizard-hipped and bird-hipped dinosaurs have different shapes and point in different directions.

A hip bone called a pubis points forward in lizard-hipped dinosaurs.

Pubis points backward in bird-hipped dinosaurs.

BIRD-HIPPED DINOSAURS

MARGINOCEPHALIANS

Pachycephalosaurus

Protoceratops

Triceratops

Pachyrhinosaurus

Centrosaurus

Psittacosaurus

Styracosaurus

Diabloceratops

ORNITHOPODS

Edmontosaurus

Hadrosaurus

Corythosaurus

Parasaurolophus

Shantungosaurus

Iguanodon

Tenontosaurus

THYREOPHORANS

Euoplocephalus

Stegosaurus

Borealopelta

Scutellosaurus

Miragaia

Polacanthus

LIZARD-HIPPED DINOSAURS

THEROPODS

Yutyrannus

Albertosaurus

Carcharodontosaurus

Baryonyx

Tyrannosaurus rex

Utahraptor

SAUROPODOMORPHS

Bajadasaurus

Amargasaurus

Saltasaurus

Argentinosaurus

Apatosaurus

Diplodocus

Tarbosaurus

Liliensternus

Citipati

Velociraptor

Monoykus

Caudipteryx

Compsognathus

Microraptor

Allosaurus

Torvosaurus

Spinosaurus

Therizinosaurus

Masiakasaurus

Brachiosaurus

Shunosaurus

Isanosaurus

Anchisaurus

Thecodontosaurus

Alamosaurus

Lufengosaurus

Giraffatitan

Plateosaurus

Massospondylus

Mamenchisaurus

Camarasaurus

Dicraeosaurus

143

T. REX
skeleton

Striding through the forests of western North America 66 million years ago was a fearsome meat-eating dinosaur called *Tyrannosaurus rex*, or *T. rex*. Its strong skeleton supported its massive head, body, and tail.

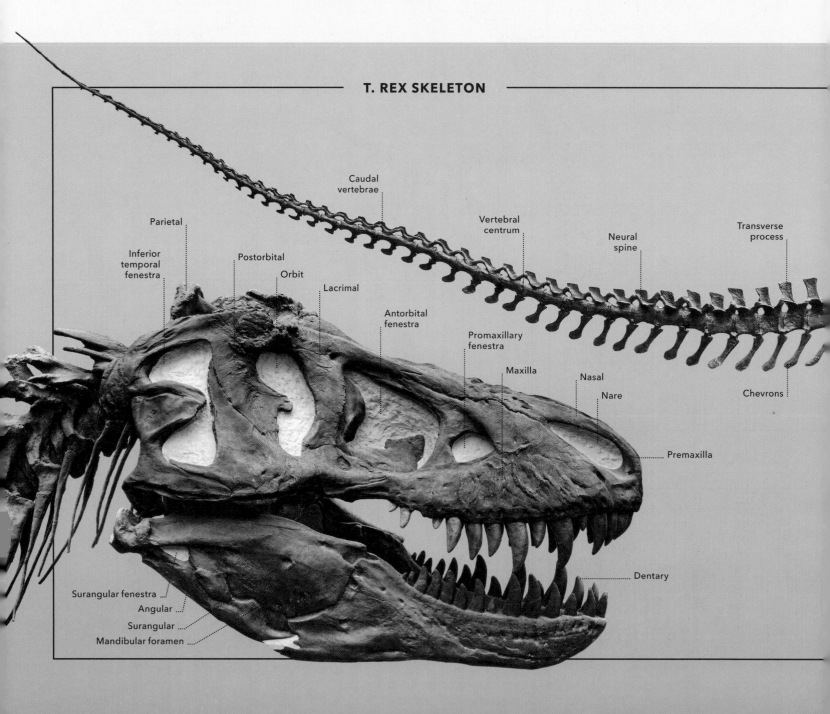

T. REX SKELETON

Caudal vertebrae

Parietal

Vertebral centrum

Neural spine

Transverse process

Inferior temporal fenestra

Postorbital

Orbit

Lacrimal

Antorbital fenestra

Promaxillary fenestra

Maxilla

Nasal

Nare

Chevrons

Premaxilla

Dentary

Surangular fenestra

Angular

Surangular

Mandibular foramen

While it wasn't the biggest dinosaur of its time, *T. rex* was as long as a school bus, at 40 ft (12 m), and as heavy as an African elephant, weighing in at 9,000–15,000 lb (4,000–7,000 kg).

Its most striking feature was its massive head. The skull, or cranium, was about 4.3 ft (1.3 m) long and weighed around 160 lb (73 kg). It also had very powerful jaws—which gave it the strongest bite force of any land animal in history. Armed with 60 banana-size, serrated teeth, *T. rex* could crush bone easily. Its skeleton contained 380 bones (humans have 206), including more than 40 in its tail, called caudal vertebrae. These bones, which could be as long as 6 in (15 cm), helped balance the rest of the dinosaur's body. Each of its hind legs had a very thick femur, tibia, and fibula. *T. rex*'s legs were supported by powerful muscles that helped this animal walk and balance. *T. rex* probably couldn't walk faster than 12 mph (19 kph).

A slice through a *T. rex* bone reveals its age, like the rings in tree bark.

The dinosaur's forelimbs were not very long. The upper arm bone, or humerus, was around 16 in (40 cm) long, and with the lower ulna and radius, the whole arm was only around 3 ft (1 m) long in total.

Air pockets in *T. rex*'s bones made them lightweight, helping this mega predator lift its huge head and gigantic tail while catching prey or fighting off other predators.

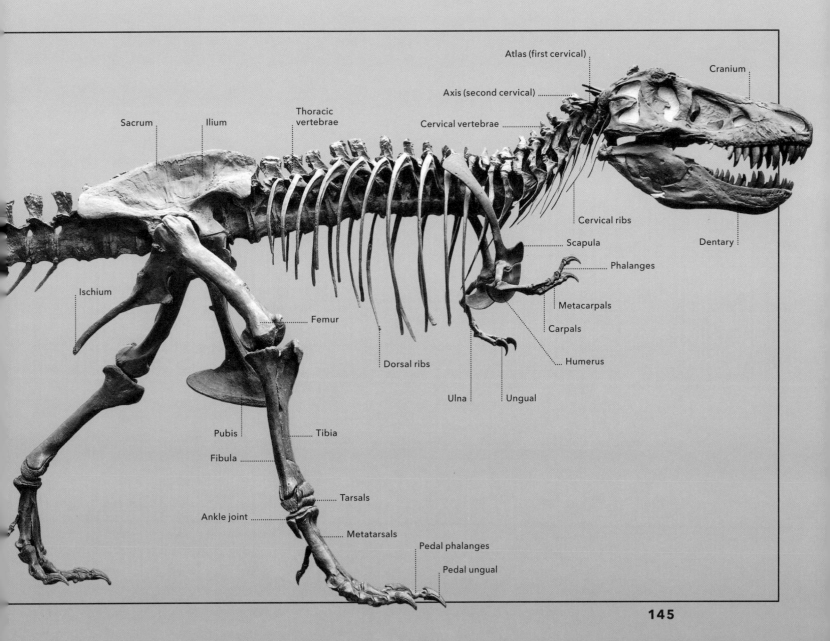

Atlas (first cervical)
Cranium
Axis (second cervical)
Cervical vertebrae
Sacrum
Ilium
Thoracic vertebrae
Cervical ribs
Dentary
Scapula
Ischium
Phalanges
Femur
Metacarpals
Carpals
Dorsal ribs
Humerus
Ulna
Ungual
Pubis
Tibia
Fibula
Tarsals
Ankle joint
Metatarsals
Pedal phalanges
Pedal ungual

SCIENCE

Science "OLOGIES"

"Ology" means "the study of" in Ancient Greek, and is used to describe a surprising number of science subjects, from the study of ears to ants!

Because science is such a massive subject, experts like to break it down into different areas, or disciplines. The natural sciences, for example, cover things such as astronomy, physics, biology, and chemistry, while the social sciences explore topics like economics and psychology. Each discipline can be broken down even more, where a person specializes in a particular "ology," studying that one particular area rather than trying to understand everything about the whole science subject.

> Epistemology is the study of knowledge itself.

Most of the bigger "ologies" can be split out into smaller "ologies," which are themselves often subdivided further. Biology, for example, is the study of all living things and their behavior. Within biology are a number of subfields, such as physiology, which is the study of how the human body works. And within physiology are many other "ologies," including cytology (the study of cells), myology (the study of muscles), and cardiology (the study of the heart).

The "ologies" shown here are just a selection of the hundreds that it's possible to learn about. Over time, as our knowledge of science grows and becomes more and more specialized, more and more "ologies" will be added to the collection.

Biology
The study of life

Cytology
The study of cells

Myology
The study of muscles

Hematology
The study of blood and blood disorders

Nephrology
The study of the kidneys

Urology
The study of the urinary tract

Psychology
The study of the human mind

Psychopathology
The study of mental illness or disorders

Sexology
The study of human sexuality

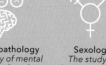
Allergology
The study of allergies

Traumatology
The study of wounds and injuries

Rheumatology
The study of rheumatic diseases

Herpetology
The study of reptiles and amphibians

Ichthyology
The study of fish

Ornithology
The study of birds

Lepidopterology
The study of butterflies and moths

Acarology
The study of ticks and mites

Coleopterology
The study of beetles

Planktology
The study of plankton

Anthropology
The study of humans

Ecology
The study of the relationships between living organisms and their environment

Agrology
The study of soil and the growing of crops

Herbology
The study of the medicinal use of plants

Toxicology
The study of poisons

Ichnology
The study of fossil footprints, tracks, and burrows

Hydrology
The study of water

Glaciology
The study of glaciers

Seismology
The study of earthquakes

Typology
The study of classification

Criminology
The study of crime using science

SCIENCE "OLOGIES"

Cardiology
The study of the heart

Gastrology
The study of the stomach and intestines

Hepatology
The study of the liver

Gynecology
The study of the female reproductive system

Pulmonology
The study of lung diseases

Endocrinology
The study of the body's hormones and glands

Neurology
The study of nerves

Craniology
The study of the human skull

Osteology
The study of bones

Proctology
The study of the lower part of the digestive system

Dermatology
The study of the skin

Rhinology
The study of the nose

Otology
The study of the ear

Audiology
The study of hearing

Odontology
The study of the teeth

Ophthalmology
The study of the eyes

Trichology
The study of hair and the scalp

Physiology
The study of living organisms

Neonatology
The study of newborn infants

Anesthesiology
The study of pain relief

Somnology
The study of sleep

Phonology
The study of vocal sounds

Immunology
The study of the immune system

Epidemiology
The study of the origin and spread of diseases

Pathology
The study of illness

Radiology
The study of imaging technology to diagnose and treat disease

Pharmacology
The study of drugs

Oncology
The study of cancer

Microbiology
The study of microorganisms

Bacteriology
The study of bacteria

Virology
The study of viruses

Parasitology
The study of parasites

Helminthology
The study of parasitic worms

Nematology
The study of roundworms

Zoology
The study of animals

Zoopathology
The study of animal diseases

Oology
The study of eggs

Mammalogy
The study of mammals

Hippology
The study of horses

Primatology
The study of primates

Cynology
The study of dogs

Felinology
The study of cats

Cetology
The study of cetaceans (e.g., whales)

Entomology
The study of insects

Arachnology
The study of spiders

Formicology
The study of ants

Orthopterology
The study of crickets and grasshoppers

Apiology
The study of bees

Dipterology
The study of flies

Odonatology
The study of dragonflies and damselflies

Coprology
The study of excrement

Malacology
The study of mollusks

Conchology
The study of shells

Mycology
The study of fungi

Bioecology
The study of the interaction of life in the environment

Phytology
The study of plants

Dendrology
The study of trees

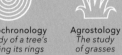

Dendrochronology
The study of a tree's age using its rings

Agrostology
The study of grasses

Phytopathology
The study of plant diseases

Pomology
The study of fruits

Palynology
The study of pollens

Xylology
The study of wood

Geology
The study of Earth

Geochronology
The study of the age of Earth

Geomorphology
The study of present-day landforms

Lithology
The study of rocks

Mineralogy
The study of minerals

Gemology
The study of gemstones

Archaeology
The study of the past by excavation

Archeozoology
The study of ancient animal remains at archaeological sites

Paleontology
The study of fossilized animals and plants

Aerology
The study of the atmosphere

Climatology
The study of the climate

Meteorology
The study of weather

Nephology
The study of clouds

Oceanology
The study of oceans

Kymatology
The study of waves

Orology
The study of mountains

Speleology
The study of caves

Volcanology
The study of volcanoes

Metrology
The study of measurements

Cryology
The study of very cold temperatures

Thermology
The study of heat

Heliology
The study of the sun

Selenology
The study of the moon

Planetology
The study of the planets

Areology
The study of Mars

Astrobiology
The study of life in the universe

Xenobiology
The study of extraterrestrial life

149

SCIENTIFIC SCALES

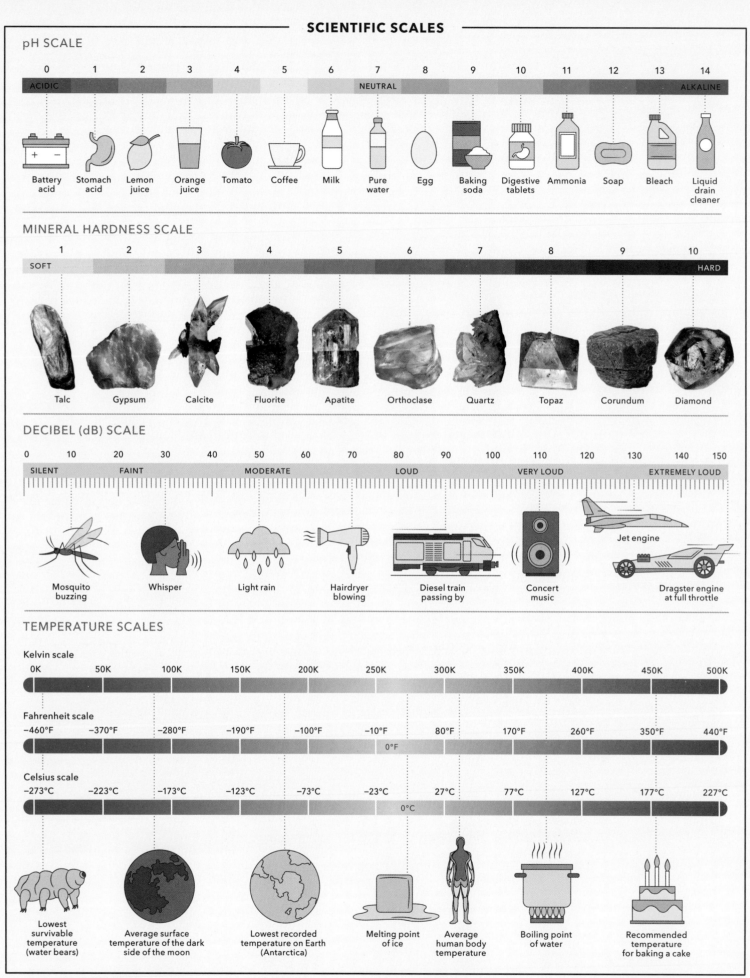

pH SCALE

0	1	2	3	4	5	6	7	8	9	10	11	12	13	14

ACIDIC   NEUTRAL   ALKALINE

Battery acid · Stomach acid · Lemon juice · Orange juice · Tomato · Coffee · Milk · Pure water · Egg · Baking soda · Digestive tablets · Ammonia · Soap · Bleach · Liquid drain cleaner

MINERAL HARDNESS SCALE

1	2	3	4	5	6	7	8	9	10

SOFT   HARD

Talc · Gypsum · Calcite · Fluorite · Apatite · Orthoclase · Quartz · Topaz · Corundum · Diamond

DECIBEL (dB) SCALE

0	10	20	30	40	50	60	70	80	90	100	110	120	130	140	150

SILENT   FAINT   MODERATE   LOUD   VERY LOUD   EXTREMELY LOUD

Mosquito buzzing · Whisper · Light rain · Hairdryer blowing · Diesel train passing by · Concert music · Jet engine · Dragster engine at full throttle

TEMPERATURE SCALES

Kelvin scale

0K	50K	100K	150K	200K	250K	300K	350K	400K	450K	500K

Fahrenheit scale

−460°F	−370°F	−280°F	−190°F	−100°F	−10°F	80°F	170°F	260°F	350°F	440°F

0°F

Celsius scale

−273°C	−223°C	−173°C	−123°C	−73°C	−23°C	27°C	77°C	127°C	177°C	227°C

0°C

Lowest survivable temperature (water bears) · Average surface temperature of the dark side of the moon · Lowest recorded temperature on Earth (Antarctica) · Melting point of ice · Average human body temperature · Boiling point of water · Recommended temperature for baking a cake

Scientific
SCALES

Most scientific work involves measuring and comparing things. Scientists have designed a number of different scales to measure things accurately and make comparisons easier.

Each scientific scale is used to measure something particular—for example, a temperature scale can only be used to measure temperature, not sound, or speed, or anything else. The scales on the left are just a few of the many scales we use.

The pH scale is used to measure how acidic or alkaline a substance is. The scale begins at 0, which is very acidic, and goes up to 14, very alkaline. In the middle of the scale is 7, which shows when a substance is neutral—neither acidic nor alkaline. The pH of a substance is often checked using a special paper coated with a dye (color), called a litmus. When it is dipped in acid, the litmus paper turns pink, and if the substance is an alkali, it turns blue.

The mineral hardness scale is also known as the Mohs hardness scale. It is used to show how hard or soft a mineral is, based on how easy it is to scratch with another mineral. The scale shows ten "guide" minerals, arranged from softest to hardest. Each of them is given a number, with higher numbers showing harder minerals. Harder minerals on the scale can scratch softer minerals, but softer minerals can't scratch harder ones. To assess the hardness of a substance or a mineral not on the scale, it is scratched with each of the "guide" minerals to see which ones are harder than it. For instance, if it can be scratched by apatite (number 5 on the scale) but not by fluorite (number 4 on the scale), then its hardness lies between 4 and 5. Only minerals harder than it will be able to scratch it.

The decibel scale shows how loud a sound is. It starts at zero for silence, and the numbers get bigger as sounds become louder. In this scale, the units increase exponentially—which means a 10 decibel (dB) increase measures a doubling in loudness but a ten-fold rise in intensity. So, a 40 dB sound is 1,000 times more intense than a sound measuring 10 dB and eight times as loud. Sounds above 120 dB do immediate damage to our ears.

There are three different scales that are commonly used for measuring temperature. Fahrenheit and Celsius are used in day-to-day life, such as in weather forecasts or for cooking. Most parts of Europe, Asia, and Africa tend to use Celsius, while the US uses Fahrenheit. The Kelvin scale is mostly used by scientists.

Strong acids and alkalis can damage skin and eat through metal.

At 310 dB, the 1883 eruption of the Krakatau volcano was the loudest sound ever recorded.

NUMBER systems

Counting and numbering things helped people keep track of time, determine how many people were in a group, and figure out how to exchange things fairly. Today's numbers developed from ancient systems.

Early humans would have had words for the numbers of things, but it was quite a long time later that they invented a system of symbols to write down and record numbers. Once a symbol for 1 had been chosen, this symbol could be repeated for other, higher numbers. To record small numbers, simple marks were usually used for each unit, but when counting to numbers higher than 10, a different symbol was often used to indicate a group unit or "base." Using a base of 10 makes sense because humans have eight fingers and two thumbs on their hands. Some cultures developed other bases—20 was used by the Maya, 60 by the Babylonians.

In ancient Babylonia (modern-day Iraq), numbers were recorded using a stylus, or pointed writing tool, on wet clay tablets. The stylus left an arrowhead-shape in the soft clay. Ancient Egyptians used simple lines to record the numbers, with special symbols for higher numbers. The Maya had a similar system which used a combination of dots for numbers up to four and lines for five. The ancient Greeks used initial letters to represent their numbers, and the Romans used a similar system, which had a combination of letters and numbers. Each letter indicated a value: V for five; X for 10; C for 100; and M for 1,000. The Roman number system is subtractive, meaning that 4 is written IV (one from five) and 9 is IX (one from 10).

Some systems, such as Brahmi and Hebrew, are known as ciphered numeral systems. These use a symbol for units up to nine, for tens, and for hundreds. To use the system efficiently, a person needs to learn all the symbols.

Modern number systems developed from the ancient ones. Most modern ones use simple symbols and notably include a symbol for zero. In ancient times, people thought zero was just an empty space. It was invented around the 3rd century BCE by the Babylonians. Separately, the Maya also came up with a symbol to indicate zero in the 4th century CE. In India, it first appeared in the 5th century, and in China and Southwest Asia (the Middle East) at the end of the 8th century. Muslim mathematician Al-Khwarizmi studied Indian ideas and realized the importance of zero. His writings helped spread the Hindu-Arabic numeral system, using digits for 0-9, on which modern number systems are based.

The term "number" comes from the Latin word *numerus,* meaning "quantity."

The Babylonians invented one of the earliest known number systems.

ANCIENT NUMBER SYSTEMS

	1	2	3	4	5	6	7	8	9	10	100	1,000
BABYLONIAN	𒁹	𒈫	𒐈	𒐋	𒐊	𒐋	𒐍	𒐏	𒐑	𒌋	𒐏	𒐏
ANCIENT EGYPTIAN	I	II	III	IIII	II/III	III/III	III/IIII	IIII/IIII	IIII/IIIII	∩	ϙ	𓆼
ANCIENT GREEK	Α	Β	Γ	Δ	Ε	Ϛ	Ζ	Η	Θ	Ι	Ρ	ʹΑ
MAYA	•	••	•••	••••	—	•̄	••̄	•••̄	••••̄	═	(shell)	(shell •)
ROMAN	I	II	III	IV	V	VI	VII	VIII	IX	X	C	M
BRAHMI	—	=	≡	+	(symbol)	(symbol)	(symbol)	(symbol)	(symbol)	α	(symbol)	9

MODERN NUMBER SYSTEMS

	0	1	2	3	4	5	6	7	8	9	10	100	1,000
ENGLISH	0	1	2	3	4	5	6	7	8	9	10	100	1,000
	Zero	One	Two	Three	Four	Five	Six	Seven	Eight	Nine	Ten	Hundred	Thousand
ARABIC	`	١	٢	٣	٤	٥	٦	٧	٨	٩	١٠	١٠٠	١٠٠٠
	Sifr	Wahid	Ithnan	Thalathah	Arba`a	Khamsa	Sitta	Sab`a	Thamaniya	Tis`a	Ashra	Mi`ah	Alf
BENGALI	০	১	২	৩	৪	৫	৬	৭	৮	৯	১০	১০০	১০০০
	Shunyo	Ak	Dui	Teen	Char	Panch	Chhoy	Saath	Aath	Noi	Dosh	Ak-show	ak-hajar
CHINESE	零	一	二	三	四	五	六	七	八	九	十	百	千
	Ling	Yī	Èr	Sān	Sì	Wǔ	Liù	Qī	Bā	Jiǔ	Shí	Yì bǎi	Yì qiān
KOREAN	○	하나	둘	셋	넷	다섯	여섯	일곱	여덟	아홉	열	온	즈믄
	Yeong	Ha-na	Dool	Seht	Neht	Da-sut	Yuh-suht	Il-gohp	Yuh-dul	Ah-hope	Yul	On	Chun
BURMESE	၀	၁	၂	၃	၄	၅	၆	၇	၈	၉	၁၀	၁၀၀	၁၀၀၀
	Su.nya.	Tac	Hnac	Sum:	Le:	Nga:	Hkrauk	Hku.nac	Hrac	Kui:	Hcai	Ya	Taon
HEBREW	אפס	א	ב	ג	ד	ה	ו	ז	ח	ט	י	ק	ʹא
	Efes	Alef	Bet	Gimel	Dalet	He	Vaf	Zayin	Het	Tet	Yod	Qof	Elef

A selection of number systems from around the world

Elements in the
PERIODIC TABLE

This table divides the 118 known chemical elements into ten types that are arranged in a carefully organized grid. It is called "periodic" because the elements have characteristics that follow repeating patterns.

ELEMENTS IN THE PERIODIC TABLE

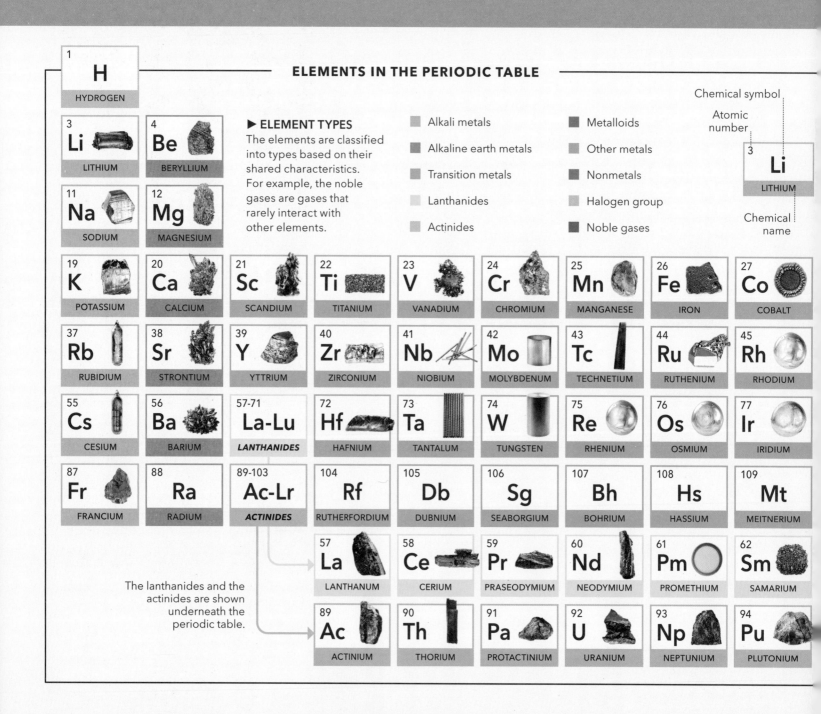

▶ **ELEMENT TYPES**
The elements are classified into types based on their shared characteristics. For example, the noble gases are gases that rarely interact with other elements.

- Alkali metals
- Alkaline earth metals
- Transition metals
- Lanthanides
- Actinides
- Metalloids
- Other metals
- Nonmetals
- Halogen group
- Noble gases

Chemical symbol
Atomic number
Chemical name

The lanthanides and the actinides are shown underneath the periodic table.

| 1 H HYDROGEN |
3 Li LITHIUM	4 Be BERYLLIUM
11 Na SODIUM	12 Mg MAGNESIUM
19 K POTASSIUM	20 Ca CALCIUM	21 Sc SCANDIUM	22 Ti TITANIUM	23 V VANADIUM	24 Cr CHROMIUM	25 Mn MANGANESE	26 Fe IRON	27 Co COBALT
37 Rb RUBIDIUM	38 Sr STRONTIUM	39 Y YTTRIUM	40 Zr ZIRCONIUM	41 Nb NIOBIUM	42 Mo MOLYBDENUM	43 Tc TECHNETIUM	44 Ru RUTHENIUM	45 Rh RHODIUM
55 Cs CESIUM	56 Ba BARIUM	57-71 La-Lu LANTHANIDES	72 Hf HAFNIUM	73 Ta TANTALUM	74 W TUNGSTEN	75 Re RHENIUM	76 Os OSMIUM	77 Ir IRIDIUM
87 Fr FRANCIUM	88 Ra RADIUM	89-103 Ac-Lr ACTINIDES	104 Rf RUTHERFORDIUM	105 Db DUBNIUM	106 Sg SEABORGIUM	107 Bh BOHRIUM	108 Hs HASSIUM	109 Mt MEITNERIUM

| 57 La LANTHANUM | 58 Ce CERIUM | 59 Pr PRASEODYMIUM | 60 Nd NEODYMIUM | 61 Pm PROMETHIUM | 62 Sm SAMARIUM |
| 89 Ac ACTINIUM | 90 Th THORIUM | 91 Pa PROTACTINIUM | 92 U URANIUM | 93 Np NEPTUNIUM | 94 Pu PLUTONIUM |

Elements are the fundamental building blocks of the universe. Each element is made up of tiny units called atoms. Atoms contain three types of even smaller particles—neutrons, protons, and electrons. Every element has its own unique atomic number, which is the number of protons in its atoms. Hydrogen's atomic number is 1 because each of its atoms has 1 proton. The periodic table lists all the elements, in order of their atomic number. The numbering starts with hydrogen on the top left, then goes from left to right across the table, then row by row. However, it isn't quite as simple as that, or the table would just be a rectangular grid. Similar elements are grouped based on their physical and chemical properties, which is reflected in the shape of the table and the colors used in the key for the different types of element.

We can learn a lot about an element just by looking at its position in the periodic table. For example, potassium's atomic number is 19, which means it is an alkali metal. Like the other elements in its group, potassium is a soft metal that melts at fairly low temperatures.

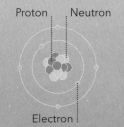

Proton   Neutron

Electron

◄ STRUCTURE OF A CARBON ATOM
The neutrons and protons form the central "nucleus" around which electrons revolve.

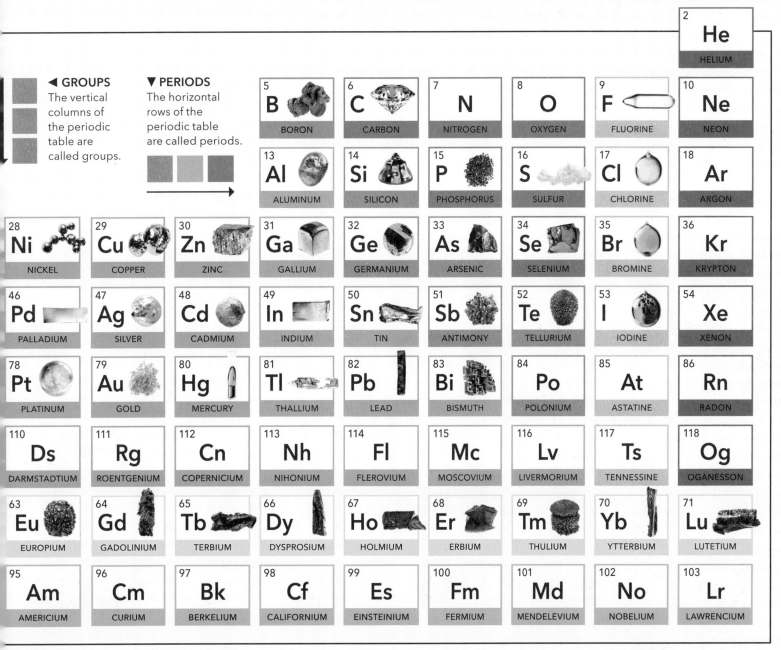

◄ GROUPS
The vertical columns of the periodic table are called groups.

▼ PERIODS
The horizontal rows of the periodic table are called periods.

| 2 He HELIUM |
5 B BORON	6 C CARBON	7 N NITROGEN	8 O OXYGEN	9 F FLUORINE	10 Ne NEON
13 Al ALUMINUM	14 Si SILICON	15 P PHOSPHORUS	16 S SULFUR	17 Cl CHLORINE	18 Ar ARGON
28 Ni NICKEL	29 Cu COPPER	30 Zn ZINC	31 Ga GALLIUM	32 Ge GERMANIUM	33 As ARSENIC	34 Se SELENIUM	35 Br BROMINE	36 Kr KRYPTON
46 Pd PALLADIUM	47 Ag SILVER	48 Cd CADMIUM	49 In INDIUM	50 Sn TIN	51 Sb ANTIMONY	52 Te TELLURIUM	53 I IODINE	54 Xe XENON
78 Pt PLATINUM	79 Au GOLD	80 Hg MERCURY	81 Tl THALLIUM	82 Pb LEAD	83 Bi BISMUTH	84 Po POLONIUM	85 At ASTATINE	86 Rn RADON
110 Ds DARMSTADTIUM	111 Rg ROENTGENIUM	112 Cn COPERNICIUM	113 Nh NIHONIUM	114 Fl FLEROVIUM	115 Mc MOSCOVIUM	116 Lv LIVERMORIUM	117 Ts TENNESSINE	118 Og OGANESSON
63 Eu EUROPIUM	64 Gd GADOLINIUM	65 Tb TERBIUM	66 Dy DYSPROSIUM	67 Ho HOLMIUM	68 Er ERBIUM	69 Tm THULIUM	70 Yb YTTERBIUM	71 Lu LUTETIUM
95 Am AMERICIUM	96 Cm CURIUM	97 Bk BERKELIUM	98 Cf CALIFORNIUM	99 Es EINSTEINIUM	100 Fm FERMIUM	101 Md MENDELEVIUM	102 No NOBELIUM	103 Lr LAWRENCIUM

Simple
MACHINES

While we wouldn't be able to lift a very heavy weight with our hands, we could do this easily using a pulley, which is a simple machine. Simple machines are tools that increase the force we can make with our body.

SIMPLE MACHINES

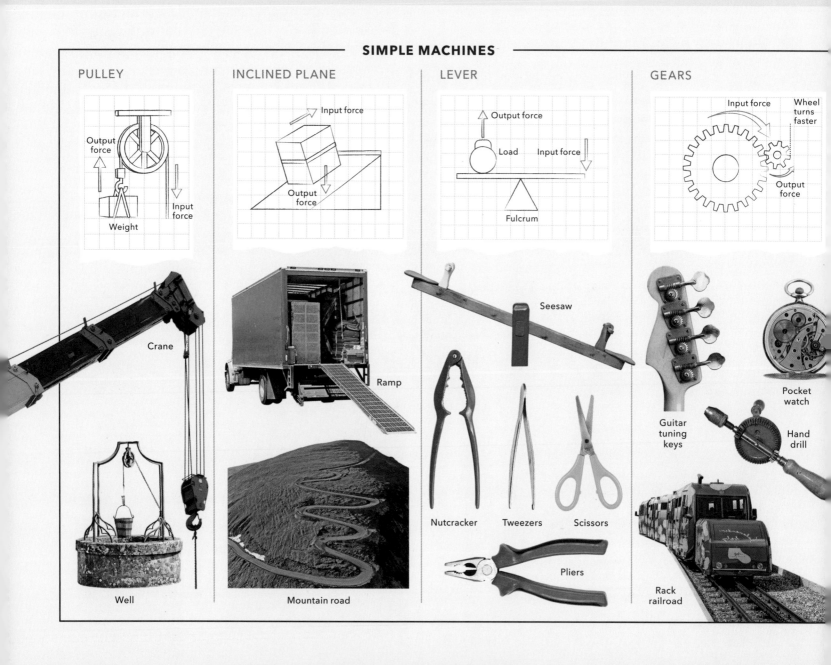

PULLEY

Output force
Input force
Weight

Crane

Well

INCLINED PLANE

Input force
Output force

Ramp

Mountain road

LEVER

Output force
Load
Input force
Fulcrum

Seesaw

Nutcracker
Tweezers
Scissors

Pliers

GEARS

Input force
Wheel turns faster
Output force

Guitar tuning keys

Pocket watch

Hand drill

Rack railroad

Simple machines make it easier for us to do work or change the direction in which we apply a force. Tools such as hammers are simple machines. Bigger machines such as cranes have smaller parts that are simple machines.

There are many types of simple machine. A pulley is a rope looped around one or more wheels that reduces the lifting force and makes it easier to lift a weight with less effort than if we picked it up. An inclined plane is a slope, which connects a low area and a higher one. Sliding an object up or down the slope requires less force than lifting it.

Wheels and gears help increase either force or speed at a time. A wheel and axle are connected, so moving the axle, which has a smaller diameter, moves the bigger wheel faster and farther than the axle but with less force. Turning the wheel makes the axle move with more force. Gears are rotating wheels of different sizes with teeth on the outsides that link up with each other. A large gear can make a smaller one move faster with less force, while a smaller one can make a large one move slower but with more force. A lever is a bar that sits across a fixed point—fulcrum—and magnifies a pushing or pulling force.

A screw is an inclined plane wrapped around in a spiral. Screws can change a turning action into a push or pull, or hold things together. Wedges have a narrow edge that can be used to split things open. In hydraulic machines, pipes filled with liquids make it easier to move or lift heavy things.

The first known simple machine is a Stone Age ax.

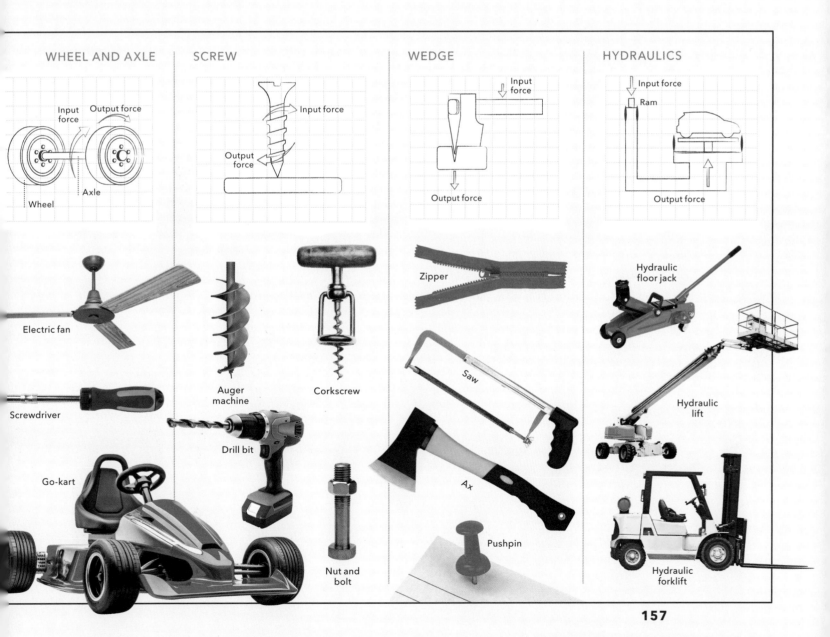

WHEEL AND AXLE

Input force
Output force

Wheel
Axle

Electric fan

Screwdriver

Go-kart

SCREW

Input force

Output force

Auger machine

Drill bit

WEDGE

Input force

Output force

Zipper

Saw

Ax

Pushpin

Nut and bolt

Corkscrew

HYDRAULICS

Input force
Ram

Output force

Hydraulic floor jack

Hydraulic lift

Hydraulic forklift

Hand
TOOLS

Humans have created an astonishing array of tools to fix, file, measure, carve, cut, or tighten things around the home.

Early hand tools were probably rocks, stones, and sticks used by humans to break objects or dig out things. Today there are thousands of tools used around the world, and each has been specially adapted to make it just right for the job at hand.

A common job at home is to take measurements, using a tape measure or a carpenter's ruler that folds up. Calipers can measure inside and outside a small space or the diameter of a round object. Once measurements are made, it's possible to make a mark using an awl, or a hole using a punch.

To split a log, we need an ax; to cut wood, we need a handsaw; and to shape it, we use a draw knife. Hacksaws slice through metal or plastic, and tin snips cut metal sheets. Wire strippers remove the outer coating of wires, and wire cutters snip through them.

A plane is required to smooth wood, and a rasp or riffler will file away a smaller area. Other hand tools for wood include chisels, which need to be struck by a hammer to push them along the surface of wood or stone.

Tools that fasten and affix include pliers to grip and clamps (in an F or a G shape) to hold things steady. Hammers are useful to drive in nails. Then there are tools for tightening or loosening screws, nuts, or bolts. These include screwdrivers with different-shaped heads, and wrenches in many sizes.

There are more than 20 types of screwdriver.

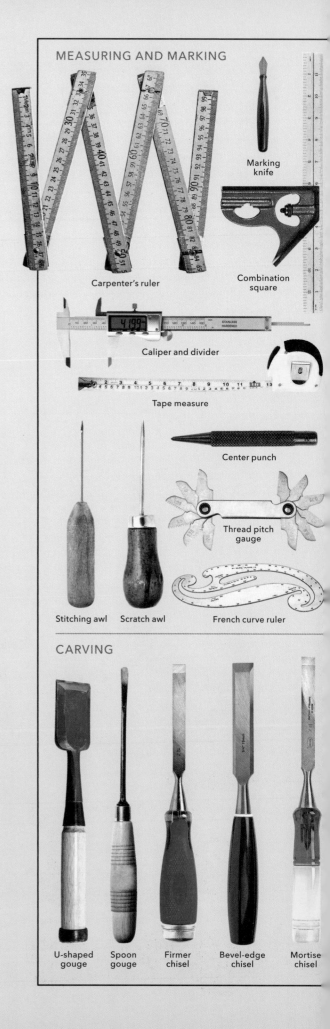

MEASURING AND MARKING

Carpenter's ruler

Marking knife

Combination square

Caliper and divider

Tape measure

Center punch

Thread pitch gauge

Stitching awl   Scratch awl   French curve ruler

CARVING

U-shaped gouge   Spoon gouge   Firmer chisel   Bevel-edge chisel   Mortise chisel

FASTENING AND FIXING

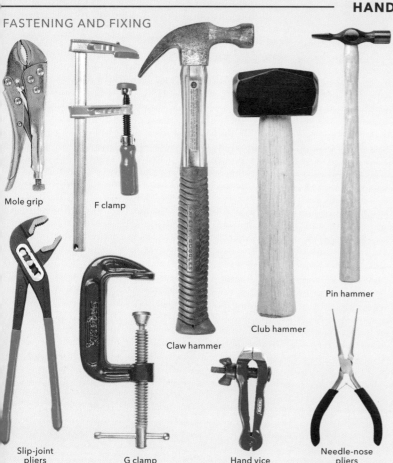

Mole grip

F clamp

Claw hammer

Club hammer

Pin hammer

Slip-joint pliers

G clamp

Hand vice

Needle-nose pliers

CUTTING

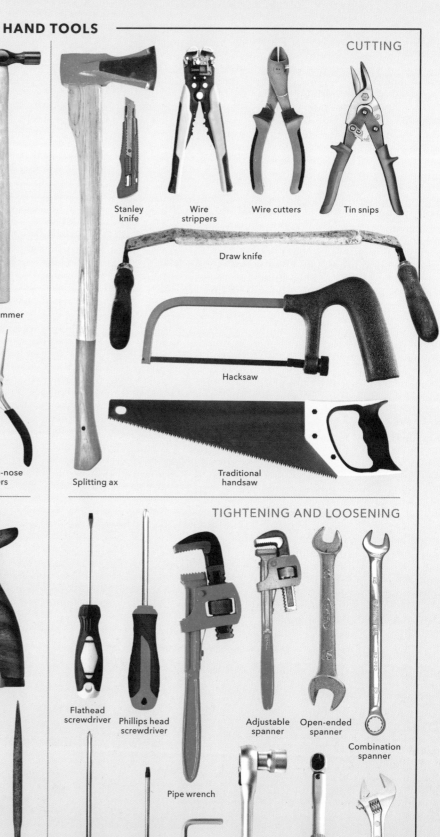

Stanley knife

Wire strippers

Wire cutters

Tin snips

Draw knife

Hacksaw

Splitting ax

Traditional handsaw

FILING / SMOOTHING / SHAPING

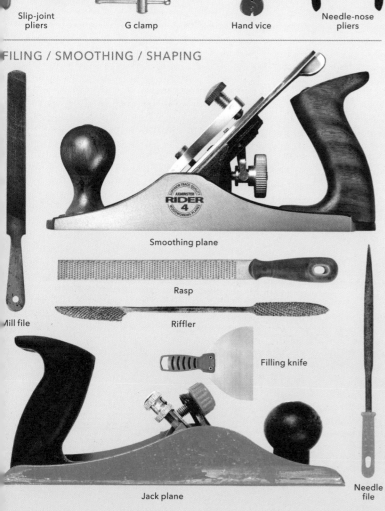

Smoothing plane

Rasp

Mill file

Riffler

Filling knife

Jack plane

Needle file

TIGHTENING AND LOOSENING

Flathead screwdriver

Phillips head screwdriver

Adjustable spanner

Open-ended spanner

Combination spanner

Pipe wrench

Pozidriv screwdriver

Torx screwdriver

Allen key

Socket wrench

Torque wrench

Monkey wrench

ELECTROMAGNETIC
spectrum

Light is a type of energy. All the light we can see is just a small part of a much larger range of energy, called the electromagnetic (EM) spectrum.

ELECTROMAGNETIC SPECTRUM

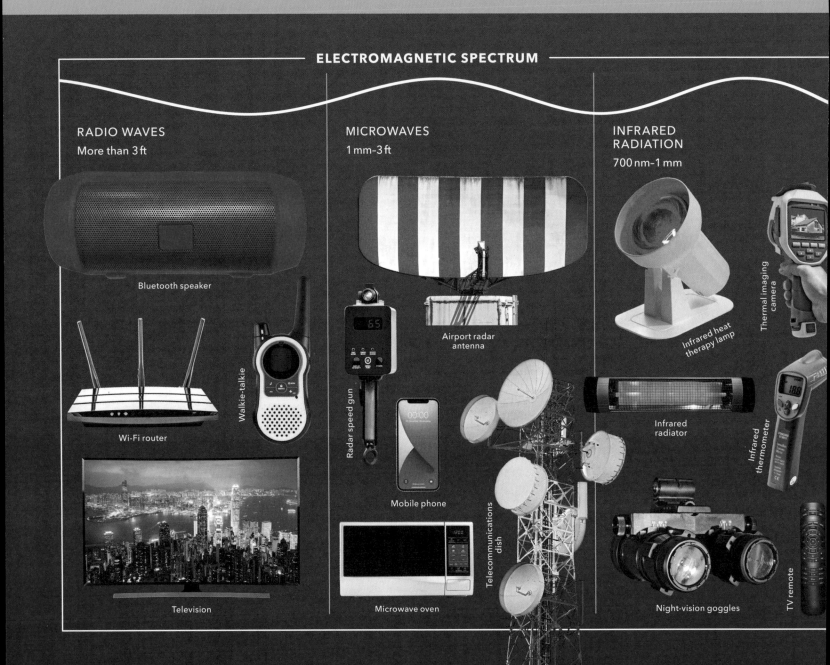

RADIO WAVES
More than 3 ft

Bluetooth speaker

Wi-Fi router

Walkie-talkie

Television

MICROWAVES
1 mm–3 ft

Airport radar antenna

Radar speed gun

Mobile phone

Telecommunications dish

Microwave oven

INFRARED RADIATION
700 nm–1 mm

Thermal imaging camera

Infrared heat therapy lamp

Infrared radiator

Infrared thermometer

Night-vision goggles

TV remote

The electromagnetic spectrum includes several different types of electromagnetic radiation—energy that travels in waves and can cross huge distances extremely quickly. Within the spectrum, light is classified as "visible light" because it is the only form of electromagnetic radiation that we can see with our eyes.

The EM spectrum is organized in order of wavelength—the distances between the crests of each energy's wave. The longest wavelengths, radio waves, can be yards or even miles long, and transfer fairly low amounts of energy. The shortest wavelengths, gamma rays, are smaller than atoms, and transfer higher amounts of energy.

Visible light sits in the middle of the spectrum, with longer wavelengths to its left, and shorter wavelengths to its right. It can be divided into the colors of the rainbow, and these colors themselves have different wavelengths: red is longest and violet shortest.

> **Ultraviolet rays emitted by the sun can burn our skin.**

The different wavelengths give all the types of radiation different properties, which can be very useful to us. The four longest types of wave in the EM spectrum are used for communication, which can be transmitted or received by radios, mobile phones, Wi-Fi, and GPS. Other parts of the spectrum allow us to heat food (microwaves), look inside our bodies (X-rays), and zap cancerous cells (gamma rays).

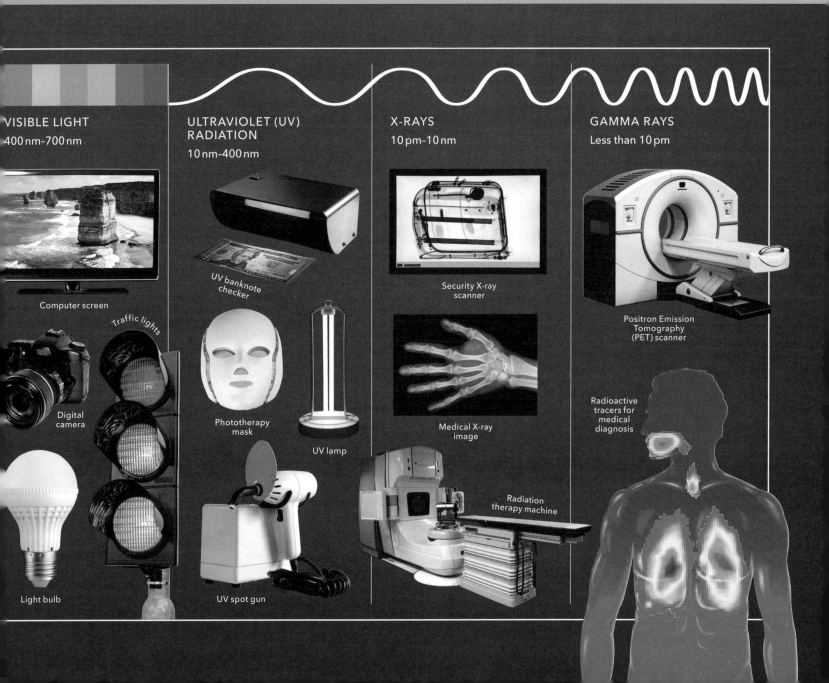

VISIBLE LIGHT
400 nm–700 nm

Computer screen

Traffic lights

Digital camera

Light bulb

ULTRAVIOLET (UV) RADIATION
10 nm–400 nm

UV banknote checker

Phototherapy mask

UV lamp

UV spot gun

X-RAYS
10 pm–10 nm

Security X-ray scanner

Medical X-ray image

Radiation therapy machine

GAMMA RAYS
Less than 10 pm

Positron Emission Tomography (PET) scanner

Radioactive tracers for medical diagnosis

COLOR
models

When we design a poster or birthday invitation on the computer, the program may give us two choices of color: RGB and CMYK. The first is used to view colors on a screen, and the second is used in print.

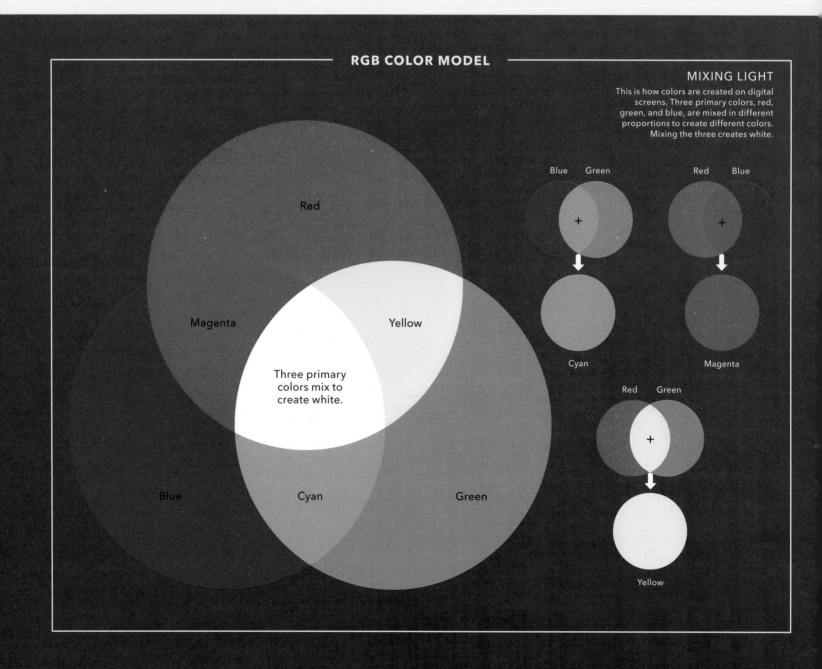

RGB COLOR MODEL

MIXING LIGHT

This is how colors are created on digital screens. Three primary colors, red, green, and blue, are mixed in different proportions to create different colors. Mixing the three creates white.

Red

Magenta

Yellow

Three primary colors mix to create white.

Blue

Cyan

Green

Blue + Green → Cyan

Red + Blue → Magenta

Red + Green → Yellow

The colors we see all around us are all contained in the visible light from the sun. We see this when raindrops split the sun's rays to make a rainbow. Images on a computer monitor, smart phone screen, and digital camera use varying amounts of the three main, or primary, light colors—Red, Green, and Blue. Hence color on screen is known as the RGB color model (see below left). The model is described as "additive" because by adding together red, green, and blue, we get white—as can be seen in the center of the overlapping circles. On screen, black is created by blocking all light from reaching the screen.

It is impossible to print on paper using RGB colors because there is no black, making most darker colors impossible to print. Therefore, printing color on paper involves a different model: CMYK. Here, the primary colors mixed are Cyan (a shade of blue), Magenta (a pink), and Yellow. The K in CMYK stands for black, which comes from a printers' term meaning "key color." The CMYK model is described as "subtractive" because by combining cyan, magenta, and yellow it creates black—as seen in the center of the three overlapping circles below right. This is why most home printers have just four cartridges: cyan, magenta, yellow, and black (key).

> **On screen, the RGB formula for black is R=0, G=0, and B=0.**

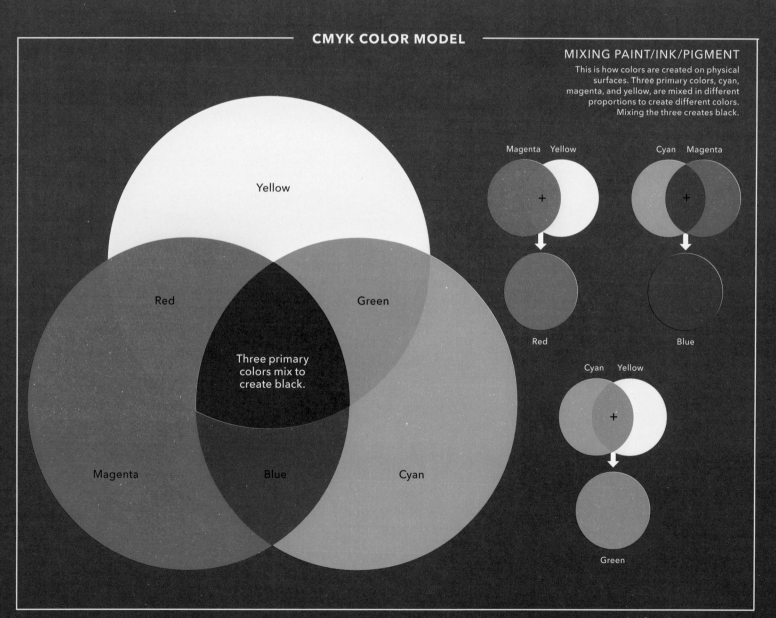

CMYK COLOR MODEL

MIXING PAINT/INK/PIGMENT
This is how colors are created on physical surfaces. Three primary colors, cyan, magenta, and yellow, are mixed in different proportions to create different colors. Mixing the three creates black.

Yellow

Red

Green

Three primary colors mix to create black.

Magenta

Blue

Cyan

Magenta Yellow
+
Red

Cyan Magenta
+
Blue

Cyan Yellow
+
Green

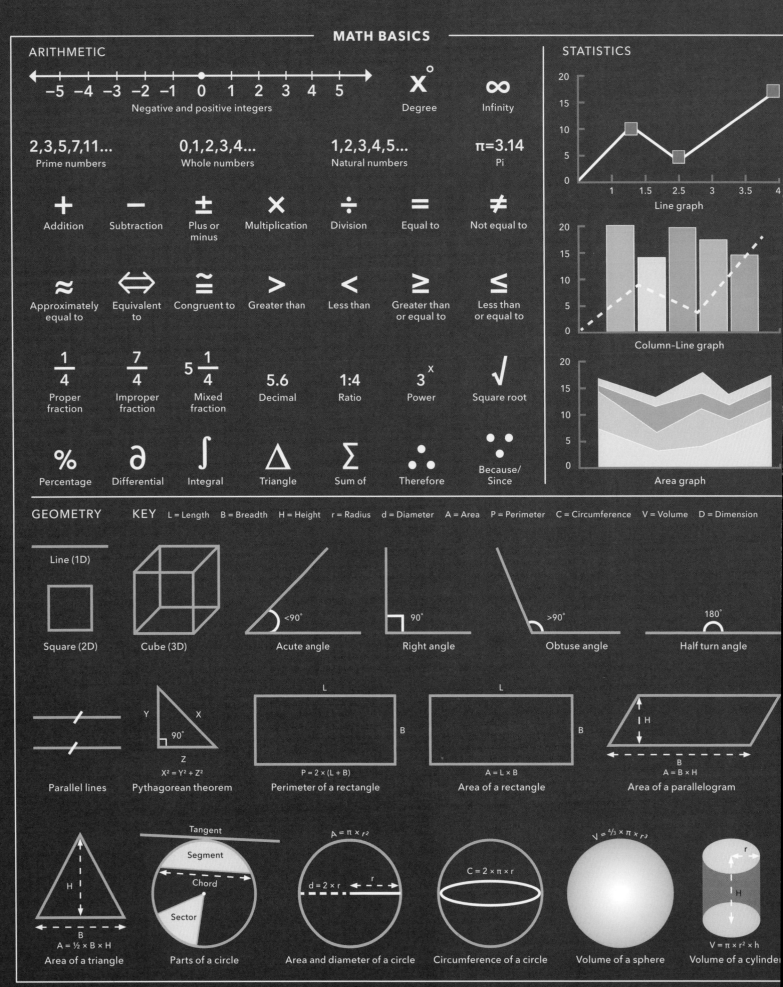

MATH BASICS

ARITHMETIC

-5 -4 -3 -2 -1 0 1 2 3 4 5
Negative and positive integers

$x°$
Degree

∞
Infinity

2,3,5,7,11...
Prime numbers

0,1,2,3,4...
Whole numbers

1,2,3,4,5...
Natural numbers

$\pi = 3.14$
Pi

$+$ Addition

$-$ Subtraction

$\pm$ Plus or minus

$\times$ Multiplication

$\div$ Division

$=$ Equal to

$\neq$ Not equal to

$\approx$ Approximately equal to

$\Leftrightarrow$ Equivalent to

$\cong$ Congruent to

$>$ Greater than

$<$ Less than

$\geq$ Greater than or equal to

$\leq$ Less than or equal to

$\frac{1}{4}$ Proper fraction

$\frac{7}{4}$ Improper fraction

$5\frac{1}{4}$ Mixed fraction

5.6 Decimal

1:4 Ratio

3^x Power

$\sqrt{}$ Square root

$\%$ Percentage

∂ Differential

$\int$ Integral

$\triangle$ Triangle

$\sum$ Sum of

$\therefore$ Therefore

$\because$ Because/ Since

STATISTICS

Line graph

Column-Line graph

Area graph

GEOMETRY

KEY L = Length   B = Breadth   H = Height   r = Radius   d = Diameter   A = Area   P = Perimeter   C = Circumference   V = Volume   D = Dimension

Line (1D)

Square (2D)

Cube (3D)

Acute angle ($<90°$)

Right angle ($90°$)

Obtuse angle ($>90°$)

Half turn angle ($180°$)

Parallel lines

Pythagorean theorem
$X^2 = Y^2 + Z^2$

Perimeter of a rectangle
$P = 2 \times (L + B)$

Area of a rectangle
$A = L \times B$

Area of a parallelogram
$A = B \times H$

Area of a triangle
$A = \frac{1}{2} \times B \times H$

Parts of a circle
Tangent, Segment, Chord, Sector

Area and diameter of a circle
$A = \pi \times r^2$
$d = 2 \times r$

Circumference of a circle
$C = 2 \times \pi \times r$

Volume of a sphere
$V = \frac{4}{3} \times \pi \times r^3$

Volume of a cylinder
$V = \pi \times r^2 \times h$

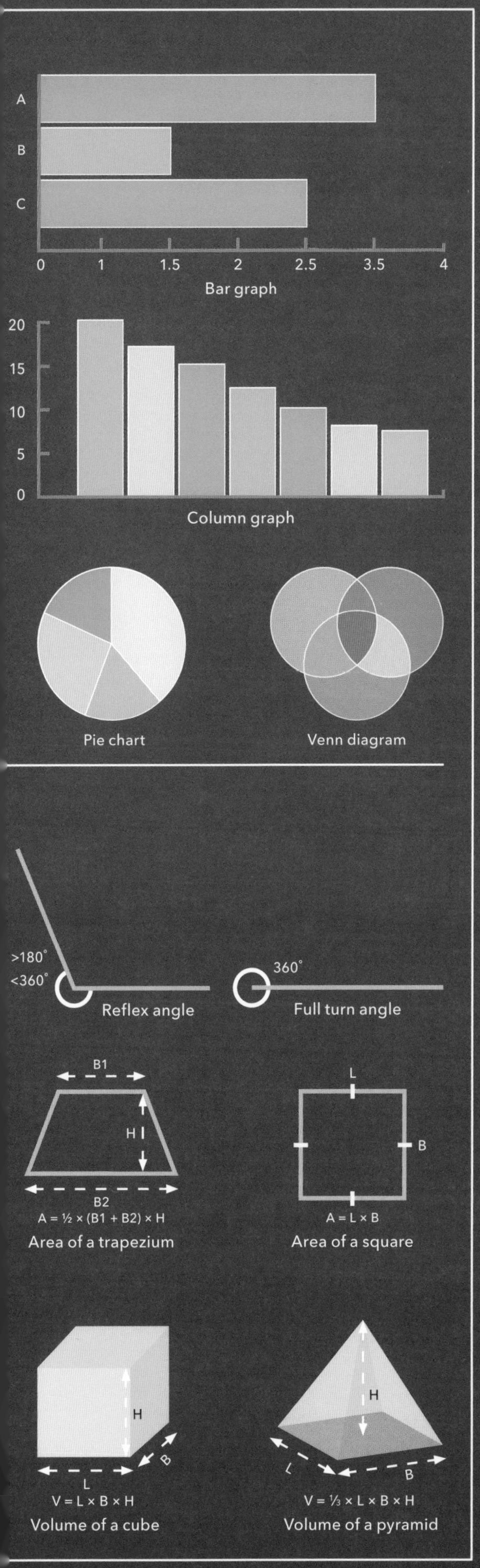

A
B
C

0   1   1.5   2   2.5   3.5   4
Bar graph

20
15
10
5
0
Column graph

Pie chart

Venn diagram

>180°
<360°
Reflex angle

360°
Full turn angle

B1
H
B2
$A = ½ × (B1 + B2) × H$
Area of a trapezium

L
B
$A = L × B$
Area of a square

H
L
B
$V = L × B × H$
Volume of a cube

H
L
B
$V = ⅓ × L × B × H$
Volume of a pyramid

MATH
basics

Math or mathematics is the study of numbers, shapes, and data. It includes arithmetic, statistics, and geometry and uses symbols and formulas.

Arithmetic looks at numbers and their properties, and the ways of calculating—including addition, subtraction, multiplication, and division. These and other operations are represented by a set of numbers and symbols. Symbols make things easier and quicker to write, such as the symbol for "equal to" or for the square roots of numbers.

Statistics involves collecting and analyzing large amounts of numeric data (collected information). A bar graph, for example, shows the values of different things in comparison to one another, while a Venn diagram shows the shared properties between different things that are represented by overlapping circles.

Geometry deals with lines, angles, and shapes, including two-dimensional (2D) shapes and three-dimensional (3D) shapes. A 2D shape can only be measured in two directions while a 3D shape can be measured in three directions—length, breadth, and height. A triangle, square, and circle are 2D shapes; a pyramid, cube, and sphere are 3D shapes. The properties of different shapes can be explained using sets of letters and numbers called formulas, such as the perimeter of a rectangle—which is the result of multiplying the sum of its length and breadth by two and is written as $P = 2 × (L + B)$.

> **A prime number can only be divided by one and by itself.**

Geometric
SHAPES

Geometry is the study of shapes. These can be flat and two-dimensional (2D) or solid and three-dimensional (3D).

Shapes are formed by lines that meet at angles. Most shapes have sides. Flat 2D shapes have only length and breadth but no thickness, while 3D shapes have length, breadth, and depth and take up space. There are different kinds of shape based on the lengths of their lines and their angles. Shapes where all sides and angles are equal are called regular and those where the sides and angles vary are called irregular.

2D shapes can have straight or curved sides or a mixture of both. A circle is a 2D shape made of just one line that curves to meet itself and has no angles. Polygons are 2D shapes with many sides and angles. An equilateral triangle and a rectangle are regular polygons, while a scalene triangle and a trapezoid are irregular polygons. Shapes such as circles and regular polygons are also symmetrical, which means they can be divided into two identical parts.

3D shapes can also have straight and curved sides. Polyhedrons are 3D shapes with many sides or surfaces that are 2D polygons. For example, an octahedron has eight surfaces and an icosahedron has 20 surfaces. They may be solids that are tilted to one side, such as oblique cylinders or oblique prisms. The shape of the base of the solid may be different from the shape of the top, as in cones or square-based pyramids.

Impossible shapes, such as a blivet or Penrose triangle, are optical illusions—a shape is drawn to look like a 3D shape, but it could not exist as a solid object.

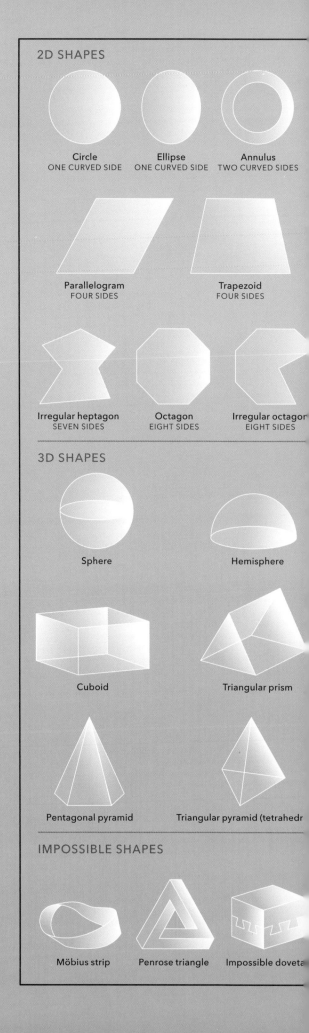

2D SHAPES

Circle
ONE CURVED SIDE

Ellipse
ONE CURVED SIDE

Annulus
TWO CURVED SIDES

Parallelogram
FOUR SIDES

Trapezoid
FOUR SIDES

Irregular heptagon
SEVEN SIDES

Octagon
EIGHT SIDES

Irregular octagon
EIGHT SIDES

3D SHAPES

Sphere

Hemisphere

Cuboid

Triangular prism

Pentagonal pyramid

Triangular pyramid (tetrahedr

IMPOSSIBLE SHAPES

Möbius strip

Penrose triangle

Impossible doveta

GEOMETRIC SHAPES

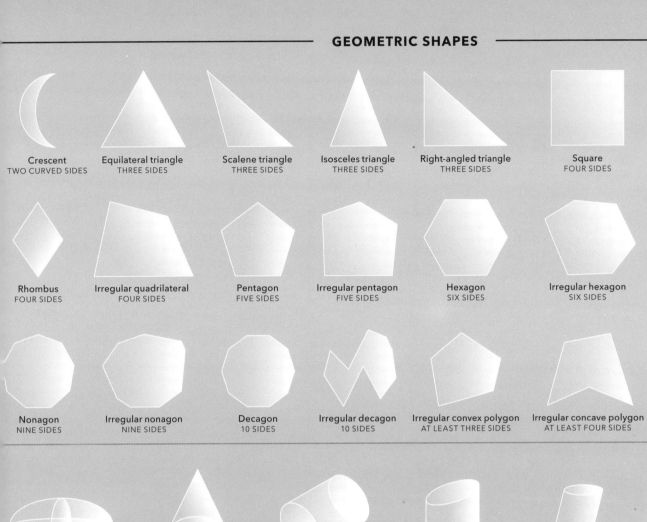

Crescent
TWO CURVED SIDES

Equilateral triangle
THREE SIDES

Scalene triangle
THREE SIDES

Isosceles triangle
THREE SIDES

Right-angled triangle
THREE SIDES

Square
FOUR SIDES

Rectangle
FOUR SIDES

Rhombus
FOUR SIDES

Irregular quadrilateral
FOUR SIDES

Pentagon
FIVE SIDES

Irregular pentagon
FIVE SIDES

Hexagon
SIX SIDES

Irregular hexagon
SIX SIDES

Heptagon
SEVEN SIDES

Nonagon
NINE SIDES

Irregular nonagon
NINE SIDES

Decagon
10 SIDES

Irregular decagon
10 SIDES

Irregular convex polygon
AT LEAST THREE SIDES

Irregular concave polygon
AT LEAST FOUR SIDES

Icosagon
20 SIDES

Ellipsoid

Cone

Cylinder

Elliptical cylinder

Oblique cylinder

Cube

Rectangular prism

Right prism

Oblique prism

Pentagonal prism

Hexagonal prism

Square-based pyramid

Double tetrahedron

Octahedron

Dodecahedron

Icosahedron

Polyhedron

Torus

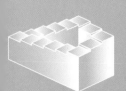
Impossible staircase

Blivet

Impossible cube

Impossible waterfall

Borromean rings

Impossible figure cuboid

Unfeasible fence

Human
CELLS

There are more cells in the human body than there are stars in the Milky Way and each one has an important role to play. These tiny units are the building blocks of all life.

Cells carry oxygen around our body, build bone and muscle, fight off infection, transmit messages to and from our organs, and produce new human beings, which will carry in their cells all the information they need for life. All cells have an outer membrane, or skin, that holds them together. This membrane is semipermeable, which means that it allows some substances to pass in and out. Each cell is filled with a jellylike substance called cytoplasm, in which float tiny cell structures called organelles, such as the nucleus and mitochondria. The nucleus holds most of a cell's DNA, the material containing our genetic information. A mitochondrion is often called the "powerhouse of a cell." Mitochondria produce energy, which is then carried to other parts of the cell.

Other types of organelle include ribosomes, which help create protein, the substance used to build and repair bone, muscle, and tissue. Proteins are processed and transported by the curly pouches of the Golgi apparatus. The endoplasmic reticulum, another wiggly structure, also carries and modifies proteins. Although most cells have these features in common, there are many types of cell, each designed to do a different job in the body. Red blood cells transport oxygen from the lungs through a network of veins and arteries, and lack many organelles so they can carry as much oxygen as possible. Nerve cells in the brain receive information from our senses and process it to figure out a response. For example, if nerve cells in the hand sense they are touching something hot, they send this information to the brain, which sends a message to muscles in the arm to quickly move the hand away from the heat source.

Energy is stored in fat cells, which also help protect the body's organs and keep us warm. Sex cells are sperm cells and egg cells—one sperm needs to combine with one egg cell to create a baby.

Stem cells have a really important job. These amazing cells can reproduce many of the 200 different cell types in a human body. If a bone or muscle cell is damaged, for example, stem cells can make a replacement. The body also produces more cells as it grows. A 10-year-old child's body contains around 17 trillion cells, but an adult male body will be composed of more than double this.

> There are 36 trillion cells in an average adult male and 28 trillion in an average adult female.

> White blood cells live for 13 days, liver cells for 18 months, and brain cells for a whole lifetime.

PARTS OF A HUMAN CELL

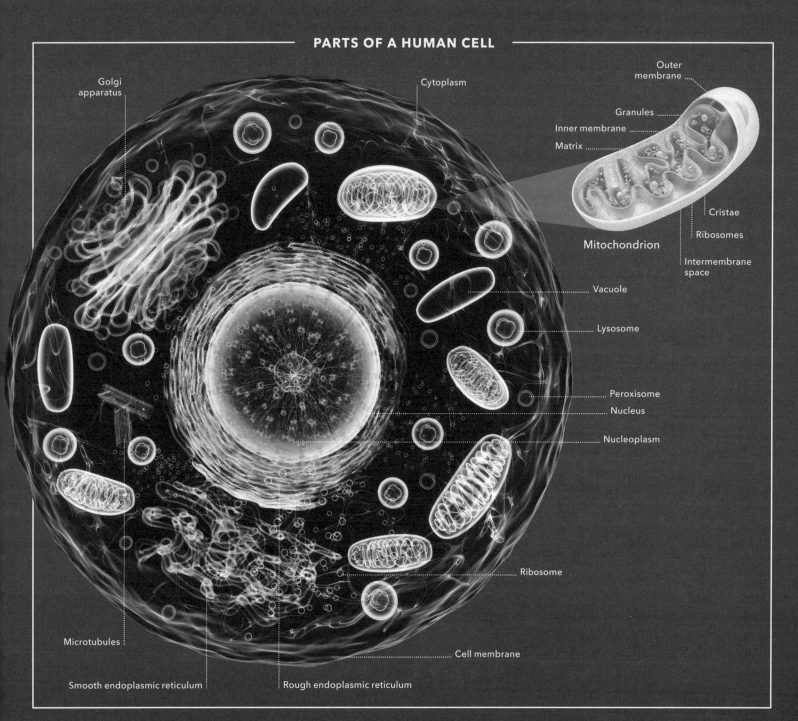

Golgi apparatus

Cytoplasm

Outer membrane

Granules

Inner membrane

Matrix

Cristae

Ribosomes

Intermembrane space

Mitochondrion

Vacuole

Lysosome

Peroxisome

Nucleus

Nucleoplasm

Ribosome

Microtubules

Cell membrane

Smooth endoplasmic reticulum

Rough endoplasmic reticulum

MAJOR TYPES OF HUMAN CELL

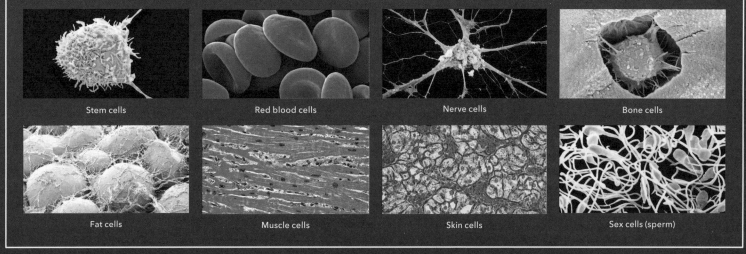

Stem cells

Red blood cells

Nerve cells

Bone cells

Fat cells

Muscle cells

Skin cells

Sex cells (sperm)

There are more than 200 different human cell types. This selection shows eight of them.

Human
SYSTEMS

Within each of us are many different systems all operating together to keep us alive; help us grow; defend ourselves from sickness; and let us run, think, dance, or study. Each system, made of one or more organs, has its own job to do, but they all rely on each other to keep us healthy.

HUMAN SYSTEMS

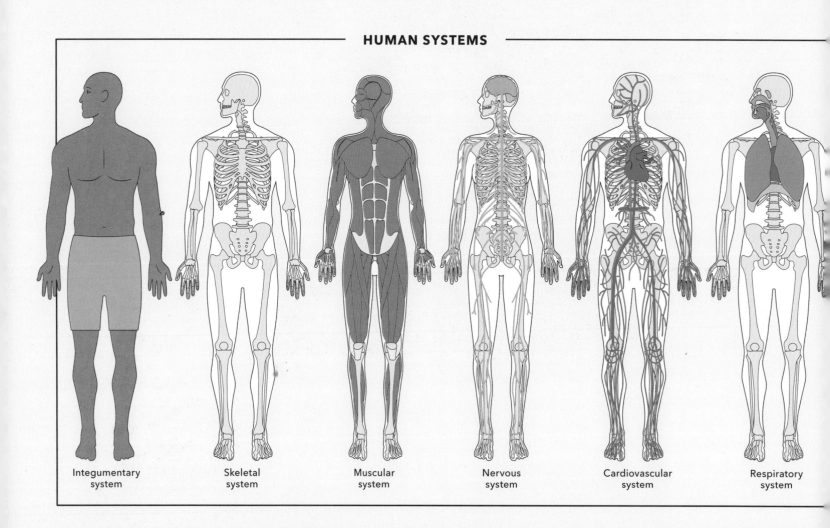

Integumentary system

Skeletal system

Muscular system

Nervous system

Cardiovascular system

Respiratory system

Our body's covering of skin, hair, and nails is part of the integumentary system, which protects our organs and regulates our body temperature. Our skeletal system of more than 200 bones forms the body's framework. The muscles in our muscular system, which are attached to the bones and cartilage (a tough connective tissue), allow the body to move. Muscles are controlled by the nervous system, which is the body's messaging network—sending information from the brain via the spinal cord and nerves to the body and back.

The cardiovascular system is the network of arteries and veins stemming from the heart that carries blood around our body. The respiratory system helps us breathe. We take air into our lungs, absorbing oxygen to produce energy in our cells, and breathing out carbon dioxide. Our digestive system breaks down food into tiny particles that are absorbed by the blood. Any food we cannot use is excreted as feces. Waste water is expelled as urine and this is carried out by the urinary system. It is based around the kidneys, which filter our blood and remove anything harmful.

The functions of some organs and body systems are controlled by hormones—chemicals produced by glands, which are a type of organ. These glands form the endocrine system. For example, the pancreas produces insulin, which controls glucose (sugar) levels in our blood. Our lymphatic system, which includes bone marrow, defends the body against infections.

Our reproductive system produces the cells we need to create a baby. The female body carries the baby, which will have all the systems shown here, ready to develop in its body as it grows.

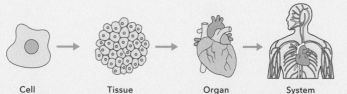

Cell   Tissue   Organ   System

◄ **BODY SYSTEMS**
Our body systems begin at a cell level. The cells form tissues, which in turn make up our organs.

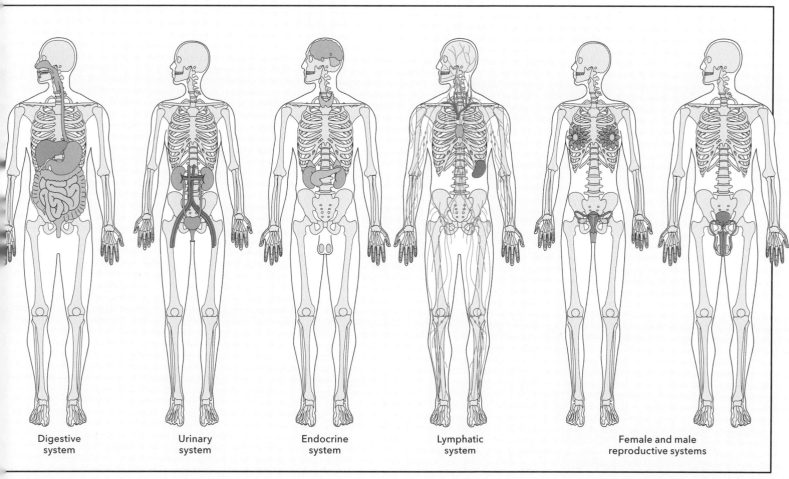

Digestive system

Urinary system

Endocrine system

Lymphatic system

Female and male reproductive systems

Human
SKELETON

Inside every person, holding their body up and allowing them to move around, is a linked network of bones—the skeleton. This skeleton is what gives the body shape and protects organs such as the brain.

The human skeleton gives the body support—without it, we would be a puddle of flesh and organs. The separate bones are linked together at moving points called joints. Different types of joint allow the bones to move in different ways—for example, in just one direction, like the knee joint, or in a circular motion, as seen in the shoulder joint.

The skeleton also provides protection for the most delicate organs. The brain is protected by the hard dome of the skull, and the heart and lungs are shielded by the rib cage. The top seven pairs of ribs are attached to the sternum at the front, and the vertebral column (spine) at the back. The spine contains the spinal cord, which carries messages from the brain to the rest of the body, and vice versa.

The femur is the longest and strongest bone in the skeleton.

There are several different types of bone in the body. Long bones such as the humerus, femur, and tibia contain mainly hard, compact bone. Short bones, such as the carpals and tarsals, are found in the wrists and ankles respectively, and contain mainly light, spongy bone. Flat bones are usually curved and thin, such as the parietal and occipital bones in the skull. Any bones that do not fit into these groups are called irregular bones. They include the vertebrae that protect the spine, the mandible or lower jawbone, and the tiny bones inside the ears.

The skull is made up of several bones fused together. They include the frontal, temporal, and nasal bones. Humans are born with around 300 bones but as they age, the bones grow, harden, and fuse together. Wavy lines on the skull's surface show where the separate bones have fused together since birth. This fusing happens across the body, but most particularly in the skull, so that by the time humans reach adulthood, the skeleton has only 206 bones.

Bone marrow   Blood vessels   Spongy bone   Compact bone

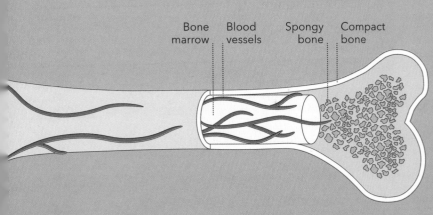

◄ INSIDE A BONE
Bones have a hard outer layer and a lighter inner layer. Blood cells are formed in the bone marrow.

HUMAN SKELETON

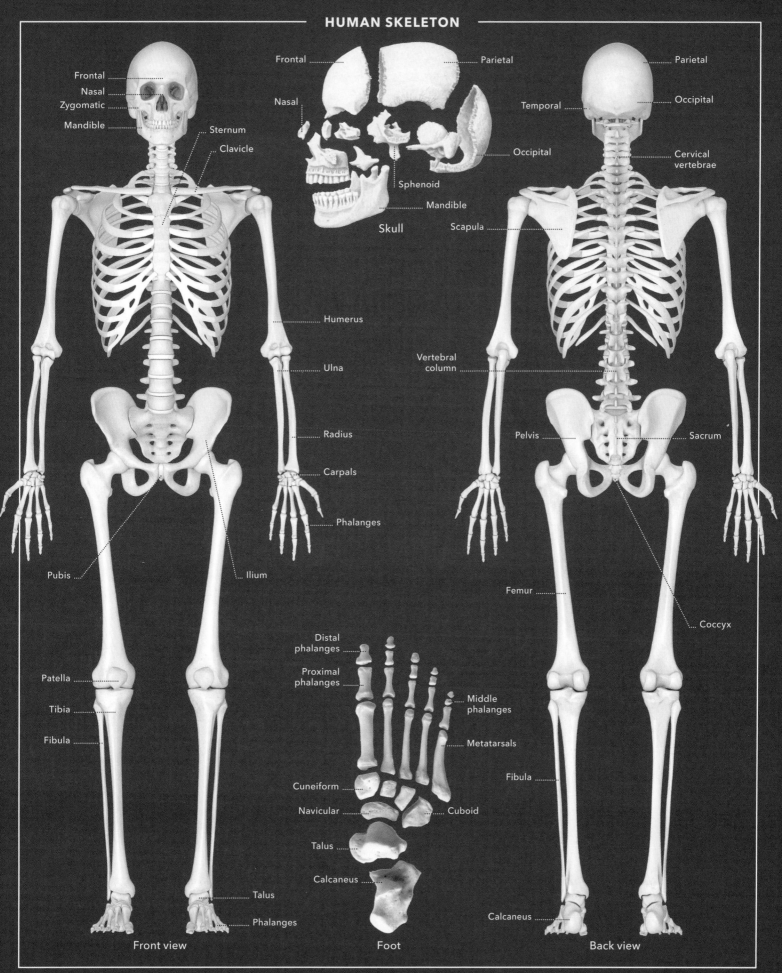

Frontal
Nasal
Zygomatic
Mandible

Sternum
Clavicle

Humerus

Ulna

Radius

Carpals

Phalanges

Pubis

Ilium

Patella

Tibia

Fibula

Talus

Phalanges

Front view

Frontal

Nasal

Parietal

Occipital

Sphenoid

Mandible

Skull

Distal
phalanges

Proximal
phalanges

Middle
phalanges

Metatarsals

Cuneiform

Navicular

Cuboid

Talus

Calcaneus

Foot

Parietal

Temporal

Occipital

Scapula

Parietal

Occipital

Cervical
vertebrae

Vertebral
column

Pelvis

Sacrum

Femur

Coccyx

Fibula

Calcaneus

Back view

MUSCLES IN THE HUMAN BODY

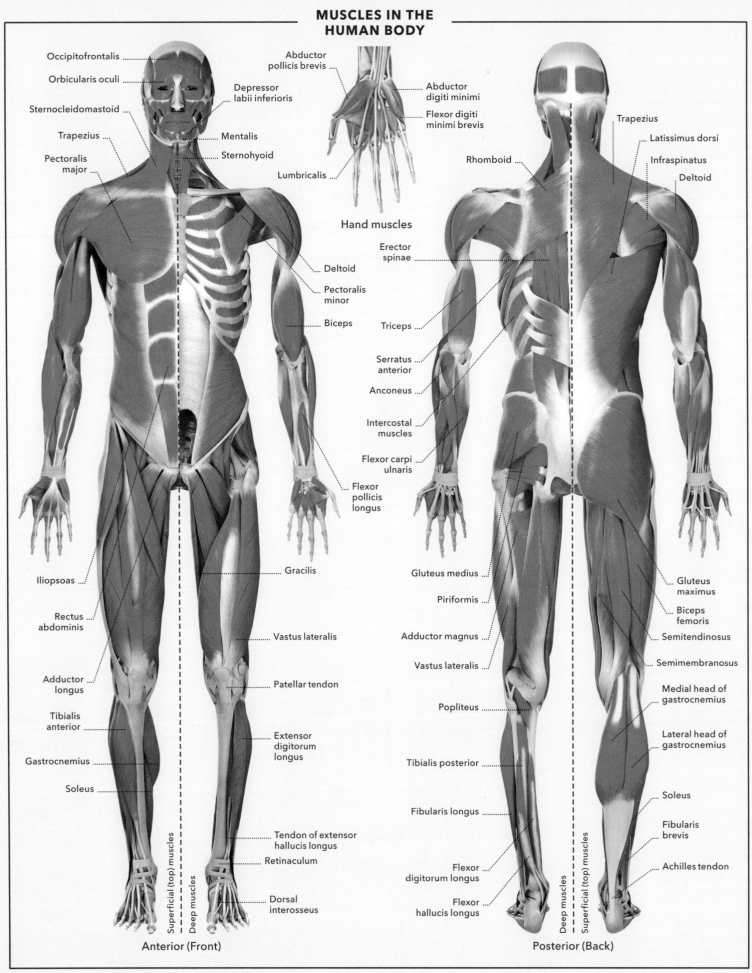

Occipitofrontalis

Orbicularis oculi

Sternocleidomastoid

Trapezius

Pectoralis major

Abductor pollicis brevis

Depressor labii inferioris

Mentalis

Sternohyoid

Abductor digiti minimi

Flexor digiti minimi brevis

Lumbricalis

Trapezius

Rhomboid

Latissimus dorsi

Infraspinatus

Deltoid

Hand muscles

Deltoid

Pectoralis minor

Biceps

Erector spinae

Triceps

Serratus anterior

Anconeus

Intercostal muscles

Flexor carpi ulnaris

Flexor pollicis longus

Iliopsoas

Rectus abdominis

Adductor longus

Tibialis anterior

Gastrocnemius

Soleus

Gracilis

Vastus lateralis

Patellar tendon

Extensor digitorum longus

Tendon of extensor hallucis longus

Retinaculum

Dorsal interosseus

Gluteus medius

Piriformis

Adductor magnus

Vastus lateralis

Popliteus

Tibialis posterior

Fibularis longus

Flexor digitorum longus

Flexor hallucis longus

Gluteus maximus

Biceps femoris

Semitendinosus

Semimembranosus

Medial head of gastrocnemius

Lateral head of gastrocnemius

Soleus

Fibularis brevis

Achilles tendon

Superficial (top) muscles

Deep muscles

Deep muscles

Superficial (top) muscles

Anterior (Front)

Posterior (Back)

MUSCLES
in the human body

The human body is moved around by stretchy cords called muscles. They allow people to smile, frown, blink, run, and throw. They also control things such as heartbeat and digestion.

All the muscles in the human body are collectively known as the muscular system. Inside the muscular system are three different types of muscle: skeletal, smooth, and cardiac muscle. Some of these are under a person's conscious control—the person decides which muscle to move, and when. Other muscles are not under their conscious control, and work constantly, without the person ever having to think about what they are doing.

Skeletal muscles are found throughout the body and together make up nearly half of the body weight. They include the muscles that help make facial expressions, the muscles that help the lungs fill with air, the ones that hold the body upright, and those that move the arms and legs when we need to walk.

The skeleton is covered in several crisscrossing layers of skeletal muscles. They are attached to the bones by thin, tough fibers called tendons. Each muscle is only able to contract (pull) and relax. When they contract they get shorter and fatter, and when relaxed they are longer and narrower. Moving a bone needs at least two skeletal

> The gluteus maximus is the largest muscle in the human body.

muscles. Complex parts of the body, such as the hands, require many muscles for movement.

Smooth muscle works without being told what to do. This type of muscle is found in many body parts, including the blood vessels, stomach, intestines, and eyes. It pushes blood and food around the body, and automatically controls the amount of light entering the eyes, helping a person see clearly.

The cardiac muscle is only found in one place—the heart. It pumps blood, which carries oxygen through arteries in the body and takes away waste through veins. The cardiac muscle works on its own, pumping blood continuously, even when we are asleep.

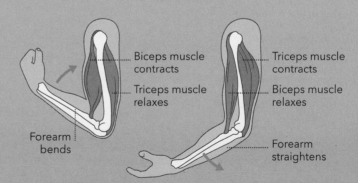

Biceps muscle contracts
Triceps muscle relaxes
Triceps muscle contracts
Biceps muscle relaxes
Forearm bends
Forearm straightens

▲ MUSCLE MOVEMENT
Muscles work in pairs to bend and straighten a joint: one contracts to move a bone one way, and the other contracts to move it back.

Types of PATHOGEN

All around and even inside us are forms of life so tiny we cannot usually see them without a microscope. These are microscopic organisms. Some of them are harmful to humans—we call them pathogens.

Humans can be infected by many types of pathogen, examples of which are shown on the right.

Some worms can live inside us. They may live in the digestive system, or in blood vessels, or under the skin. Many of them, such as roundworms, are big enough to see without a microscope.

Most fungi are harmless to humans, and live on rotting vegetation or soil, but a few types can live in or on us. Ringworm is an example—it is a skin infection caused by a fungus called *Microsporum canis* that creates itchy marks on the skin.

Protozoa are organisms with just one cell. Some of them are parasites—animals that live on or in other life forms and do them harm. They can cause diseases in humans—for example, *Giardia lamblia* causes giardiasis, which may give someone diarrhea. This pathogen is spread by drinking contaminated water and by infected people and animals.

Bacteria are a different type of single-celled life. Many of them are harmless, or even good for us. But some cause diseases such as food poisoning and even plague. Tuberculosis is caused by bacteria in the lungs. It is spread when infected people cough or sneeze.

Scientists don't think of viruses as life forms—they don't even have proper cells. To reproduce, a virus infects a host cell, using it to make copies of itself. Viruses spread a wide range of diseases, from colds and flu to AIDS and COVID-19.

Prions are not organisms, but rather proteins whose shape gets twisted. These begin affecting other proteins in the brain making them fold up abnormally. They can cause BSE (or mad cow disease) in cows—a disease that can spread to humans as Creutzfeldt-Jakob syndrome.

There are around 1,400 pathogens that infect humans.

▶ **HOW A VIRUS REPRODUCES**
Viruses reproduce by breaking their way into a host cell, which then creates and releases copies of the virus.

Virus attaches itself to the host cell.

Host cell swallows up the virus.

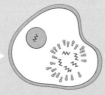

The virus uses the host cell to make copies of its parts.

New viruses form inside the host cell.

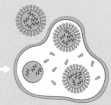

New viruses are released while the cell keeps making copies of the virus.

TYPES OF PATHOGEN

WORMS

Threadworm
ENTEROBIASIS

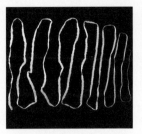

Beef tapeworm
TAENIASIS

Roundworm
ASCARIASIS

Schistosoma mansoni
SCHISTOSOMIASIS

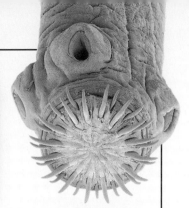

Pork tapeworm
CYSTICERCOSIS

FUNGI

Trichophyton mentagrophytes
ATHLETE'S FOOT

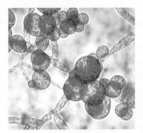

Candida auris
CANDIDIASIS

Histoplasma capsulatum
HISTOPLASMOSIS

Microsporum canis
RINGWORM

Aspergillus clavatus
ASPERGILLOSIS

PROTOZOA

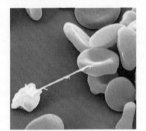

Plasmodium falciparum
MALARIA

Giardia lamblia
GIARDIASIS

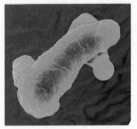

Entamoeba histolytica
AMOEBIASIS

Toxoplasma gondii
TOXOPLASMOSIS

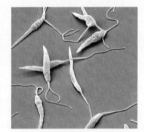

Leishmania
LEISHMANIASIS

BACTERIA

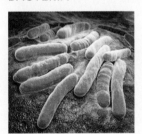

Mycobacterium tuberculosis
TUBERCULOSIS

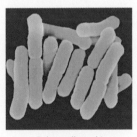

Salmonella typhi
TYPHOID FEVER

Vibrio cholerae
CHOLERA

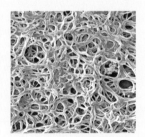

Borrelia burgdorferi
LYME DISEASE

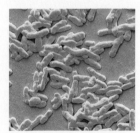

Mycobacterium leprae
LEPROSY

VIRUSES

Varicella zoster virus
CHICKENPOX

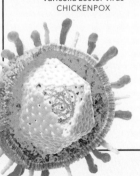

Hepatitis B
HEPATITIS

SARS-CoV-2
COVID-19

HIV
AIDS

PRIONS

BSE prion
MAD COW DISEASE

TRANSPORTATION and COMMUNICATION

Types of
BICYCLE

This two-wheeled, personal form of transportation is powered by its rider using pedals. The pedals turn the back wheel, pushing the bicycle forward. Different bicycles have different features based on their use.

Bicycles first appeared in the early 19th century. The earliest versions were quite different to the ones we have now—they didn't have pedals, and the rider had to move them along by pushing their feet against the ground.

Pedals were added in the 1860s and could propel the bicycle without the rider needing to run. They were initially affixed to the front wheel, which made for a very bumpy and unstable ride—so bumpy that these bikes were called "boneshakers." Some inventors used very large front wheels to try and make bicycles more stable. These bicycles were called "penny-farthings" as their wheels looked like a large penny and a smaller farthing—types of British coins. They were more stable, but the high seat was dangerous.

In 1885, a "safety bicycle" was invented, which had same-size wheels and pedals directly below the rider, with a chain from the pedals to the back wheel. Turning the pedals made the back wheel turn, pushing the bicycle forward. This made bicycles much safer and easier to ride.

By the 1890s, bicycles had become popular throughout Europe and the US. They offered freedom and mobility to anyone who could get ahold of one—particularly women, many of whom were able to travel by themselves for the first time. Bicycles were also useful for traveling in crowded areas—firefighters could cycle to fires on bikes that had a housing for the fire hose. Even today, many people around the world use bicycles for their daily commute.

Modern bicycles still follow the same general approach as the safety bicycle, though their design and materials have been fine-tuned over the years. There are now many different styles of bike, designed to fill a wide range of roles. For example, folding bikes are designed to be collapsed and carried onto public transit, and the ice bike has a sled in place of a front wheel, with spikes on the back wheel to dig into frozen surfaces.

The fastest cyclists can reach speeds of more than 155 mph (250 kph).

▶ **HOW GEARS WORK**
Modern bicycles use gears to reduce the effort needed by the cyclist. The bigger the rear sprocket, the lower the gear. Gears control how far the rear wheel moves with each turn of the pedals. Cycling in a lower gear requires less force but more pedaling, and vice versa.

Cassette with different-size sprockets (wheels with teeth) that the chain fits over

Pedals move the chain.

The chain connects the pedals to the back wheel.

PARTS OF A BICYCLE

Seat

Seat post

Top tube

Handlebars

Stem

Brake lever

Seat stay

Chain

Down tube

Brake cables

Road and track bike

Seat tube

Water bottle holder

Tire valve, for inflating the tire

Fork blade

Hub

Rim

Rubber wheel

Pedal

Chain ring

Cassette with sprockets

Front derailleur

Brake

Spoke

Rear derailleur

TYPES OF BICYCLE

Boneshaker

Penny-farthing

Ice bike

Firefighter bike

Folding bike

Electric bike

BMX bike

Recumbent bike

Mountain bike

Touring bike

Racing bike

Tandem bike

Cruising bike

Fat bike

Aerodynamic time-trial bike

Delivery bike

Types of
MOTORBIKE

A fast, two-wheeled vehicle—a motorbike or motorcycle—is essentially a bicycle powered by a motor. There are many kinds of motorbike, some built for speed, some for comfort, and some for utility.

The motorbike was born when inventors began attaching engines to bicycle frames in the late 19th and early 20th centuries. The very first motorbikes used steam engines attached to early pedal-less bicycles. However, these could be dangerous and had limited use, so they did not become popular.

By the 1890s, the internal combustion engine had been invented. This engine used liquid fuel, and could be made much smaller and more compact than steam engines. In 1894, three German engineers teamed up to create the "motorrad," which was a bicycle powered by a small combustion engine.

The Hildebrand & Wolfmüller Motorrad was the first motorbike to be produced in bulk and sold to the general public. Engineers around the world continued to work on motorbike designs, and gradually moved away from the bicycle-like shape. Scooters were invented around 1915, with a design that allowed the rider to step on board and sit down in a chair-like seat. The maxi scooter was a further development on this design, with a larger and more powerful engine.

Today, there is a huge range of different types of motorbike. They are popular all over the world, in many different forms. Generally, motorbikes and scooters are cheaper than cars, easier to park, and able to drive through narrow spaces: all these things make them very appealing to people living in busy cities. Mopeds are motorbikes with small wheels and small engines—they are specifically designed for city life, rather than for cruising the open road.

Motorbikes are also popularly used for sports: they can reach incredibly high speeds and are easy to maneuver around tight corners. A few notable motorbike sports include dirt biking, road racing, motocross, hill climbing, and ice racing.

> **Motocross bikes can reach speeds of 100 mph (160 kph).**

2. Spark plug ignites the fuel, pushing piston down.

Piston

1. Fuel enters the engine.

3. Piston moves crankshaft, which moves the wheel.

5. Burned fuel gases expelled

4. Piston moves up.

▲ HOW A MOTORBIKE ENGINE WORKS
Motorbikes use internal combustion engines—like cars. Fuel is sucked into the engine and lit, which creates a reaction that turns a piston. This moves a crankshaft connected to the wheels.

TYPES OF MOTORBIKE

Rex Rexette 5
HP 1905

Hildebrand & Wolfmüller
Motorrad 1894

Perks and Birch
Motorwheel 1900

Werner 1901

Bayliss Thomas
Excelsior 1902

Ariel 4F Square
Four 1931

Indian Sport
Scout 1937

Sunbeam Model
S7 Deluxe 1949

Electric

Chopper

Scrambler

Streetfighter

Dual sport

Roadster

Retro

Café racer

Motocross

Cruiser

Maxi scooter

Off-road

Moped

Naked

Off-road
adventure

Supermoto

Scooter

Sports

Sports tourer

Adventure

Enduro

Custom

Touring

CAR

types

Since the Motorwagen was invented in 1885, cars have helped us get around on the road. A car usually has four wheels, four doors, a roof, and a windshield, but there are many variations on this basic shape.

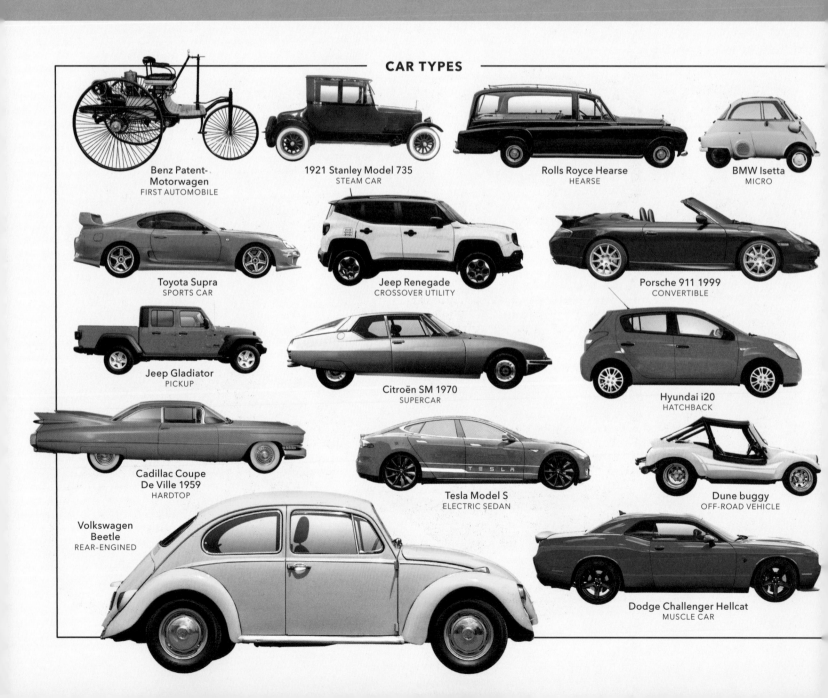

CAR TYPES

Benz Patent-Motorwagen
FIRST AUTOMOBILE

1921 Stanley Model 735
STEAM CAR

Rolls Royce Hearse
HEARSE

BMW Isetta
MICRO

Toyota Supra
SPORTS CAR

Jeep Renegade
CROSSOVER UTILITY

Porsche 911 1999
CONVERTIBLE

Jeep Gladiator
PICKUP

Citroën SM 1970
SUPERCAR

Hyundai i20
HATCHBACK

Cadillac Coupe De Ville 1959
HARDTOP

Tesla Model S
ELECTRIC SEDAN

Dune buggy
OFF-ROAD VEHICLE

Volkswagen Beetle
REAR-ENGINED

Dodge Challenger Hellcat
MUSCLE CAR

Most of us have seen the four-door sedan, but it is just one of many types of car. The coupe, first designed in the 1950s, has only two doors and a sloping, streamlined shape. Some even have extra trim, such as rear fins, to enhance their look. In contrast, a broad, boxy outline is typical of the powerful muscle cars, which became popular in the 1960s.

Convertibles can come in any shape, but they all have a folding or sliding roof so occupants can enjoy the fresh air. More practical adaptations are the hatchbacks, where the back seating folds down to provide a larger trunk area, and the SUVs (sports utility vehicles), which sit higher off the road and have lots of space for storage. Another vehicle designed to carry lots of luggage or many people is a microbus, such as the VW T2 microbus.

Cars with chunky tires, such as the Dune buggy, are made for off-road adventures, while sports cars with stripped-back interiors and high-powered engines are built for racing.

More than 85 million cars are produced every year.

Some cars have been designed for specific functions, such as the hearse—with a flat area to carry a coffin at the rear—or pickups, which are open at the back with an area to store equipment. The Lincoln Town Car is an extra-long limousine with a large area where passengers can lie on sofas.

The next generation of cars, such as the Tesla models, run on electricity rather than gasoline or diesel, so they are less polluting and really quiet.

Ford Model T 1924
TOURING CAR

Mercedes-Benz SLC
ROADSTER

BMW M2
COUPE

Maruti Suzuki Ertiga
MULTI-UTILITY VEHICLE (MUV)

Nissan X-Trail
SPORTS UTILITY VEHICLE (SUV)

VW T2
MICROBUS

Lincoln Town Car
LIMOUSINE

Mazda MX-5
TARGA TOP

Smart ForTwo
TWO-SEATER CAR

Volvo V60
ESTATE

Bugatti Chiron 2016
HYPERCAR

Large land
VEHICLES

Buses carrying people or trucks hauling loads are a common sight on the road. Other large land vehicles include fire engines and ambulances rushing to emergencies, heavy construction vehicles, and those helping on farms.

Large vehicles typically carry heavy loads or a large number of people. Different types of large land vehicle are designed for different purposes. A selection of these vehicles is shown on the following pages.

All over the world, buses carry people to work or school, or across cities. Buses are fueled by diesel, electricity, or a mixture of the two. Trolley buses, which usually run in cities, are powered by electricity running through cables connected to the roof. If they need to hold more people, buses may have another deck upstairs (a double-decker) or be double the length, with a flexible joint or articulation in the middle that allows the bus to bend around corners. In cold regions with heavy snowfall, buses are sometimes modified to become snow buses that are able to travel over rough, snowy terrain.

Trucks transport large quantities of supplies. They might carry liquids such as fuel or milk, wet cement, logs, or garbage, and are adapted to do the job safely. Oil or gas tankers have a large tank to safely contain the liquid and prevent it spilling. Concrete trucks have a large rotating drum that keeps the ingredients of the concrete well mixed. Garbage trucks are equipped to empty household bins into the back of the truck and compress the contents inside.

Emergency vehicles, such as fire trucks, ambulances, and police vans, are usually brightly painted and have flashing lights and sirens to alert other road users to get out of their way. They carry machinery to tackle specific emergencies—for example, ambulances carry life-saving equipment such as defibrillators to restart a stopped heart.

There are specialized vehicles that are made to carry out jobs on farms, highways, or construction sites. These include tractors and combine harvesters, which help with plowing land and harvesting crops on farms, and bulldozers and excavators, which help at construction sites. Some diggers and dumpers drive on tracks made of linked metal chains rather than wheels. These are called caterpillar tracks, and they have a larger surface area to stop the vehicle from getting stuck in mud. Military tanks and trucks use these too.

> **Log trucks can hold up to 65 large oak tree logs.**

> **At 311 ft (95 m), the Bagger 288 excavator is taller than the Statue of Liberty.**

BUSES

Trolley bus

Bi-articulated bus

Double-decker bus

Single-decker bus

Snow bus

Articulated bus

School bus

Open-top bus

Low-floor bus

Minibus

Electric bus

Charter bus

Off-road bus

TRUCKS

Semitruck

Kei truck

Log truck

Articulated truck

Tanker

Monster truck

Flatbed truck

Street cleaner truck

Garbage truck

Airport tug

Car transporter

Dump truck

CONSTRUCTION VEHICLES

Concrete truck

Bulldozer

Compactor

Backhoe loader

Excavator

Crane truck

Haul truck

Front loader

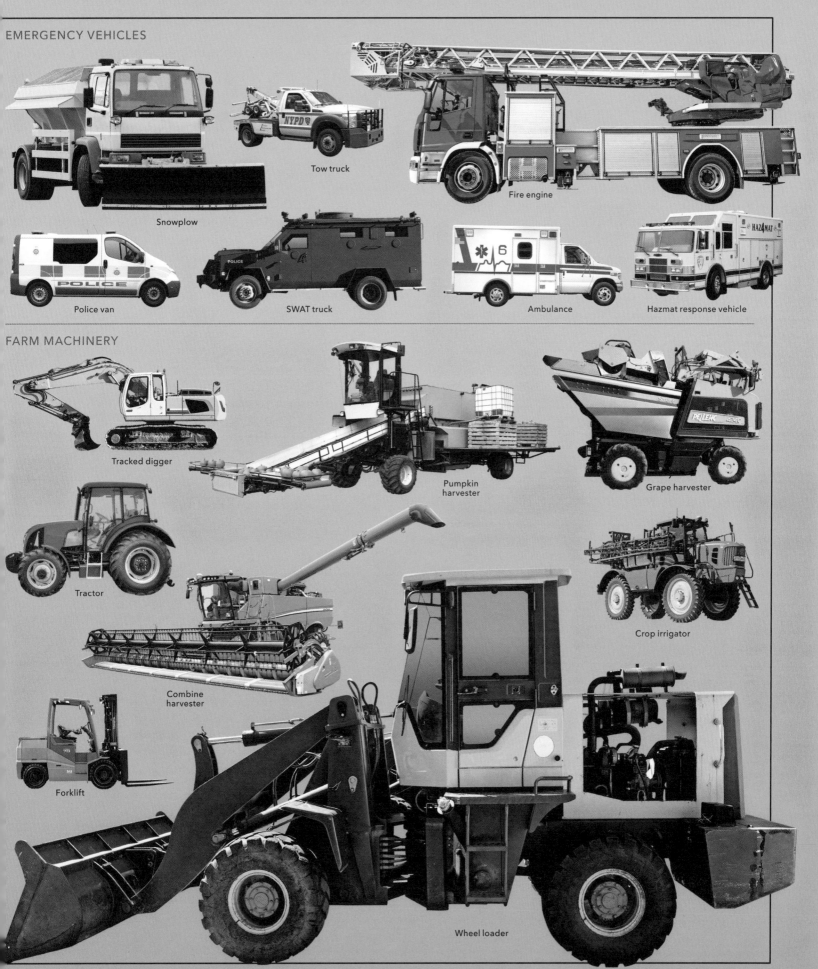

EMERGENCY VEHICLES

Snowplow

Tow truck

Fire engine

Police van

SWAT truck

Ambulance

Hazmat response vehicle

FARM MACHINERY

Tracked digger

Pumpkin harvester

Grape harvester

Tractor

Crop irrigator

Combine harvester

Forklift

Wheel loader

TRAINS
through time

People and goods have been traveling by train for more than 200 years. Over time, changes in engine design and methods of moving a train have led to faster transportation over greater distances.

Trains are a great option for people to move between places quickly. They are vehicles that move along fixed tracks and have sections called cars, which are pushed or pulled along by locomotives (engines). Their invention sparked a transportation revolution, helping connect places and opening up entire regions for explorers and settlers.

The first trains were powered by steam: coal was burned in the locomotive, to heat up water and create steam, which pushed pistons to turn its wheels. These steam engines were many times faster than the horses and carts people had previously used. They revolutionized travel and trade, as people and goods were able to move farther and faster than ever before. The first steam-powered train was used in 1804 at Pen-y-Darren Colliery, Wales. Governments and companies all over the world quickly began to build networks of train tracks. In 1825, *Locomotion No 1* ran along the world's first passenger line in England. Within a few decades, Hawthorne No 9 *Blackie* ushered in the steam age in South Africa.

Around the middle of the 20th century, trains powered by diesel, a liquid fuel, began to replace steam trains. The diesel engine spun a generator, which created electricity to turn the locomotive's wheels. Diesel trains used less fuel than steam trains, and could move fast without damaging the tracks. The CB&Q *Pioneer Zephyr*, which could reach speeds of 110 mph (177 kph), carried letters for the US Mail. After diesel trains came electric trains, which were faster. They ran on electricity without the need to burn fuel in the locomotive. Electricity was supplied either by cables above the tracks, such as in the Series 0 Shinkansen, or by a "live" rail in the track. The more recent maglev trains move faster than electric trains by using powerful magnets.

Mallard, the world's fastest steam engine, ran at a speed of 126 mph (203 kph).

▶ **TYPES OF PROPULSION**
Most trains move using steam, diesel, electricity, magnets, or a combination of these things.

Steam
A steam engine is powered by steam, which is produced by burning coal.

Diesel
A diesel engine works by burning diesel, which turns the wheels.

Electric
An electric train is powered by electricity, which runs a motor that drives the wheels.

Maglev
Magnets make a maglev train float over its track and move forward.

TRAINS THROUGH TIME

Pen-y-Darren locomotive
1804

Puffing Billy
1813

Locomotion No 1
1825

Seguin's locomotive
1829

Tom Thumb
1830

John Bull
1831

Stephenson's *Rocket*
1829

Adler
1835

B&O *Lafayette*
1837

Südbahn Class 23 GKB 671
1860

Metropolitan Railway
A class steam locomotive No 23
1860s

John Steven's *Steam Wagon*
1825

GWR Iron Duke Class locomotive *Sebastopol*
1855

Hawthorne No 9 *Blackie*
1859

CP No 60 *Jupiter*
1868

Gross Lichterfelde Tramway
1881

EIR No 22 *Fairy Queen*
1855

LNER Class A3 4472
Flying Scotsman
1923

CB&Q *Pioneer*
Zephyr
1934

Wuppertaler Schwebebahn
1901

LNER Class A4 4468 *Mallard*
1938

Akkuschleppfahrzeug ASF
1966

EMD FT 6000
1939

DRG Class SVT 877 *Hamburg Flyer*
1933

Series 0 Shinkansen
1964

SNCF TGV Sud-Est
1981

ER200
1984

FS Class ETR 212
1937

Birmingham
International
Maglev shuttle
1985

SMT
Transrapid
2002

Types of AIRCRAFT

Humans first took to the air in a controlled aircraft in 1903, when brothers Wilbur and Orville Wright launched their *Flyer* plane. As technology evolved, people made a range of different aircraft.

The *Flyer* was a biplane with two stacked wings on either side. This type of plane took part in World War I (1914–1918) along with triplanes, which had three wings on either side.

The invention of the jet engine in the 1940s led to a new generation of aircraft for military use and later for carrying passengers and cargo. The Bell X-1 was a rocket-powered aircraft launched in 1947 from a Boeing B-29 aircraft, and it flew higher and faster than any plane before it.

By the 1950s, turboprop aircraft had become popular. These burn fuel to power a turbine that drives a propeller. Amphibious aircraft, which can land on both land and water, are also propeller-driven—the DHC-3 Turbine Otter plane has either wheels, floats, or skis to land on a runway, water, or snow.

Other ways of getting airborne use different technology. Autogyros and helicopters use long spinning blades to move air over a rotor and generate lift. Helicopters can get into tight spaces because they don't need a runway to take off or land. Air ambulances can land in a park or on the roadside, and search and rescue helicopters can hover over someone at sea or on a mountainside, drop down a winch, and haul them aboard.

Modern jet planes have been adapted for different purposes. Some have large interior spaces to carry cargo and troops, others can have huge fuel tanks to refuel planes mid-flight, and still others are fitted with radar equipment to detect craft at sea or in the air.

Concorde was a commercial jet that flew at supersonic (faster than sound) speeds in the 1970s. It had triangular (delta) wings that allowed it to fly fast. Modern fighter jets also have delta wings. Some of these planes have stealth technology that makes them almost invisible to radar.

▶ **TURBOPROPS AND JETS**
Turboprop planes have a propeller on the outside of the engine. In modern jet planes, the fan blades are inside the engine housing.

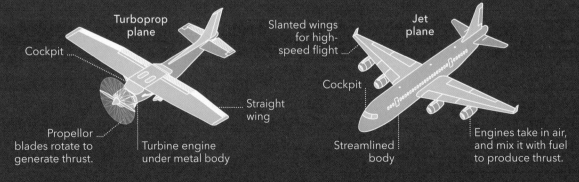

Turboprop plane

Cockpit

Propellor blades rotate to generate thrust.

Turbine engine under metal body

Straight wing

Slanted wings for high-speed flight

Jet plane

Cockpit

Streamlined body

Engines take in air, and mix it with fuel to produce thrust.

TYPES OF AIRCRAFT

Antonov An-225 Mriya
CARGO PLANES

Antonov An-124 Ruslan
CARGO AND PARATROOP TRANSPORT PLANES

Leonardo AW139
AIR AMBULANCES

Paramotor
POWERED PARAGLIDERS

Westland Sea King HAR3
SEARCH AND RESCUE HELICOPTERS

Boeing Dreamliner
PASSENGER JETS

Concorde
SUPERSONIC JETS

Boeing E-3 Sentry
EARLY WARNING AND CONTROL PLANES

Boeing KC-135 Stratotanker
REFUELING PLANES

De Havilland Q400
TURBOPROP AIRCRAFT

McDonnell Douglas Harrier
VERTICAL SHORT TAKE OFF AND LANDING PLANES

Sea Harrier
NAVAL JET FIGHTERS

F-117 Night Hawk
BOMBERS AND STRIKE PLANES

Bombardier 415
WATER BOMBERS

Bell 206B JetRanger III
TRANSPORT HELICOPTERS

DHC-3 Turbine Otter
AMPHIBIOUS AIRCRAFT

Fokker Dr.I
TRIPLANES

Bell X-1
ROCKET PLANES

Lockheed U-2
RECONNAISSANCE PLANES

F-22 Raptor
FIGHTER JETS (AIR TO AIR)

1918 Sopwith Camel
BIPLANES

Wallis WA-116
AUTOGYROS

Schempp-Hirth Arcus
GLIDERS

Pitts Special
AEROBATIC PLANES

Aeros flexwing
MICROLIGHTS

Piper PA-28-161
PISTON-ENGINE PLANES

PZL-106 Kruk
CROP-DUSTING PLANES

193

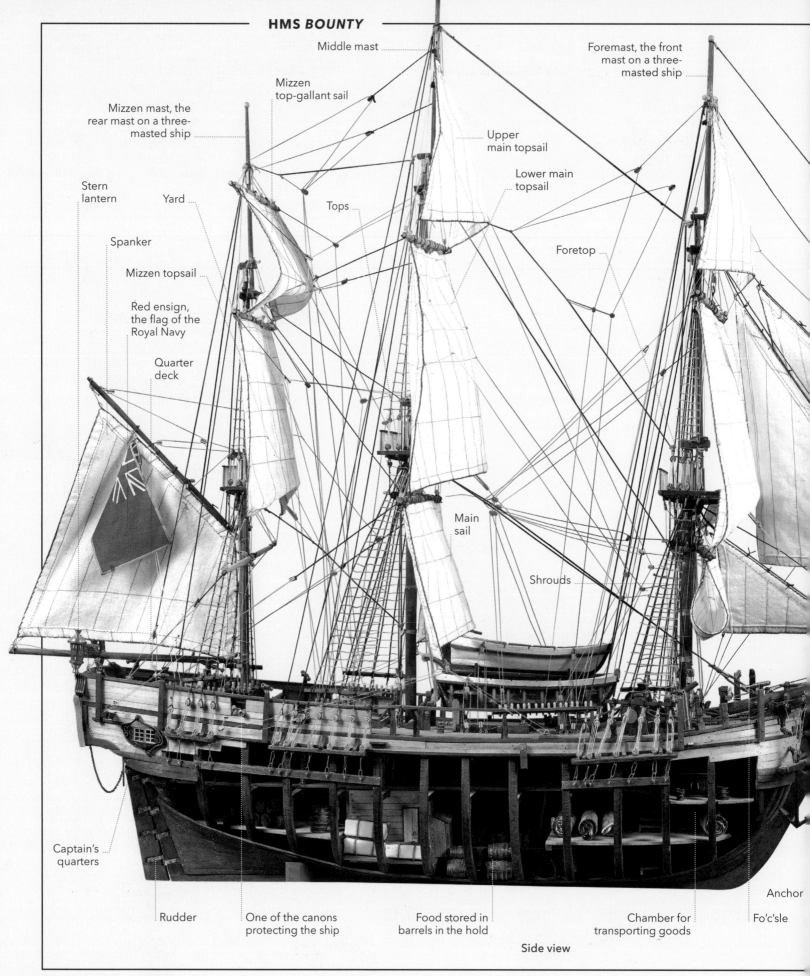

HMS *BOUNTY*

Middle mast

Foremast, the front mast on a three-masted ship

Mizzen top-gallant sail

Mizzen mast, the rear mast on a three-masted ship

Upper main topsail

Lower main topsail

Stern lantern

Yard

Tops

Spanker

Foretop

Mizzen topsail

Red ensign, the flag of the Royal Navy

Quarter deck

Main sail

Shrouds

Captain's quarters

Anchor

Rudder

One of the canons protecting the ship

Food stored in barrels in the hold

Chamber for transporting goods

Fo'c'sle

Side view

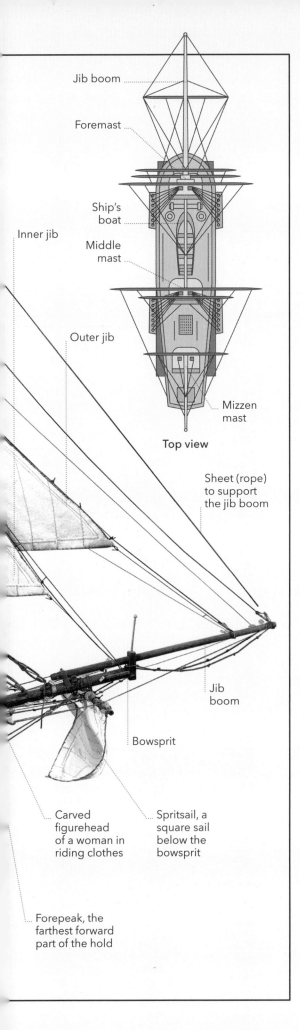

Jib boom

Foremast

Ship's boat

Inner jib

Middle mast

Outer jib

Mizzen mast

Top view

Sheet (rope) to support the jib boom

Jib boom

Bowsprit

Carved figurehead of a woman in riding clothes

Spritsail, a square sail below the bowsprit

Forepeak, the farthest forward part of the hold

Parts of a
SAILING SHIP

The 18th century was the "golden age of sail." Consisting of just wood, rope, and canvas, beautifully built ships like this one ruled the waves!

In 1787, HMS *Bounty* set sail from England, bound for Tahiti in the South Pacific. A Royal Navy ship measuring 89 ft (27 m) in length and weighing 247 tons (224 metric tons), *Bounty* was a three-masted merchant, or trading, vessel. She was full-rigged, meaning there were three layers of sails on each mast. The mizzen mast was at the rear, or stern, of the ship, followed by the middle mast (the tallest) and the foremast at the front, or bow. The lowermost sail on each mast was called the main sail. Above it were the topsails. Sails hung from the masts on horizontal wooden bars called yards, held in place by shrouds. These were part of the rigging, the collection of ropes, chains, and lines that kept the sails and masts secure. Sailors climbed the rigging to reach the tops, the platforms partway up the masts from which they could spot land or enemy ships.

> Ship figureheads helped sailors identify their vessel in busy ports.

At the ship's bow, the bowsprit and the jib boom held ropes to support the sails. At the stern, the rudder and a sail called a spanker helped steer the ship. The captain slept in his quarters at the stern, while the crew slept in the fo'c'sle (or forecastle) in the bow.

Types of
BRIDGE

The mighty spans of bridges sweep across rivers and valleys, bringing places together. They look calm and static, but these monumental structures are in a tug-of-war between immense forces.

TYPES OF BRIDGE

BEAM

Donghai Bridge
CHINA

Faidherbe Bridge
SENEGAL

King Fahd Causeway
BAHRAIN AND SAUDI ARABIA

Shiziguan Floating Bridge
CHINA

TRUSS

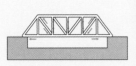

Ikitsuki Bridge
JAPAN

Auckland Harbor Bridge
NEW ZEALAND

Dashengguan Yangtze River Bridge
CHINA

Astoria-Megler Bridge
US

ARCH

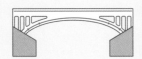

Rialto Bridge
ITALY

Stari Most
BOSNIA AND HERZEGOVINA

Dragon Bridge
VIETNAM

Sydney Harbor Bridge
AUSTRALIA

KEY
- ■ Compression
- ■ Tension

Every bridge is unique, but all bridges work by resisting forces—the weight of the bridge, the load it bears, and forces from wind and water. Some parts of a bridge are stretched (in tension), while others are squashed (in compression). The secret of a well-designed bridge lies in the way the tension and compression balance perfectly. Bridges balance the forces acting on them in many different ways. The deck (main section) of a beam bridge, such as the Donghai in China, is stretched along the bottom and squeezed across the top, and squashes down on its supports. In a truss bridge, such as Japan's Ikitsuki, the deck hangs from a crisscross framework of metal bars. An arch bridge, such as the Rialto in Italy, is supported mainly by forces of compression, as the tension below the arch is negligible. It balances on a curve of stones squashed by the load pushing down. A cantilever bridge, such as Scotland's Forth, has truss sections supporting beams in between. In suspension bridges, such as the Golden Gate in California, a vast bridge deck hangs from a swooping curve of strong metal ropes stretched between tall towers. The towers are squashed down and the metal ropes stretched tight. A cable-stayed bridge, such as the Russky in Russia, is similar, but the deck hangs directly from the towers using fans of stretched cables.

Often, several of these features—beams, arches, trusses, and cables—are combined in the same bridge.

> **Nongriat, India, has a suspension bridge made of living roots.**

CANTILEVER

Howrah Bridge
INDIA

Tokyo Gate Bridge
JAPAN

Forth Bridge
SCOTLAND

Québec Bridge
CANADA

SUSPENSION

Golden Gate Bridge
US

Tsitsikamma Bridge
SOUTH AFRICA

Osman Gazi Bridge
TÜRKIYE (TURKEY)

Ulsan Bridge
SOUTH KOREA

CABLE-STAYED

Russky Bridge
RUSSIA

Normandy Bridge
FRANCE

Samuel Beckett Bridge
IRELAND

Newton Navarro Bridge
BRAZIL

Most spoken
LANGUAGES

Our languages are a huge part of how we communicate, both in writing and by speaking to each other. Here is how to say "good morning" in the 40 most spoken languages.

MOST SPOKEN LANGUAGES

Good morning
Good morning
ENGLISH
1.45 BILLION SPEAKERS WORLDWIDE

早上好
Zǎo shàng hǎo
CHINESE (MANDARIN)
1.13 BILLION

शुभ प्रभात
Shubh prabhaat
HINDI
609 MILLION

Buenos días
Buenos días
SPANISH
559 MILLION

Bonjour
Bonjour
FRENCH
310 MILLION

Selamat pagi
Selamat pagi
INDONESIAN
199 MILLION

Guten Morgen
Guten Morgen
STANDARD GERMAN
133 MILLION

おはようございます
Ohayoh gozaimasu
JAPANESE
123 MILLION

Gud morning
Gud morning
NIGERIAN PIDGIN
121 MILLION

صباح الخير
Sabah el khear
EGYPTIAN ARABIC
102 MILLION

早晨
Zou san
YUE CHINESE
87 MILLION

Chào buổi sáng
Chào buoi sáng
VIETNAMESE
86 MILLION

儂早
Nóng zao
WU CHINESE
83 MILLION

Magandang umaga
Magandang umaga
TAGALOG
83 MILLION

좋은 아침이에요
Joh-eun achim-ieyo
KOREAN
82 MILLION

سویرا بخیر
Śavēra bakhair
WESTERN PUNJABI
67 MILLION

સુપ્રભાત
Suprabhāta
GUJARATI
62 MILLION

สวัสดีตอนเช้า
Sawatdee tohn chao
THAI
61 MILLION

ಶುಭೋದಯ
Śubhōdaya
KANNADA
59 MILLION

እንደምን አደሩ
Endämen addäru
AMHARIC
58 MILLION

The first language someone learns as they are growing up is called their "mother tongue." Those who have two mother tongues are called bilingual, and there are many people who can speak multiple languages.

Most countries in the world have at least one "official" language—the language that is used by their government and is taught in schools. But there are usually a number of other languages spoken too—for example, in Spain the official language is Spanish, but it also has many regional languages such as Catalan and Basque. In the US, English is used for all official purposes but is not labeled as an official language. It is spoken along with many other languages, including Spanish, Chinese, and Tagalog.

The number of people who speak a language in any region depends on a wide range of factors. Countries with large native populations are likely to be home to people who speak the same language. This explains why Chinese is second on the list and Hindi, which is spoken in India, is third.

English is first on the list because the British Empire once controlled much of the world, and the people who lived in the countries colonized by the British learned English. Today, English is often used for business and in the media, with English-language films and TV shows popular all over the world.

> There are 573 "dead" languages that are no longer spoken.

صباح الخير

Subaah al-kheir

STANDARD ARABIC
274 MILLION

সুপ্রভাত

Suprabhāt

BANGLA
273 MILLION

Bom dia

Bom dia

PORTUGUESE
264 MILLION

доброе утро

Dobroye utro

RUSSIAN
255 MILLION

صبح بخیر

Subha bakhair

URDU
232 MILLION

शुभ सकाळ

Śubh sakal

MARATHI
99 MILLION

శుభోదయం

Śubhōdayam

TELUGU
96 MILLION

Günaydın

Günaydın

TURKISH
90 MILLION

காலை வணக்கம்

Kālai vanakkam

TAMIL
87 MILLION

صبح به خیر

Sobh bekheir

IRANIAN PERSIAN
79 MILLION

Barka da safiya

Barka da safiya

HAUSA
79 MILLION

Habari za asubuhi

Habari za asubuhi

SWAHILI
72 MILLION

ꦱꦸꦒꦼꦁꦌꦤ꧀ꦗꦁ

Sugeng enjang

JAVANESE
68 MILLION

Buongiorno

Buongiorno

ITALIAN
68 MILLION

शुभ प्रभात

Subh prabhat

BHOJPURI
52 MILLION

ਸ਼ੁਭ ਸਵੇਰ

Śubha savēra

EASTERN PUNJABI
52 MILLION

賢早

Gâu-chá

MIN NAN CHINESE
50 MILLION

早上好

Zăo shàng hăo

JIN CHINESE
48 MILLION

صباح الخير

Subaah al-kheir

LEVANTINE ARABIC
48 MILLION

Ẹ káàróò

Ẹ káàróò

YORUBA
46 MILLION

Indo-European
LANGUAGES

All over Europe and parts of Asia, people speak languages that are different, but share some features with their neighbors' languages. This is because these languages all have an ancestor in common.

Languages are essential to our lives—they allow us to share ideas, agree trades, and build friendships and communities. Languages are also dynamic—they change and develop over time as they are used.

A language family is a group of languages that all developed from a shared parent language. The Indo-European languages are a group of languages that are spoken across Europe and in large parts of southern and southwestern Asia. They are thought to have developed from a parent language that would have been spoken north of the Black Sea more than 5,000 years ago.

The speakers of this parent language traveled out and away from their original home, carrying their language with them. The Black Sea is positioned between Europe and Asia—continents that are joined together, creating the largest land mass on Earth. The Indo-European speakers were able to go around the Black Sea, traveling long distances on land, without having to cross water.

The Indo-European speakers set up new communities in different places, and traded with the people they met,

> There are 446 living Indo-European languages.

talking as they went. As time passed, the Indo-European languages used in these places slowly changed, and new groups or families of languages developed in different areas. For example, the Balto-Slavic languages are spoken in eastern Europe, and include Polish, Czech, Latvian, Ukrainian, and Russian. They are separate languages, but there are similarities in some of their grammar and words. For instance, the Polish word *brutto* and the Latvian word *bruto* both mean "bad." In the same way, there are similarities in words between the Pahari languages, which include Nepali, Sinhalese, Kumaoni, Garhwali, and Dogri. The speakers of this family live in a range of places in southern Asia, including in Nepal, India, and Sri Lanka.

The main language families that developed from Indo-European are highlighted opposite. Most of these language families continued changing over time, creating new languages that are related but distinct from each other. Those languages are shown here too, with links to the languages that they descended from (in black boxes).

> Indo-European languages have more speakers than any other language group.

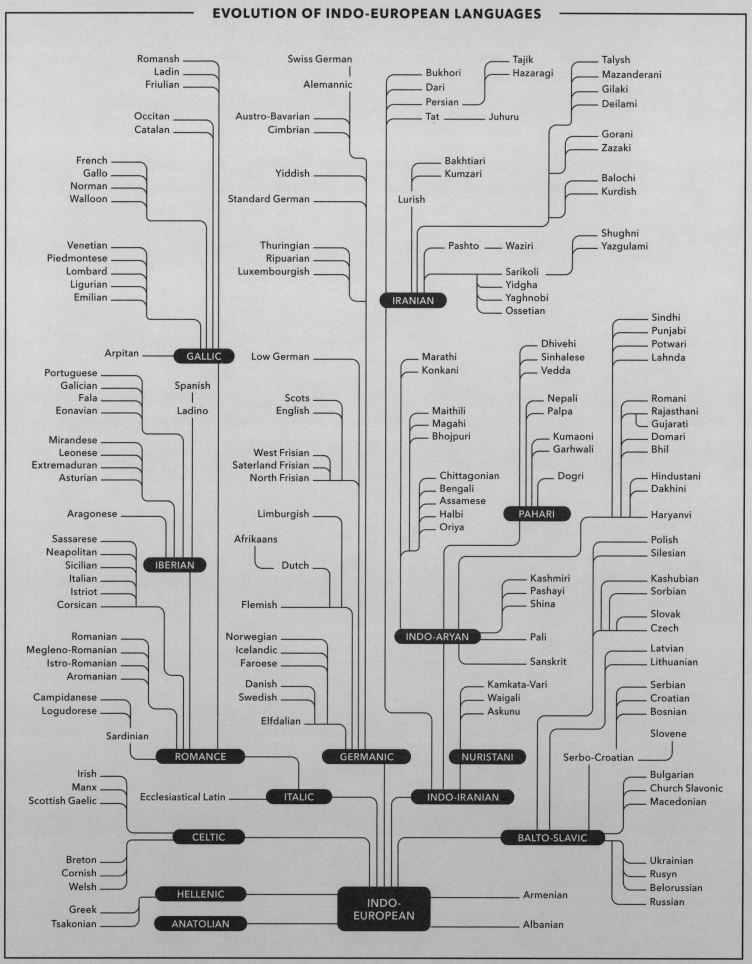

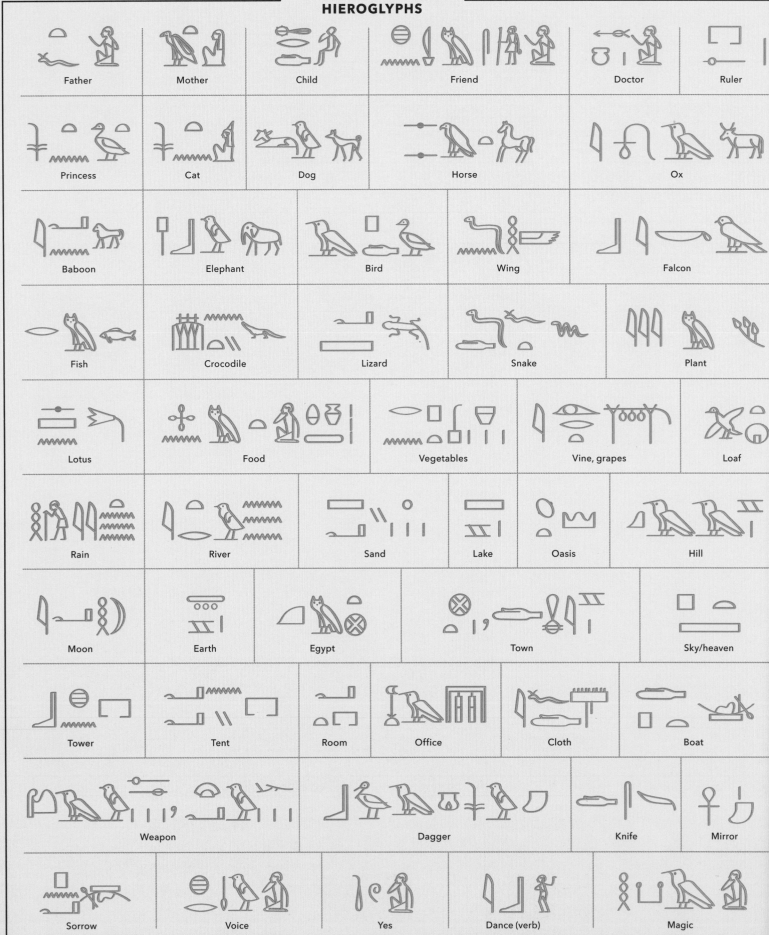

Father Mother Child Friend Doctor Ruler

Princess Cat Dog Horse Ox

Baboon Elephant Bird Wing Falcon

Fish Crocodile Lizard Snake Plant

Lotus Food Vegetables Vine, grapes Loaf

Rain River Sand Lake Oasis Hill

Moon Earth Egypt Town Sky/heaven

Tower Tent Room Office Cloth Boat

Weapon Dagger Knife Mirror

Sorrow Voice Yes Dance (verb) Magic

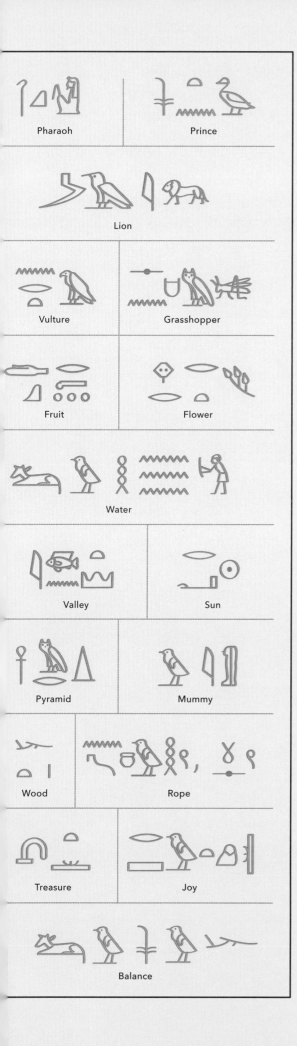

Egyptian
HIEROGLYPHS

Many ancient Egyptian monuments are covered in tiny pictures that are not just decorative, but a form of writing called hieroglyphics.

Hieroglyphs are not straightforward to read, and there are several different ways of saying the same thing. Hieroglyphic symbols can be arranged in rows or columns, and read from the left or from the right, or from top to bottom or bottom to top. To find out which way to read them, the reader must look to see which direction the people or animal hieroglyphs are facing.

For the ancient Egyptians, hieroglyphs were a gift from the gods—they were called *medu-neter*, or "god's words." Each hieroglyph represented how a part of a word was spoken. We call these signs phonograms. For example, the image of an open mouth stands for the sound of the letter "r," and a forearm represents the sound "ay." Putting these together makes the ancient Egyptian word for the sun—*re*.

Sometimes another picture was added at the end of a word to depict an animal or object being shown, such as a round circle with a dot in the middle representing the sun or a horse after the phonograms spelling "horse." These additional signs were not meant to be spoken out, but instead worked to indicate the thing being spoken about. They are called determinatives. They also helped to separate words because there was no space between words in ancient Egyptian writing.

More than 700 hieroglyphs have been found and translated so far.

Communicating in
BRAILLE

This is a method of communication in which letters, words, and numbers are represented as tiny bumps on a page. It allows people who are blind or have low vision (BLV) to read, by using their fingers to feel the bumps.

The Braille method was developed by French inventor Louis Braille in 1824. Braille had become blind as a child, at the age of three. He attended a school for blind children in Paris, France, where he learned about "night writing"—a system of writing using dots, which was designed to help soldiers send messages in the dark.

When he was just 15 years old, Braille took this night writing system and simplified it, creating a method that was far easier to use. His code used a "cell" of six dots to represent each character. He numbered the position of each dot in the cell, starting from the top left and reading downward. The dots could then be either "raised" as bumps on the page or "not raised" (flat). Combining all the different possibilities of a cell's six dots being raised or not gave a total of 64 Braille characters, which could be "read" by a person using their fingertips.

Different languages have their own versions of Braille. Each letter of the English alphabet has its own cell arrangement in Braille, but they are all lower case. To make a letter into a capital, a dot six (a raised dot in the sixth position of a cell) is added in front of the letter. Adding two dot sixes shows that the whole following word should be capitalized.

The cells used to show numbers are the same as those used for the first ten letters of the English alphabet. To make clear that a cell is a number and not a letter, a # sign is used, which raises dots three, four, five, and six.

Some short, everyday words have their own Braille arrangements, which make reading quicker for the reader than if every word were spelled out. Adding a space—an "empty cell" with no dots raised—on either side of a Braille letter means that the cell stands for a word. For example, when there is a space before and after "b" in Braille, it is read as the word "but." Almost all Braille books use these arrangements, which are known as contractions. Today, there are also Braille emojis, which use a 3 × 3 cell, rather than the traditional 3 × 2. These were created by Belgian designer Walda Verbaenen as an experiment, called "Braille meets emoticons."

▼ **READING BRAILLE**
To read Braille, a user gently runs their fingertips over the printed bumps, allowing them to feel which dots are raised and which are flat.

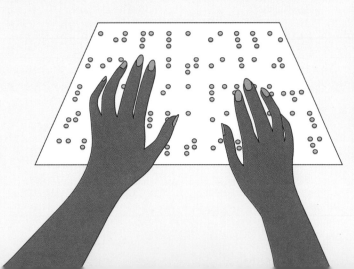

COMMUNICATING IN BRAILLE

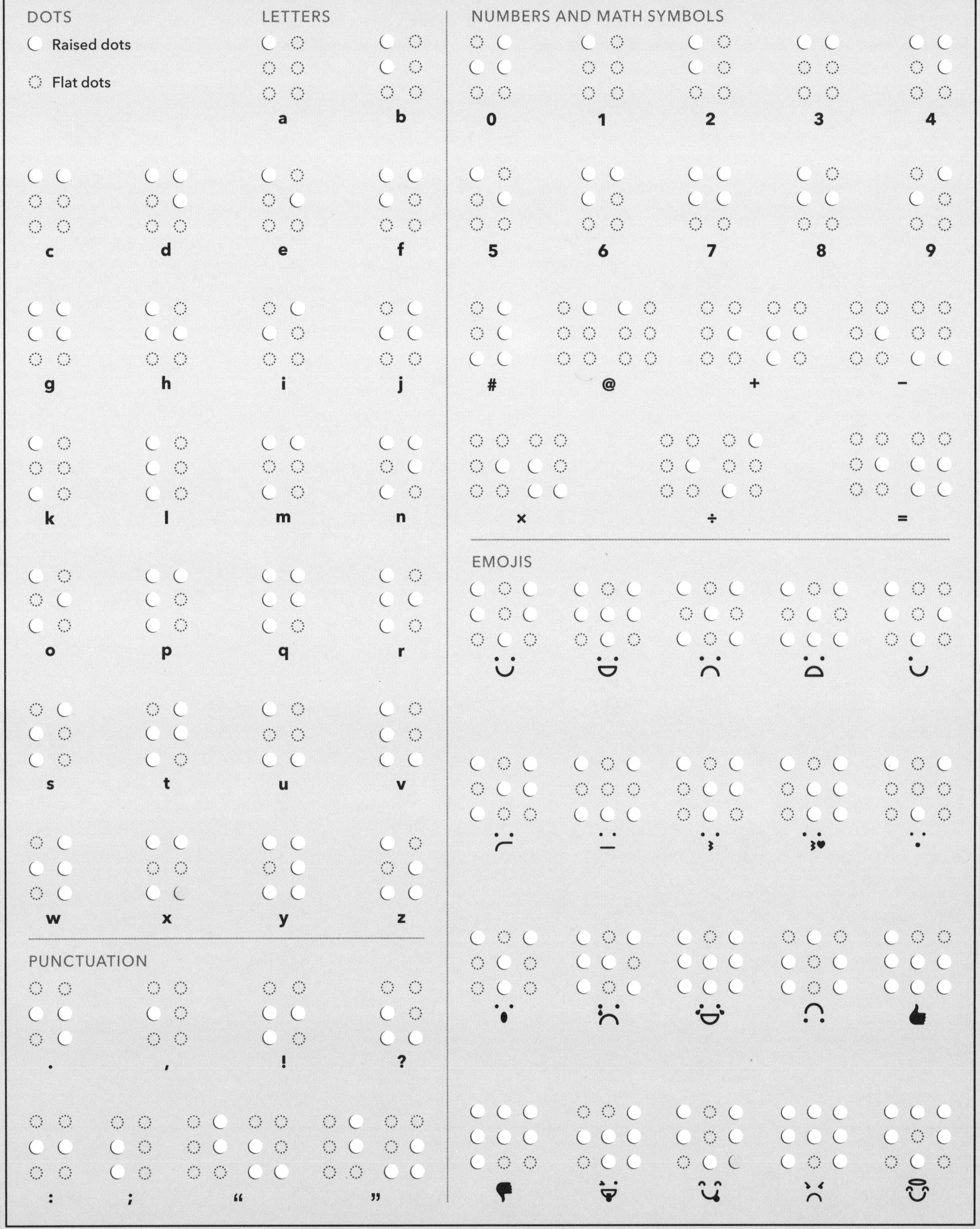

DOTS

○ Raised dots

○ Flat dots

LETTERS

a   b

c   d   e   f

g   h   i   j

k   l   m   n

o   p   q   r

s   t   u   v

w   x   y   z

PUNCTUATION

.   ,   !   ?

:   ;   "   "

NUMBERS AND MATH SYMBOLS

0   1   2   3   4

5   6   7   8   9

\#   @   +   −

×   ÷   =

EMOJIS

205

LETTERS

A	·—	N	—·
B	—···	O	———
C	—·—·	P	·——·
D	—··	Q	——·—
E	·	R	·—·
F	··—·	S	···
G	——·	T	—
H	····	U	··—
I	··	V	···—
J	·———	W	·——
K	—·—	X	—··—
L	·—··	Y	—·——
M	——	Z	——··

NUMBERS

1	·————	6	—····
2	··———	7	——···
3	···——	8	———··
4	····—	9	————·
5	·····	0	—————

PUNCTUATIONS AND SYMBOLS

.	·—·—·—	@	·——·—·
,	——··——	(	—·——·
?	··——··	)	—·——·—
!	—·—·——	+	·—·—·
'	·————·	−	—····—
"	·—··—·	×	—··—
:	———···	/	—··—·
&	·—···	=	—···—

DISTRESS SIGNAL

SOS ···———···

ACCENTED AND NON-ENGLISH LETTERS (IN INTERNATIONAL MORSE CODE)

À Å	·——·—	Ń Ñ	——·——
Ä Ą Æ	·—·—	Ó Ö Ø	———·
Ć Ĉ Ç	—·—··	Ś	···—···
Đ É Ę	··—··	Ŝ	···—·
È Ł	·—··—	Þ	·——··
Ĝ	——·—·	Ü Ŭ	··——
Ĥ Š	————	Ź	——··—·
Ĵ	·———·	Ż	——··—

MORSE
code

For much of history, hand-delivered messages over long distances would take weeks to be received. With the invention of the telegraph, Morse code could be used to send messages in minutes.

In Morse code, each letter, number, or symbol is represented by a unique combination of short or long signals—this could be short or long taps on a telegraph machine (or the dots or dashes on paper while decoding a telegraph message), short or long beeps over short-wave radio, short or long flashes of light, or even short or long puffs of smoke. Each word or sentence is spelled out by the sender and receiver of a message.

Morse code was invented by US inventor Samuel Morse. He had learned about a new phenomenon, electricity, and wanted to use it to communicate over long distances. Between 1835 and 1837, he built a machine to do this—the telegraph. Several other scientists had made telegraphs before, but Morse's was simpler and quicker thanks to the unique way it sent and received coded messages using a single wire. The earliest attempts by Morse to send wired messages featured numbered lists of words. This was refined by Morse and US inventor Alfred Vail, who devised a code of short dots and long dashes for each letter of the English alphabet (always in upper case). The dots and dashes could be sent as electrical signals, through the telegraph wires (and later, wirelessly). A dot was created by pressing a button (or tapping) on the telegraph machine very briefly, while a dash was created by holding the button longer. The person sending a message would convert each letter or number into Morse code, and use the telegraph machine to tap the message in and send it. Then, at the other end of the wire, the message would be received as dots and dashes on a strip of paper. The receiver would decode the message back into letters and words, and the spaces between them.

This system allowed messages to be sent and received almost instantly. A telegrapher needed to learn each combination of dots and dashes by heart, in order to be able to quickly send and receive messages. Telegrams (telegraph messages) were generally kept short because telegraph services were expensive.

A variation of Morse code that includes accented letters is now taught and used globally as International Morse Code by many, including the armed forces of several countries.

The Titanic was the first ship to send out a distress signal in Morse code.

One of the longest messages ever sent in Morse code contained 16,543 words.

SEMAPHORE
signals

In this system of communication, a person holds a pair of flags at different positions, relaying a letter, number, or instruction. A second person at a distance is able to "read" this message.

In the days before modern technology, flag signals enabled people to communicate across distances that were much farther than they could ever shout. The semaphore system was used by ships to "talk" with each other, including in the wars between the ancient Greeks and the Persian Empire around 2,500 years ago. Today, sailors on ships use semaphore signals if they are unable to communicate via radio.

Every letter of the alphabet or number is represented by the unique combination of positions of the two flags in semaphore signals. Flag positions or movements can also represent some general concepts such as "ready to signal" or "error."

To send a message today, a signaler holds the flags in the "attention" position. When the receiver signals "ready to receive," the sender starts moving the flags to form a message. Signalers have to make clear, precise movements with their arms, to ensure that the correct message is sent. Ten of the flag positions have two different meanings—representing both a letter and a number. To be clear which of these is meant, the signaler uses the "numeral" signal before beginning to signal numbers. Similarly, the "J" sign is used to signal the start of letters.

The modern semaphore system grew out of a signaling device created by French inventor Claude Chappe in the 1790s. He built "semaphore telegraphs"— a series of towers topped with a signaling device with two swinging blades or "arms." Each signaler would receive a message, then send it along to the next signaler, allowing messages to be sent between French cities.

Chappe's signaling system was then adapted to be used with handheld flags—each flag signaler held a brightly-colored flag in each hand, and moved them into different positions to represent letters and numerals.

> In ancient Greek, "semaphore" means "apparatus for signaling."

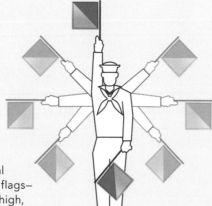

▶ **FLAG POSITIONS**
There are eight potential positions of semaphore flags—up and down, and then high, out, and low for each hand.

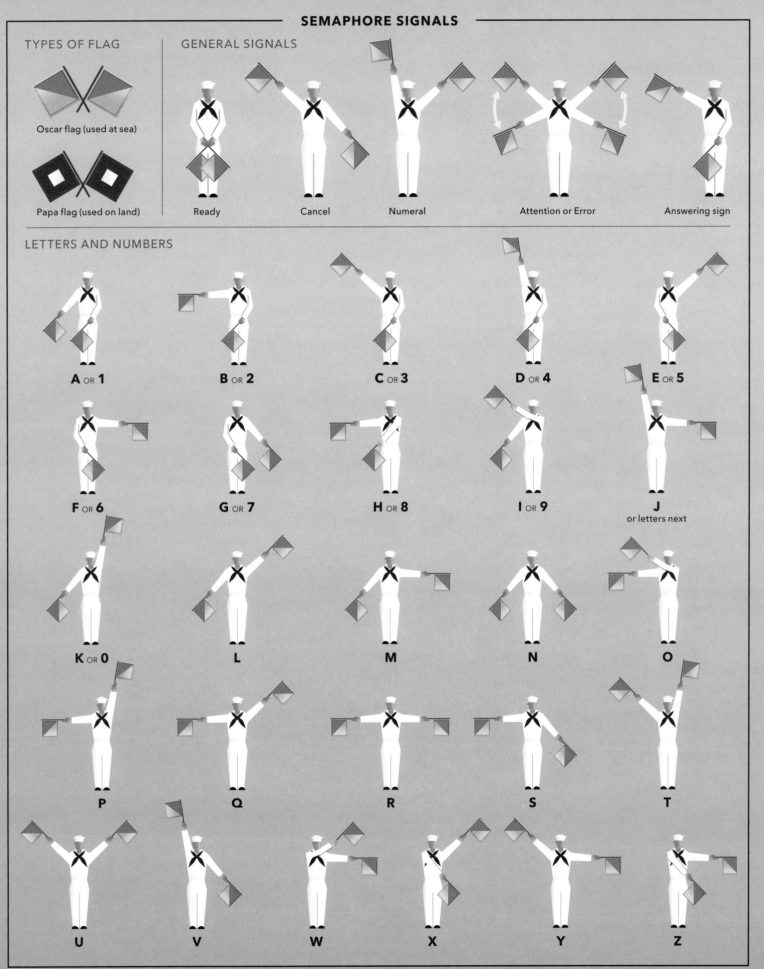

SEMAPHORE SIGNALS

TYPES OF FLAG

Oscar flag (used at sea)

Papa flag (used on land)

GENERAL SIGNALS

Ready

Cancel

Numeral

Attention or Error

Answering sign

LETTERS AND NUMBERS

A OR **1**

B OR **2**

C OR **3**

D OR **4**

E OR **5**

F OR **6**

G OR **7**

H OR **8**

I OR **9**

J
or letters next

K OR **0**

L

M

N

O

P

Q

R

S

T

U

V

W

X

Y

Z

Types of FLAG

Flags come in many different shapes and sizes. A flag can be a powerful symbol of pride and passion for an identity or a nation, city, or organization, often tied to its history.

Flags were originally used by armies to rally their troops during warfare. Today, every country has its own flag, a selection of which are shown on the right. Each of these flags has its own unique design. Some types of design are more common than others.

There are three types of striped flag—bicolors, with a pair of vertical or horizontal stripes in two different colors; tricolors, with stripes in three different colors; and tribar, or triband, with three stripes, two of which have the same color. These colors often carry symbolic meanings. For example, the three colors of the Indian flag represent courage (saffron), peace (white), and growth (green).

Dividing lines on flag designs appear in different ways. Triangle flags are divided by a different-colored triangle, which is usually on the staff side of the flag. Bend flags are divided by a diagonal stripe that can either go from left to right or the other way. A serration is a flag that has areas of two colors, separated by a serrated (zigzag) line.

Some types of flag are classified as cross. These can have different designs of crosses, such as a regular cross in the center or a Scandinavian cross, which is set off-center toward the staff. The saltire type has a diagonal cross, which connects the corners of the flag.

The shape on a flag can be significant to a particular culture, for example the green "Y" shape on the South African flag represents the coming together of people who were previously divided. This has a special meaning in a country with a history of apartheid (discrimination against people of color by separating them from white people and denying them privileges). Flag designs may also be associated with a country's history. For instance, the canton flag of the United States of America has one quarter that is colored differently and features 50 stars, each representing one of the 50 states.

> The study of flags is called vexillology.

▶ **PARTS OF A FLAG**
Flags are usually made of a light material that can blow freely in the wind. The different parts of a flag have specific terms to describe them.

Emblem or charge

Field (background)

Staff

Fly (end farthest from the staff)

The flag of Kiribati

TYPES OF FLAG

BICOLOR

Haiti

Vatican City

Angola

Indonesia

Singapore

Poland

San Marino

Portugal

TRICOLOR

India

Mexico

Guinea

Ecuador

France

Lithuania

Kenya

Lesotho

TRIBAR

Canada

Austria

Argentina

Spain

Honduras

Latvia

Nigeria

TRIANGLE

Vanuatu

The Bahamas

Zimbabwe

South Africa

São Tomé and Príncipe

Guyana

Philippines

BEND

St. Kitts & Nevis

Trinidad & Tobago

Republic of the Congo

Tanzania

Namibia

Solomon Islands

Brunei

PLAIN WITH EMBLEM

Brazil

China

Japan

Somalia

Palau

SERRATION

Qatar

Bahrain

CROSS

Switzerland

Dominican Republic

Dominica

Georgia

SCANDINAVIAN CROSS

Iceland

Denmark

Norway

Sweden

CANTON

USA

Samoa

Australia

BORDERED

Grenada

Montenegro

Sri Lanka

QUARTERED

Panama

SALTIRE

Jamaica

UNIQUE SHAPES AND COMBINATIONS

Bhutan
EMBLEM ON
DIAGONAL
BICOLOR

Antigua &
Barbuda
EMBLEM,
TRIANGLES,
TRICOLOR

United
Kingdom
CROSS ON
SALTIRE

Nepal
TRIANGLE
SHAPE

HISTORY and CULTURE

Human EVOLUTION

Humans are an animal species, with the scientific name *Homo sapiens*. We are the only human species alive today, but a number of others existed before us, and even alongside us.

Human evolution has not been a straightforward process—there is no clear chain showing one species evolving from another since an early ape ancestor. Instead, the group of hominins (modern humans, extinct human species, and human ancestors) is shaped more like a tree, with several branches—featuring different human species—heading off in different directions from the main trunk. The branches evolved in parallel with each other in Africa. Most branches ended when their species died out.

Scientists divide hominins into four main genera (branches), shown by the different colors on the right. At the bottom is the oldest branch—they were forest-dwelling apes that could walk upright, but still spent much of their time living in trees. They were followed by the *Australopithecus* and *Paranthropus* branches, who both walked on two legs as their main way of getting around.

Humans in the *Homo* branch walked upright at all times. This freed their hands to carry and throw things, and allowed *Homo habilis* to make tools. Walking upright also allowed members of the branch to see farther and move out from forests into open grasslands.

Homo erectus was the first hominin to have the same body size as modern humans (*Homo sapiens*). Members of the species moved into Asia, made hand axes, and learned to control fire. Fire meant that they could cook meat and not spend long hours chewing raw foods. As a result, their jaws and teeth grew smaller and brains grew bigger.

Homo sapiens is the only species still living today, but in prehistory, other *Homo* species existed at the same time as us. Most of us might even have some DNA from the Neanderthals (*Homo neanderthalensis*).

The Denisovans are a recently discovered species that have yet to be placed on the human tree.

▶ **CHANGING SKULLS**
Over millions of years, the human brain has developed significantly, becoming much larger. The skull has had to adapt and grow to make space for a large brain.

Australopithecus "southern ape"

Homo habilis "handy human"

Homo erectus "upright human"

Homo neanderthalensis "human from the Neander Valley"

Homo sapiens "wise human"

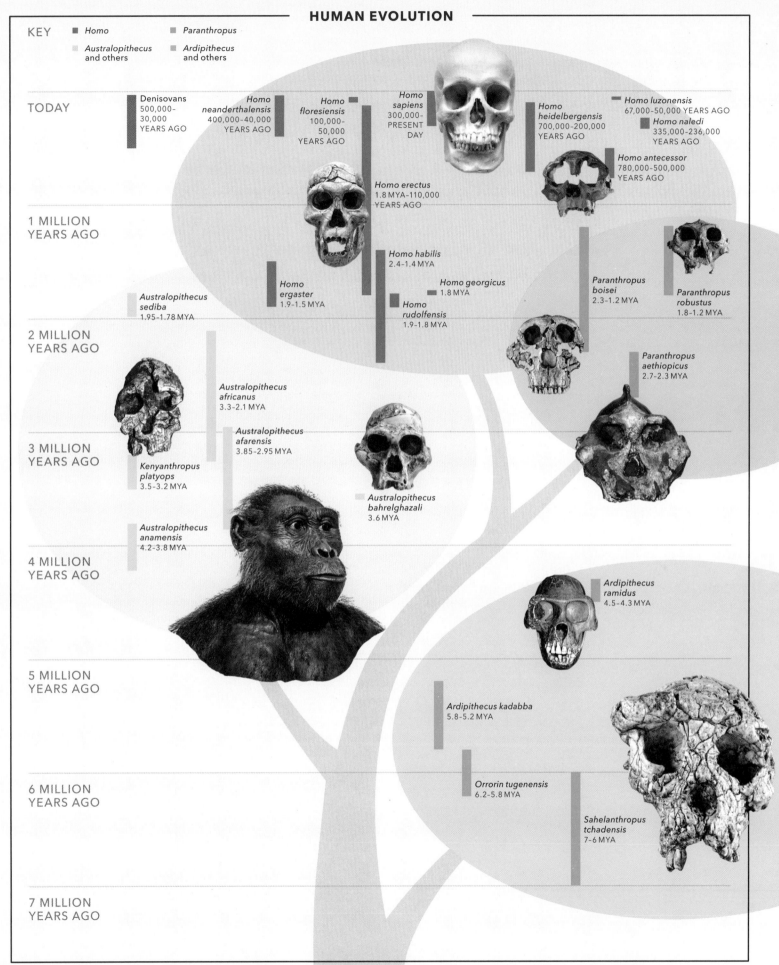

HUMAN EVOLUTION

KEY
■ *Homo*
■ *Paranthropus*
■ *Australopithecus* and others
■ *Ardipithecus* and others

TODAY

Denisovans
500,000–
30,000
YEARS AGO

Homo neanderthalensis
400,000–40,000
YEARS AGO

Homo floresiensis
100,000–
50,000
YEARS AGO

Homo sapiens
300,000–
PRESENT
DAY

Homo heidelbergensis
700,000–200,000
YEARS AGO

Homo luzonensis
67,000–50,000 YEARS AGO

Homo naledi
335,000–236,000
YEARS AGO

Homo antecessor
780,000–500,000
YEARS AGO

Homo erectus
1.8 MYA–110,000
YEARS AGO

1 MILLION YEARS AGO

Homo habilis
2.4–1.4 MYA

Homo ergaster
1.9–1.5 MYA

Homo georgicus
1.8 MYA

Homo rudolfensis
1.9–1.8 MYA

Paranthropus boisei
2.3–1.2 MYA

Paranthropus robustus
1.8–1.2 MYA

Australopithecus sediba
1.95–1.78 MYA

2 MILLION YEARS AGO

Paranthropus aethiopicus
2.7–2.3 MYA

Australopithecus africanus
3.3–2.1 MYA

Australopithecus afarensis
3.85–2.95 MYA

3 MILLION YEARS AGO

Kenyanthropus platyops
3.5–3.2 MYA

Australopithecus bahrelghazali
3.6 MYA

Australopithecus anamensis
4.2–3.8 MYA

4 MILLION YEARS AGO

Ardipithecus ramidus
4.5–4.3 MYA

5 MILLION YEARS AGO

Ardipithecus kadabba
5.8–5.2 MYA

6 MILLION YEARS AGO

Orrorin tugenensis
6.2–5.8 MYA

Sahelanthropus tchadensis
7–6 MYA

7 MILLION YEARS AGO

215

HISTORY
of the world

For most of our history, humans moved from place to place, as hunter-gatherers. Then, around 12,000 years ago, people began to settle down. Settlements grew into civilizations and empires.

People began staying in the same areas once they started farming because it meant planting crops and taking care of them. Permanent homes were built, which often grew into villages, then larger settlements. These were often built near rivers and lakes, so there was plenty of water for the growing crops. The rivers also offered a good option for travel and trade—it was easier to move people and goods around on boats than over land. Farming led to a rise in population.

Villages grew into towns and later cities. This led to the rise of civilizations—highly developed societies, with laws; organized religion, with priests and temples; and buildings designed to look good, not just to keep people safe. Not everyone needed to farm, so some people took on other roles, for example as blacksmiths. This led to the rise of different classes in society, with peasants among the poorest, and monarchs at the top. Trade flourished and record-keeping became important, so writing systems were invented. By 2500 BCE, the Indus Valley people had built complex cities with multilevel buildings, traded goods, and produced elaborate arts and crafts such as

The very first cities grew up in Mesopotamia (modern-day Iraq).

beaded jewelery. Other early advanced civilizations developed in Egypt, China, and Central America.

Civilizations emerged in different parts of the world at similar times. For example, the Minoans were building palaces in Crete in the Mediterranean at the time when Pharaoh Senusret II (1897-1878 BCE) was ruling ancient Egypt. Some civilizations lasted for thousands of years; others, only for a short time. Many were followed by newer civilizations, which built upon what had been created before them.

In some civilizations, the people were ruled by lines of rulers who were related to each other, with power being passed down from one family member to the next. These lines were called dynasties.

Other civilizations fought to take over their neighbors. We call these larger, multi-state groups "empires." Empires existed alongside each other for much of history, and occasionally conquered each other in order to gain land and resources. From the 18th century onward, some European empires, such as the British Empire, covered huge swathes of the world, colonizing many Indigenous peoples. But by the 20th century, most of them had broken apart.

The Olmecs left behind huge carved stone heads.

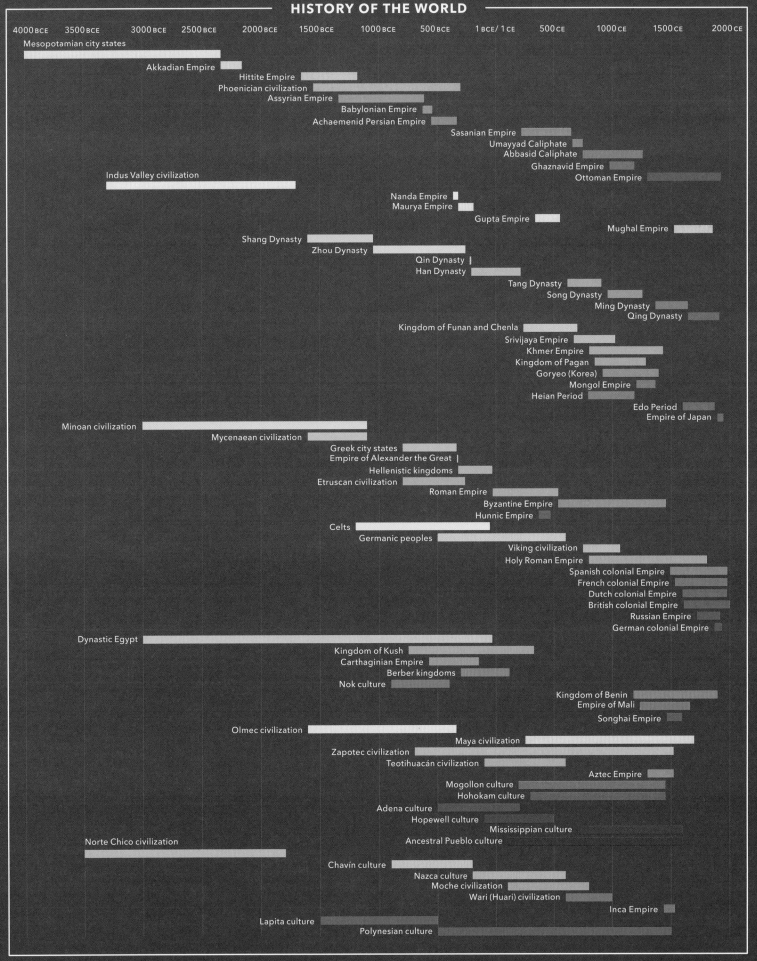

HISTORY OF THE WORLD

4000 BCE 3500 BCE 3000 BCE 2500 BCE 2000 BCE 1500 BCE 1000 BCE 500 BCE 1 BCE/ 1 CE 500 CE 1000 CE 1500 CE 2000 CE

Mesopotamian city states

Akkadian Empire

Hittite Empire

Phoenician civilization

Assyrian Empire

Babylonian Empire

Achaemenid Persian Empire

Sasanian Empire

Umayyad Caliphate

Abbasid Caliphate

Ghaznavid Empire

Ottoman Empire

Indus Valley civilization

Nanda Empire

Maurya Empire

Gupta Empire

Mughal Empire

Shang Dynasty

Zhou Dynasty

Qin Dynasty

Han Dynasty

Tang Dynasty

Song Dynasty

Ming Dynasty

Qing Dynasty

Kingdom of Funan and Chenla

Srivijaya Empire

Khmer Empire

Kingdom of Pagan

Goryeo (Korea)

Mongol Empire

Heian Period

Edo Period

Empire of Japan

Minoan civilization

Mycenaean civilization

Greek city states

Empire of Alexander the Great

Hellenistic kingdoms

Etruscan civilization

Roman Empire

Byzantine Empire

Hunnic Empire

Celts

Germanic peoples

Viking civilization

Holy Roman Empire

Spanish colonial Empire

French colonial Empire

Dutch colonial Empire

British colonial Empire

Russian Empire

German colonial Empire

Dynastic Egypt

Kingdom of Kush

Carthaginian Empire

Berber kingdoms

Nok culture

Kingdom of Benin

Empire of Mali

Songhai Empire

Olmec civilization

Maya civilization

Zapotec civilization

Teotihuacán civilization

Aztec Empire

Mogollon culture

Hohokam culture

Adena culture

Hopewell culture

Mississippian culture

Ancestral Pueblo culture

Norte Chico civilization

Chavín culture

Nazca culture

Moche civilization

Wari (Huari) civilization

Inca Empire

Lapita culture

Polynesian culture

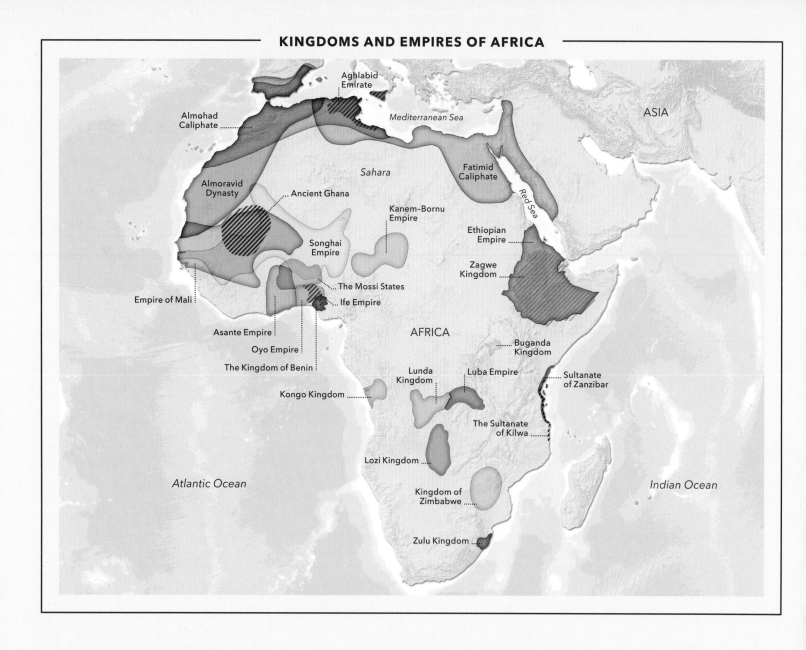

Aghlabid Emirate

Almohad Caliphate

Mediterranean Sea

ASIA

Sahara

Fatimid Caliphate

Almoravid Dynasty

Ancient Ghana

Kanem-Bornu Empire

Red Sea

Ethiopian Empire

Songhai Empire

Zagwe Kingdom

The Mossi States

Empire of Mali

Ife Empire

AFRICA

Asante Empire

Buganda Kingdom

Oyo Empire

The Kingdom of Benin

Lunda Kingdom

Luba Empire

Sultanate of Zanzibar

Kongo Kingdom

The Sultanate of Kilwa

Lozi Kingdom

Atlantic Ocean

Indian Ocean

Kingdom of Zimbabwe

Zulu Kingdom

Kingdoms and Empires of
AFRICA

Africa has been home to many empires and kingdoms. Some of these are shown on the map and chart above, but all have left their mark on the great continent and on the wider world.

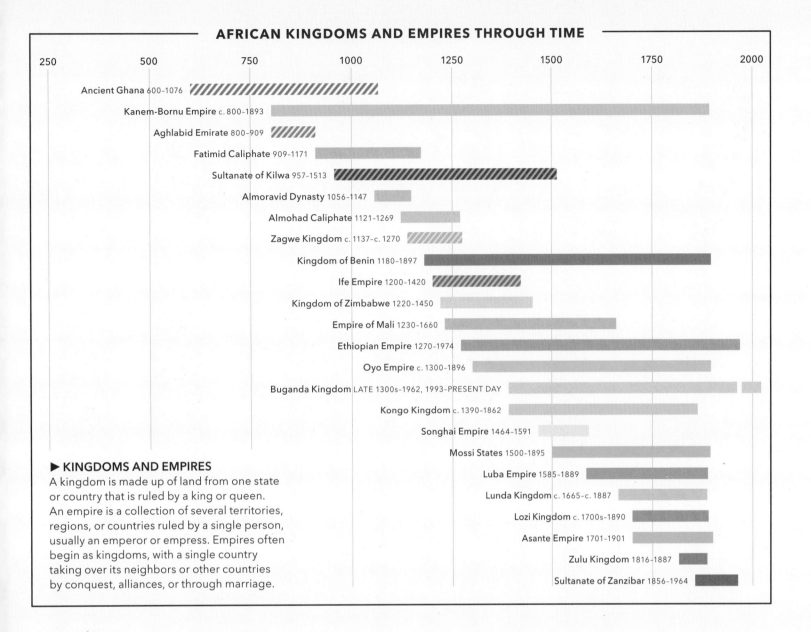

250	500	750	1000	1250	1500	1750	2000

Ancient Ghana 600-1076
Kanem-Bornu Empire c. 800-1893
Aghlabid Emirate 800-909
Fatimid Caliphate 909-1171
Sultanate of Kilwa 957-1513
Almoravid Dynasty 1056-1147
Almohad Caliphate 1121-1269
Zagwe Kingdom c. 1137-c. 1270
Kingdom of Benin 1180-1897
Ife Empire 1200-1420
Kingdom of Zimbabwe 1220-1450
Empire of Mali 1230-1660
Ethiopian Empire 1270-1974
Oyo Empire c. 1300-1896
Buganda Kingdom LATE 1300s-1962, 1993-PRESENT DAY
Kongo Kingdom c. 1390-1862
Songhai Empire 1464-1591
Mossi States 1500-1895
Luba Empire 1585-1889
Lunda Kingdom c. 1665-c. 1887
Lozi Kingdom c. 1700s-1890
Asante Empire 1701-1901
Zulu Kingdom 1816-1887
Sultanate of Zanzibar 1856-1964

▶ KINGDOMS AND EMPIRES

A kingdom is made up of land from one state or country that is ruled by a king or queen. An empire is a collection of several territories, regions, or countries ruled by a single person, usually an emperor or empress. Empires often begin as kingdoms, with a single country taking over its neighbors or other countries by conquest, alliances, or through marriage.

The Ancient Ghana Empire grew rich by trading in gold, textiles, and salt across the Sahara. Islam spread across the north from the late 7th century. The Kanem-Bornu Empire built some of Africa's earliest mosques, while the Almoravid Dynasty made Marrakesh in Morocco its capital and conquered parts of Spain and African territory as far south as Senegal. The richest state was the Empire of Mali. When its ruler Mansa Musa died in the 1330s, he was said to be the wealthiest man that ever lived, due to his control of

Mali's gold and salt mines that had once been part of the Ancient Ghana Empire. Education also flourished in the Empire of Mali, particularly in Timbuktu between the 13th and 16th centuries.

Christianity held sway in other parts of Africa. The Zagwe Kingdom carved great churches from solid rock, and the rulers of the Ethiopian Empire claimed descent from King Solomon. Elsewhere, Indigenous beliefs flourished alongside Christianity or Islam, as in Benin.

But it was commerce that motivated most of Africa's empires. The Kongo and

Zimbabwe kingdoms and the Sultanate of Kilwa, for example, lay on major trade routes to and from Asia, Europe, and North and South America, through which passed gold, silver, ivory, copper—and enslaved Africans. European powers enslaved more than 12.5 million Africans when they colonized the continent. Africa's empires and kingdoms resisted imperialism, most famously the Zulu Kingdom in the late 1800s, but the colonial powers conquered most of them. A few survive to this day, such as the kingdom of Buganda in Uganda.

DYNASTIES OF ANCIENT EGYPT

Palette of Pharaoh Narmer

1st Dynasty
c. 3000–2890 BCE

Pharaoh Khasekhemwy

2nd Dynasty
2890–2686 BCE

Pharaoh Djoser

3rd Dynasty
2686–2613 BCE

Pharaoh Menkaure and queen

4th Dynasty
2613–2494 BCE

Pharaoh Userkaf

5th Dynasty
2494–2345 BCE

Pharaoh Pepy II and his mother Queen Ankhesenpepi II

6th Dynasty
2345–2181 BCE

Pharaoh Sekhemre-Wepmaat Intef

17th Dynasty
c. 1580–1550 BCE

Sculpture of goddess Hathor

16th Dynasty
1650–1580 BCE

Seal of Pharaoh Apophis

15th Dynasty
1650–1550 BCE

Scarab of Pharaoh Nehesy

14th Dynasty
1773–1650 BCE

Pharaoh Sobekhotep V

13th Dynasty
1773–c. 1650 BCE

Pharaoh Senusret III

12th Dynasty
1985–1773 BCE

Pharaoh Hatshepsut

18th Dynasty
1550–1295 BCE

Pharaoh Ramses II

19th Dynasty
1295–1186 BCE

Window grille from a palace of Pharaoh Ramses III

20th Dynasty
1186–1069 BCE

Mummy-board of Henettawy

21st Dynasty
1069–945 BCE

Pendant from tomb of Prince Sheshonq

22nd Dynasty
945–715 BCE

Gold pectoral of Queen Kama

23rd Dynasty
818–715 BCE

Pharaoh Cleopatra VII Philopator

Ptolemaic Dynasty
305–30 BCE

Alexander the Great

Macedonian Dynasty
332–310 BCE

Relief of a winged sphinx

31st Dynasty
343–332 BCE

Shabti (figurine) of Pharaoh Nectanebo II

30th Dynasty
380–343 BCE

Sphinx of Pharaoh Nepherites I

29th Dynasty
399–380 BCE

Papyrus from the reign of Pharaoh Amyrtaeus

28th Dynasty
404–399 BCE

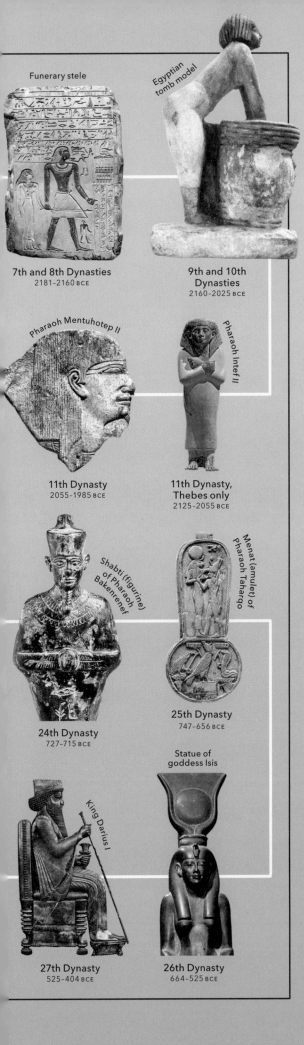

Funerary stele

7th and 8th Dynasties
2181–2160 BCE

Egyptian tomb model

9th and 10th Dynasties
2160–2025 BCE

Pharaoh Mentuhotep II

11th Dynasty
2055–1985 BCE

Pharaoh Intef II

11th Dynasty, Thebes only
2125–2055 BCE

Shabti (figurine) of Pharaoh Bakenrenef

24th Dynasty
727–715 BCE

Menat (amulet) of Pharaoh Taharqo

25th Dynasty
747–656 BCE

King Darius I

27th Dynasty
525–404 BCE

Statue of goddess Isis

26th Dynasty
664–525 BCE

Dynasties of
ANCIENT EGYPT

The banks of the Nile River saw the rise of ancient Egypt, which was ruled over by pharaohs from 33 different dynasties (family lines).

For 3,000 years, ancient Egypt was ruled by pharaohs, making this the longest and most stable system of royal rule in the world. The dynasties to which they belonged are known by their number, except for the last two (when Egypt was ruled by outsiders from Macedonia), which have descriptive names. These dynasties are seen on the left, each represented by an object from its heyday. The pharaohs were seen as gods, whose rule ensured that the Nile River flooded regularly and crops grew in the fields.

Ancient Egypt flourished under a pharaoh in three main periods: the Old Kingdom (3rd–6th dynasties), the Middle Kingdom (11th–14th dynasties), and the New Kingdom (18th–20th dynasties). Old Kingdom pharaohs ruled from Memphis and were buried in pyramids. The capital moved to Thebes during the Middle Kingdom. New Kingdom pharaohs were warriors who created an empire in Asia, and who were buried in underground tombs in the desert. In between these periods were times of unrest, when there was no clear ruler, or when several pharaohs competed to rule.

Most pharaohs were male, including Tutankhamen, the boy pharaoh whose tomb was full of treasure. Female pharaohs included Hatshepsut, a great builder, and Cleopatra VII, who was the ruler before the Romans conquered Egypt.

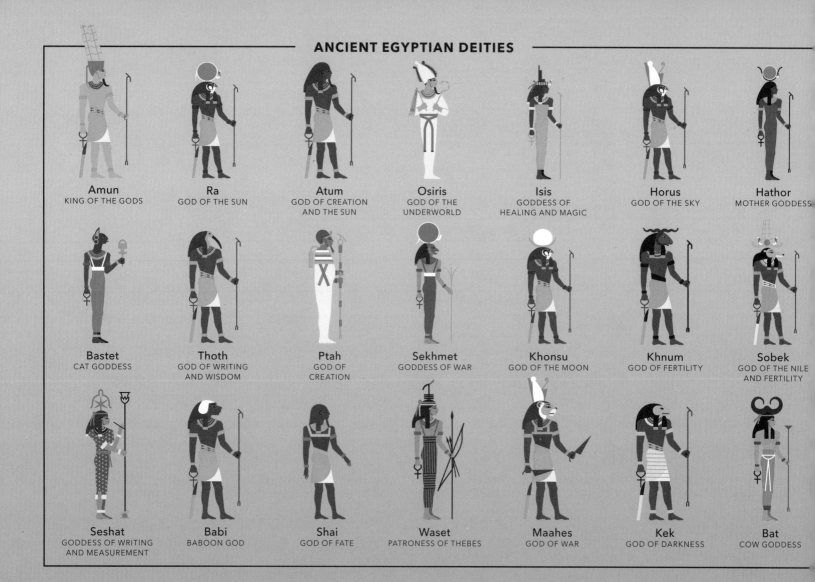

Amun
KING OF THE GODS

Ra
GOD OF THE SUN

Atum
GOD OF CREATION
AND THE SUN

Osiris
GOD OF THE
UNDERWORLD

Isis
GODDESS OF
HEALING AND MAGIC

Horus
GOD OF THE SKY

Hathor
MOTHER GODDESS

Bastet
CAT GODDESS

Thoth
GOD OF WRITING
AND WISDOM

Ptah
GOD OF
CREATION

Sekhmet
GODDESS OF WAR

Khonsu
GOD OF THE MOON

Khnum
GOD OF FERTILITY

Sobek
GOD OF THE NILE
AND FERTILITY

Seshat
GODDESS OF WRITING
AND MEASUREMENT

Babi
BABOON GOD

Shai
GOD OF FATE

Waset
PATRONESS OF THEBES

Maahes
GOD OF WAR

Kek
GOD OF DARKNESS

Bat
COW GODDESS

Ancient Egyptian
DEITIES

The ancient Egyptian civilization flourished for
thousands of years. Religion was very important to
the Egyptian people, and worship of their deities
(gods and goddesses) was a key part of their daily
lives. Over the centuries, many different deities
gained and lost popularity among the people.

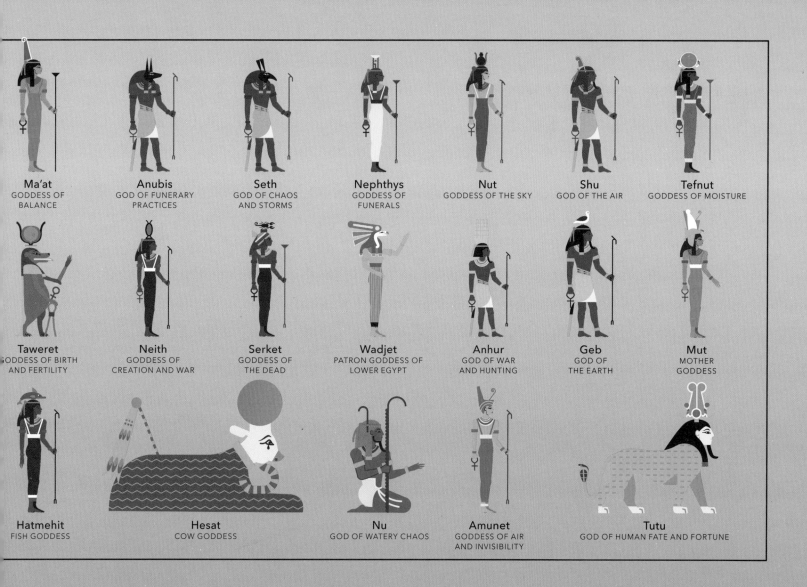

Ma'at
GODDESS OF BALANCE

Anubis
GOD OF FUNERARY PRACTICES

Seth
GOD OF CHAOS AND STORMS

Nephthys
GODDESS OF FUNERALS

Nut
GODDESS OF THE SKY

Shu
GOD OF THE AIR

Tefnut
GODDESS OF MOISTURE

Taweret
GODDESS OF BIRTH AND FERTILITY

Neith
GODDESS OF CREATION AND WAR

Serket
GODDESS OF THE DEAD

Wadjet
PATRON GODDESS OF LOWER EGYPT

Anhur
GOD OF WAR AND HUNTING

Geb
GOD OF THE EARTH

Mut
MOTHER GODDESS

Hatmehit
FISH GODDESS

Hesat
COW GODDESS

Nu
GOD OF WATERY CHAOS

Amunet
GODDESS OF AIR AND INVISIBILITY

Tutu
GOD OF HUMAN FATE AND FORTUNE

Each deity had their own particular role in ancient Egyptian life. Some deities were important to the people, and were worshipped across Egypt, while others were worshipped only in certain parts of the country. A selection of the most important gods and goddesses is shown above.

One god who was worshipped widely was the Sun God, Ra. He was thought to have created himself and the other deities, and was closely linked with Egypt's rulers, the pharaohs. Other deities included Osiris (god of the underworld), Isis (wife of Osiris), and Horus (son of Isis and Osiris). Isis, the most powerful goddess in Egypt, was the deity of magic and healing, and known for bringing Osiris back to life after the god Seth killed him.

The powers and characteristics of the deities, such as strength, were like those of animals that lived in Egypt. So, many Egyptian gods were shown as animals, or with animal heads on human bodies. For example, Sekhmet, the war goddess, had the head of a fierce lioness. In many places, animals linked to gods—including cats, lions, hawks, and cobras—were worshipped as living versions of the gods.

> **More than 2,000 deities were worshipped across ancient Egypt.**

CHINESE
dynasties

For much of Chinese history, the country was ruled over by dynasties—lines of rulers who were related to each other, with power being passed down from one family member to the next.

China has been a world power for more than 2,000 years. The ancient Chinese believed that dynasties ruled thanks to divine approval, called the Mandate of Heaven. Every dynasty since the Zhou claimed to have received the Mandate of Heaven. Some of them ruled for only a few years, others for centuries. Over time, these dynasties saw the rise of inventions such as paper, printing, the compass, and gunpowder, and new religions such as Confucianism and Taoism.

The earliest dynasty was the Xia. They are known only from legends, and historians disagree about whether they really existed. Legend has it that the last Xia ruler was overthrown by Zi Lü, who founded the Shang Dynasty. The Shang used engraved animal shells and bones in religious rituals. These engravings form the oldest known Chinese script, which led to the development of modern Chinese characters.

From 476 BCE, China was divided into many rival kingdoms, which were always at war with each other. By the 4th century BCE, only seven kingdoms remained. In 221 BCE, one of these kingdoms, the Qin, emerged victorious and its ruler called himself Shi Huangdi ("first emperor"). From the Qin Dynasty onward, China was a single enormous country—an empire, with rulers known as emperors.

Shi Huangdi's son was unseated in 206 BCE by Liu Bang, who set up the Han Dynasty. Trade flourished as the Han established the Silk Route, connecting China to the Roman Empire in the west. The next great dynasty to rise was the Tang, under whom China developed new forms of art and poetry, while their vast empire stretched into Central Asia. The Song Dynasty brought arts and literature to the people. The Chinese population prospered and doubled under the Ming Dynasty, and trade flourished, with Chinese porcelain exploding in popularity.

The last Chinese dynasty was the Qing. The Qing were Manchu people, who had helped the Ming Dynasty fight rebels in 1644, then took power for themselves. The empire was large and strong under the Qing for many years, but then grew gradually weaker in the 19th century. In 1912, the Qing were overthrown by a revolution— China became a republic, with no imperial family and no emperor.

The longest-reigning Chinese dynasty was the Zhou, who ruled for almost 800 years.

The first emperor, Shi Huangdi, was buried with 7,000 terra-cotta soldiers.

CHINESE DYNASTIES

Jade plaque
Xia Dynasty
c. 2070–1600 BCE

Engraved tortoise shell
Shang Dynasty
c. 1600–1046 BCE

Kang Hou gui (vessel)
Western Zhou Dynasty
c. 1045–771 BCE

Gold tomb ware
Eastern Zhou Dynasty
c. 770–256 BCE

Spade money
Warring states
c. 476–221 BCE

Jade comb
Eastern Han Dynasty
c. 25–220 CE

Bronze mirror
Xin Dynasty
c. 9–23 CE

Jade burial suit
Western Han Dynasty
c. 206 BCE–9 CE

Kneeling archer
Qin Dynasty
c. 221–206 BCE

Pottery chickens
The Three Kingdoms
c. 220–279 CE

Mural brick
Western Jin Dynasty
c. 265–316 CE

Chicken-headed ewer
Eastern Jin Dynasty
c. 317–420 CE

Clay sculpture of a bodhisattva
The Northern and Southern dynasties
c. 420–589 CE

Wu Zhu (coin)
Sui Dynasty
c. 581–618 CE

Buddhist gold art
Liao Dynasty
c. 916–1125 CE

Black plaque
Southern Song Dynasty
c. 1127–1279 CE

Wooden figure of a bodhisattva
Northern Song Dynasty
c. 960–1127 CE

Stone bowl
Five Dynasties and Ten Kingdoms
c. 907–979 CE

Figurine of a dancer
Tang Dynasty
c. 618–907 CE

Bronze coin
Xi Xia Dynasty
c. 1038–1227 CE

Dragon textile
Jin Dynasty
c. 1115–1234 CE

War helmet
Yuan Dynasty
1279–1368 CE

Enamel jar
Ming Dynasty
1368–1644 CE

Hexagonal teapot or wine pot
Qing Dynasty
1644–1912 CE

Ancient and medieval
INDIA

The subcontinent of India has an ancient and rich history. Home to many of the world's great religions, it has produced some of the finest art and architecture the world has ever seen.

TIMELINE OF ANCIENT AND MEDIEVAL INDIA

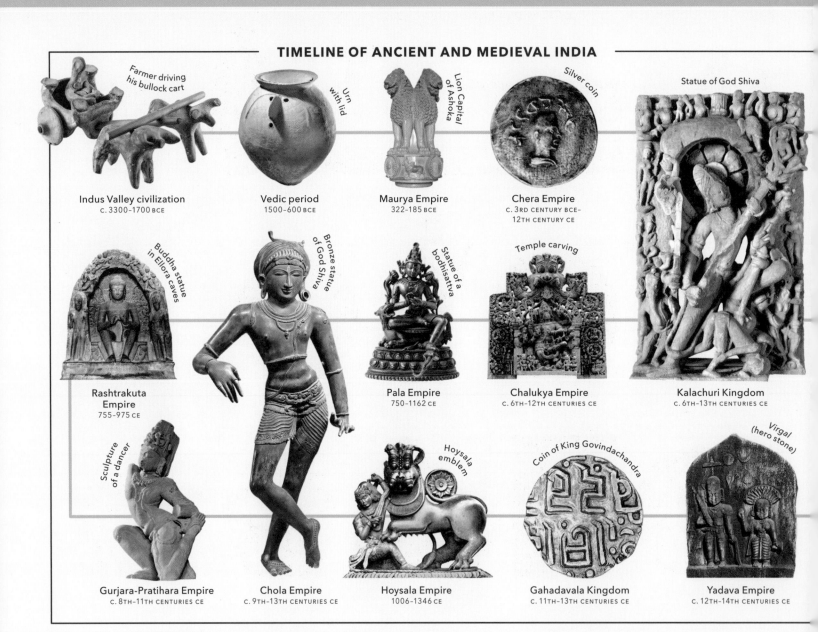

Farmer driving his bullock cart

Indus Valley civilization
c. 3300–1700 BCE

Urn with lid

Vedic period
1500–600 BCE

Lion Capital of Ashoka

Maurya Empire
322–185 BCE

Silver coin

Chera Empire
c. 3RD CENTURY BCE–12TH CENTURY CE

Statue of God Shiva

Buddha statue in Ellora caves

Rashtrakuta Empire
755–975 CE

Bronze statue of God Shiva

Statue of a bodhisattva

Pala Empire
750–1162 CE

Temple carving

Chalukya Empire
c. 6TH–12TH CENTURIES CE

Kalachuri Kingdom
c. 6TH–13TH CENTURIES CE

Sculpture of a dancer

Gurjara-Pratihara Empire
c. 8TH–11TH CENTURIES CE

Chola Empire
c. 9TH–13TH CENTURIES CE

Hoysala emblem

Hoysala Empire
1006–1346 CE

Coin of King Govindachandra

Gahadavala Kingdom
c. 11TH–13TH CENTURIES CE

Virgal (hero stone)

Yadava Empire
c. 12TH–14TH CENTURIES CE

The Indus Valley civilization in what is today India and Pakistan lasted from 3300–1700 BCE. Its people created mud brick buildings, dockyards, and drainage systems; and made clay and bronze sculptures, jewelery, and complex tools, some of which still survive.

Hinduism developed in the Vedic period (1500–600 BCE). By its end, the Maurya Empire had expanded until most of India was under the control of Ashoka the Great (d. 232 BCE). At the same time, Buddhism spread down from the north of the subcontinent.

When the Maurya Empire ended, it broke up into many small states. One, the Kushana Empire, traded with the Romans. The Gupta Empire brought in a Golden Age, with advances in science, art, and literature.

For the next seven centuries, empires and kingdoms such as the Gurjara-Pratihara, Pala, Chola, and Hoysala conquered much of the north, northeast, and south of India

(and Sri Lanka) respectively, leaving behind many architectural marvels, Buddhist and Hindu temples, and artworks. Muslim rulers founded the Delhi Sultanate in 1206, gradually expanding their empire to control much of India for 300 years. Buddhism was fading in popularity by this time, leaving Hinduism and Islam as India's two main religions, which they still are today.

The country name "India" derives from the Indus River.

Satavahana Empire
230 BCE–220 CE
Silver coin

Shunga Empire
185–73 BCE
Fragment of a stupa

Kushana Empire
30–375 CE
Statue of Emperor Kanishka

Vakataka Kingdom
C. 3RD–6TH CENTURIES CE
Bronze statue of Buddha

Pallava Empire
C. 3RD–9TH CENTURIES CE
Statue of God Vishnu

Kadamba Kingdom
C. 4TH–6TH CENTURIES CE
Temple entrance sculpture

Delhi Sultanate
1206–1526 CE
Painting showing Sultan Ala al-Din Khalji

Pandya Kingdom
4TH–14TH CENTURIES CE
Garuda statue

Gupta Empire
320–550 CE
Gold coin

Kakatiya Kingdom
C. 12TH–14TH CENTURIES CE
Sculpture of God Vishnu

Vijayanagara Empire
1336–1646 CE
Ugra Narasimha sculpture

Bahmani Sultanate
1347–1538 CE
Copper coin

MUGHAL

emperors

From 1526 to 1857, a line of Muslim emperors called the Mughals ruled over most of the Indian subcontinent thanks to their military might. They left behind a legacy of stunning art and architecture.

Over the centuries of Mughal rule, eighteen emperors sat on the Mughal throne. The first Mughal emperor was Babur, a Turko-Mongol leader from Central Asia who commanded his forces as they conquered what is now Afghanistan and the north of India. He defeated the sultans of Delhi to set up the Mughal Empire in 1526. When Babur died, he was succeeded by his son Humayun, who was soon forced into exile by the Afghan ruler Sher Shah Suri. Humayun returned in 1555 to reconquer the lost lands and restore Mughal rule in India.

Humayun's son Akbar became one of the greatest Mughal emperors. During his reign, the Mughal Empire stretched from modern-day Afghanistan in the west to the Bay of Bengal in the east. Akbar's effective administrative system held it together. His subjects included followers of religions other than Islam. Akbar encouraged them to practice their religion. He was a patron of the miniature style of painting (vividly colored paintings made with delicate brushstrokes). Court scenes and animals were usually drawn in this style, and so were portraits, as seen in the paintings on the right. His son, Jahangir, who ruled after the death of his father,

> Akbar I was proclaimed emperor at 13.

continued to encourage art and architecture. But it was during the rule of Jahangir's son, Shah Jahan, that many historic buildings, including Delhi's Red Fort and Agra's Taj Mahal, were built. These exceptional examples of Mughal architecture have towering minarets and beautiful arches and domes.

The empire saw its greatest extent under Aurangzeb, a son of Shah Jahan. But his intolerance toward other faiths led to uprisings, and the empire began to decline after his death. Each Mughal emperor after him ruled for only a short time and the empire began to break up. By the 1800s, British colonizers had grown powerful in India. They forced the last emperor, Bahadur Shah Zafar, into exile in 1857, ending over three centuries of Mughal rule in India.

Some remarkable women played a significant role in Mughal history. Humayun's sister, Gulbadan Begum, wrote an account of his life in her book *Humayun-nama*. Jahangir's wife, Nur Jahan, was a powerful force in her husband's court. Shah Jahan's wife, Mumtaz Mahal, worked to help poor people. When she died, the grief-stricken emperor built the Taj Mahal as a grand tomb for her.

> Princess Zeb-un-Nissa secretly wrote poetry under the name Makhfi ("the hidden one").

MUGHAL EMPERORS

Babur
REIGNED 1526–1530

Humayun
1530–1540 AND 1555–1556

Akbar I
1556–1605

Jahangir
1605–1627

Shah Jahan I
1628–1658

Aurangzeb
1658–1707

Azam Shah
1707

Bahadur Shah I
1707–1712

Jahandar Shah
1712–1713

Farrukhsiyar
1713–1719

Rafi ud-Darajat
1719

Shah Jahan II
1719

Muhammad Shah
1719–1748

Ahmad Shah Bahadur
1748–1754

Alamgir II
1754–1759

Shah Alam II
1759–1806

Akbar Shah II
1806–1837

Bahadur Shah Zafar
1837–1857

INFLUENTIAL MUGHAL QUEENS AND PRINCESSES

Gulbadan Begum
1523–1603

Mariam-uz-Zamani
1542–1623

Nur Jahan
1577–1645

Mumtaz Mahal
1593–1631

Jahanara Begum
1614–1681

Zeb-un-Nissa
1639–1702

A selection of six out of many influential Mughal women

Ancient civilizations of
MESOAMERICA AND SOUTH AMERICA

Over thousands of years, many civilizations thrived in the central and southern parts of the Americas. Some of the most famous are the Inca, Aztecs, and Maya.

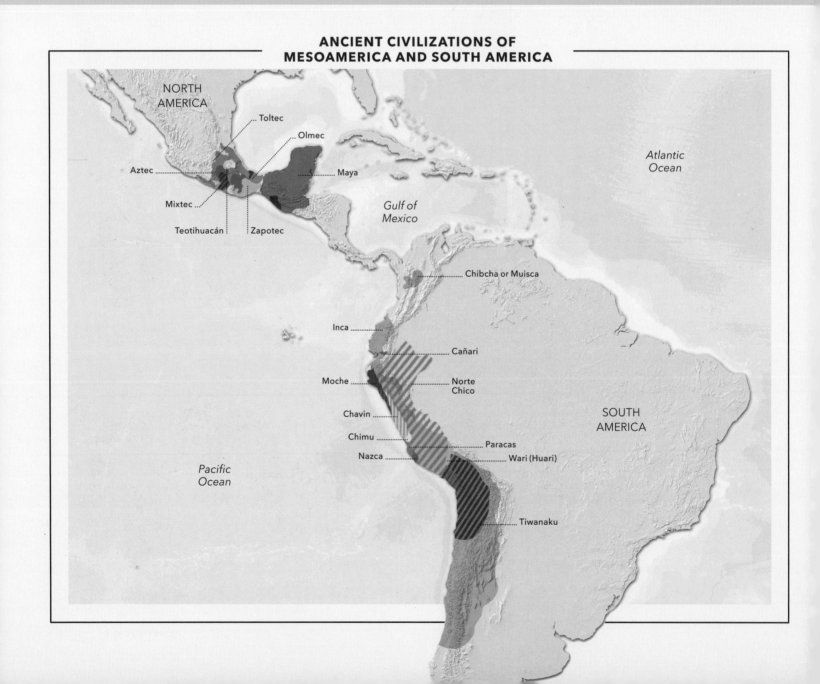

**ANCIENT CIVILIZATIONS OF
MESOAMERICA AND SOUTH AMERICA**

NORTH AMERICA

Toltec

Olmec

Aztec

Maya

Mixtec

Teotihuacán

Zapotec

Gulf of Mexico

Atlantic Ocean

Chibcha or Muisca

Inca

Cañari

Moche

Norte Chico

Chavin

SOUTH AMERICA

Chimu

Paracas

Nazca

Wari (Huari)

Pacific Ocean

Tiwanaku

There were two main clusters of ancient civilizations (highly developed, organized societies) in the central and southern parts of the Americas: one in Mesoamerica (parts of Mexico and Central America) and the other between South America's Pacific coast and the Andes Mountains.

The Norte Chico people, who lived on the coast of modern-day Peru, had one of the first civilizations in these regions. They built cities, such as Caral, with a central plaza and pyramid-shaped temples. The Olmecs were the first civilization in modern-day Mexico, and traded rubber across Mesoamerica. They may have developed the first writing in the Americas. Teotihuacán, centered near modern-day Mexico City, was the site of another civilization. Their city had a population of around 25,000.

The Maya lived in small kingdoms, each based around a city ruled by a king. One of their major cities was Chichén Itzá, which was home to 35,000 people. The Maya built great stepped pyramids as temples to the gods. Some of these also served as tombs to kings, such as the Temple of the Inscriptions at Palenque, where King Pacal was buried.

South America's Inca Empire was highly organized. Cuzco, the capital, was located in the Andes, and as many as 200,000 people might have lived there. Unlike the Inca Empire, the Aztecs of Mexico did not directly rule over the people they had conquered. Tenochtitlán, their capital, was built on an island in the middle of a lake.

These civilizations were destroyed by Spanish colonizers in the early 16th century, who brought with them European diseases such as smallpox and measles. These killed 90 percent of the local Indigenous populations.

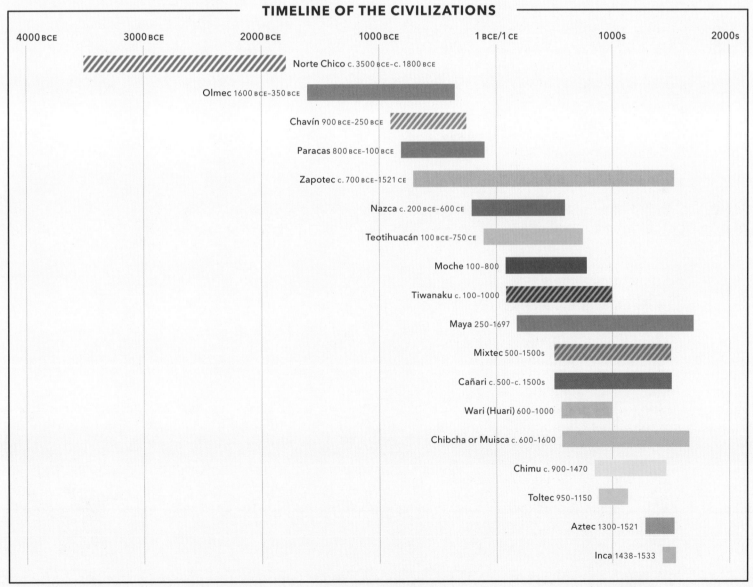

TIMELINE OF THE CIVILIZATIONS

4000 BCE	3000 BCE	2000 BCE	1000 BCE	1 BCE/1 CE	1000s	2000s

Norte Chico c. 3500 BCE–c. 1800 BCE
Olmec 1600 BCE–350 BCE
Chavín 900 BCE–250 BCE
Paracas 800 BCE–100 BCE
Zapotec c. 700 BCE–1521 CE
Nazca c. 200 BCE–600 CE
Teotihuacán 100 BCE–750 CE
Moche 100–800
Tiwanaku c. 100–1000
Maya 250–1697
Mixtec 500–1500s
Cañari c. 500–c. 1500s
Wari (Huari) 600–1000
Chibcha or Muisca c. 600–1600
Chimu c. 900–1470
Toltec 950–1150
Aztec 1300–1521
Inca 1438–1533

Greco-Roman
DEITIES

The ancient Greeks and later the Romans worshipped a large family of deities, who argued, fell in love, and sometimes harmed each other.

According to ancient Greek mythology, the first deity to emerge from the void before creation was Gaia, who gave birth to Ouranos. Gaia and Ouranos had children, including the powerful Titans. These included Kronos and Rhea, who were the parents of the main gods of ancient Greece—Poseidon, Hades, Demeter, Hera, Hestia, and their youngest brother Zeus, who became the king of the gods. There were 12 deities who were mainly worshipped in ancient Greece. They were said to live on Mount Olympus and so were known as the Olympian gods. A family tree of the deities is shown on the right. They had many human characteristics, good and bad, such as empathy, love, and jealousy.

> **Prometheus stole fire from the gods and gave it to humans.**

Zeus was married to Hera, who was also his sister and queen of the gods. Their children included Hebe, Hephaestus, and Ares, but Zeus also had the twins Apollon and Artemis with Leto. Dionysus, the son of Zeus and a mortal woman named Semele, was the youngest of the Olympian gods.

The Romans later worshipped the same gods but gave them different names. Many of the Roman names for the gods became the names of the planets, such as Mars (for Ares); Neptune (for Poseidon); Venus (for Aphrodite); and Mercury (for Hermes).

Kronos / Saturn
KING OF THE TITANS

Rhea / Cybele
QUEEN OF THE TITANS

Poseidon / Neptune
GOD OF THE SEAS

Hades / Pluto
GOD OF THE UNDERWORLD

Demeter / Ceres
GODDESS OF GRAIN

Hestia / Vesta
GODDESS OF THE HEARTH

Persephone / Proserpina
QUEEN OF THE UNDERWORLD

Hephaestus / Vulcan
GOD OF FIRE AND METALWORK

Each entry has two names—the first one is Greek, the second one is Roman

GRECO-ROMAN DEITIES

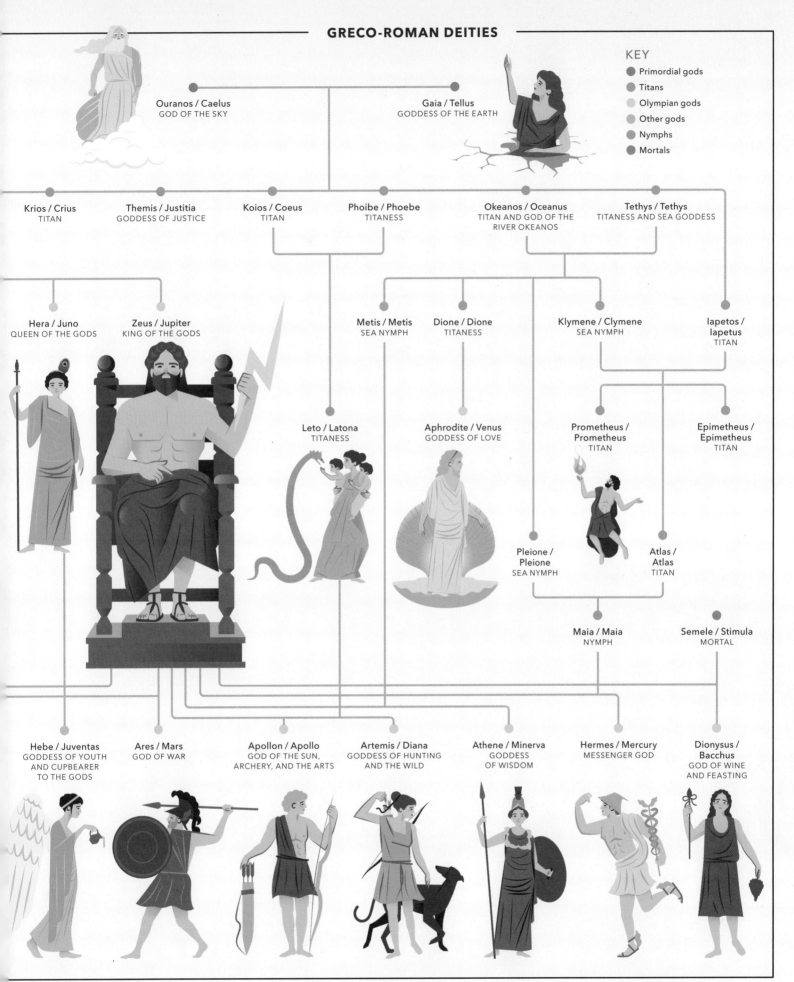

KEY
- Primordial gods
- Titans
- Olympian gods
- Other gods
- Nymphs
- Mortals

Ouranos / Caelus
GOD OF THE SKY

Gaia / Tellus
GODDESS OF THE EARTH

Krios / Crius
TITAN

Themis / Justitia
GODDESS OF JUSTICE

Koios / Coeus
TITAN

Phoibe / Phoebe
TITANESS

Okeanos / Oceanus
TITAN AND GOD OF THE
RIVER OKEANOS

Tethys / Tethys
TITANESS AND SEA GODDESS

Hera / Juno
QUEEN OF THE GODS

Zeus / Jupiter
KING OF THE GODS

Metis / Metis
SEA NYMPH

Dione / Dione
TITANESS

Klymene / Clymene
SEA NYMPH

Iapetos / Iapetus
TITAN

Leto / Latona
TITANESS

Aphrodite / Venus
GODDESS OF LOVE

Prometheus / Prometheus
TITAN

Epimetheus / Epimetheus
TITAN

Pleione / Pleione
SEA NYMPH

Atlas / Atlas
TITAN

Maia / Maia
NYMPH

Semele / Stimula
MORTAL

Hebe / Juventas
GODDESS OF YOUTH
AND CUPBEARER
TO THE GODS

Ares / Mars
GOD OF WAR

Apollon / Apollo
GOD OF THE SUN,
ARCHERY, AND THE ARTS

Artemis / Diana
GODDESS OF HUNTING
AND THE WILD

Athene / Minerva
GODDESS
OF WISDOM

Hermes / Mercury
MESSENGER GOD

Dionysus / Bacchus
GOD OF WINE
AND FEASTING

ROMAN EMPERORS

Augustus
27 BCE–14 CE

Tiberius
14–37 CE

Caligula
37–41 CE

Claudius
41–54 CE

Nero
54–68 CE

Galba
68–69 CE

Otho
69 CE

Vitellius
69 CE

Pescennius Niger
193–194 CE

Didius Julianus
193 CE

Pertinax
193 CE

Commodus
177–192 CE

Marcus Aurelius (with
Verus and Commodus)
161–180 CE

Lucius Verus
161–169 CE

Antoninus Piu
138–161 CE

Septimius Severus
193–211 CE

Caracalla
198–217 CE

Geta
209–211 CE

Macrinus
217–218 CE

Diadumenian
218

Elagabalus
218–222 CE

Severus Alexander
222–235 CE

Maximinus I
235–238 CE

Gordian I and
Gordian II
238 CE

Probus
276–282 CE

Florianus
276 CE

Tacitus
275–276 CE

Aurelian
270–275 CE

Quintillus
270 CE

Claudius II
268–270 CE

Gallienus
253–268 CE

Valerian
253–260

Carus
282–283 CE

Numerianus
283–284 CE

Carinus
283–285 CE

Diocletian
284–305 CE

Maximian (West)
286–305 CE

Galerius (East)
305–311 CE

Constantius I (West)
305–306 CE

Maxenti
(West)
306–312

Valentinian II
(West)
375–392 CE

Gratian (West)
367–383 CE

Valens (East)
364–378 CE

Valentinian (West)
364–375 CE

Jovian
363–364 CE

Julian
361–363 CE

Gallus (East)
351–354 CE

Constantius
337–361 CE

Theodosius I (East)
379–395 CE

Eugenius (West)
392–394 CE

Honorius (West)
393–423 CE

Arcadius (East)
395–408 CE

Theodosius II
(East)
408–450 CE

Constantius III
(West)
421 CE

John (West)
423–425 CE

Valentinian III (We
425–455 CE

Anastasius I (East)
491–518 CE

Romulus Augustulus
(West) 475–476 CE

Zeno (East)
474–491 CE

Julius Nepos (West)
474–475 CE

Glycerius (West)
473–474 CE

Olybrius (West)
472 CE

Anthemius (We
467–472 CE

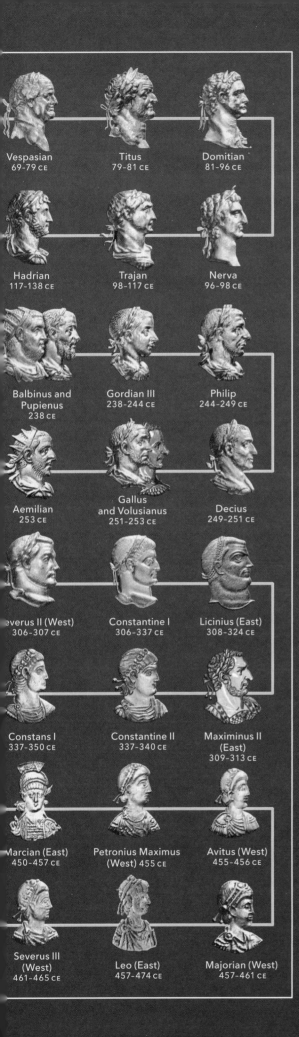

Vespasian
69-79 CE

Titus
79-81 CE

Domitian
81-96 CE

Hadrian
117-138 CE

Trajan
98-117 CE

Nerva
96-98 CE

Balbinus and
Pupienus
238 CE

Gordian III
238-244 CE

Philip
244-249 CE

Aemilian
253 CE

Gallus
and Volusianus
251-253 CE

Decius
249-251 CE

everus II (West)
306-307 CE

Constantine I
306-337 CE

Licinius (East)
308-324 CE

Constans I
337-350 CE

Constantine II
337-340 CE

Maximinus II
(East)
309-313 CE

Marcian (East)
450-457 CE

Petronius Maximus
(West) 455 CE

Avitus (West)
455-456 CE

Severus III
(West)
461-465 CE

Leo (East)
457-474 CE

Majorian (West)
457-461 CE

ROMAN
emperors

Ninety emperors ruled over ancient Rome in a period of 545 years. Sometimes two or more people ruled at the same time.

Rome was the greatest empire ever, stretching from Mesopotamia (present-day Iraq) in the east to England's Atlantic waters in the west. Incredibly it was ruled by a single person—an emperor. Roman emperors commanded the army, made laws, and were great builders. From 27 BCE to 518 CE, the Roman Empire was ruled by a succession of 90 emperors.

Gaius Octavius, also known as Augustus, became the first emperor. Rulers such as Augustus and Hadrian were strong and successful, while others such as Caligula and Nero were so unfit to rule that they were overthrown. After the fall of Nero, there was a civil war, in which four emperors came to power in a single year.

Under Diocletian, the empire was split into Eastern and Western parts with emperors for each, but the Roman Empire was united again under Constantine I, who established the Eastern capital at Byzantium (present-day Istanbul). After his death, the empire split in two once again. The Western Empire weakened over time, and its final ruler, Romulus Augustulus, was overthrown. In the East, the descendants of Anastasius I continued to rule until 1453 as emperors of the Byzantine Empire.

> **Augustus ruled for 40 years—more than any other Roman emperor.**

MONARCHS
of England and Britain

Over a period of more than 1,000 years, nearly 60 monarchs have ruled over England and Britain. Those years have seen conflicts, revolts, battles, and plenty of political skulduggery.

Fifty-nine monarchs have ruled over England and Britain since the first "Ruler of all England," the Anglo-Saxon Athelstan in 927 CE. The Vikings regularly attacked England, and in 1013, the Danish king Sweyn "Forkbeard" ruled for 40 days. Three other Danish kings took the throne between then and 1042, when the Anglo-Saxons regained their kingdom, only to be conquered by the Normans in 1066.

Power shifted to the House of Plantagenet, whose first king, Henry II, ruled England and much of France. Later, Richard "the Lionheart" invaded Southwest Asia (the Middle East) to fight Muslims for Christian dominion of the Holy Land, in brutal wars called the Crusades that devastated the region. The House of Lancaster, a branch of the Plantagenet family, rose to power when Henry IV killed his cousin Richard II.

Henry IV's son Henry V won a decisive battle against the French at Agincourt, which strengthened his rule. Henry VI brought chaos and the Wars of the Roses between the vying dynasties of York and

Lancaster until Lancastrian Henry VII founded a new dynasty, the Tudors. Henry VIII, his successor, unified England and Wales. He also broke with the Catholic Church, becoming head of a new Church of England. His daughter Elizabeth I left no heir, so her cousin, King James of Scotland, founded the Stuart Dynasty, and brought the nations of England and Scotland together. His son Charles I's refusal to give Parliament real power led to two civil wars. He was executed, and England briefly became a republic under Oliver Cromwell until the return of the monarchy with Charles II.

Queen Anne unified England and Scotland into Great Britain but had no heir, so the crown went to the German Hanoverians, who were related to the Stuarts. Nearly 150 years later, Victoria ruled over a global colonial empire. Elizabeth II of the House of Windsor reigned in the mid-20th century, and was followed by her son, Charles III.

> *Elizabeth II's 70-year reign was the longest of any British ruler.*

▶ **ENGLISH ROYAL FAMILIES**
Rule of England, and later, Britain, has been fought over by many royal families.

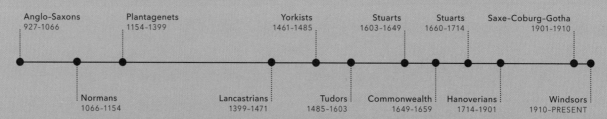

| Anglo-Saxons 927-1066 | | Plantagenets 1154-1399 | | Yorkists 1461-1485 | | Stuarts 1603-1649 | Stuarts 1660-1714 | | Saxe-Coburg-Gotha 1901-1910 |
| Normans 1066-1154 | Lancastrians 1399-1471 | Tudors 1485-1603 | Commonwealth 1649-1659 | Hanoverians 1714-1901 | Windsors 1910-PRESENT |

MONARCHS OF ENGLAND AND BRITAIN

Athelstan
REIGNED 927-939

Edmund I
939-946

Eadred
946-955

Eadwig
955-959

Edgar
959-975

Edward the Martyr
975-978

Aethelred II
978-1013, 1014-1016

Sweyn
1013-1014

Edmund II
1016

Canute
1016-1035

Harold I
1035-1040

Hardicanute
1040-1042

Edward the Confessor
1042-1066

Harold II
1066

William the Conqueror
1066-1087

William II
1087-1100

Henry I
1100-1135

Stephen
1135-1154

Henry II
1154-1189

Richard I
1189-1199

John
1199-1216

Henry III
1216-1272

Edward I
1272-1307

Edward II
1307-1327

Edward III
1327-1377

Richard II
1377-1399

Henry IV
1399-1413

Henry V
1413-1422

Henry VI
1422-1461, 1470-1471

Edward IV
1461-1470, 1471-1483

Edward V
1483

Richard III
1483-1485

Henry VII
1485-1509

Henry VIII
1509-1547

Edward VI
1547-1553

Lady Jane Grey
1553

Mary I
1553-1558

Elizabeth I
1558-1603

James I
1603-1625

Charles I
1625-1649

Oliver Cromwell
1653-1658

Richard Cromwell
1658-1659

Charles II
1660-1685

James II
1685-1688

William III of Orange
and Mary II 1689-1694

William III
1694-1702

Anne
1702-1714

George I
1714-1727

George II
1727-1760

George III
1760-1820

George IV
1820-1830

William IV
1830-1837

Victoria
1837-1901

Edward VII
1901-1910

George V
1910-1936

Edward VIII
1936

George VI
1936-1952

Elizabeth II
1952-2022

Charles III
2022-

Oliver Cromwell and Richard Cromwell ruled as Lord Protectors during the Commonwealth

TYPES OF ARMOR

Helmet

Visor

Mail sewn onto the doublet or a mail shirt

Collar to protect neck

Plackart (torso plate)

Couter (elbow guard)

Vambrace (forearm guard)

Gauntlet (glove)

Cuisse (thigh guard)

Poleyn (knee guard)

Greave (leg guard)

Sabbaton (foot guard)

German steel armor
16TH CENTURY

Gilt copper etchings of Buddhist prayers on helmet

Decorative metal studs

Polished and engraved steel plates

Throat protector

Dragons stood for power, protection, and good luck.

Gold thread embroidery

Coat lined with overlapping metal plates on the inside

Ankle-length skirt

Metal rivets secured metal plates within.

Single-edged blade

Boots were lined with thick fabric.

Flat-heeled boots

Chinese ceremonial armor
18TH CENTURY

238

Mycenaean
bronze armor
15TH CENTURY BCE

Greek hoplite
8TH–4TH CENTURIES BCE

Roman
legionnaire
suit of armor
509 BCE–476 CE

Mongolian
armor
13TH–14TH
CENTURIES

Italian armor
c. 1400–1450
AND LATER

Aztec
ichcahuipilli
EARLY 1540s

Central Asian
lamellar armor
16TH–17TH CENTURIES

Japanese
samurai gusoku
18TH CENTURY

Turkish armor
18TH CENTURY

Jodhpuri mail
armor (India)
18TH–19TH CENTURIES

Kiribati
armor
1800s

Tlingit armor
(North America)
19TH CENTURY

Types of ARMOR

Hard strong clothing that protects the body during combat by blocking or deflecting attacks is called armor. It has many types.

Humans have been fighting each other for thousands of years. Historically, that has meant hand-to-hand combat with weapons such as clubs and swords. If a soldier is fighting other soldiers up-close like this, it is very useful for them to have some sort of protection for their body.

In early days, armor was made by attaching overlapping plates of metal over cloth. Mycenaean bronze armor was made this way and could be quite heavy. Lighter armor, such as the Aztec ichcahuipilli armor, was made by sewing together layers of thick, fibrous cotton and fabric.

Materials used to make armor also varied according to what was available. Jodhpuri mail armor was made by sewing iron rings to fabric or leather. In Kiribati, a Pacific island nation, armor was made from coconut fibers and shells easily available on the island.

Armor was also ceremonial and it was often decorated to reflect the wealth of its wearer. The Mycenaean armor was made of expensive bronze, and its helmet was made of 40–50 boar tusks (long teeth), which could only be afforded by a rich aristocrat. The 18th-century Chinese ceremonial armor shown here was made for a high-ranking official. It is made from steel and copper, decorated with silk, gold, and embroidery.

> An English knight's armor could weigh up to 55 lb (25 kg).

PRESIDENTS OF THE US

George Washington
1789-1797

John Adams
1797-1801

Thomas Jefferson
1801-1809

James Madison
1809-1817

James Monroe
1817-1825

John Quincy Adams
1825-1829

Andrew Jackson
1829-1837

Martin Van Buren
1837-1841

William Henry Harrison
1841

John Tyler
1841-1845

James K. Polk
1845-1849

Zachary Taylor
1849-1850

Millard Fillmore
1850-1853

Franklin Pierce
1853-1857

James Buchanan
1857-1861

Abraham Lincoln
1861-1865

Andrew Johnson
1865-1869

Ulysses S. Grant
1869-1877

Rutherford B Hayes
1877-1881

James A. Garfield
1881

Chester A. Arthur
1881-1885

Grover Cleveland
1885-1889, 1893-1897

Benjamin Harrison
1889-1893

William McKinley
1897-1901

Theodore Roosevelt
1901-1909

William Howard Taft
1909-1913

Woodrow Wilson
1913-1921

Warren G. Harding
1921-1923

Calvin Coolidge
1923-1929

Herbert Hoover
1929-1933

Franklin D. Roosevelt
1933-1945

Harry S. Truman
1945-1953

Dwight D. Eisenhower
1953-1961

John F. Kennedy
1961-1963

Lyndon B. Johnson
1963-1969

Richard M. Nixon
1969-1974

Gerald Ford
1974-1977

Jimmy Carter
1977-1981

Ronald Reagan
1981-1989

George H. W. Bush
1989-1993

Bill Clinton
1993-2001

George W. Bush
2001-2009

Barack Obama
2009-2017

Donald Trump
2017-2021

Joe Biden
2021-

US Presidents at the time of publication of this book

PRESIDENTS
of the US

The government of the United States of America is led by a president, who is elected by the people and their representatives. There have been 46 US presidencies since the very first one in 1789.

On July 4, 1776, following the American Revolution (1775-1783), 13 British colonies in North America declared their independence and called themselves the United States of America. They set up a government and, on February 4, 1789, they elected George Washington as the first president. It was the president's job to lead the executive branch of the country's government. The executive is responsible for enforcing laws, running the economy, and negotiating treaties with other nations.

There was a clear link between the first four presidents, who came to be known as the founding leaders. John Adams, Thomas Jefferson, and James Madison all served in Washington's cabinet.

In the early years, a father and son each became president. John Adams became the second president in 1797. In 1825, John Quincy Adams, his son, became the sixth president. In more recent times, George H. W. Bush held office from 1989 to 1993. His son, George W. Bush, was president from 2001 to 2009.

US presidents usually serve terms of four years. However, there were three different presidents in office in 1841,

and again in 1881. When William Henry Harrison took over from Martin Van Buren in 1841, he served for only 31 days before becoming the first president to die in office. He was succeeded by his vice president, John Tyler. In 1881, Rutherford Hayes was succeeded by James Garfield, who was assassinated. His vice president, Chester A. Arthur, then became the 21st president.

Theodore Roosevelt was the 25th president, and the youngest to take office—at the age of 42. A distant cousin of his, Franklin D. Roosevelt, who was elected four times in succession, spent the most days in office—4,423. After Dwight D. Eisenhower became president in 1953, the law was amended to limit the number of terms anyone could be president to two.

In 2009, Barack Obama became the first Black president. In 2021, Joe Biden became the oldest president to take office. Though Joe Biden is known as the 46th president, because Grover Cleveland was in office on two separate occasions, only 45 different men have been US president to date, as seen on the left.

Twenty-one presidents have served two terms.

Two presidents survived assassination attempts: Roosevelt in 1912 and Reagan in 1981.

ART MOVEMENTS

*The Miracle of the Child
Falling From the Balcony*
by Simone Martini
EARLY ITALIAN RENAISSANCE
13TH–16TH CENTURIES

The Arnolfini Portrait
by Jan van Eyck
NORTHERN RENAISSANCE
c. 1420–1550

Creation of Adam
by Michelangelo
HIGH RENAISSANCE
c. 1420–1550

*Rudolf II of Hapsburg
as Vertumnus*
by Giuseppe Arcimboldo
MANNERISM
c. 1420–1550

*Self-Portrait as Saint Catherine of
Alexandria* by Artemisia Gentileschi
ITALIAN BAROQUE
17TH–18TH CENTURIES

The Night Watch
by Rembrandt van Rijn
DUTCH BAROQUE
17TH–18TH CENTURIES

*Portrait of Madame
de Pompadour*
by François Boucher
FRENCH ROCOCO
18TH–19TH CENTURIES

L'Allegro
by Thomas Cole
ROMANTICISM
1800–1850

Chestnut Tree in Blossom
by Pierre-Auguste Renoir
IMPRESSIONISM
1867–1886

*Madam Stuart Merrill–
Mysteriosa* by Jean Delville
SYMBOLISM
18TH–19TH CENTURIES

Mäda Primavesi
by Gustav Klimt
FIN DE SIÈCLE
1890–1910

The Starry Night
by Vincent van Gogh
POST-IMPRESSIONISM
1890–1920

The Black Women
by Marianne von Werefkin
EXPRESSIONISM
1905–1920

Still Life With a Guitar
by Juan Gris
CUBISM
1910s–1935

Lobster Fishermen
by Marsden Hartley
AMERICAN MODERNISM
1910s–1935

*Construction for Noble
Ladies* by Kurt Schwitters
DADAISM
1917–1920s

Oath of the Horatii
by Jacques-Louis David
NEOCLASSICISM
c. 1750–1850

Girl Screening Grain
by Gustave Courbet
REALISM
1840s–20TH CENTURY

Rooftops, Paris
by Henry Lyman Saÿen
FAUVISM
1890–1920

A Center
by Wassily Kandinsky
ABSTRACT ART
1905–1920

Mobile Device
by Pierre Roy
SURREALISM
1917–1920s

World's Fair Mural
by James Rosenquist
POP ART
1950s ONWARD

A selection of some of the many Western art movements

ART
movements

Humans have been creating art for thousands of years as a way of making beautiful things and of sharing ideas and beliefs.

For the last thousand years, the story of Western art has largely been one of a series of "movements," or styles of painting, that follow each other. Sometimes, these movements have complemented each other; often, they have been a radical change of style. The Renaissance, which began in Italy, saw artists create increasingly realistic paintings, usually on religious or mythological themes. The Mannerist movement that followed did this too, in a more stylized way. Baroque was darker in tone, while Rococo was lighter and less serious. Both often focused on portraiture, in contrast to the more colorful Neoclassicism, which celebrated ancient Greece and Rome. In the early 19th century, Romanticism looked back to an imagined and happy past, and Realism depicted gritty daily life.

The Impressionists were obsessed with the ever-changing nature of light; the Post-Impressionists, Expressionists, Fauvists, Symbolists, Fin de Siècle, and Abstract artists explored emotions and ideas. Surrealists looked at the mysteries of the human mind, while Cubists, Pop Artists, and Dadaists painted the world in new, surprising, and sometimes funny ways.

> The term Renaissance comes from the French word for "rebirth".

Styles of
ARCHITECTURE

Architecture is the designing and building of a beautiful and sturdy structure. It requires both artistic skill and a grasp of scientific principles.

The earliest buildings were simple shelters, used to keep people dry and out of the wind. Later, as more advanced and permanent civilizations grew up, structures slowly became more elaborate. Across history, many amazing buildings have been constructed in different styles of architecture—some of these old and new architectural marvels are shown here.

At first, buildings were often designed for religious reasons, such as temples for worship, or as palaces and castles for the nobility. They were also made from materials available locally—for example, the Ziggurat of Ur in Mesopotamia (modern-day Iraq) was made not of large stones but of clay bricks, because clay was easily available in the region.

Around the world, different cultures developed their own building styles. The Konark Sun temple of India was built in the 13th century, a few years before construction began for the Florence Cathedral in Italy. Both are places of worship but they look nothing alike. The Konark Sun temple is built of stone and designed in the shape of a chariot drawn by horses, while the Florence Cathedral has the largest brick dome ever constructed.

Today, modern technology allows architects to design structures that reach high into the sky—such as the Chrysler Building in the US—with strong steel supports to hold them up. The development of newer materials has also allowed architects to explore new shapes, such as the Sydney Opera House in Australia, which was built with a series of concrete sails on its roof.

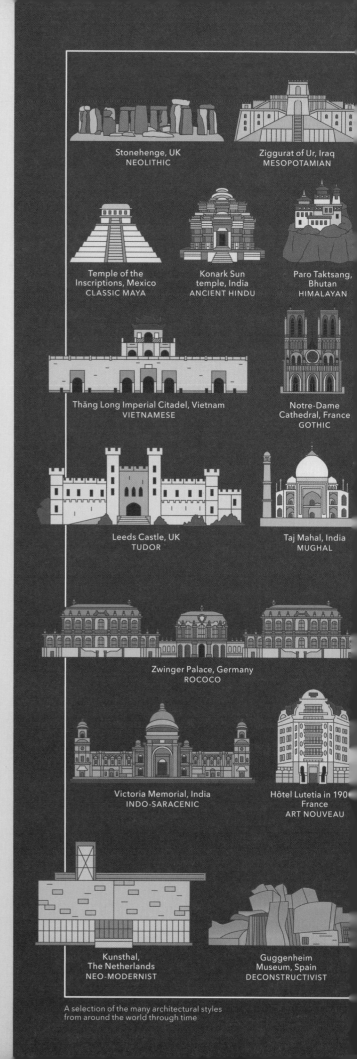

Stonehenge, UK
NEOLITHIC

Ziggurat of Ur, Iraq
MESOPOTAMIAN

Temple of the Inscriptions, Mexico
CLASSIC MAYA

Konark Sun temple, India
ANCIENT HINDU

Paro Taktsang, Bhutan
HIMALAYAN

Thăng Long Imperial Citadel, Vietnam
VIETNAMESE

Notre-Dame Cathedral, France
GOTHIC

Leeds Castle, UK
TUDOR

Taj Mahal, India
MUGHAL

Zwinger Palace, Germany
ROCOCO

Victoria Memorial, India
INDO-SARACENIC

Hôtel Lutetia in 190 France
ART NOUVEAU

Kunsthal, The Netherlands
NEO-MODERNIST

Guggenheim Museum, Spain
DECONSTRUCTIVIST

A selection of the many architectural styles from around the world through time

STYLES OF ARCHITECTURE

Great temple at Abu Simbel, Egypt
ANCIENT EGYPTIAN

The Great Bath, Pakistan
HARAPPAN

Parthenon, Greece
ANCIENT GREEK

Colosseum, Italy
ANCIENT ROMAN

Tāq Kasrā, Iraq
PERSIAN

Great Stupa at Sanchi, India
ANCIENT BUDDHIST

Hagia Sophia, Türkiye (Turkey)
BYZANTINE

Great Mosque of Samarra, Iraq
ISLAMIC

Great Mosque of Kairouan, Tunisia
MOORISH

Angkor Wat, Cambodia
KHMER

Basilica of St. Sernin, France
ROMANESQUE

Church of Saint George (Lalibela), Ethiopia
ETHIOPIAN

Temple of Heaven, China
MING DYNASTY

King's Palace, Rwanda
WEST AFRICAN AND BANTU

Tāne-nui-ā-Rangi, New Zealand
MĀORI

Florence Cathedral, Italy
RENAISSANCE

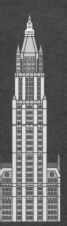

Woolworth Building, USA
NEO-GOTHIC

Royal Palace of Amsterdam, The Netherlands
BAROQUE

Independence Hall, USA
AMERICAN COLONIAL

Bacon's Castle, USA
JACOBEAN

Himeji Castle, Japan
EDO PERIOD

US Capitol, USA
NEOCLASSICAL

Federal Hill, USA
FEDERAL

Metropolitan Museum of Art, USA
BEAUX ARTS

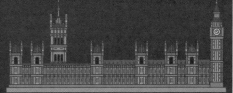

Palace of Westminster and the Houses of Parliament, UK
VICTORIAN

Seagram Building, USA
INTERNATIONAL STYLE

National Assembly in Dhaka, Bangladesh
LATE MODERNIST

Goetheanum, Switzerland
EXPRESSIONIST

MI6 Building, UK
POST MODERNIST

Sydney Opera House, Australia
MODERN EXPRESSIONIST

Chrysler Building, USA
ART DECO

Heydar Aliyev Cultural Center, Azerbaijan
PARAMETRICIST

245

MUSICAL
instruments

The earliest musical instruments made simple sounds, and were used while hunting or to warn others. Over time, instruments became far more complicated, able to make a huge range of different sounds.

Musical instruments are organized into groups based on how they produce a sound. These groups are: woodwind, brass, keyboard, string, and percussion.

Woodwind instruments have mouthpieces, which make a sound when we blow into them. This is done by blowing across a hole (for a flute or a shehnai), or by blowing into a mouthpiece that has a reed inside it (as in a clarinet or an oboe). The reed vibrates against wood or another reed, creating a smooth, slightly buzzing effect. Different musical notes are made by holding down different keys or by covering different holes on the body of the instrument, which changes the strength and flow of air being blown into the mouthpiece.

Keyboard instruments have a range of keys, which each play a different note. The notes can be created in different ways. In a piano or a harmonium, each key causes a hammer to hit a string, while in an organ, each key pushes air through a tuned pipe.

Brass instruments, such as a tuba or trombone, are defined by the way the sound is made and not by whether the instrument is made from brass. These instruments are blown into, like the woodwinds, but the instrument itself is made from metal, which creates a very different sound. The mouthpiece is usually cup-shaped, and the player must purse and vibrate their lips in order to produce a note. Different notes are created by moving the lips, and by pressing different keys.

String instruments make a sound when their strings are plucked (as on a guitar), or when a bow is pulled across them (like a cello). Different notes are made by holding the strings down at certain points, to make the strings shorter.

Percussion instruments make sounds when they are struck, either with the hands or with a stick or beater of some sort. Some forms of percussion are tuned, and can play different notes (like a xylophone); others make sound effects without playing any particular note (like cymbals).

As well as these five traditional groups of instruments, we now have more recent, experimental types of musical instruments, which are usually electronic—they produce sounds using computerized effects. Some examples include the DJ turntable, the Eigenharp, and the theremin.

The oldest known musical instrument, a bone-flute, is 60,000 years old.

The study of musical instruments and their classification is called organology.

WOODWIND

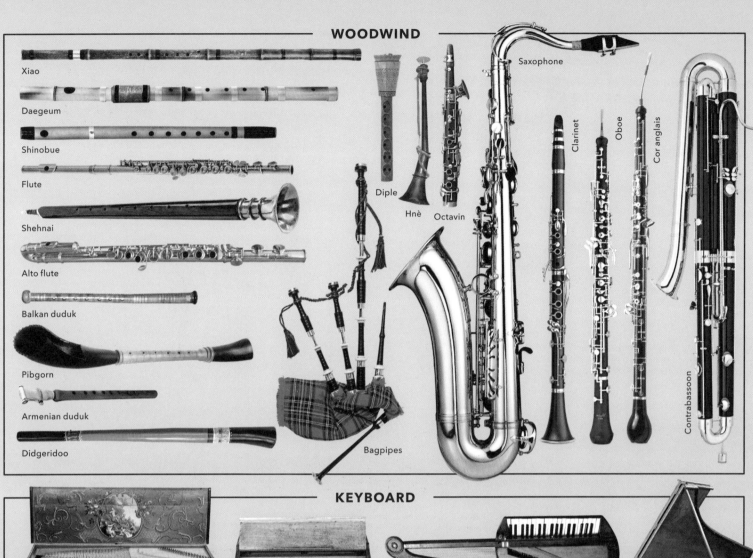

Xiao

Daegeum

Shinobue

Flute

Shehnai

Alto flute

Balkan duduk

Pibgorn

Armenian duduk

Didgeridoo

Diple

Hnè

Octavin

Bagpipes

Saxophone

Clarinet

Oboe

Cor anglais

Contrabassoon

KEYBOARD

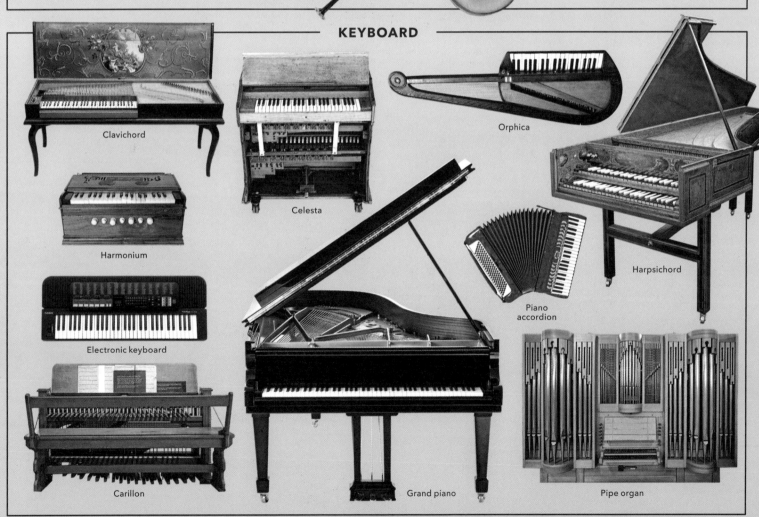

Clavichord

Harmonium

Electronic keyboard

Carillon

Celesta

Orphica

Grand piano

Piano accordion

Harpsichord

Pipe organ

BRASS

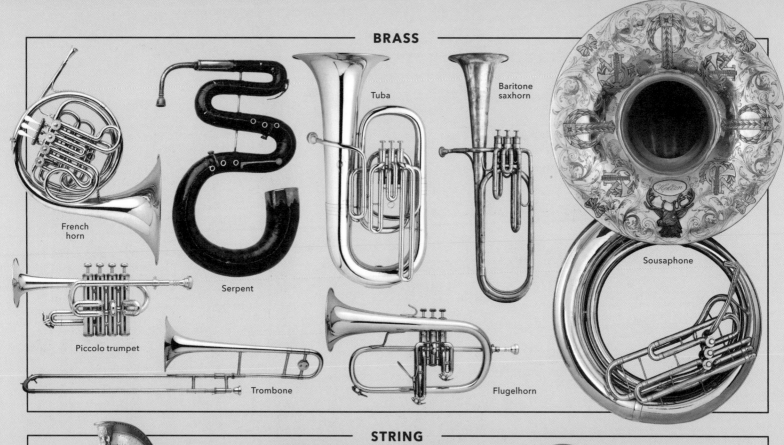

French horn

Serpent

Tuba

Baritone saxhorn

Sousaphone

Piccolo trumpet

Trombone

Flugelhorn

STRING

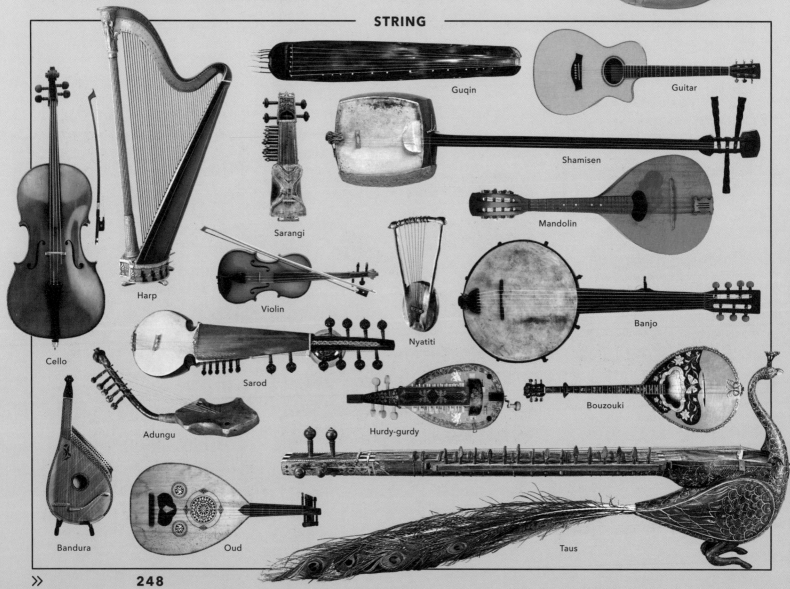

Guqin

Guitar

Shamisen

Harp

Sarangi

Mandolin

Violin

Nyatiti

Banjo

Cello

Sarod

Hurdy-gurdy

Bouzouki

Adungu

Bandura

Oud

Taus

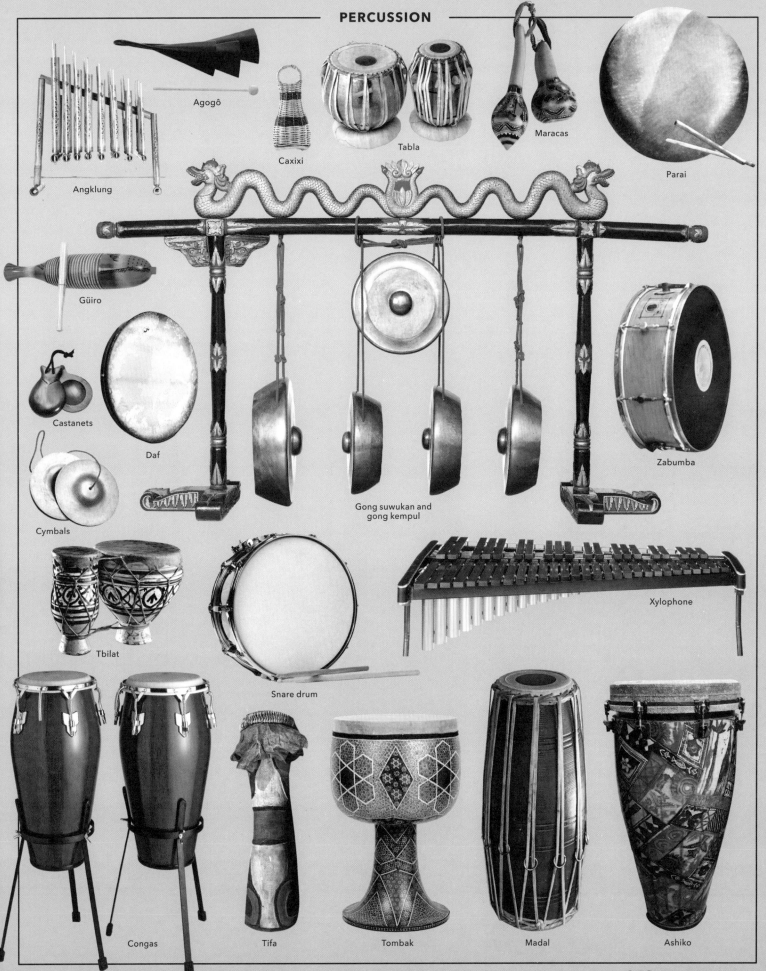

Angklung

Agogô

Caxixi

Tabla

Maracas

Parai

Güiro

Castanets

Daf

Gong suwukan and gong kempul

Zabumba

Cymbals

Tbilat

Snare drum

Xylophone

Congas

Tifa

Tombak

Madal

Ashiko

SECTIONS OF A SYMPHONY ORCHESTRA

PERCUSSION

Marimba

Timpani

Cymbals

BRASS

Horn

Trumpet

Trombone

WOODWIND

Piccolo

Flute

Oboe

Bass clarinet

Clarinet

Bassoon

Cor anglais

Grand piano

STRINGS

Harp

First violin

Second violin

Viola

Cello

Conductor

Chimes

Bass drum

Tuba

Contrabassoon

Double bass

The
ORCHESTRA

The main sections of a typical orchestra are strings, woodwind, brass, and percussion, with the strings often accounting for more than half the total instruments.

Just as a choir includes a variety of different voices, the wide-ranging sounds of the instruments in an orchestra are combined to create a rich, balanced musical experience. Wherever an orchestra plays, it always follows the same general seating plan. The arrangement places similar instruments together and puts the quieter instruments at the front and the louder instruments at the back.

A large-scale orchestra may have as many as 30 violins.

The four main sections—strings, woodwinds, brass, and percussion—are arranged in arcs, so all the musicians can see the conductor. Stringed instruments, including violins, violas, cellos, and bass, are near the front. The woodwinds, with flutes, clarinets, and bassoons, sit behind. The brass section comes next, with trumpets, trombones, and horns. Then, right at the back, is the percussion section, with timpani and cymbals. This placement has existed since the 1830s, when symphony orchestras were first established.

The word "orchestra" can describe two different ensembles; a symphony orchestra, which plays larger venues and can include up to 100 instruments, and a chamber orchestra, which plays smaller venues and usually has 40 instruments.

Musical
NOTES

Music is a combination of sounds, rhythms, and melodies that can be written down using lines, dots, and symbols. These notations show exactly when and how each note should be played.

Music is written on sets of lines, which are called staves. Musical notes are shown as little ovals on or in between the lines. Once a clef is added to the stave, we can work out which note is which by looking at the line or space it is positioned on or in.

The notes have names, which are the letters of the alphabet from A to G (or sometimes the sequence *do, re, mi, fa, so, la, ti*). They can also be written in Braille for blind people.

Notes are drawn differently to show how long they should be physically held for—some are solid black while others are hollow outlines. Shorter notes such as quavers can be joined together by beams, if there are a lot of them. Each length of note also has an equivalent-length rest. These rests are used to show when there is a gap in the music and nothing should be played.

Other notation is used to show whether notes should smoothly blend into each other, or stand out individually. Time signatures show how many beats there are in each bar (section) of the music. The beat is a steady, constant pulse that underlies a whole piece of music—a little like a heartbeat. The time signature 3 over 4 shows that there are three crotchets in each bar.

Music can be played in different keys (scales)—groups of pitches. In a piece of music these are indicated with a key signature, which shows the sharps and flats a musician will need to play. Any notes outside the key signature are shown with accidentals on the stave.

The earliest known musical notation is from 1400 BCE.

Key signature

Allegro means that this should be played fast.

The slur here shows that these notes should smoothly blend into each other.

The clef is the first thing shown on the stave.

Accidental

Allegro

▶ HOW TO READ MUSIC
Every single element of a written piece of music tells the musician performing it something about how the music should be played.

mp

Time signature shows the number of beats in a bar.

Vertical lines show where each bar starts and ends.

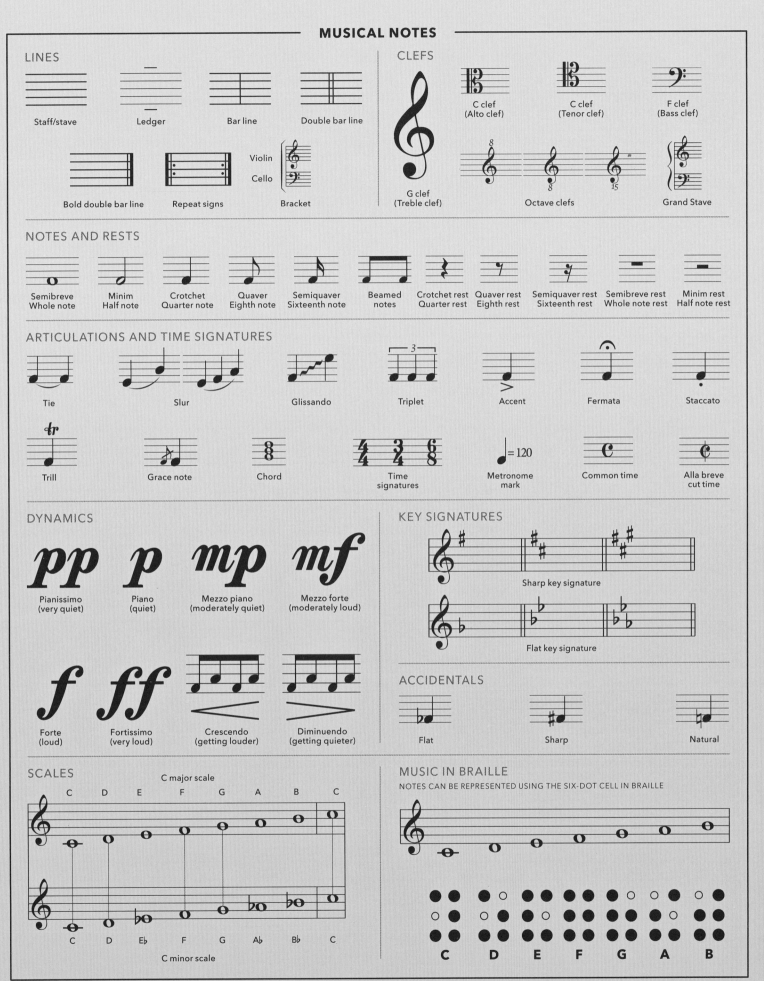

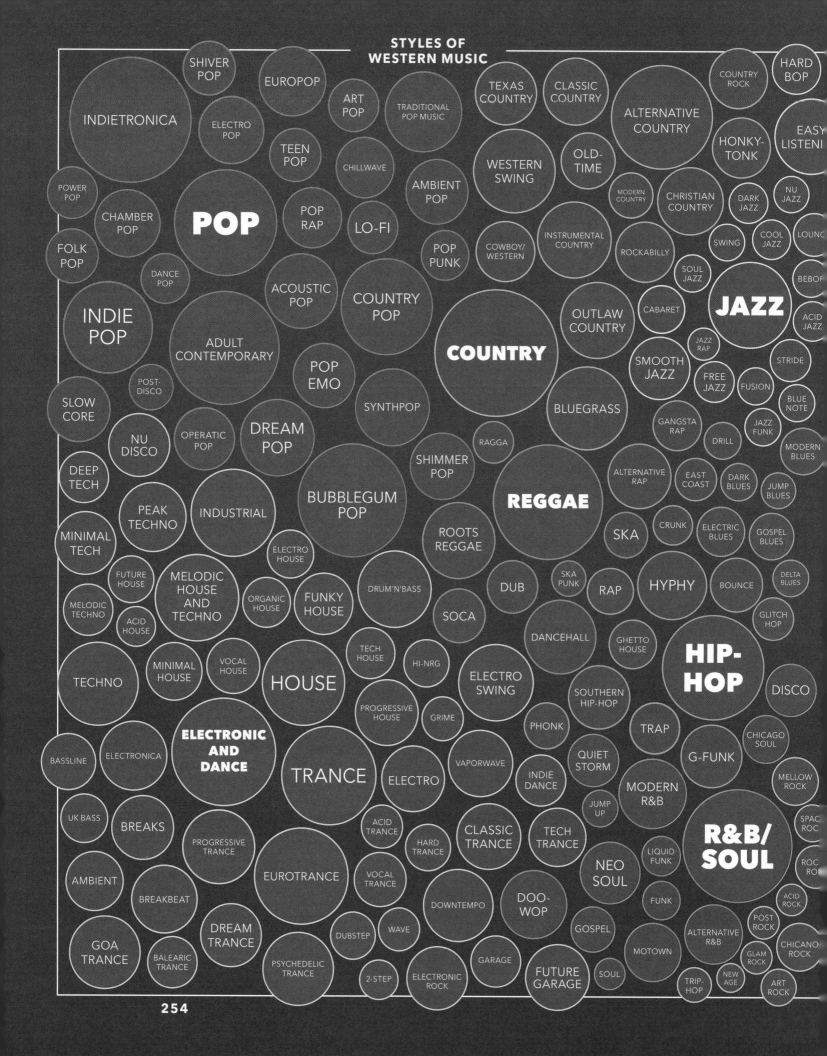

STYLES OF
WESTERN MUSIC

254

Styles of
WESTERN MUSIC

Popular music from the West can be divided into several main styles, but boundaries may be blurred—music can shift and change between them.

Popular Western music comes from Europe, or from countries that were once part of European empires and have been influenced by European cultures. These places include the US and Latin America (countries in North or South America in which the main languages spoken are Spanish and Portuguese, both of which come from Latin). Some of the main styles of popular Western music are shown on the left. Each of these styles covers a wider group of more specific types of music. For example, electronic and dance music includes techno, trance, house, and more.

Some styles of music are linked with particular countries. Country music began in the southern states of the US, while reggae comes from Jamaica. Jazz developed among Black musicians in the southern US, who took inspiration from African rhythmic music. Many forms of electronic and dance music have roots in the US and Europe. Today, all these musical styles are played all over the world.

Different styles of music have moved in and out of fashion over time. Jazz and blues were some of the first forms of non-classical music, and were very popular in the 1920s and 1930s. Pop music took off in the 1950s and rock in the 1960s. Particular styles of music can form a backdrop to a period of time, for example shoegaze is an alternative music style that was popular in the early 1990s.

A selection of some of the many popular Western music styles

Zaouli
CÔTE D'IVOIRE

Highland dancing
SCOTLAND

Hula
USA

Irish stepdance
IRELAND

Bharatanatyam
INDIA

Kathakali
INDIA

Odissi
INDIA

Bhangra
INDIA

Ghoomar
INDIA

Fan dance
CHINA

Ballet
ITALY

Nihon-buyō
JAPAN

Raqs sharqi
EGYPT

Break dance
USA

Khon
THAILAND

Tap dance
USA

Flamenco
SPAIN

Foxtrot
USA

Tarantella
ITALY

Pasodoble
SPAIN

Tango
ARGENTINA

Mazurka
POLAND

Cha-cha-cha
CUBA

Dragon dance
CHINA

Can-can
FRANCE

Kuchipudi
INDIA

Samba
BRAZIL

Hopak
UKRAINE

Jive
USA

Lindy Hop
USA

Salsa
CUBA

Marinera
PERU

Waltz
AUSTRIA

Tinikling
PHILIPPINES

Khorovod
RUSSIA

Dabkeh
THE LEVANT

Haka
NEW ZEALAND

A selection of dance styles from around the world

Styles of
DANCE

Moving the body rhythmically to music is enjoyed in many forms by people all over the world, either as a way of expression or to entertain others.

People have danced for thousands of years. Over time, hundreds of types or styles of dance have developed. People dance for joy, for exercise, and to showcase their skills.

Some dances are performed solo, such as the classical Bharatanatyam from India, while others, such as the Cuban Cha-cha-cha, are danced in pairs. Still others, such as the Russian Khorovod, are danced in large groups, where each person performs the same action at the same time. Dancers often wear a costume for the dance. This can be for many reasons, including ease of movement, as part of a cultural tradition, or to tell a story.

> **Ballet has been popular for more than 400 years.**

Styles of dance come from many parts of the world, and they are often an important way for communities to show their unique identity. The Zaouli is performed with seven masks, each one representing a character from the Guro people's legends, and the dancers spend years learning the moves. Traditional dances, such as the Haka of the Māori people, are a form of living history, while newer ones evolve along with new types of music. For example, break dance began on the streets of New York City, but is popular all over the world. Also popular is Classical ballet—its rigorous techniques and set movements are still the same as they were in the 17th century.

Types of
SPORTS

Many of us play sports of some sort, for our fitness or just for fun. Sports can be categorized into different forms and can be played individually or in teams. All sports are competitive.

The earliest sports often developed from hunting or warfare. For example, people practiced throwing rocks or running fast, and then enjoyed testing their skills against each other. Over time, these early competitions became more specific, with particular rules. People didn't just throw rocks but a whole range of different objects, such as sharp javelins, round and heavy shot puts, and the disk-shaped discus.

Today, there is a huge range of sports that can be split into different categories. Sports are open to everyone to enjoy.

Athletics is a group of sports that are usually undertaken on a track or field. Running events, such as sprints and hurdles, take place on the track. Throwing events, such as javelin, and jumping events, such as the high jump, take place on the field.

Gymnastics is a group of events that involve moving through a wide range of carefully controlled exercises. Some gymnastic disciplines are performed on the floor, others on equipment such as trampolines and rings. In weights, athletes try to lift up as much weight as possible in different ways.

> Wrestling may be one of the world's oldest sports.

In team sports, two teams face off against each other, usually with an objective—such as getting a ball into the other team's goal, as seen in soccer, or scoring runs, such as in cricket. A racket is used to hit a ball or shuttlecock in racket sports, while target sports involve hitting a target with an object, such as an arrow in archery or a bowling ball in bowling. On the other hand, combat sports, such as fencing and sumo, involve one-on-one fighting.

Some sports need a specific environment, such as water sports, which include swimming and boat racing, or ice and snow sports, which include bobsledding and snowboarding.

Motor sports showcase the high speed thrills of racing machines, while sports on wheels display the skill of riders on non-powered wheeled vehicles. Although all sports have a possibility of injury, the most dangerous are the extreme sports, which involve a high degree of risk.

Today, people can watch live or recorded games on television or other devices. Star athletes have legions of fans, and major sports teams and events attract billions in advertising, making sports a huge global industry.

> Soccer is the world's most popular sport, with around 3.5 billion fans.

TYPES OF SPORTS

ATHLETICS

Pole vault

Sprints

High jump

Hammer

Triple jump

Long jump

Middle-distance running

Relay

Shot put

Hurdles

Discus

Javelin

GYMNASTICS

Rings

Trampolining

Beam

Rhythmic gymnastics

Pommel horse

Sports acrobatics

Vault

Sports aerobics

Floor exercises

Bar events

WEIGHTS

Weightlifting

Powerlifting

TEAM SPORTS

Soccer

Football

Blind soccer

Rugby Union

Baseball

Lacrosse

Field hockey

Ice hockey

Bandy

Cricket

Volleyball

Basketball

A selection of sports from each category

TYPES OF SPORT

RACQUET SPORTS

Pelota

Badminton

Tennis

Squash

Racquetball

Pickleball

Jianzi

Para table tennis

Paddle tennis

COMBAT SPORTS

Karate

Taekwondo

Judo

Kendo

Boxing

Kung fu

Kickboxing

Sumo

Wheelchair fencing

Sombo

WATER SPORTS

Water polo

Kayaking

Diving

Rowing

Underwater hockey

Swimming

Surfing

Sailing

Dragon boat racing

ICE AND SNOW SPORTS

Bobsleigh

Speed skating

Luge

Skeleton

Ski jumping

Cross-country skiing

Ice dancing

Para snowboarding

Figure skating

Nordic combined

TARGET SPORTS

Curling

Lawn bowls

Tenpin bowling

Golf

Darts

Para archery

Croquet

Pool

Snooker

MOTOR SPORTS

Snowmobiling

Air racing

Truck racing

Road racing

NASCAR

Off-road motorcycling

Drag racing

Karting

Formula 1

SPORTS ON WHEELS

BMX

Skateboarding

Road racing

Roller skating

Roller hockey

Mountain biking

Track cycling

EXTREME SPORTS

Skydiving

Parkour

Paragliding

Extreme climbing

Land yachting

Cliff diving

Free diving

White water rafting

Freeride mountain biking

SUMMER AND WINTER
Olympics and Paralympics

Every couple of years, sportspeople from around the globe come together to showcase their skills in a spectacular competition: the Olympics. The Paralympics run alongside the Olympics.

SUMMER

OLYMPICS

3x3 Basketball	Basketball	Baseball/ Softball	Beach volleyball	Football	Handball	Hockey	Rugby sevens	Volleyball
Badminton	Table tennis	Tennis	Golf	Swimming	Marathon swimming	Artistic swimming	Diving	Water polo
Surfing	Rowing	Sailing	Canoe sprint	Canoe slalom	Cycling mountain bike	Cycling road	Cycling track	Cycling BMX freestyle
Cycling BMX racing	Boxing	Judo	Tae kwon do	Fencing	Wrestling	Artistic gymnastics	Rhythmic gymnastics	Trampoline
Athletics	Archery	Shooting	Sport climbing	Skateboarding	Modern pentathlon	Triathlon	Weightlifting	Equestrian

Olympic and Paralympic sports are shown above. Every Games creates its own set of pictograms for the sports being played in it. These are our own pictograms.

The first Olympic Games were held in ancient Greece from the 8th century BCE to the 4th century CE. In 1896, they were revived as the modern Olympic Games. They developed into several different Olympic Games at different times of the year, and for disabled and non-disabled people. The largest games are the Summer Olympics, which covers a range of summer sports, and are held every four years. Winter sports are covered in the Winter Olympics, held in snowy locations. The Winter Olympics also occur every four years, but two years after the Summer Olympics. All the Olympic Games are organized by an International Olympic Committee. The Summer and Winter Paralympics feature sports for physically disabled athletes. These games are held in the same years as the Summer and Winter Olympics. Sports that are featured at the Olympics and Paralympics are represented by pictures below. Since 1968, there has also been a Special Olympics for intellectually disabled athletes. The Special Olympic World Games are held every two years, switching between summer and winter. They feature many of the same sports as the Olympic Games.

Some sports have a number of different events, while others have only one. Some sports feature only in certain years—karate was included at the Tokyo Games in 2020, while flag football is set to be included in the Los Angeles Games in 2028.

The first Paralympic Games were held in Rome, Italy, in 1960.

PARALYMPICS

Para badminton

5-a-side blind football

Boccia

Goalball

Sitting volleyball

Para table tennis

Wheelchair basketball

Wheelchair rugby

Wheelchair tennis

Para swimming

Para canoe

Para rowing

Para cycling

Para judo

Para tae kwon do

Wheelchair fencing

Para athletics

Para archery

Shooting para sport

Para triathlon

Para powerlifting

Para equestrian

WINTER

OLYMPICS

Alpine skiing

Biathlon

Cross-country skiing

Freestyle skiing

Nordic combined

Ski jumping

Ski mountaineering

Snowboard

Bobsled

Curling

Figure skating

Ice hockey

Luge

Short track speed skating

Skeleton

Speed skating

PARALYMPICS

Para alpine skiing

Para biathlon

Para cross-country skiing

Para snowboard

Para ice hockey

Wheelchair curling

BALLS
used in sports

Many different sports are played using a ball, which is either struck with a part of the body or with an object such as a racket, stick, or bat. These balls can be solid or filled with air.

The earliest balls for play were made from inflated animal parts such as a pig's bladder or seal's stomach, or a buckskin bag filled with seeds. Over time, the shape and weight of balls became more specialized so they better suited the way they were struck or thrown. Modern sports balls are made of leather, rubber, or plastics.

Air-filled balls are lighter and suitable for hitting with hands, feet, or the head. Sports where the ball is caught or thrown to another player—such as rugby, football, or water polo—use air-filled balls, as do the sports in which the ball is kicked, such as soccer.

Football, rugby, and Australian rules football are played with an oval ball, which is carried, thrown to other players, and kicked. A kin-ball is the largest air-filled sports ball and is lightweight and easy to bounce. When a soccer player kicks a ball across the pitch to their teammate, they need to factor in the effect of air-resistance and temperature and bend the ball so it will find its mark. Soccer balls are slightly smaller and lighter than netballs. The smallest ball is used in squash—it is 1.56–1.59 in (39.5–40.5 mm) in diameter. The lightest ball is used in table tennis—it weighs just 0.095 oz (2.7 g).

In sports where the ball is hit with a bat, racket, or stick, the balls tend to be solid and heavier. Smaller, heavier balls are easier to control with a cue in snooker or pool, or with a bat in cricket or baseball. They offer much less air resistance and can be struck with great accuracy. Pétanque and bowling balls are heavy for their size so they stay near the ground when they are thrown at their target. Baseballs, lacrosse balls, cricket balls, and hockey balls are all roughly the same size and weight, while softballs are a little bigger. Within the solid balls, the largest and heaviest is a 10-pin bowling ball, which weighs from 10 lb (4.5 kg) to 16 lb (7.2 kg).

> **A pelota ball can reach speeds of up to 186 mph (300 kph) during a game of jai alai.**

▶ BALL TYPES
Solid and air-filled balls are made differently. Golf balls usually have three or four layers, with a core of solid rubber. Soccer balls are air-filled and can be inflated using a valve to keep them firm and bouncy.

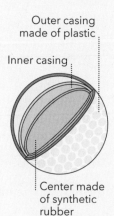

Outer casing made of plastic

Inner casing

Center made of synthetic rubber

Solid ball

Outer casing made of synthetic leather

Bladder containing pressurized air

Air-filled ball

BALLS USED IN SPORTS

AIR-FILLED BALLS

Goalball

Soft tennis

Horse ball

Squash

Cycle ball

Beach tennis

Water polo

Floorball

Gaelic football

Pickleball

Football

Table tennis

Soccer

Basketball

Racquetball

Volleyball

Futsal

Kin-ball

Wiffle ball

Dodgeball

Sepak Takraw

Netball

Tennis

Australian football

Fistball

Korfball

Rugby

OMNIKIN® OFFICIAL KIN-BALL®

Burley

SOLID BALLS

Golf

Pelota

Pétanque

Klootschieten

Pool

Snooker

Billiards

Polo

Lacrosse

Tenpin bowling

Rounders

Baseball

Bandy

Softball

Hockey

Bocce

Hurling

Cricket

Croquet

Real tennis

Lawn bowling

Types of
YOGA ASANA

Yoga is an ancient practice that combines exercises to calm our thoughts and breathing, as well as postures—asanas—including the 108 shown here. Some were performed centuries ago, many are modern adaptations.

No one knows exactly how the practice of yoga began, although its roots reach back to South Asia and the 12th to 15th centuries BCE. At that time, it looked very different to what we think of as yoga today. For ancient yogis (practitioners of yoga), the physical side was designed to prepare the body to sit still for hours on end to meditate. One early source, *Patanjali's Yoga Sutras* (325–425 CE), could be described as a blueprint for life through eight steps, or limbs (see below). The few physical poses mentioned were mainly seated asanas, such as Padmasana (lotus pose). Yet we know from paintings and manuscripts that strong arm balances were practiced at least 2,000 years ago, including Mayurasana (peacock pose) and Sirsasana (headstand).

Modern yoga has a greater focus on physical asanas and fitness, with many styles of yoga emerging over the last century as different schools create their own sequences and variations. Most postures aim to move the spine in different directions, building a healthy, supple yet strong body. A well-rounded yoga session would include something from all the categories of asana shown here.

Some are more challenging, such as Hanumanasana (monkey pose), and others are more restorative, such as Viparita Karani (legs up the wall). Many postures can be practiced in a chair and adapted for people with restricted mobility, while yogis often use blocks and other props for support.

There has never been a definitive list of postures, and yoga remains an ever-evolving practice. Here, we are showing 108 asanas because this is a sacred number for some yogis. Special occasions may be marked with 108 chants or Sun Salutations. Importantly, there are 108 beads on a mala, a garland used to help focus the mind during meditation.

> *Yoga comes from Sanskrit and means "to unite" mind, body, and spirit.*

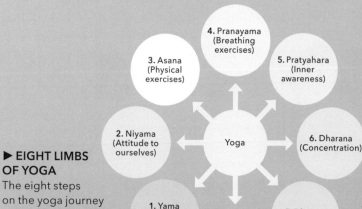

▶ EIGHT LIMBS OF YOGA
The eight steps on the yoga journey begin with being kind to others and the environment, and being kind to ourselves.

- 4. Pranayama (Breathing exercises)
- 3. Asana (Physical exercises)
- 5. Pratyahara (Inner awareness)
- 2. Niyama (Attitude to ourselves)
- Yoga
- 6. Dharana (Concentration)
- 1. Yama (Attitude to others)
- 7. Dhyana (Meditation)
- 8. Samadhi (Enlightenment)

TYPES OF YOGA ASANA

STANDING

Mountain pose
TADASANA

Chair pose
UTKATASANA

Chair twist pose
PARIVRTTA
UTKATASANA

Tree pose
VRKSASANA

Standing forward
fold pose
UTTANASANA

Big toe pose
MODIFIED
PADANGUSTHASANA

Wide leg forward
fold pose PRASARITA
PADOTTANASANA

Extended
triangle pose
UTTHITA
TRIKONASANA

Revolved triangle
pose PARIVRTTA
TRIKONASANA

Downward-facing dog pose
ADHO MUKHA SVANASANA

Downward-facing
dog pose with chair
ADHO MUKHA
SVANASANA WITH CHAIR

Upward-facing dog pose
URDHVA MUKHA
SVANASANA

Intense side
stretch pose
PARSVOTTANASANA

Goddess squat pose
UTKATA KONASANA

Warrior pose I
VIRABHADRASANA I

Warrior pose II
VIRABHADRASANA II

Warrior pose III
VIRABHADRASANA III

Reverse warrior pose
VIPARITA
VIRABHADRASANA

Extended side angle
pose with block
UTTHITA PARSVAKONASANA
WITH BLOCK

Revolved side angle pose
PARIVRTTA
PARSVAKONASANA

Humble warrior
pose
BADDHA
VIRABHADRASANA

Revolved half
moon pose
PARIVRTTA ARDHA
CHANDRASANA

Half moon pose
with block
ARDHA
CHANDRASANA
WITH BLOCK

Eagle pose
GARUDASANA

Extended hand to big
toe pose with belt
UTTHITA HASTA
PADANGUSTHASANA
WITH BELT

Extended hand
to big toe pose II
UTTHITA HASTA
PADANGUSTHASANA II

Dancer pose
NATARAJASANA

Bird of
paradise pose
SVARGA
DVIJASANA

FROM THE FLOOR

Cat pose
MARJARYASANA

Cow pose
BITILASANA

Balancing table pose
DANDAYAMANA
BHARMANASANA

Crescent lunge pose
ANJANEYASANA

Gate pose
PARIGHASANA

Plank pose
KUMBHAKASANA

Four-limbed
staff pose
CHATURANGADANDASANA

Side plank pose
VASISTHASANA

Sage
Visvamitra's pose
VISVAMITRASANA

A selection of yoga asanas is shown. Each entry has two names—
the first one is in English and the second one is in Sanskrit.

TYPES OF YOGA ASANA

SEATED

Easy pose
SUKHASANA

Accomplished pose
SIDDHASANA

Lotus pose
PADMASANA

Fire log pose
AGNISTAMBHASANA

Hero pose
VIRASANA

Thunderbolt pose
VAJRASANA

Boat pose
PARIPURNA NAVASANA

Staff pose
DANDASANA

Marichi's pose I
MARICHYASANA I

Marichi's pose II
MARICHYASANA II

Marichi's pose twist
MARICHYASANA III

Marichi's pose IV twist
MARICHYASANA IV

**Wide-angled seated
forward fold pose B**
UPAVISTHA KONASANA B

Bharadvaja's twist pose
BHARADVAJASANA

**Modified Bharadvaja's
twist pose**
MODIFIED
BHARADVAJASANA

Child's pose
BALASANA

Tortoise pose
KURMASANA

**Wide-angled seated
forward fold pose A**
UPAVISTHA KONASANA A

Pigeon pose
EKA PADA (RAJA)
KAPOTASANA

ARM BALANCES

Crane pose
BAKASANA

Side crane pose
PARSVA BAKASANA

Sage Koundinya's pose
EKA PADA KOUNDINYASANA I

Two-legged Sage Koundinya's pose
DWI PADA KOUNDINYASANA

Sage Koundinya's pose II
EKA PADA KOUNDINYASANA II

Peacock pose
MAYURASANA

**Forearm balance
pose** PINCHA
MAYURASANA

Dolphin pose
ARDHA PINCHA
MAYURASANA

ON THE FLOOR

Cobra pose
BHUJANGASANA

King cobra pose
RAJA BHUJANGASANA

**Modified reclining
hand to big toe pose**
MODIFIED SUPTA
PADANGUSTHASANA

Sphinx pose
SALAMBA
BHUJANGASANA

**Upward-facing
bow pose**
URDHVA
DHANURASANA

Bow pose
DHANURASANA

Camel pose
USTRASANA

Sleeping Vishnu pose
ANANTASANA

Locust pose
SALABHASANA

Revolved belly pose
JATHARA PARIVARTANASANA

Crocodile pose
MAKARASANA

Head to knee pose
JANU SIRSASANA

Revolved head to knee pose
PARIVRTTA JANU SIRSASANA

Heron pose
KROUNCHASANA

Seated forward fold pose
PASCHIMOTTANASANA

Modified Bharadvaja's
twist pose II
MODIFIED
BHARADVAJASANA II

Half lord of the fish pose
ARDHA MATSYENDRASANA

Bound angle pose
BADDHA KONASANA

Seated pigeon pose
EKA PADA (RAJA)
KAPOTASANA
IN CHAIR

Garland pose
MALASANA

Monkey pose
HANUMANASANA

Mermaid pose
NAGINYASANA

Sundial pose
SURYA YANTRASANA

Cow face pose
GOMUKHASANA

Handstand pose
ADHO MUKHA
VRKSASANA

Shoulder stand pose
SALAMBA
SARVANGASANA

Headstand pose
SIRSASANA

Tripod headstand
pose SALAMBA
SIRSASANA

Firefly pose
TITTIBHASANA

Flying pigeon pose
EKA PADA
GALAVASANA

Plow pose
HALASANA

Frog pose
BHEKASANA

Half frog pose
ARDHA BHEKASANA

Fish pose
MATSYASANA

Happy baby pose
ANANDA BALASANA

Legs up the wall
pose VIPARITA
KARANI

Upward
plank pose
PURVOTTANASANA

Supine splits pose
SUPTA TRIVIKRAMASANA

Reclining bound
angle pose
SUPTA BADDHA
KONASANA

Reclining hero pose
SUPTA VIRASANA

Bridge pose
SETU BANDHASANA

Eye of the needle pose
SUCIRANDHRASANA

Melting heart pose
ANAHATASANA

Corpse pose
SAVASANA

TIME

around the world

There is a reason why the day is 24 hours long and not more or less—and why the time of day is not the same in every part of the world. It is all about how our planet spins around in space.

It takes Earth 24 hours to make one rotation around its axis. As it turns, it faces toward and away from the sun. It is why we have day and night. In 1884, the countries of the world agreed to divide the planet into 24 time zones, one for every hour of the day. Each zone was separated by an imaginary line, called a meridian (or line of longitude), running from the North Pole to the South Pole.

Because time had to "begin" somewhere, the Royal Observatory in Greenwich, London, UK, was chosen as the site for the first, or prime, meridian. From there, the time all over the world is measured against what is known as Greenwich Mean Time (GMT). The meridians east of the line in Greenwich are ahead of it in time and those west of it are behind; when it is midday in London, the time at the next meridian to its east—for example in Paris or Rome—is 13:00. In the next meridian it is 14:00, and so on. It works the other way too: in the first meridian west of London at midday, such as in Reykjavik, Iceland, it is 11:00.

Some countries, such as the US and Russia, are so large that they are spread over several time zones. But not all big countries do this. China, seven hours ahead of the UK, has just one time zone, mainly because this makes communication easier. India, most of which lies between the +5 and +6 hour meridians, decided to split the difference, and the time there is 5.5 hours ahead of the UK.

Halfway around the world from Greenwich and in the middle of the Pacific Ocean is another imaginary marker called the International Date Line. This is the place where the day officially ends and a new day begins when it is midday in London. If a person crosses this line traveling east, they will find themselves starting the day that just ended all over again; if they go over the line moving to the west, they will have moved one day forward. In this way it is possible to "jump" 24 hours in just a few seconds!

> The International Space Station uses GMT. Noon in London is noon in space.

▶ **NORTH AMERICAN TIME ZONES**
There are six time zones across North America, ranging from four to nine hours behind the time in London (GMT).

TIME AROUND THE WORLD

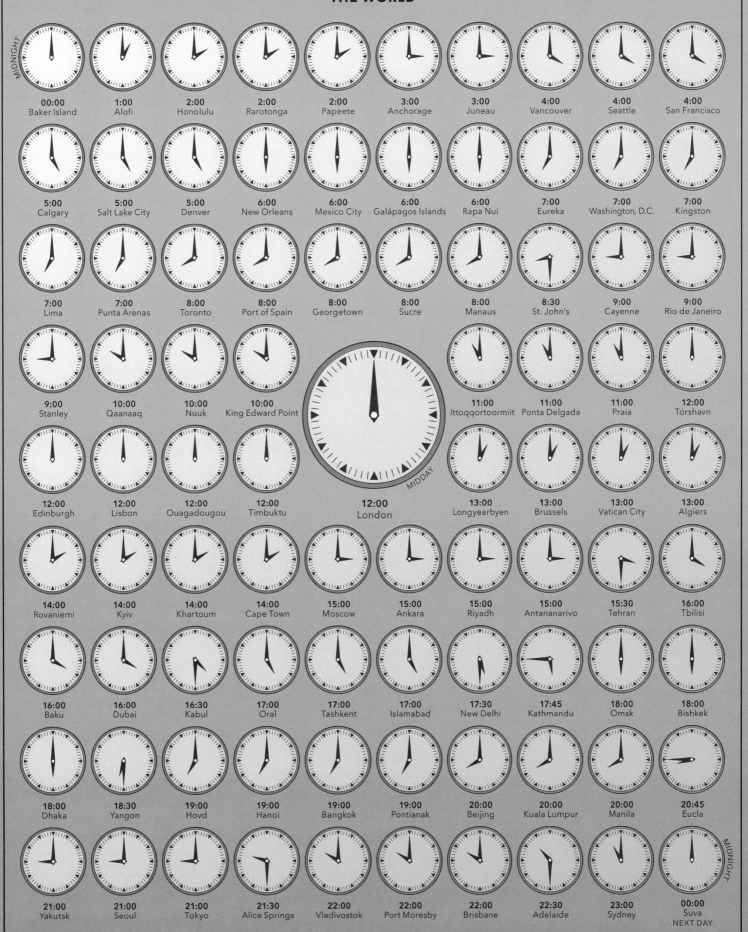

MIDNIGHT

| 00:00 Baker Island | 1:00 Alofi | 2:00 Honolulu | 2:00 Rarotonga | 2:00 Papeete | 3:00 Anchorage | 3:00 Juneau | 4:00 Vancouver | 4:00 Seattle | 4:00 San Francisco |

| 5:00 Calgary | 5:00 Salt Lake City | 5:00 Denver | 6:00 New Orleans | 6:00 Mexico City | 6:00 Galápagos Islands | 6:00 Rapa Nui | 7:00 Eureka | 7:00 Washington, D.C. | 7:00 Kingston |

| 7:00 Lima | 7:00 Punta Arenas | 8:00 Toronto | 8:00 Port of Spain | 8:00 Georgetown | 8:00 Sucre | 8:00 Manaus | 8:30 St. John's | 9:00 Cayenne | 9:00 Rio de Janeiro |

| 9:00 Stanley | 10:00 Qaanaaq | 10:00 Nuuk | 10:00 King Edward Point | 12:00 London | 11:00 Ittoqqortoormiit | 11:00 Ponta Delgada | 11:00 Praia | 12:00 Tórshavn |

MIDDAY

| 12:00 Edinburgh | 12:00 Lisbon | 12:00 Ouagadougou | 12:00 Timbuktu | | 13:00 Longyearbyen | 13:00 Brussels | 13:00 Vatican City | 13:00 Algiers |

| 14:00 Rovaniemi | 14:00 Kyiv | 14:00 Khartoum | 14:00 Cape Town | 15:00 Moscow | 15:00 Ankara | 15:00 Riyadh | 15:00 Antananarivo | 15:30 Tehran | 16:00 Tbilisi |

| 16:00 Baku | 16:00 Dubai | 16:30 Kabul | 17:00 Oral | 17:00 Tashkent | 17:00 Islamabad | 17:30 New Delhi | 17:45 Kathmandu | 18:00 Omsk | 18:00 Bishkek |

| 18:00 Dhaka | 18:30 Yangon | 19:00 Hovd | 19:00 Hanoi | 19:00 Bangkok | 19:00 Pontianak | 20:00 Beijing | 20:00 Kuala Lumpur | 20:00 Manila | 20:45 Eucla |

| 21:00 Yakutsk | 21:00 Seoul | 21:00 Tokyo | 21:30 Alice Springs | 22:00 Vladivostok | 22:00 Port Moresby | 22:00 Brisbane | 22:30 Adelaide | 23:00 Sydney | 00:00 Suva NEXT DAY |

MIDNIGHT

Clocks from every time zone at exactly the same moment on the 1st of January

ZODIAC SYSTEMS

MAYA ZODIAC

13 PERIODS OF 20 DAYS EACH

AHAU (Flower) DAY 20
CAUAC (Storm) DAY 19
ETZNAB (Knife) DAY 18
CABAN (Earth) DAY 17
CIB (Vulture) DAY 16
MEN (Eagle) DAY 15
IX (Jaguar) DAY 14
BEN (Reed) DAY 13
EB (Grass) DAY 12
CHUEN (Monkey) DAY 11
OC (Dog) DAY 10
MULUC (Water) DAY 9
LAMAT (Rabbit) DAY 8
MANIK (Deer) DAY 7
CIMI (Death) DAY 6
CHICCHAN (Serpent) DAY 5
KAN (Lizard) DAY 4
AKBAL (House) DAY 3
IK (Wind) DAY 2
IMIX (Crocodile) DAY 1

WESTERN ZODIAC

12 MONTH-LONG PERIODS

ARIES (Ram) MAR 21– APR 19
TAURUS (Bull) APR 20– MAY 20
GEMINI (Twins) MAY 21– JUN 21
CANCER (Crab) JUN 22– JUL 22
LEO (Lion) JUL 23– AUG 22
VIRGO (Maiden) AUG 23– SEPT 22
LIBRA (Scales) SEPT 23– OCT 23
SCORPIO (Scorpion) OCT 24– 21 NOV
SAGITTARIUS (Archer) NOV 22– DEC 21
CAPRICORN (Goat) DEC 22– JAN 19
AQUARIUS (Water Bearer) JAN 20– FEB 18
PISCES (Fish) FEB 19– MAR 20

CHINESE ZODIAC

12-YEAR CYCLE, WITH A SIGN FOR EACH YEAR

SHU (Rat) 1984, 1996, 2008, 2020
NIU (Ox) 1985, 1997, 2009, 2021
HU (Tiger) 1986, 1998, 2010, 2022
TU (Rabbit) 1987, 1999, 2011, 2023
LONG (Dragon) 1988, 2000, 2012, 2024
SHE (Snake) 1989, 2001, 2013, 2025
MA (Horse) 1990, 2002, 2014, 2026
YANG (Goat) 1991, 2003, 2015, 2027
HOU (Monkey) 1992, 2004, 2016, 2028
JI (Rooster) 1993, 2005, 2017, 2029
GOU (Dog) 1994, 2006, 2018, 2030
ZHU (Pig) 1995, 2007, 2019, 2031

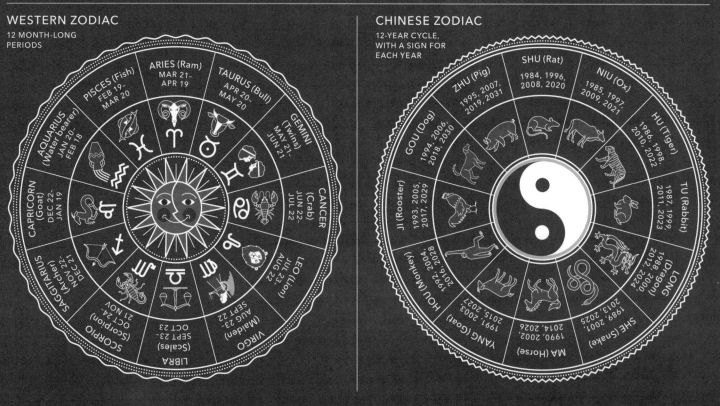

272

ZODIAC
systems

A zodiac is a traditional calendar related to astrology that suggests people will have certain characteristics depending on when they were born. Different zodiacs have been used throughout history in different places.

Many cultures and civilizations have studied astrology and created zodiacs. The earliest zodiac we know of was developed in Babylon (modern-day Iraq), around 4,000 years ago. Today, many people all over the world believe in zodiac systems and use them to help guide their lives. For example, they might check the zodiac prediction for their birth sign before making an important decision. On these pages are just three of the most well-known zodiac systems.

The calendar of the Maya people from Mesoamerica divides the year into 13 periods of 20 days each. There are 20 signs in the Maya zodiac: one for each day of the 20-day cycle. The sign of the day someone is born on is said to reveal their strengths, weaknesses, and main characteristics. A person born on the day of Ik (the wind), which is the second-day sign, is considered to be lively, intelligent, and skilled at many tasks. Someone born on the day of Kan (the lizard)—the fourth-day sign—is said to be powerful, intelligent, and good at understanding feelings.

The zodiac from the West (western Europe and parts of North America and Australasia) is based on 12 groups of stars called constellations. These appear in a band-shaped area of the sky that contains the path the sun appears to follow over the year. Each constellation is a "sign of the zodiac," and everyone has their own zodiac sign—the one that the sun was positioned in on the day they were born. In this zodiac, a person's sign is also linked to their character and talents. For example, a person born under the sign Sagittarius (the archer) will be optimistic and forward-looking. The signs of the Western zodiac are also linked to the ancient idea of the four basic elements—earth, fire, wind, and water.

The Chinese zodiac has 12 signs, all of which are animals. According to legend, one of the most important Chinese deities, the Jade Emperor, organized a race for animals, and picked 12 winners. Each Chinese New Year has one of these animals assigned to it, in a repeating cycle of 12 years. A person's birth year is thought to influence their character, luck, career, and even who they will marry. Someone born in the year of Long (the dragon) is said to be lucky, honorable, and successful, while a person born in the year of Tu (the rabbit) is kind, polite, and thoughtful.

> *Reading the position of stars in the sky to predict the future is called astrology.*

> *"Zodiac" comes from the Greek word zodiakos meaning "circle of animals."*

Shapes of FIREWORKS

Early fireworks had no bright colors, no spectacular shapes—they were just a series of small explosions. But today, fireworks can be designed to explode in extraordinary displays of color and shape.

Modern fireworks create explosive, colorful displays as a result of many chemical reactions. Fireworks are bundles of chemicals and gunpowder packed together in a shell, which explodes to form bright sparkling shapes when lit. Some fireworks are designed to shoot high into the sky, while others are burned on the ground. When an aerial firework's fuse is lit, the flame travels into its compartmentalized body. One of these compartments is packed with gunpowder. This explodes and pushes the firework upward. The explosion also lights a time-delayed fuse within the firework, which ignites a "burst" charge connected to a compartment packed with pellets of metal salts and other compounds, known as "stars." When the burst charge is ignited, the stars explode outward, bursting open the casing of the shell. And it is these stars that are responsible for creating the firework's shapes.

The stars can be arranged to create distinct shapes when a firework explodes, including flowers, smiley faces, hearts, and even words. The stars will often be laid out into the desired pattern on a piece of cardboard, which is then inserted into the firework shell.

> **Different metal salts in fireworks produce different colors in the sky.**

One of the most common aerial firework shapes is a peony flower design, where a shell explodes into a flowerlike series of falling sparks. Here, the inside of the firework is packed with stars in ever-expanding circles. When the firework bursts, the innermost circle explodes and pushes out the stars in the outer circles after a slight delay. A palm-shaped firework has stars arranged in the shape of a trunk, with "leaves" at the other end. A willow-shaped firework has slow-burning sparks that fall in the shape of willow tree branches. Unlike more traditional firework shapes, where the stars burst outward in a single direction, crossette stars are designed to split apart mid-flight, creating multiple trails of sparks that shoot off in different directions.

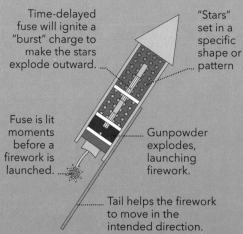

Time-delayed fuse will ignite a "burst" charge to make the stars explode outward.

"Stars" set in a specific shape or pattern

Fuse is lit moments before a firework is launched.

Gunpowder explodes, launching firework.

Tail helps the firework to move in the intended direction.

◀ **INSIDE A FIREWORK**
A firework contains gunpowder as well as "stars" (pellets of metal compounds) to help it launch into the sky and explode in the desired shape.

Comet

Peony

Chrysanthemum

Rising tail

Stars

Palm

Dragon eggs

Glitter

Spider

Brocade

Crackle

Strobe

Pattern shells

Dahlia

Crossette

Willow

Pistil

Fish

Bees

Strings

Ground spinner

Snake

Fountain

M-80

Catherine wheel

Sparkler

TYPES OF KNOT

STOPPER KNOTS
STOP A ROPE FROM UNRAVELING

Overhand knot

Slipped overhand knot

Double overhand knot

Figure-eight

Slipped figure-eight

Manrope knot

Stopper knot

Sink stopper knot

Diamond knot

Stevedore knot

BINDING KNOTS
BIND LOOSE ITEMS TOGETHER

Reef knot

Double-slipped reef knot

Turquoise turtle

Granny knot

Surgeon's knot

Thief knot

Boa knot

Clove hitch

HITCHES AND LASHINGS
SECURE A ROPE TO AN OBJECT

Bachmann knot

Sheer lashing

Square lashing

Diagonal lashing

Cow hitch

Timber hitch

Rolling hitch

Wagoner's hitch

LOOPS
ALLOW ROPE TO GO AROUND THINGS OR ATTACH ROPES TO OTHER THINGS

Angler's loop

Spanish bowline

Overhand loop

Alpine butterfly loop

Jury mast knot

Bowline

Buntline hitch

Round turn and two half hitches

Highwayman's hitch

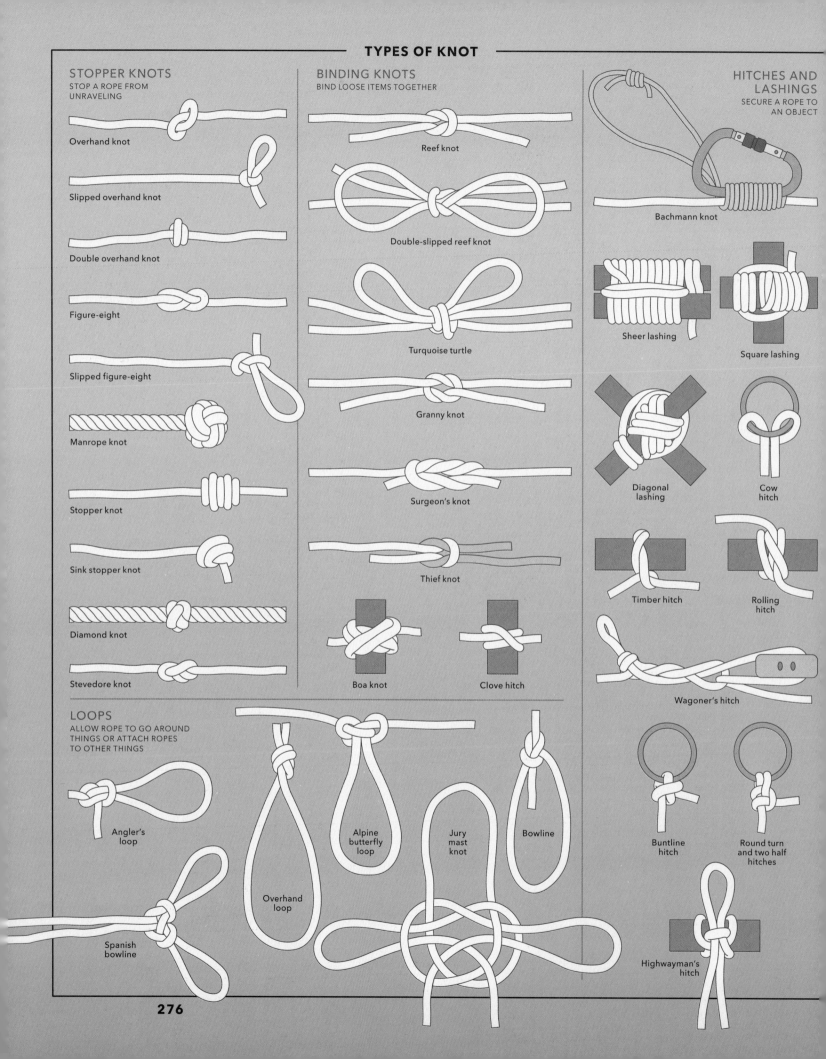

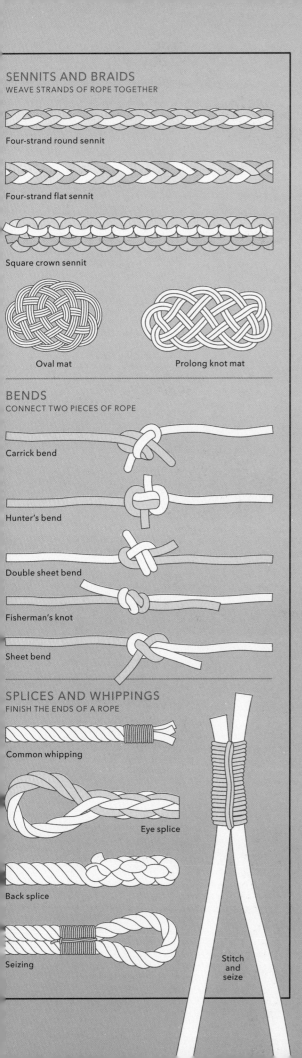

SENNITS AND BRAIDS
WEAVE STRANDS OF ROPE TOGETHER

Four-strand round sennit

Four-strand flat sennit

Square crown sennit

Oval mat

Prolong knot mat

BENDS
CONNECT TWO PIECES OF ROPE

Carrick bend

Hunter's bend

Double sheet bend

Fisherman's knot

Sheet bend

SPLICES AND WHIPPINGS
FINISH THE ENDS OF A ROPE

Common whipping

Eye splice

Back splice

Seizing

Stitch and seize

Types of KNOT

A knot is a tightened twist and tuck in a piece of string or rope. There are many types of knot, used in different situations, from climbing to fishing.

The way a knot is tied can stop a rope or string from moving, attach it to another object, allow it to move in a particular way, and so on. It's an everyday skill we use often without thinking about it—even tying one's shoelaces needs a knot (a type of reef knot).

Stopper knots are tied at the end of a piece of rope, to stop the rope being pulled through a hole or unraveling. They are usually tied using the whole rope, but a few are tied with just the strands of the rope. Some stopper knots can also be decorative.

> The reef knot is the most commonly tied knot on the planet.

Loops allow rope to go around things or to attach ropes to other things, such as hooks and sticks. They are often used by climbers, sailors, and those out fishing or angling.

Binding knots are used to keep things in place, for example by tying bundles of wood together. Hitches and lashings are another way of attaching a rope to another object. Sennits and braids are made by weaving strands of rope or threads together. They are usually used to create pretty, decorative items such as table mats.

Bends are used to connect two pieces of rope together. Splices and whippings are different ways of finishing the ends of a rope, to stop it unraveling. A splice splits the rope and weaves the ends in, while a whipping involves binding the end of the rope.

FRAGRANCE INGREDIENTS

KEY ■ Top note ■ Heart note ■ Base note

FLORAL

■ Jasmine

■ Damask rose

■ Ylang ylang

■ Orange flower

■ Tuberose

■ Neroli

■ Strawberry

■ Peach

■ Osmanthus

■ Pear

■ Tea

■ Fig

■ Coconut

■ Geranium

■ Lilac

FRESH

■ Spearmint

■ Anise

■ Carrot seed

■ Mandarin

■ Thyme

■ Violet leaf

■ Bergamot

■ Eucalyptus

■ Peppermint

■ Lemon

■ Clary sage

■ Bitter orange

■ Green mandarin

■ Blood orange

■ Lavender

AMBER

■ Tonka beans

■ Myrrh

■ Cinnamon

■ Cistus

■ Vanilla

■ Ginger

■ Benzoin

■ Frankincense

■ Black pepper

■ Clove

■ Pink peppercorn

■ Cardamom

■ Hay

WOODY

■ Vetiver

■ Oakmoss

■ Sandalwood

■ Atlas cedar

■ Patchouli

■ Cedar virginia

■ Guaiac wood

MUSK AND LEATHER

■ Ambrette seed

■ Musk

■ Leather

278

FRAGRANCE
ingredients

Liquid fragrances called perfumes can't be seen when sprayed, but they linger in the air and on the skin to create a pleasant-smelling scent. Some fragrances are light and floral, others are warmer and musky.

Perfumers, or perfume makers, create their fragrances by combining alcohol and oils with mixtures of ingredients that complement each other. Some aromas only last a short time while others last longer.

Perfumers draw from groups of ingredients depending on the effect they are seeking to achieve. Musky aromas are considered more sophisticated and take time to mature, while floral scents such as jasmine, lilac, or orange flowers are simpler and more instant. Citrus ingredients such as bitter orange, bergamot, and lemon are fresh and pungent, and evaporate quickly. Amber tones include cloves, vanilla, and benzoin resin, and they have a "warmer" smell, which gives a feeling of comfort. Woody ingredients such as sandalwood and cedar last the longest.

There are many flowers that lend their aromas to floral perfumes, and flowers such as rose and ylang ylang have beautiful heady aromas. Black tea and sweet fruits, such as pears and peaches, have a similar floral fragrance, and are also part of this group.

Along with the fresh scents of citrus fruits go mints, lavender, and eucalyptus—these are also clear and bright aromas that feel refreshing to wear, but don't last very long. The warmer amber scents tend to come from spices, such as black pepper, ginger, and cardamom, or from resins, such as myrrh and frankincense. These linger for around an hour on the skin.

Woody aromas come from trees, moss, and plants, and all linger for a few hours. Vetiver (a grass), oakmoss (a lichen), and guaiac wood (a tree) all have earthy smells, which conjure up nature. The animal smells of leather and musk oil can be too overpowering on their own, so are usually mixed with lighter odors to create a pleasing smell.

Perfumers also create "layers" in their fragrances so the scent changes as different ingredients evaporate at different times.

> **Tapputi, a woman from Mesopotamia (modern-day Iraq), was the world's first perfumer.**

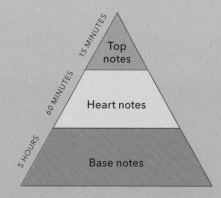

◄ FRAGRANCE PYRAMID
Perfume ingredients can be categorized based on how fast they evaporate. Top notes last about 15 minutes, heart notes about an hour, while base notes can endure for up to five hours.

FOOD

Edible
FRUITS

All plants bear fruit, but edible fruits are those that humans can eat safely, often without cooking. They fall into six groups, based on the structure of the fruit.

Fruits are ripened flower ovaries that contain a plant's seeds. Botanists (scientists who study plants) categorize fruits by how they develop.

The six categories are: citrus fruit, berry, melon, core fruit, pit fruit, and accessory fruit. Citrus fruits, berries, and melons have multiple seeds. Citrus fruits are a form of fruit called a hesperidium. Each citrus fruit has segments with seeds packed among swollen juice sacs. Its rind contains oil glands and is used as zest (flavoring).

A berry is a fleshy fruit formed from a flower with a single ovary (female reproductive structure that develops into a fruit with seeds). Berries include kiwi, blueberries, and black currants, where the fleshy layer is almost liquid, as well as bananas, which have a solid starchy layer where seeds would normally be found. Commercial bananas, however, are seedless varieties, with only small black spots in place of seeds. Some fruits such as strawberries and raspberries, which we call berries, aren't considered berries by botanists because they aren't fruits formed from a single ovary.

Melons are a type of fruit called a pepo, with a thick rind and watery flesh. This group includes fruits such as watermelons and cantaloupes. Accessory and core fruits do not develop from the ovary of a flower, but from other tissues. In core fruits, such as apples, the base of the flower, or receptacle, swells and engulfs the ovary to create a large fleshy fruit around it.

Accessory fruits, such as strawberries, form when the receptacle swells, leaving individual true fruits as the pips on the outside. Breadfruit and jackfruit develop from the petals of hundreds of individual flowers, while the cashew plant grows a fleshy cashew apple at the base of the true fruit, the cashew nut.

Pit fruits have a single seed at the center, protected by the hard pit. They include cherries. Blackberries and raspberries are also pit fruits, despite their name. They consist of many small fruits, each of which has a single seed.

> The citrus fruit kumquat is very rich in vitamin C.

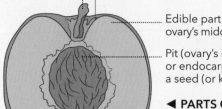

Stem, or peduncle, supports the fruit.

Outer skin, or exocarp, protects the fruit.

Edible part of the fruit is the ovary's middle layer, or mesocarp.

Pit (ovary's inner layer, or endocarp) encloses a seed (or kernel).

◄ PARTS OF A PIT FRUIT
A pit fruit, such as a peach, consists of three layers. The hard pit protects the seed until it lands in the right place to sprout.

EDIBLE FRUITS

CITRUS FRUIT

Orange

Lime

Lemon

Kumquat

Clementine

Yuzu

Pomelo

CORE FRUIT

Pear

Rowan

Apple

Medlar

Loquat

Cherimoya

Quince

Crabapple

BERRIES

Blueberry

Cloudberry

Kiwi

Gooseberry

Cranberry

Blackcurrant

Banana

PIT FRUIT

Cherry

Plum

Apricot

Rambutan

Raspberry

Blackberry

Peach

Mango

Lychee

ACCESSORY FRUIT

Strawberry

Fig

Cashew

Jackfruit

Breadfruit

Pineapple

MELONS

Cantaloupe

Kiwano

Cucamelon

Winter melon

Gac

Watermelon

Do not eat any unripe fruits, rambutan and lychee seeds, or cashew nuts off the tree, because they can be toxic

CITRUS FRUITS

POMELOS

Sarawak pomelo

Honey pomelo

Pomelo

Tahitian pomelo

Siamese sweet pomelo

Chandler pomelo

Jaffa sweetie

Pomelit pomelo

Ugli fruit

CITRONS

Lemon

Etrog citron

Buddha's Hand

Lime

Balady citron

Cedruna citron

Sicilian citron

Diamante citron

Yemenite citron

Mediterranean mandarin

MANDARIN ORANGES

Tangerine

Satsuma

King mandarin

Tangelo

Clementine

Tangor

Common mandarin

HYBRIDS

African cherry orange

Volkamer lemon

Chinotto

Rangpur lime

Sweet orange

Navel orange

Red grapefruit

Blood orange

Rough lemon

CITRUS
fruits

Fruits classified as "citrus" are a specialized form of fruit called hesperidium. Citrus fruits have tough and leathery peels, and are divided inside into segments, each holding seeds embedded among juicy fruit sacs.

Citrus fruits have a long history of cultivation. From a handful of original species, growers have developed some types for their specific traits. More recently, they have artificially created hybrid varieties by cross-breeding, using different parent fruits, in a process called hybridization.

Wild citrus species and their relatives may have originated in the regions of Asia that get heavy monsoon rains—from the Indian subcontinent through China to New Guinea and even as far south as Australia. It is thought that the mandarin group appeared in southern China, while the citron group probably originated in the Himalayan foothills.

People growing these fruits traveled through Asia and, as they exchanged their varieties, new forms appeared in each group. Over thousands of years, the range of varieties increased, from limes to the Buddha's Hand in the citron group, and from tangelos to satsumas in the mandarin group.

As citrus fruits were taken to new places, new varieties appeared, which were better suited to the local climates. For example, the Tahitian pomelo is believed to have originated in Polynesia, whereas the tangelo (a cross between a tangerine and a pomelo) originated in the Caribbean. Once several types of citrus fruits were grown together, it gave growers a chance to hybridize them.

Oranges are hybrids of mandarins and pomelos. All oranges get their fruit color from the mandarin and have varying degrees of sweetness, depending on which parent has the larger effect. Grapefruit arose from hybridizing the same two parents as oranges, but here the pomelo is dominant, with its sharp taste and large size. Rough lemons are a hybrid of mandarin and citron.

In recent years, fruit breeders have combined the characteristics of several varieties and existing hybrids into new types of citrus fruit. These complex fruits are hard to classify, but are often seedless and easy to peel, making them favorites with consumers worldwide.

> **Unlike many fruits, citrus fruits do not ripen if picked early.**

▼ ACIDITY LEVEL OF CITRUS FRUIT
Citrus fruits contain citric acid, the acidity of which can be measured by the pH scale. Fruits with lower pH values are more acidic and so have a more bitter taste.

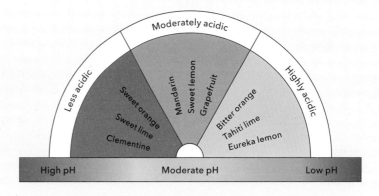

Moderately acidic

Less acidic

Highly acidic

Sweet orange
Sweet lime
Clementine

Mandarin
Sweet lemon
Grapefruit

Bitter orange
Tahiti lime
Eureka lemon

| High pH | Moderate pH | Low pH |

APPLE VARIETIES

Red Delicious
US

Tropical Beauty
SOUTH AFRICA

Pacific Rose
NEW ZEALAND

Firiki Piliou
GREECE

McIntosh
CANADA

Idared
US

Ambrosia
CANADA

Baldwin
US

Cortland
US

Kaiser
Alexander
UKRAINE

Spartan
CANADA

Enterprise
US

Queen
NEW ZEALAND

Cripps Pink
AUSTRALIA

Dabinett
ENGLAND

Common apple
WORLDWIDE

Belle de Boskoop
NETHERLANDS

Honeycrisp
US

Elstar
NETHERLANDS

Brettacher
GERMANY

Braeburn
NEW ZEALAND

Jazz
NEW ZEALAND

Empire
US

Black
Diamond
CHINA

Fuji
JAPAN

Cosmic Crisp
US

Reglindis
GERMANY

Sekai Ichi
JAPAN

Opal
CZECHIA

Golden Delicious
US

Gala
NEW ZEALAND

Cox's Orange Pippin
ENGLAND

Landsberger Reinette
POLAND

Grimes Golden
US

Jonathan
US

Porter
US

Rhode Island Greening
US

Granny Smith
AUSTRALIA

APPLE
varieties

Apples once grew in the wild and were found only in Kazakhstan in central Asia. People began cultivating them around 8,000 years ago, and today more than 7,500 varieties of apples have been developed.

Ancient Egyptians were growing apples along the Nile River in 1300 BCE and historical records tell us that the Romans brought apples with them to England around 200 BCE. Through thousands of years of cultivation, apple varieties have been bred to suit many different types of climate and region—from the cold and wet climate of northern Europe to the sunny summers of southern Europe, New Zealand, and South Africa.

Apples grown from seeds may not have the same characteristics as their parent plant. Because of this, apples are usually grown by grafting—an apple tree stem with growing buds is planted onto another apple tree. This makes the stem grow fruit with the best qualities of both trees.

The long history of apple cultivation has also allowed chance seedlings to appear in orchards. These seedlings are created when there is unintentional cross-pollination between apple varieties. This kind of pollination has led to many new and famous varieties such as the English Bramley Seedling, which first appeared in 1809.

Growing apples globally means that they can be available all year round. Keeping the harvested fruit in special stores, where the atmosphere is carefully controlled, also allows for apples to be stored for up to eight months before being eaten.

Apple varieties come in a large range of colors. While many have red, green, or golden outer skins, the Australian Cripps Pink apple has a pink coloring and the Chinese Black Diamond has a deep purple color.

This fruit can vary in flavor and sweetness, from the extremely sweet Japanese Fuji to the ultra-sour ones, such as the English Dabinett, that are used mostly for cooking or making cider. Some people love acidic apples such as the Australian Granny Smith, while many prefer the sweetness of the New Zealand Gala or the Red Delicious from the US. Many varieties are used in famous dishes, such as the Austrian apple strudel, the French tarte tatin, or the American apple pie.

> **More than 100 million tons of apples are grown globally each year.**

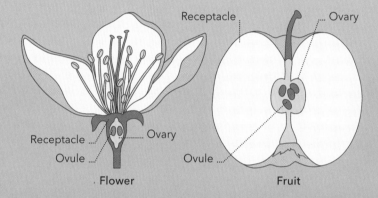

Receptacle

Ovary

Receptacle

Ovary

Ovule

Flower

Ovule

Fruit

▲ FROM FLOWER TO FRUIT
In many plants, the ovary wall forms its fruit. In apples, the base of the flower (the receptacle) swells around the ovary, to become the fleshy fruit.

Types of
VEGETABLE

Vegetables are plants or parts of plants that can be used as food. Many can be eaten raw, while others are only edible once they have been cooked. Some plants we call vegetables are actually fruits!

Vegetables have been part of the human diet for many thousands of years. Of the 1,000 or so vegetable species, few are entirely edible. It is why they are classified by the part of the plant that is consumed. Bulb vegetables (that look like a bulb), such as garlic, onions, and leeks, and root vegetables like carrots, potatoes, yams, and beets, are so called because those are the main parts of them we eat. They contain lots of vitamins and minerals because they grow underground, protected from bad weather, storing up nutrients so the plant can develop quickly when conditions improve.

A less commonly edible part of a plant is the stem, or stalk. Stem vegetables include rhubarb, celery,

and asparagus. They usually contain lots of fiber. Kohlrabi, also known as a German turnip, is a stem vegetable whose root and stalks can both be eaten, raw or cooked.

In addition to roots, bulbs, and stems, the green leaves of "crucifers" (also called Brassicas) such as cabbage and bok choy are also good to eat, as are the upper stems, or florets, of other crucifers like broccoli. Many green vegetables grow in winter and, in the past, provided vitamins, minerals, and disease-fighting substances called antioxidants in the cold months when there was less to eat. Because they can now be flown in from around the world, they are available in stores all year, as are "summer" salad greens such as lettuce and endive.

Vegetables that grow in pods are very nourishing. With peas and fava beans, just the seeds are usually eaten; for runner beans and green beans, the whole pod is consumed.

Usually thought of as vegetables, items such as cucumbers, tomatoes, and zucchini are actually fruits. This is because, like other fruits, they contain seeds. Unlike "normal" fruit, however, they are usually savory, not sweet.

> **More onions are produced and eaten around the world each year than any other vegetable.**

▶ ANATOMY OF AN ONION
The inside layers of an onion bulb are not its only edible part. The flowers, stem, and leaves can all be eaten. The roots suck up nutrients from the soil and the skin protects the bulb.

Flowers, or buds

Stem, with tender leaves

Skin, or scale, is dry and papery.

Roots grow from the basal plate.

Fibrous (stringy) roots are inedible.

Taro
ROOT

Ginseng
ROOT

Ginger
RHIZOME
(UNDERGROUND STEM)

Cassava
ROOT

Jicama
BULB

Miniature turnip
ROOT

Skirret
ROOT

Italian flat
onion
BULB

Jerusalem
artichoke
ROOT

Sweet
potato
ROOT

Shallot
BULB

Onion
BULB

Green onion
BULB

Yam
ROOT

Potato
STEM TUBER

Black radish
ROOT

Salsify
ROOT

Carrot
ROOT

Celeriac
ROOT

Red radish
ROOT

Parsnip
ROOT

Rutabaga
ROOT

Beet
ROOT

Black Spanish
radish
ROOT

Globe beet
BULB

Yellow turnip
BULB

Garlic
BULB

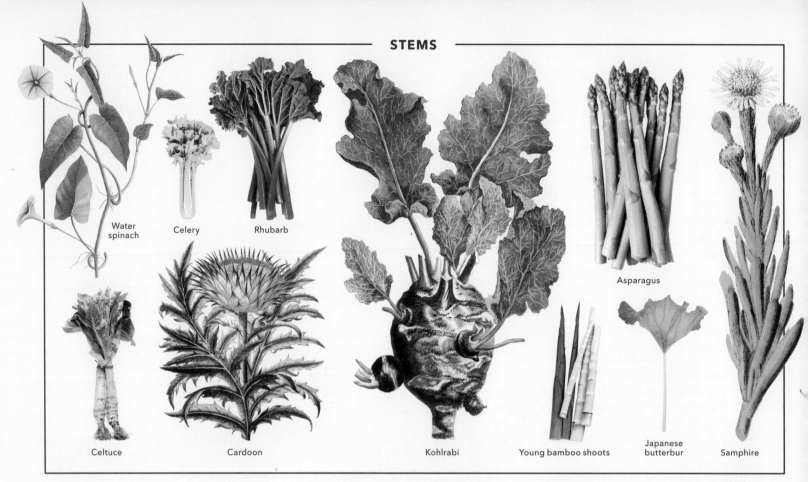

Water spinach

Celery

Rhubarb

Asparagus

Celtuce

Cardoon

Kohlrabi

Young bamboo shoots

Japanese butterbur

Samphire

LEAVES

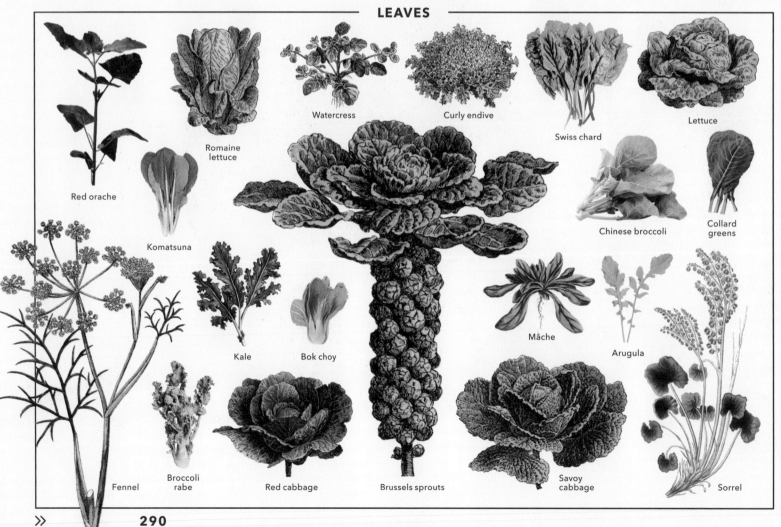

Red orache

Romaine lettuce

Watercress

Curly endive

Swiss chard

Lettuce

Komatsuna

Chinese broccoli

Collard greens

Fennel

Kale

Bok choy

Mâche

Arugula

Broccoli rabe

Red cabbage

Brussels sprouts

Savoy cabbage

Sorrel

SEED POD, FLOWER, AND BUD

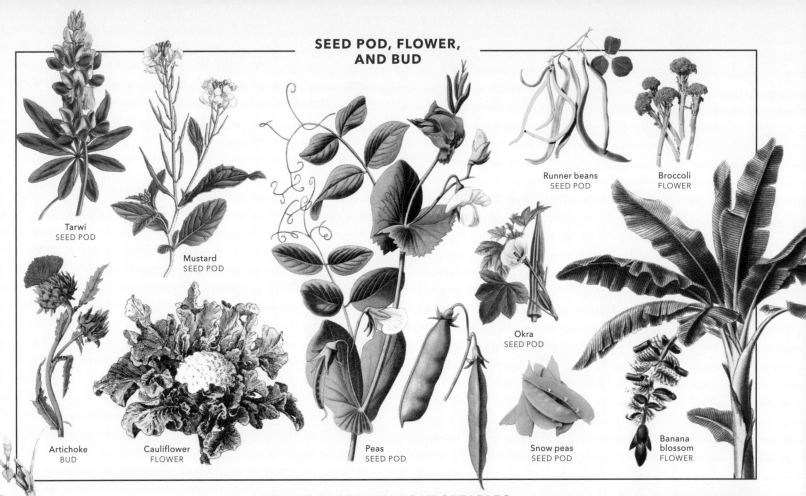

Tarwi
SEED POD

Mustard
SEED POD

Runner beans
SEED POD

Broccoli
FLOWER

Okra
SEED POD

Artichoke
BUD

Cauliflower
FLOWER

Peas
SEED POD

Snow peas
SEED POD

Banana blossom
FLOWER

FRUITS MISTAKEN AS VEGETABLES

Tomato

Corn

Cucumber

Eggplant

Bell pepper

Bitter melon

Pumpkin

Zucchini

291

BRASSICA
varieties

The plants we farm for food today are very different from those that grow naturally. The wild cabbage, for example, has been cultivated into remarkably different varieties, from cabbages to kale.

All the plants we call brassicas have been cultivated from just one single plant—the wild cabbage (known scientifically as *Brassica oleracea*). This includes vegetables such as green cabbage and tenderstem broccoli.

People practiced artificial selection as they grew wild cabbages—they selected plants that had the features they liked best. In some places, it was the leaves. In others, it was the stems or buds. Each time a new crop was planted, these features became more obvious, a little at a time. Eventually, the plants themselves changed due to this selection, and became a range of new, different varieties of the same plant, with different traits. Where plants were selected for their flower

buds, those buds became larger and larger, becoming the plants we know as broccoli and cauliflower. There is a wide range of different broccoli and cauliflower, but all of them feature dense clusters of edible flower buds.

The wild cabbage has leaf buds in different places along its stems, and different types of plant developed from differently placed buds. Brussels sprouts came from lateral leaf buds (buds on the sides of the stalks), and cabbages from terminal leaf buds (buds at the tip of the stalks). Kale and collards formed when wild cabbage plants with large leaves were chosen to be grown. Kohlrabi was formed when plants with thick stems were chosen.

Today, there are dozens of types of farmed brassicas. They only exist because of human farming methods, and all of them are descended from one parent plant. Further selection has created a huge range of different shapes, sizes, and colors, even within the main groups—for example, cauliflower can now be white, green, orange, or purple. Some varieties, such as the Japanese flowering kale, are also used as ornamental plants in gardens. Its leaves come in colors of green, cream, and purple.

> Cabbages have been farmed for more than 4,000 years.

▼ MANY VARIANTS
Modern varieties of the wild cabbage were developed from different parts of this plant.

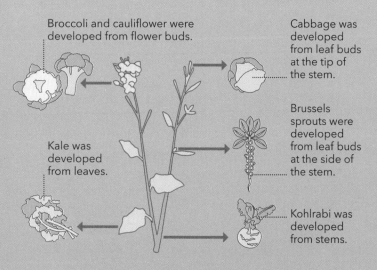

Broccoli and cauliflower were developed from flower buds.

Cabbage was developed from leaf buds at the tip of the stem.

Kale was developed from leaves.

Brussels sprouts were developed from leaf buds at the side of the stem.

Kohlrabi was developed from stems.

BRASSICA VARIETIES

BROCCOLI AND CAULIFLOWER
(FLOWER BUDS)

Chinese broccoli

Calabrese broccoli

Romanesco cauliflower

Rapini

Graffiti cauliflower

Purple sprouting broccoli

Cheddar cauliflower

Tenderstem broccoli

Vitaverde cauliflower

BRUSSELS SPROUTS
(LATERAL LEAF BUDS)

Nautic

Jade Cross

Nelson

Diablo

Redarling

CABBAGE
(TERMINAL LEAF BUDS)

Buscaro cabbage

Cone cabbage

Chinese cabbage

White cabbage

Melissa cabbage

Green cabbage

Choy sum

Red cabbage

Cannonball cabbage

January King cabbage

KALE AND COLLARD
(LEAVES)

Chinese kale

Redbor kale

Blue Curled Scotch kale

Red Russian kale

Dwarf green curled kale

Cavolo nero

Georgia collard green

White Russian kale

Japanese flowering kale

Baby kale

Purple kale

KOHLRABI
(STEMS)

Purple Delicacy

Early White Vienna

Gigante

Kossak

Kolibri

A selection of brassica varieties grown from wild cabbage

Edible
SEEDS

Seeds are the tiny parcels of nutrients from which new plants grow. Many seeds are edible (safe to eat) for humans, and have been a part of our diet for centuries. They include grains, legumes, pulses, and nuts.

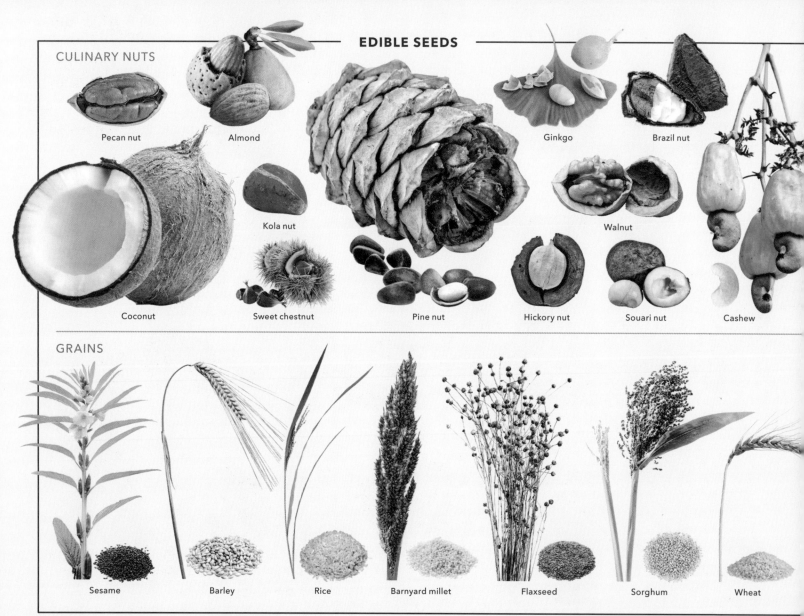

EDIBLE SEEDS

CULINARY NUTS

Pecan nut

Almond

Ginkgo

Brazil nut

Coconut

Kola nut

Walnut

Sweet chestnut

Pine nut

Hickory nut

Souari nut

Cashew

GRAINS

Sesame

Barley

Rice

Barnyard millet

Flaxseed

Sorghum

Wheat

Do not eat cashew nuts off the tree or the seeds inside ginkgo nuts, because they are toxic. Always cook sweet chestnuts and dried legumes before eating.

Many plant groups have seeds that humans can eat. They can be divided into three categories based on how the seeds develop: legumes grow inside pouches, called pods; grains grow many all together, clustered at the top of the plant's stem; and nuts are single seeds that develop inside a hard cover.

Nuts include cashews, pecans, and walnuts. They are very nutritious—their hard seeds are packed with proteins, fats, and carbohydrates.

Legumes and pulses are all the seeds of one plant family—the peas. They are distinctive in having two large cotyledons (food reserves to nourish the developing seedling) and pods that split open, in two halves, when the seeds are ripe. If eaten while still green, these edible seeds are termed legumes (like peas), but if eaten when ripe and dry, they are called pulses (like many beans). A few pulses, including alfalfa and mung beans, are left to grow and sprout before we eat their seedlings. Fox nuts are often roasted until they pop like popcorn before they are eaten.

Grains are mostly the seeds from plants in the grass family, which are called cereals, but other plants included here, such as quinoa, have similar seeds and are called pseudo-cereals. They all have small, or even tiny, seeds in large heads. These seeds often need to be milled or ground to release their nutrients for cooking or eating. Over many years, each grain has been selectively bred to make the seeds bigger and easier to harvest.

Each year, about 2.7 million tons of grains are harvested.

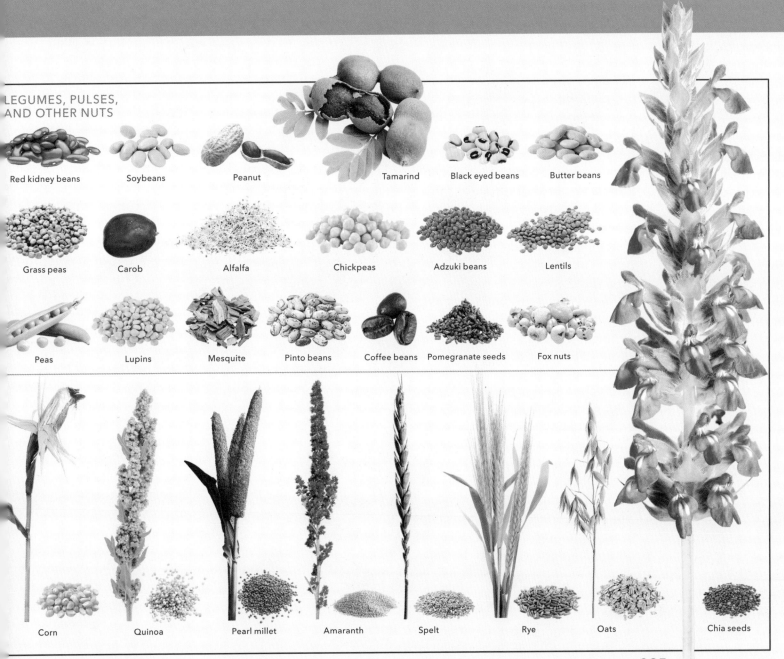

LEGUMES, PULSES, AND OTHER NUTS

Red kidney beans • Soybeans • Peanut • Tamarind • Black eyed beans • Butter beans

Grass peas • Carob • Alfalfa • Chickpeas • Adzuki beans • Lentils

Peas • Lupins • Mesquite • Pinto beans • Coffee beans • Pomegranate seeds • Fox nuts

Corn • Quinoa • Pearl millet • Amaranth • Spelt • Rye • Oats • Chia seeds

TYPES OF HERB

HERBS USED RAW

Calendula

Smooth sumac berries

Chervil

Rosemary

Lavender

Dill

Ginkgo

Indian snakeroot flower

Mint

Indian snakeroot

HERBS USED RAW AND COOKED

Lemon

Angelica

Parsley

Arugula

Celery

Neem

Tamarind

Basil

Goji berries

Oregano

Borage

Anise hyssop

Pomegranate

Cilantro

Prickly pear

Fennel flowers and seeds

Chives

Tarragon

HERBS USED COOKED

Chamomile

Tea tree

Lemongrass

Sage

Stinging nettle

Bay

Elder flowers and berries

Thyme

Wild bergamot

Types of
HERB

An herb is any plant whose leaves, seeds, or flowers are used for flavoring food, as a medicine, or in perfume. They can be used raw or cooked and differ from spices in that they are often used fresh.

There are many sources of herbs, which are found wild across much of the globe. Every culture has found native herbs to use, with many having been cultivated for thousands of years. People have spread herbs far away from their origins as they traveled, adding to the local herbs used. Although most herbs are the leaves of plants, there are some stems, fruits, flowers, and roots used as well. While some can be dried to preserve them when fresh herbs are unavailable, most are used and preferred fresh.

Most herbs can be used either raw or cooked, depending on the dish they are added to. The essential oils that help protect these plants from hot, dry conditions and repel pests are the key ingredient in making them valuable as herbs. For example, more than 60 types of basil are grown in warmer climates and used to add a fresh, sweet flavor to sauces and curries around the world.

Some herbs are only used cooked, such as stinging nettle and bay laurel leaves. Nettle stings are neutralized by cooking, making this herb edible, with a pleasant, spinachlike flavor and medicinal properties that can help arthritis. Bay leaves can be picked fresh or used dried, but their aromatic flavor is only released by the heat of cooking. Herbs such as chamomile have an ancient history. In England, chamomile was mentioned in Nicholas Culpeper's 17th-century book *Complete Herbal*. It has well-known medicinal properties. It is used to make a calming tea or as an ingredient in beer making.

Very often, several herbs are used in combination, to add a particular taste to a dish. In Europe, and particularly in Mediterranean cooking, cilantro, parsley, and celery are indispensable in many dishes. While celery is often added at the start of cooking, parsley and cilantro are added at the end, so they retain their unique flavors.

In Southwest Asia (the Middle East), the health benefits of sumac berries are well understood and make this powerful herb a valuable addition to many dishes. Persian and Islamic cuisines add pomegranate seeds to dishes for medicinal, as well as culinary, benefits, because they have antibacterial and other beneficial properties, as well as a sharp, fruity taste. In southern Asia, neem is widely grown and used for a variety of medicinal remedies. All parts of the tree can be used, so much so that it is known as the "village pharmacy."

> More than 100 species of herbs are used globally.

> Mexicans traditionally use prickly pear to treat obesity and diabetes.

SPICE
flavors

People have used parts of plants as spices to add flavor to food for thousands of years. Spices can be grouped according to the type of flavors they add.

Leaves, bark, roots, fruits, seeds, and even flowers can be dried and used as spices. Based on the flavor they add, spices can be of twelve types. Each type of spice adds a different tang to a dish. Some are mild and sweet, such as the gently warming flavor of cinnamon. Others can be fiery and peppery, like chile, creating a burning sensation on the tongue. Spice combinations have come to characterize the cuisines of different regions. Many Indian dishes are flavored with turmeric, chile, cumin, coriander, paprika, and ginger, while Mexican dishes, such as mole sauce, will feature allspice, cacao, and cloves.

Spices aren't only used in food. The ancient Egyptians used spices such as cinnamon and cumin during the mummification process. Historically, many spices were also used for medicinal purposes—often to treat colds or digestive issues. The Romans used nutmeg to treat indigestion and headaches, while in 3rd-century China, ginger was used to treat nausea and stomach problems.

These days, most spices are relatively cheap and easy to source, but historically they were extremely valuable. In medieval Europe, peppercorns were so valuable they were used to pay rent. It wasn't until the 13th century that spices first came to Europe from Asia. Explorer Marco Polo brought new spices, such as ginger, cinnamon, and pepper, back from his travels—marking the beginning of the global spice trade. In the 15th century, Christopher Columbus sailed to the Americas and encountered a wealth of new spices, including chile, allspice, and vanilla. One spice that remains highly valuable today is saffron. It is incredibly labor-intensive to harvest and as a result very expensive. Its nickname is "red gold" because an ounce of saffron is more expensive than an ounce of gold.

Asafoetida is called "devil's dung" because its smell is so pungent.

India produces nearly 80 percent of the world's turmeric.

▶ **FLAVOR STORES**

Most of the flavor in a spice is stored inside bubbles of oil or fat. Damaging the plant, by bruising, grinding, or heating it, releases this oil as well as the flavor compounds inside the spice.

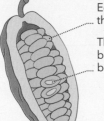

Edible pulp surrounds the cacao beans.

The fleshy, fat-filled beans are roasted to bring out the flavor.

Cacao pod

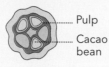

Pulp

Cacao bean

Cacao pod top cross-section

SPICE FLAVORS

GENTLE WARMTH

Cassia bark · Licorice · Vanilla pods · Cinnamon · Anise · Allspice · Star anise · Mahleb

FRAGRANT

Coriander · Cardamom · Mastic · Juniper · Rose

SWEET-SOUR

Anardana · Sumac · Amchoor · Carob · Tamarind

PEPPERY

Chile · Ginger · Grains of paradise · Sichuan pepper · Black pepper

EARTHY

Nigella · Cumin · Turmeric · Onion seeds

CITRUS

Dried lime · Lemongrass · Lemon myrtle · Myristica

SULFUROUS

Asafoetida · Mustard seeds · Curry leaf · Garlic

WARM

Mace · Caraway seeds · Nutmeg · Dill seeds · Annatto

TOASTY

Sesame · Fennel seeds · Wattle · Paprika

HARD-HITTING

Grains of Selim · Cardamom · Galangal · Bay leaf

BITTER-SWEET

Celery seeds · Ajwain · Saffron · Fenugreek · Poppy seeds

FRUITY

Cloves · Cacao · Pink peppercorn · Barberry

Chile
PEPPERS

These peppers originally grew only in southern North America and South America, but they are now grown around the world. Chiles are used in a number of cuisines and bring "heat" to many popular dishes.

CHILE PEPPERS

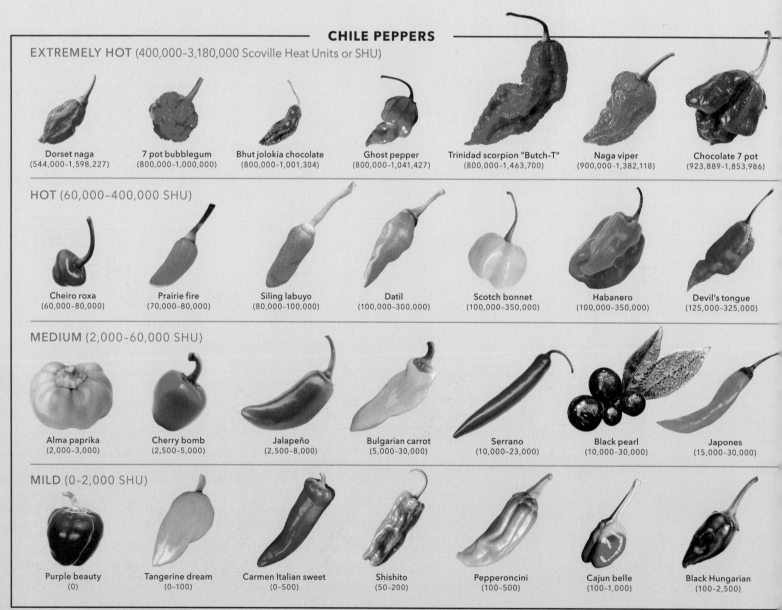

EXTREMELY HOT (400,000–3,180,000 Scoville Heat Units or SHU)

Dorset naga
(544,000–1,598,227)

7 pot bubblegum
(800,000–1,000,000)

Bhut jolokia chocolate
(800,000–1,001,304)

Ghost pepper
(800,000–1,041,427)

Trinidad scorpion "Butch-T"
(800,000–1,463,700)

Naga viper
(900,000–1,382,118)

Chocolate 7 pot
(923,889–1,853,986)

HOT (60,000–400,000 SHU)

Cheiro roxa
(60,000–80,000)

Prairie fire
(70,000–80,000)

Siling labuyo
(80,000–100,000)

Datil
(100,000–300,000)

Scotch bonnet
(100,000–350,000)

Habanero
(100,000–350,000)

Devil's tongue
(125,000–325,000)

MEDIUM (2,000–60,000 SHU)

Alma paprika
(2,000–3,000)

Cherry bomb
(2,500–5,000)

Jalapeño
(2,500–8,000)

Bulgarian carrot
(5,000–30,000)

Serrano
(10,000–23,000)

Black pearl
(10,000–30,000)

Japones
(15,000–30,000)

MILD (0–2,000 SHU)

Purple beauty
(0)

Tangerine dream
(0–100)

Carmen Italian sweet
(0–500)

Shishito
(50–200)

Pepperoncini
(100–500)

Cajun belle
(100–1,000)

Black Hungarian
(100–2,500)

Chiles with a high SHU content can be toxic, especially in large amounts

Most mammals don't like the heat of peppers, but humans love it. There are more than 4,000 varieties of chile peppers, but most are descended from a single species. It was grown for millennia in Mexico. Chile pepper seeds were taken by people to the Caribbean, from where they found their way to Europe and the rest of the world.

The chile pepper is an annual plant—which means it germinates, grows, produces fruit, and then dies within the same season. Each generation can be different, which has allowed humans to develop hotter variants over the years.

The chemical capsaicin is responsible for the "heat" felt when eating chiles. Completely absent in bell peppers, the amount of capsaicin increases significantly in the hottest chiles. In 1912, Wilbur Scoville developed a scale to measure the intensity of heat. The Scoville Heat Scale (SHU) is used in the food industry to indicate the level of spiciness and heat in peppers, sauces, and dishes. Pepper X, the world's hottest chile, has an intensity of 2,693,000 SHU. Hot sauce makers also use this scale while branding their products to attract consumers.

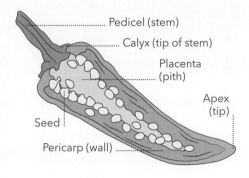

Pedicel (stem)
Calyx (tip of stem)
Placenta (pith)
Apex (tip)
Seed
Pericarp (wall)

▲ PARTS OF A PEPPER

The chile fruit is actually a berry, with many seeds. The hottest part is the placenta, but the flesh or pericarp is the part most often eaten.

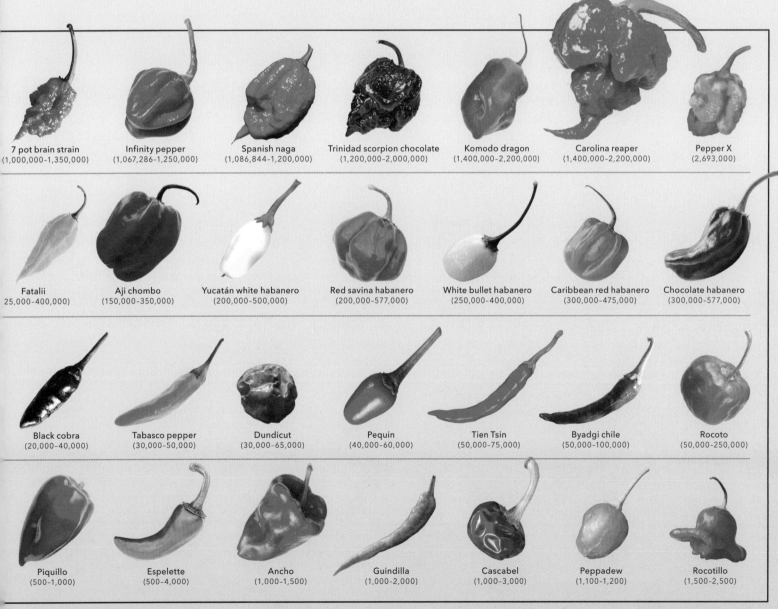

7 pot brain strain
(1,000,000–1,350,000)

Infinity pepper
(1,067,286–1,250,000)

Spanish naga
(1,086,844–1,200,000)

Trinidad scorpion chocolate
(1,200,000–2,000,000)

Komodo dragon
(1,400,000–2,200,000)

Carolina reaper
(1,400,000–2,200,000)

Pepper X
(2,693,000)

Fatalii
25,000–400,000)

Aji chombo
(150,000–350,000)

Yucatán white habanero
(200,000–500,000)

Red savina habanero
(200,000–577,000)

White bullet habanero
(250,000–400,000)

Caribbean red habanero
(300,000–475,000)

Chocolate habanero
(300,000–577,000)

Black cobra
(20,000–40,000)

Tabasco pepper
(30,000–50,000)

Dundicut
(30,000–65,000)

Pequin
(40,000–60,000)

Tien Tsin
(50,000–75,000)

Byadgi chile
(50,000–100,000)

Rocoto
(50,000–250,000)

Piquillo
(500–1,000)

Espelette
(500–4,000)

Ancho
(1,000–1,500)

Guindilla
(1,000–2,000)

Cascabel
(1,000–3,000)

Peppadew
(1,100–1,200)

Rocotillo
(1,500–2,500)

BREADS
of the world

Bread is a staple food in many cultures, and it comes in various forms. Evidence of breads and breadmaking has been found dating back 30,000 years, making it one of the oldest prepared foods.

The first step in making bread is preparing the dough—a thick, elastic paste made of flour mixed with salt and a liquid such as water, milk, or yogurt. Salt not only adds flavor to the dough, but also gives it a soft texture when it is kneaded. The dough is then left to rise, before being shaped into various forms. Many breads use a leavening (raising) agent, such as yeast (dried or fresh yeast, or wild yeast in sourdough) or baking soda, which produces a chemical reaction that makes the dough rise.

Some types of bread are unleavened, meaning they don't contain a raising agent and remain flat. Throughout Southeast Asia, flatbreads such as roti and parantha are eaten regularly. The same goes for the tortilla from Mexico, the matzah from Egypt, and the sour injera from Ethiopia.

Some flatbreads do use a raising agent, despite being flat in shape. Examples include the Indian naan and Turkish pide, both of which are sometimes stuffed with meat or herbs. Similarly, the Levantine pita is made to be split in half to create a pocket that can be filled with meat or falafels (chickpea fritters).

Different types of bread are made by using different cooking methods, or by adding extra ingredients to the dough. Many flatbreads are cooked on a single hot surface such as a skillet, which means the bread must be flipped over so both sides can be cooked. Bigger loaves of bread, such as baguettes and challah, are usually baked in ovens, which allow more than one side of the bread to be heated at once, and have space for the bread to rise up as it cooks.

Most bread uses flour milled from wheat, but not all. One type of wheat flour is bread flour, which has a higher protein content than other flour types, and is often used to make fluffy and chewy breads. Rye is a grain similar to wheat, but with a different flavor. It is milled into rye flour and used to make breads such as anadama and pumpernickel, which are usually heavier than wheat-flour breads, with a slightly sour taste.

Bagels are a doughnut-shaped type of bread roll. To make bagels, the shaped dough is boiled before it is baked. This gives the finished bagels an unusual, chewy texture compared to breads that aren't boiled.

Brioche bread has butter added to the dough, which makes the texture of the loaf rich and slightly sweet.

Remains of 8,600-year-old bread have been found in Türkiye (Turkey).

BREADS OF THE WORLD

Roti canai
SOUTHEAST ASIA

Parantha
INDIA

Nan-e-sangak
IRAN

Pita
SOUTHWEST ASIA (MIDDLE EAST)

Matzah
EGYPT

Toghach
CHINA

Lefse
NORWAY

Crispbread
FINLAND AND SWEDEN

Tortilla
MEXICO

Chapati
SOUTH ASIA

Msemmen
MOROCCO

Pan de bono
COLOMBIA

Naan
INDIA

Chawal bhakri
INDIA

Gözleme
TÜRKIYE (TURKEY)

Farinata
ITALY AND FRANCE

Simit
TÜRKIYE (TURKEY)

Youtiao
CHINA

Injera
ETHIOPIA

Fry bread
NORTH AMERICA

Pide
TÜRKIYE (TURKEY)

German pretzel
GERMANY

Damper
AUSTRALIA

Adobe bread
NORTH AMERICA

Breadsticks
ITALY

Marraqueta
CHILE

Lepinja
BOSNIA

Khubz
SOUTHWEST ASIA (MIDDLE EAST)

Focaccia
ITALY

Cong you bing
CHINA

Melon pan
JAPAN

Bagel
POLAND

Challah
CENTRAL EASTERN EUROPE

Speķrauši
LATVIA

Baguette
FRANCE

Roosterkoek
SOUTH AFRICA

Croissant
FRANCE

Pane al latte
ITALY

Brioche
FRANCE

Picos
SPAIN

Ciabatta
ITALY

Pumpernickel
GERMANY

Zopf
SWITZERLAND AND AUSTRIA

Coppia ferrarese
ITALY

Parãoa rēwena
NEW ZEALAND

Mantou
CHINA

Fan tan roll
US

Irish soda bread
IRELAND

Anadama bread
US

White bread loaf
ENGLAND

Skillet bread
SCOTLAND

Partybrot
GERMANY

303

Italian
PASTA

Pasta originated in Italy, and is now popular around the world. Pasta comes in different shapes and sizes, from long tagliatelle and stuffed tortellini to short rigatoni and tiny stellette.

Pasta is made out of dough, or "paste." There are five basic pasta shapes: long (thin strings or flat lengths), stuffed (containing tasty morsels of meat or vegetables), specialty (regional varieties), short cut (chunky shapes or tubes), and minute (tiny shapes). Examples of each shape are shown on the right. The shape is important because there is a best form of pasta for each accompanying sauce. Long pasta, such as linguine and fettuccine, need to be twirled around a fork to eat, which means that tomato or creamy sauces go well with it. Short cut, chunky pasta shapes, such as macaroni or dischi, can hold heavy cream or meat sauces. The ridges on some of these pasta such as rigatoni help oily sauces cling to them. Stuffed pasta, which is already flavorful from fillings such as cheese and spinach, might be accompanied with a very simple sauce, or no sauce—just smothered in melted butter and herbs. Minute pastas, such as orzo, are often added to soups.

Pasta names often describe their shape in Italian. Conchiglie means shells, farfalle means butterflies, stellette means stars, orecchiette

People have made pasta in Italy since at least the 4th century BCE.

means little ears, fiori means flowers, ruote means wheels, and mezzelune means half moons.

Pasta dough is made by mixing durum wheat, water, and sometimes eggs and olive oil. It is kneaded until smooth and then covered and set aside to rest. The dough is either rolled into flat sheets and cut into shapes by hand, or pressed through machines to produce different shapes. Pasta is always made with the same basic ingredients, but different foods can be added to the dough to change its color or taste. Adding squid ink creates black pasta, while the use of beets produces purple pasta. Garlic and herbs can be mixed into the dough to add a savory flavor.

Pasta comes in many sizes, which is often explained in its name. A pasta name ending in "ini" means smallest and "oni" means largest. For example, fusilli is a type of spiral pasta, so fusillini is a small type of fusilli, and fusillioni is the largest type of fusilli.

Some types of pasta are linked with a specific region of Italy—pappardelle is associated with Tuscany, and in Veneto, potato gnocchi is the favorite.

Around 3.8 million tons of pasta are produced every year in Italy alone.

ITALIAN PASTA

LONG

Lasagna

Pizzoccheri

Fusilli Lunghi

Mafalde

Pappardelle

Fettuccine

Tagliatelle

Linguine

Pici

Bigoli

Bucatini

Bavette

Bucati

Stringozzi

Spaghetti

Vermicelli

Capellini

STUFFED

Agnolotti

Cappelletti

Caramelle

Conchiglioni

Pansotti

Ravioli

Sacchettoni

Tortellini

Mezzelune

Manicotti

Fazzoletti Ripieni

Cannelloni

MINUTE

Stellette

Alfabeto

Orzo

Anelli

Merletti

Gianduietta

Tripolini

Quadrucci

Coralli

Cocciolette

Paternoster

Margheritine

Acini di Pepe

Ditalini Rigati

SPECIALTY

Abbotta pezziende

Assabesi

Ballerine

Torchio

Canestrini

Capunti

Cavatelli

Farfalle

Francesine

Funghetti

Garganelli

Gnocchi

Margherite

Nuvole

Orecchiette

Pasta al Ceppo

Busiate

Troffiette

Sagne 'Ncannulate

Passatelli

SHORT CUT

Penne Rigate

Canneroni

Cannolicchi

Cappello Napoletano

Cavatappi

Rigatoni

Chifferi rigati

Conchiglie

Creste di gallo

Dischi

Elicoidali

Fiori

Gemelli

Trottole

Gomiti

Gramigna

Lumache

Macaroni

Malloreddus

Trenne

Marziani

Pipe

Ziti

Rotini

Ruote

Sorprese Lisce

Tortiglioni

Mezze Penne

Mostaccioli

Ondule

Paccheri

Pantacce

WORLD CHEESES

COW

SOFT
Munster
Gorgonzola
Brie
Langres
Limburger
Ricotta
Camembert

SEMI-SOFT
Danbo
Tomme de Savoie
Paneer
Taleggio
Kachokabaro
Havarti
Pepper jack

SEMI-HARD
Cheddar
Provolone
Maytag Blue
Monterey Jack
Oaxaca
Gouda
Tilsit
Jarlsberg
Stilton

HARD
Emmental
Parmesan
Mahón
Grana Padano
Comté
Gruyère

SHEEP

SOFT
Brocciu
Brânză de burduf
Casu martzu
Fleur du Maquis

SEMI-SOFT
Serra da Estrela
Manouri
Feta
Caş

SEMI-HARD
Redykołka
Ossau-Iraty
Pecorino Toscano
Roquefort

HARD
Zamorano
Kasseri
Pecorino Sardo
Manchego

GOAT

SOFT
Golden Cross Cheese
Bûcheron
Cathare
Sainte-Maure de Touraine

SEMI-SOFT
Charolais
Clochette
Chabichou
Humboldt Fog

SEMI-HARD
Majorero
Rubing
Picodon

HARD
Crottin de Chavignol
Garrotxa
Payoyo

World
CHEESES

This food made from milk is popular all over the world, with different countries creating their own varieties. Cheeses can be classified based on which animal's milk is used and how moist the cheese is.

Any animal milk can be used to make cheese, but cow, sheep, and goat cheese are the most common. Cheeses are divided into types not just by the type of milk, but also based on how much moisture they contain. Soft cheeses have the most moisture and hard cheeses the least, with semi-soft and semi-hard sitting in between these two extremes. Famous examples of different kinds of cheese are shown on the left.

Milk may be pasteurized (killing bacteria in milk using heat) before making cheese, but cheese can also be made from unpasteurized milk. The first step in cheese-making is fermentation—a process that curdles the milk, separating it into solid lumps called curds and a thin liquid, called whey. This is done by adding acids such as lemon juice, vinegar, whey, or an enzyme called rennet. Once the milk is curdled, the curds are cut, stirred, and cooked.

To make a soft cheese, the curds are shaped and left, so any remaining whey can drain away. Some soft cheeses, such as ricotta, can be eaten right away, while others, such as brie, are left to ripen and develop a stronger flavor. Semi-soft cheeses ripen for 30-90 days.

They are considered the smelliest cheeses, and include ones such as Taleggio.

Parmesan is a hard cheese. To make hard cheeses, the curds are firmly pressed, squeezing out as much of the liquid as possible. They are generally left to age longer than nine months, often in the form of large cheese wheels that ripen slowly. These cheeses are dry and crumble readily, making it easy to grate them.

There are hundreds of cheese varieties around the world. Some are made in many places, while others can be produced legally only in a few places.

Many cheeses have additional flavors added to them. Blue cheese has streaks of mold running through it, created by adding mold spores (similar to seeds) to the milk after it has been curdled. The cheese is then shaped and tiny holes are made in it to let air in for the mold to grow. Smoked cheeses are made by placing the shaped cheeses into a smoker, where different types of wood, such as oak, are burned and the smoke wafted over the cheeses. Other cheeses get their flavors from extra ingredients, such as herbs, garlic, dried fruit, spices, and chiles.

Italian cheese Bitto Storico is aged for up to 18 years before it is eaten.

More than 9.9 million tons of cheese is eaten every year in Europe.

CAKES
of the world

In many parts of the world, cakes are an important part of celebrations. These are sweet desserts that are generally baked and are often decorated to make them look beautiful.

In Europe, the word "cake" used to mean a thin, round mass of baked grain or dough. These early foods were not much of a treat and weren't always sweetened. Over time, as cooking techniques developed and new baking devices were invented, cakes became more elaborate. The meaning of "cake" gradually changed as well—it is now almost always used to refer to something sweet.

Today, there is a huge range of different types and flavors of cake. Some, such as a lava cake, are everyday treats, while others are made to celebrate special occasions, such as a birthday. Cakes may be linked to important events and festivals. For example, in China, mooncakes are made to mark the Mid-Autumn Festival. They are given as gifts to friends and family, and eaten when the moon is at its brightest.

Some cakes, such as the lamington, are made of a spongy mixture of flour, butter, sugar, and eggs. Rounds of sponge cake are often piled on top of each other, and then stuck together with icing or other fillings, such as jam.

Different flavors can be added to make cakes more delicious. Honey, for example, is used to flavor a medovik,

> **The term cake comes from the old Norse word *kaka*, meaning "flatbread."**

while a sachertorte needs chocolate. The syrup made from an osmanthus flower is used to add sweetness to an osmanthus cake, while vanilla and caramelized coconut are essential for a drømmekage.

Making cakes has even become an art form—there are pastry and dessert chefs in restaurants who make and decorate cakes exquisitely. Some cakes are covered in a layer of icing, which comes in a range of varieties—from the simple cream frosting of a chaja to thick layers of fondant used to coat sponge cakes. Some cakes are decorated with chocolate or fruit, or are constructed in a way that is pleasing to the eye—a fraisier is made with a ring of carefully sliced strawberries facing outward, sandwiched between cream and sponge cake.

Cakes are loved all over the world, with each country creating its own favorite. For example, the pavlova was invented in New Zealand, the bundt cake in the US, the basbousa in Egypt, and the šakotis in Poland.

Cake recipes are shared around the world—for instance, the Victoria sponge was made in Britain but it is now enjoyed around the globe.

> **A gâteau de crêpes has more than 20 layers of crêpes and cream.**

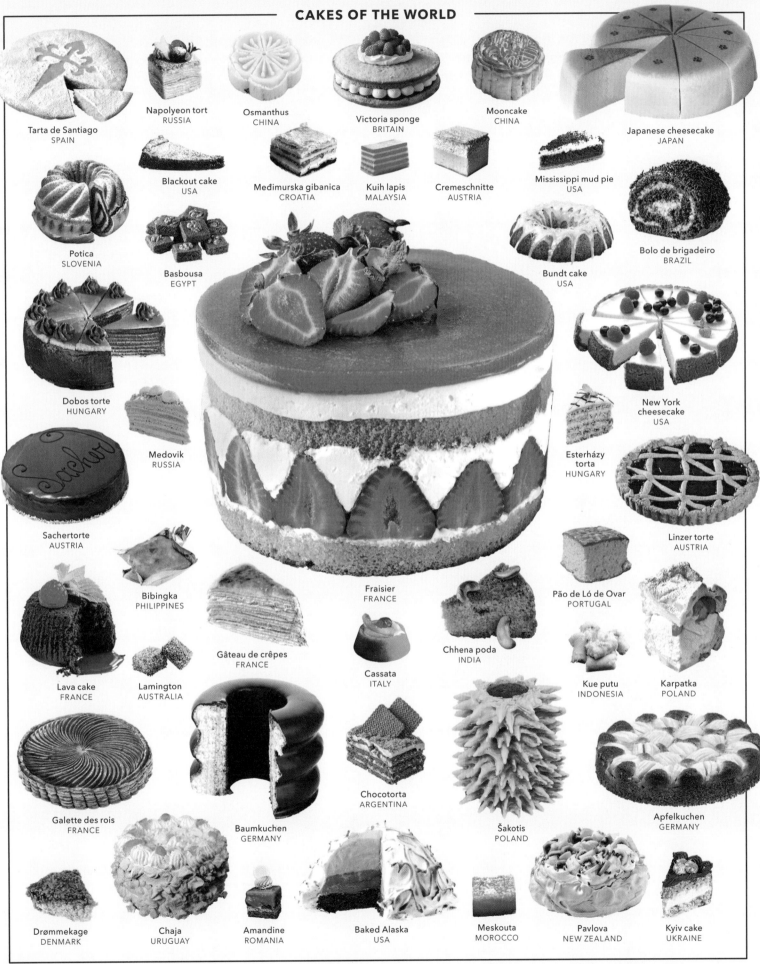

CAKES OF THE WORLD

Tarta de Santiago
SPAIN

Napolyeon tort
RUSSIA

Osmanthus
CHINA

Victoria sponge
BRITAIN

Mooncake
CHINA

Japanese cheesecake
JAPAN

Blackout cake
USA

Međimurska gibanica
CROATIA

Kuih lapis
MALAYSIA

Cremeschnitte
AUSTRIA

Mississippi mud pie
USA

Potica
SLOVENIA

Basbousa
EGYPT

Bundt cake
USA

Bolo de brigadeiro
BRAZIL

Dobos torte
HUNGARY

Medovik
RUSSIA

New York
cheesecake
USA

Sachertorte
AUSTRIA

Esterházy
torta
HUNGARY

Linzer torte
AUSTRIA

Bibingka
PHILIPPINES

Fraisier
FRANCE

Pão de Ló de Ovar
PORTUGAL

Lava cake
FRANCE

Lamington
AUSTRALIA

Gâteau de crêpes
FRANCE

Cassata
ITALY

Chhena poda
INDIA

Kue putu
INDONESIA

Karpatka
POLAND

Galette des rois
FRANCE

Baumkuchen
GERMANY

Chocotorta
ARGENTINA

Šakotis
POLAND

Apfelkuchen
GERMANY

Drømmekage
DENMARK

Chaja
URUGUAY

Amandine
ROMANIA

Baked Alaska
USA

Meskouta
MOROCCO

Pavlova
NEW ZEALAND

Kyiv cake
UKRAINE

INDEX

Page numbers in **bold** refer to main entries.

ACKNOWLEDGMENTS

Dorling Kindersley would like to thank the following people for their help with making the book: Upamanyu Das, Ian Fitzgerald, Satu Hämeenaho-Fox, Vandana Likhmania, Shahid Qureshi, Catharine Robertson, and Laura Sandford for editorial assistance; Anukriti Arora, Noopur Dalal, Chhaya Sajwan, Ira Sharma, Aanchal Singal, and Arunesh Talapatra for design assistance; Manpreet Kaur, Ridhima Sikka, Samrajkumar S, and Rituraj Singh for picture research assistance; Syed Md Farhan for Hi-Res assistance; Phil Gamble, Mark Lloyd, and Mark Ruffle for illustrations; Simon Mumford for cartographic assistance; Andiamo! Language Services Ltd. for linguistic checks; Lynne Boddy for additional consultancy; Lisa Jane Gillespie and the DK Diversity, Equity, and Inclusion Team for a sensitivity check; Laura Gardner Design Studio and Suhita Dharamjit for the jacket; Yogesh Kumar for assistance with contracts and payments; Hazel Beynon for proofreading; and Helen Peters for indexing.

The creative team would like to thank Andrew Macintyre for his continued support and creative input, as well as Jonathan Metcalf and Karen Self for their contribution to the concept and development of this book.

The publisher would like to thank the following for their kind permission to reproduce their photographs:

(Key: a-above; b-below/bottom; c-center; f-far; l-left; r-right; t-top)

1 Alamy Stock Photo: Album (cl/1); MCLA Collection (cl). **Dreamstime.com:** Arx0nt (cr/1); Chaoticmind (cr). **Getty Images:** Moment / Jasius (c). **2 Alamy Stock Photo:** agefotostock (crb/4); Nature Picture Library / Adrian Davies (tl); Chris Mattison (tr/2); Stocktrek Images, Inc. / Sergey Krasovskiy (tr/3); Stocktrek Images / HIGH-G Productions (cra/2); Derek Croucher (cl/2); Nature Picture Library / MYN / JP Lawrence (cr/3); Tristan3D (clb/1); Louise Heusinkveld (bl/1); Historic Illustrations (bc/1); Bill Gozansky (bc/3). **Depositphotos Inc:** ronnarong (bc). **Dorling Kindersley:** Tim Ridley / Robert L. Braun (clb/3); Holts Gems / Ruth Jenkinson (cla/3); National Motor Museum Beaulieu / James Mann (cr). **Dreamstime.com:** Philip Bird (cr/1); Olga Simonova (tc); Marcouliana (tr); Ivan Ekushenko (tr/1); Melinda Fawver (tl/2); Maxim Tatarinov (cla); Nevinates (cla/1); Supamas Lhakjit (cla/2); Nynke Van Holten (cra/3); Heike Rau (cl/1); Alessandro Canova (c); Chaoticmind (cr/2); Shutterfree, Llc / R. Gino Santa Maria (crb); Teddyleung (crb/3); Krzysztof Kowalczyk (bc/2). **Getty Images / iStock:** Film Studio Aves (cl). **Getty Images:** Moment / Jasius (bl). **NASA:** (clb). **naturepl.com:** Andy Sands (br). **Science Photo Library:** Pascal Goetgheluck (tl/1); Dirk Wiersma (clb/2). **4 Alamy Stock Photo:** © chrisstockphotography (crb); trinellblue82 / Stockimo (fcl); MCLA Collection (tc); Chris Mattison (ftr); Xinhua (cl/1); Nature Photographers Ltd / PAUL R. STERRY (c); Ray Evans (cb); Historic Images (fcr). **Dorling Kindersley:** David Harasti (tr). **Dreamstime.com:** Kalinin Dmitrii (cl); Robyn Mackenzie (fcla); VanderWolfImages (tl); Isselee (ftl, cra); Sergey Kolesnikov (clb); Grejak (c/1). **Getty Images / iStock:** Asim Patel (fcra). **The Metropolitan Museum of Art:** Purchase, The Rosenkranz Foundation and Shelby White Gifts, 2004 (cla). **5 Alamy Stock Photo:** Florilegius (c/1); Stocktrek Images, Inc. / Sergey Krasovskiy (ftr); M@rcel (cb); PhotoStock-Israel / Historic Illustrations (fcra); Piotr Naskrecki / Minden Pictures (cr). **Dorling Kindersley:** Bicycle Museum Of America / Gerard Brown (tl); Angela Coppola / University of Pennsylvania Museum of Archaeology and Anthropology (fcl); Natural History Museum, London / Frank Greenaway (tc); Peter Chadwick / Natural History Museum, London (cra). **Dreamstime.com:** Karass2 (tr); Ondřej Prosick (ftl); Mikumistock (fcla); Maxim Tatarinov (ca); Urospoteko (cla); Sombra12 (cla/1); Valentyn75 (c); Denis Pepin (ca/1). **6 Alamy Stock Photo:** Ed Brown Wildlife. **7 Dreamstime.com:** Diidik. **8 Alamy Stock Photo:** British Library / Album (b). **Dorling Kindersley:** Whipple Museum of the History of Science, Cambridge / Gary Ombler (tr). **9 Bridgeman Images:** The British Library Archive / Cellarius, Andreas (C.1596-1665) / German. **10 Alamy Stock Photo:** ICP / Incamerastock. **11 Alamy Stock Photo:** FineArt. **12 Science Photo Library:** Library of Congress. **13 Alamy Stock Photo:** Historic Illustrations / John Wilkes. **16 Alamy Stock Photo:** American Photo Archive (fbr); RGB Ventures / SuperStock / Tony Hallas (tl); Stocktrek Images, Inc. (tc); Scott Camazine (tr); Stocktrek Images, Inc. / Michael Miller (cla); NASA Image Collection (cb); Geopix (cra/1); UPI / NASA (fcra/1); Science History Images / Photo Researchers (fcl, fclb/1, br); Science History Images (c). **Dreamstime.com:** Julian Martinez Cando (cra); Rastan (fcla). **ESA:** Hubble & NASA / Acknowledgement: Judy Schmidt (clb); (image by C. Carreau) (ca/1); NASA, ESA, J. Olmsted (STScI), F. Summers (STScI)C. Ma (UC Berkeley); CC BY 4.0 (cl); NASA, ESA, S. Beckwith (STScI), and The Hubble Heritage Team (STScI / AURA) (fcra); NASA / ESA and The Hubble Heritage Team (fbl); NASA, CSA, STScI (bc); Hubble & NASA (crb/1); Hubble & NASA Acknowledgment: Judy Schmidt (crb). **ESO:** https://creativecommons.org/licenses/by/4.0 (fclb); IDA/Danish 1.5 m/R. Gendler, J-E. Ovaldsen, C. Thöne, and C. Feron./https://creativecommons.org/licenses/by/4.0 (ftr). **NASA and The Hubble Heritage Team (AURA/STScI):** ESA, S. Baum and C. O'Dea (RIT) (fcr). **NASA:** ESA, and C. Sarazin (University of Virginia); Processing: Gladys Kober (NASA / Catholic University of America) (cr); Goddard Space Flight Center / ESO / JPL-Caltech / DSS (ca). **17 Alamy Stock Photo:** RGB Ventures / SuperStock / NASA (clb). **ESA:** Hubble, NASA Y. Choi (NOIRLab), K. Gilbert (Space Telescope Science Institute), J. Dalcanton (Flatiron Institute and University of Washington); CC BY 4.0 (bl); NASA, ESA and the Hubble Heritage Team (STScI / AURA) (cla). **ESO:** Zdenk Bardon/https://creativecommons.org/licenses/by/4.0 (tl). **NASA:** ESA, and The Hubble Heritage Team (STScI / AURA) / Acknowledgment: M. Gregg (Univ. Calif.-Davis and Inst. for Geophysics and Planetary Physics, Lawrence Livermore Natl. Lab.) (cl). **20-21 Alamy Stock Photo:** ukasz Szczepanski (b). **21 Alamy Stock Photo:** Alan Dyer / VWPics (fcrb/1); Roth Ritter / Stocktrek Images (tl); Science History Images (tl/2, cl/2, clb/2, bc, fbr); Granger, NYC / GRANGER - Historical Picture Archive (tr); NASA Image Collection (fcla/1); Stocktrek Images, Inc. (cla/3); Roberto Colombari / Stocktrek Images (fcra/2); PSL Images (bl). **Dreamstime.com:** Milos Gagic (cla/1). **ESA:** ESA & Valentin Bujarrabal (Observatorio Astronomico Nacional, Spain) (cla/4); NASA (ca); Hubble & NASA (fcl); NASA, ESA, and J. Kastner (RIT) (c); ESA / Hubble & NASA, ESO, K. Noll (clb/1). **ESO:** Y. Beletsky (ftr); Igor Chekalin (ftl); ESO, ALMA (ESO / NAOJ / NRAO) / Wong et al., ESO / M.-R. Cioni / VISTA Magellanic Cloud survey. Acknowledgment: Cambridge Astronomical Survey Unit (clb/3); ESA / Hubble & NASA, Acknowledgement: Judy Schmidt (clb/4); ESO (fcra/1, fcla/2, crb/2). **NASA:** JPL-Caltech / STScI / CXC / SAO (crb/1); NASA and the Hubble Heritage Team (AURA / STScI); acknowledgment: D. Garnett (U. Arizona), J. Hester (ASU) and J. Westphal (Caltech) (cla/2); X-ray: NASA / CXC / RIKEN & GSFC / T. Sato et al; Optical: DSS (cra); NASA / ESA / JPL / Arizona State Univ. (cr); NASA / ESA / Hubble (br); ESA, K. Noll (STScI) (cl/1). **Shutterstock.com:** Giovanni Benintende (fcrb/2); PeopleImages.com - Yuri A (cb). **27 Alamy Stock Photo:** Joshimer Biñas (c/2); Christophe Coat (cl/1); Martin (c/1); Tristan3D (c/3, cr/5); blickwinkel / Dautel (clb); ManuelMata (fbr); NASA / digitaleye / J Marshall - Tribaleye Images (fclb). **Dorling Kindersley:** NASA (cl/3). **Dreamstime.com:** Yuri Arcurs (c); Alexandr Yurtchenko (tl); Martijn De Vries (fcla, cla, fcl); Martin Holverda (tc); Grejak (ftr); Larichev89 (cl); Ianm35 (cl/2, fcrb); Diego Barucco (cr/3); Nerthuz (fcr); Tristan Tuftnell (fclb/1); Buradaki (bc/3). **ESA:** ESA 2010 MPS for OSIRIS Team MPS / UPD / LAM / IAA / RSSD / INTA / UPM / DASP / IDA (cb); Hubble, NASA & A. Simon, A. Pagan (STScI); CC BY 4.0 (cra). **Getty Images:** imagenavi (bl); Stocktrek RF (cr/2); Universal Images Group / QAI Publishing (bc/1). **NASA:** JPL-Caltech / UCLA / MPS / DLR / IDA / PSI (crb); JPL / Space Science Institute (fcr/1); Lawrence Sromovsky, University of Wisconsin-Madison / W.W. Keck Observatory (tr). **Science Photo Library:** Jerry Lodriguss (fbl); NASA (cl/4, cr/4); US Geological Survey (cr); NASA / JPL / Space Science Institute (cr/1); VWPICS / Alan Dyer (bc); NASA / GSFC (br). **33 Alamy Stock Photo:** Associated Press / Indian Space Research Organization (fcr); Konstantin Shaklein (tl); Stocktrek Images / Adrian Mann (ftr); NASA / UPI (ca); Universal Images Group North America LLC / QAI Publishing (ca/1); Historical Picture Archive / Granger, NYC. (cra/1); Xinhua (cl); imago images / Xinhua (fcr/1); NG Images (fclb); NASA Image Collection (crb). **Dreamstime.com:** 3000ad (ftl); Eugen Dobric (cl/1); Grejak (cb); Nerthuz (br). **ESA:** ESA-D. Ducros (fbl). **Getty Images:** Pallava Bagla (cl/2); QAI Publishing / Universal Images Group (tc); Future Publishing / Adrian Mann / All About Space Magazine (cla). **NASA:** (cla/1, tc/1, fcla, c); NASA / JPL-Caltech (tr, fcl, fcrb); NASA / ARC (cra). **Science Photo Library:** NASA / JPL (cra/2); Detlev Van Ravenswaay (fcra, cr, cr/1); Paul Wootton (clb). **35 Dreamstime.com:** Scol22 (tc). **NASA:** JSC (tl, cla, cla/Apollo 14, cra, cra/Apollo 17, tr). **36 123RF.com:** (c); Corey A Ford (cb/Dragonfly). **Dorling Kindersley:** James Kuether (cb). **37 123RF.com:** Ivana van Keulen (cl/cat). **Getty Images / iStock:** 2630ben (cb). **Shutterstock.com:** Damien Che (cl). **38 Alamy Stock Photo:** John Cancalosi (c); PjrStudio (tl); Dembinsky Photo Associates / Layne Kennedy (ftl); Imagebroker / Arco / I. Schulz (clb); Nikreates (crb/1); Fossil & Rock Stock Photos (bl); Corbin17 (fbr). **Depositphotos Inc:** Lefpap (fcra). **Dorling Kindersley:** Andy Crawford Courtesy of Dorset Dinosaur Museum (cla, bc); Natural History Museum, London / Colin Keates (tc, cl, cb, cb/1); Oxford University Museum of Natural History / Gary Ombler (tr); Oxford Museum of Natural History / Gary Ombler (cr, crb); Natural History Museum / Colin Keates (fclb). **Dreamstime.com:** Boonchok75 (fcrb); Wlad74 (fbl). **Getty Images / iStock:** Gfrandsen (br). **Science Photo Library:** Science Stock Photography (bl/1). **Shutterstock.com:** Breck P. Kent (fcla); Olpo (cra). **41 Alamy Stock Photo:** agefotostock (cl, cb/2); S.E.A. Photo (fcl); Phil Degginger (c/1). **Dorling Kindersley:** Natural History Museum, London / Tim Parmenter (cr); Natural History Museum, London / Harry Taylor (fcla, crb); Oxford University Museum of Natural History / Gary Ombler (fbr). **Dreamstime.com:** 73bats (fcrb); Siimsepp (ftl); Vvoevale (tl, cra, c, cr/1); Tiu Potchana (tc); Ekaterina Kriminskaia (cr/2, fcr); Montree Nanta (clb). **Getty Images / iStock:** Tycson1 (fcrb/1). **Science Photo Library:** Dirk Wiersma (bc). **Shutterstock.com:** Yes058 Montree Nanta (cla); Aleksandr Pobedimskiy (cb). **42 Dorling Kindersley:** Holts Gems / Ruth Jenkinson (tc); Oxford University Museum of Natural History / Gary Ombler (cla); Natural History Museum, London / Colin Keates (ca, c). **Dreamstime.com:** Joools (ca/1). **44 Dorling Kindersley:** Holts Gems / Ruth Jenkinson (fcra, ca, ca/1, fcl, cl/1, fcrb, br, fbl); Natural History Museum, London / Tim Parmenter (tl, tl/1, tc, tr, cl, cr, clb, fclb, clb/1, cl/2); Holts Gems / Richard Leeney (bc). **Dreamstime.com:** Bigjo5 (c); Emma Ros (ftl); Alessandro Canova (ftr); Gfgfmoses (cra); Vvoevale (fcla, cla); Dani3315 (cla/1); Igor Kaliuzhny (cr/1, c/1); Byjeng (c/2, c/3); Martin Novak (bc/1); Toscawhi (bl); Wlad74 (cb); Phodo1 (fcl/1). **Getty Images / iStock:** E+ / benedek (fcr). **47 Alamy Stock Photo:** imageBROKER.com GmbH & Co. KG / Olaf Krüger (bc); AGF Srl / White Fox (tr); Gregory Maassen (br); Jan Wlodarczyk (crb); Zoonar GmbH / Michal Bednarek (c/1); Mabelin Santos (cl/1); Octavio Campos Salles (cr); GeorgiaFlash (ca). **Dreamstime.com:** Wirestock (cb); Staphy (tl); Photo072 (tc); SnapTPhotography (cla); Mark Baker (clb); Demerzel21 (c); Petr Kahanek (cra/1); Yuliia Bodaniuk (cl). **Getty Images / iStock:** vlad61 (bl). **55 Dreamstime.com:** Victoria L. Almgren (clb); Petro Perutskyy (tl); Richair (cla); Altitudevs (cl); John Sirlin (bl). **Getty Images / iStock:** petesphotography (fbl). **57 Dreamstime.com:** Chaoticmind (c). **63 123RF.com:** drmicrobe (clb). **Alamy Stock Photo:** BIOSPHOTO / Sylvain Cordier (cr/1); FLPA (cra/1); Adisha Pramod (fcla/2); Minden Pictures / Ingo Arndt (fcla/1); Roberto Nistri (cla/3); Premierlight Images (fcl); Juniors Bildarchiv GmbH (fcra); Iconographic Archive (fclb); Les Archives Digitales (fcrb/1); Henri Koskinen (fcrb/3); WILDLIFE GmbH (cb);. **Dorling Kindersley:** Linda Pitkin (cla/1); Richard Leeney / Whipsnade Zoo (tc). **Dreamstime.com:** Serg_dibrova (tr); Grafvision (ftl); Voislav Kolevski (tl); Isselee (tc/1, ftr); Smileus (fcr); Valeriy Kirsanov (cl); Roman Ivaschenko (cb/2); Frenta (fbr); Thomaspicture (cra/2). **Getty Images:** Cultura RM Exclusive / Alexander Semenov (tl/2). **Getty Images / iStock:** Robert Winkler (fcrb/2). **Science Photo Library:** BOB GIBBONS (c); DAVID SCHARF (cla/2); Dr Morley Read (fcla/3); EYE OF SCIENCE (fbl). **64 123RF.com:** Alfio Scisetti (fcrb). **Alamy Stock Photo:** BIOSPHOTO / Sylvain Cordier (tr); Natural History Museum, London (ftr); Westend61 GmbH (ca); Henri Koskinen (c/1); Sunny Celeste (fcr); Margery Maskell (c/2); Peter Yeeles (clb); Bob Gibbons (crb); Historic Illustrations (fbl); WILDLIFE GmbH (bc); Pictures Now (br). **Dreamstime.com:** Prapat Aowsakorn (bl); Gabriela Beres (tl); Aris Astriana (cla); Yosef Erpert (cra); Picture Partners (fcla/1); Hanna Hryharenka (cl); Digitalimagined (c); Chabkc (fbr); Krzysztof Kowalczyk (bc/1); Jocrebbin (cb). **Shutterstock.com:** ijimino (fcla). **65 Alamy Stock Photo:** José María Barres Manuel (fcl); David Whitaker (fcla). **Dorling Kindersley:** David Fenwick (cla). **Dreamstime.com:** Denys Kurylow (fbl); Smileus (clb). **Getty Images / iStock:** Sieboldianus (bl); Robert Winkler (cl). **67 Dreamstime.com:** Alisali (l); Vrozhko (r). **68 123RF.com:** Amawasri Naksakul (crb/1). **Alamy Stock Photo:** blickwinkel / Jagel (br); Nature Photographers Ltd / PAUL R. STERRY (crb); Imagebroker / Arco / Schoening (fcrb); shapencolour (fbl); C J Wheeler (fbl/1); Jacques Jangoux (fcla). **Dorling Kindersley:** Batsford Garden Centre and Arboretum / Gary Ombler (bc/2); Centre for Wildlife Gardening / London Wildlife Trust / Gary Ombler (ftr). **Dreamstime.com:** Dewins (tc/1); Valery Prokhozhy (tl, fclb); Sergey Kolesnikov (tr); Irabel8 (fcla/1); Ielit8 (fcl); Surut Wattanamaetee (cla); Olga Simonova (c); Boonchuay Iamsumang (ca, bc/1); Kwselcer (cra); Iquacu (cl); Urospoteko (clb); Tamara Kulikova (clb/2); Lev Kropotov (cb); Hellmann1 (fcrb/1); Jose Gulias Trigas (bc). **Getty Images / iStock:** ByMPhotos (bl); gianpinox (tc). **Shutterstock.com:** LAURA_VN (clb/1). **70 Mercervale Daffodils & Nursery:** (ftr). **72 Alamy Stock Photo:** Mike Booth (cb/1); The History Collection (tc); Florilegius (tr); The Picture Art Collection (ftr); Herman Vlad (fcra); Historic Images (fcr); imageBROKER.com GmbH & Co. KG / Willi Rolfes (cb); History and Art Collection (clb); John Richmond (crb/1); INTERFOTO / History (bc); Christian Hütter (br); Historic Collection (br/1). **Dorling Kindersley:** Natural History Museum, London / Colin Keates (cra); Scott Zona (fcrb). **Dreamstime.com:** Mohammed Anwarul Kabir Choudhury (crb); Valery Prokhozhy (c/1); Inna Polietaieva (cr); Troichenko (fcrb/1); Sahil Ghosh (fbr). **Getty Images / iStock:** athirati (ca/1); cturtletrax (c). **Getty Images:** Rosemary Calvert (ca). **Barry Hammel:** (fcrb/Sleumer). **73 Alamy Stock Photo:** Album (clb); Amoret Tanner Collection (tl); Blickwinkel / R. Koenig (tl/1); Biosphoto / Frederic Tournay (tc); Historic Images (tc/1, ca, fcr/1); Peter van Evert (cra/1); McPHOTO (fcra); Natural History Museum, London (c); Natural History Archive (bc); PjrNature (bl); Dorling Kindersley: Mark Winwood / RHS Wisley (cr/2); The Picture Art Collection (fclb). **Depositphotos Inc:** KaterinaLin (ftl). **Dreamstime.com:** Rinus Baak (cb/1); Panyukova Uliana (tr); Rbiedermann (tr/1); Serge Goujon (ftr); Key1234 (fcla); Kazakovmaksim (cla); Hecos255 (cra); Poonsak Pornnatwuttikul (cla/1); Oleksandr Kostiuchenko (fcl); Leo6001 (cr); Le Thuy Do (cr/1, fbl); Niels Kliim (fcr); Petrsalinger (fbr); Thomaspicture (crb); Zanozaru (crb/1); Alfio Scisetti (cb). **naturepl.com:** Will Watson (fcla/1). **Shutterstock.com:** alybaba (fbr/1); Harismoyo (ftl/1). **74 Alamy Stock Photo:** Album. **76 123RF.com:** kostiuchenko (cr); sgoodwin4813 (br). **Alamy Stock Photo:** Sandra Baker (tc); Derek Croucher (ftl); Fabiano Sodi (tc/1); John Martin (fcr); Zoonar / Andy Nowack (c). **Dorling Kindersley:** London Wildlife Trust / Gary Ombler: Centre for Wildlife Gardening (fbr). **Dreamstime.com:** Emilio100 (tl); Whiskybottle (tr); Sgoodwin4813 (bc); Picture Partners (bl); Anuwat Namkorn (bl/1). **Shutterstock.com:** Walter Erhardt (ftr). **77 Alamy Stock Photo:** Bob Gibbons (fcla); David Winger (ftl); Alfio Scisetti (tr); Tamara Kulikova (fclb). **Dreamstime.com:** Appfind (fcr); Tiantan (tl); Valery Prokhozhy (cla); Vera08 (cr); ConnectUA (fbl); Richard Griffin (br); Carlos Neto (bc). **Getty Images / iStock:** E+ / Chushkin (clb); E+ / Vidok (bl). **Getty Images:** Martin Ruegner (tc). **78 Alamy Stock Photo:** Avalon.red / Photos Horticultural (cra); Nature Picture Library / Adrian Davies (cr); Florapix (c); Petar Kostov (fbl); WILDLIFE GmbH (fclb). **Bridgeman Images:** Look and Learn (tl). **Getty Images / iStock:** bauhaus1000 (bl). **Getty Images:** Brazil Photos / LightRocket / Flavio Varricchio (fcla); Hulton Archive (ftr); Florilegius / Universal Images (tr); Heritage Art / Heritage Images (ca); Paul Starosta (fcra, fbr). **Adam Schneider:** (cl). **Shutterstock.com:** Yes058 Montree Nanta (clb). **81 Alamy Stock Photo:** ART Collection (br/1); Historic Images (c); Minden Pictures / Gerrit van Ommering / Buiten-beeld (cl); SDym Photography (cr); Iconographic Archive (ftr); Zoonar GmbH / Jürgen Vogt (cb/1); imageBROKER.com GmbH & Co. KG / Martin Dr. Baumgärtner (cb/2); Andrew Darrington (clb/2); The History Collection (bc); Buiten-Beeld / Dick Pasman (crb/2); Chris Mattison (clb/4). **Dreamstime.com:** Andersastphoto (clb); Chanchai Duangdoosan (fcl); Juan-Felipe Giraldo (tl); Matunka (tc); Corina Tintila (ca); Jennifergauld (cla); Oleh Marchak (tr/1, fbl); Anna Puhan (cra/1); Opreanu Roberto Sorin (cra/2); Musat Christian (cb); Savelov (fcrb); Christian Weinkötz (clb/1); Valeriy Kirsanov (crb/1); Laupri (br); Lukas Jonaitis (cb/3). **Getty Images / iStock:** Janice Chen (fcla); ZU_09 (fcr, fcra, fclb); Kornwipa Ponganan (bl). **Getty Images:** Science Photo Library - Steve Gschmeissner (clb/3); Paul Starosta (cra). **Nhu H. Nguyen, University of Hawai'i at Mānoa:** (fcrb/1). **Science Photo Library:** DK Images (crb); Eurelios / Massimo Brega (fbr). **Shutterstock.com:** Ressormat (tr); Wirestock Creators (cl/1). **82 Alamy Stock**

Photo: Minden Pictures / Ingo Arndt (cra/2); Roberto Nistri (tr); Genevieve Vallee (ftr); Fabrice Bettex Photography (fcra); Ethan Daniels (crb/3); imageBROKER.com GmbH & Co. KG / Norbert Probst (fcrb/2); Biosphoto / Colin Marshall (br). **Dorling Kindersley:** Linda Pitkin (crb). **Dreamstime.com:** Voislav Kolevski (crb/2); Andrey Rykov (cra/1); Yodke67 (cra/3). **Shutterstock.com:** Sean Lema (fcrb). **83 123RF.com:** arrxxx (cra/2). **Alamy Stock Photo:** agefotostock (ca/1) Nature in Stock / Jan van Arkel (clb); Helmut Corneli (cl/2); M@rcel (fcr); Roberto Nistri (tc); gustavo adolfo rojas segovia (cla/3); Nature Photographers Ltd / Paul R. Sterry (cra/3); Auscape International Pty Ltd / Mark Spencer (cra/1); Adisha Pramod (cra/5); Andrey Nekrasov (cra/6); blickwinkel / B. Trapp (fcrb). **BluePlanetArchive.com:** Marc Chamberlain (tr). **Depositphotos Inc:** MianHamza (ca/3). **Dorling Kindersley:** John Anderson (cl); Linda Pitkin (cla). **Dreamstime.com:** Wirestock (cla/2); Junyan Jiang (fcl); Manfred Ruckszio (c/1); Kateryna Kon (c/2); Suwat Sirivutcharungchit (ftl); Seadam (ca); Xiao Zhou (fcla); John Albers-mead (fcla/2); R. Gino Santa Maria / Shutterfree, Llc (fcra/2); Tatiana Saenko (br); Grafvision (crb); Isselee (crb/2). **Getty Images:** Cultura RM Exclusive / Alexander Semenov (cra); imageBROKER / Rolf von Riedmatten (fcra); Paul Starosta (clb/3). **Getty Images / iStock:** micro_photo (cra/4). **naturepl.com:** Joel Sartore / Photo Ark (fcrb/2); Sinclair Stammers (bl); MYN / Gil Wizen (fcrb/3). **Science Photo Library:** Steve Gschmeissner (fbl); Eye Of Science (fclb); David Scharf (fclb/3); Dr Morley Read (fclb/2, clb/2). **85 Alamy Stock Photo:** blickwinkel / R. Koenig (cl, fcrb); Nature Picture Library / Alex Hyde (ftr); SBS Eclectic Images (cla/5); Photo12 / Ann Ronan Picture Library (cra/2); Danita Delimont / Margaret Gaines (cra/3); Jason Edwards (fcra); Nature Photographers Ltd / Paul R. Sterry (fcla/2); Roberto Nistri (fcla/3); Wildlife Gmbh (ca); Penta Springs Limited / Artokoloro (cr); Florilegius (cb, crb/3); Custom Life Science Images (fcra/3, clb/3); PjrShells (clb/4). **Dreamstime.com:** Jan Van Bizar (cla/3); KPixMining (tl); Jeremy Campbell (tc); Eyeblink (cla/2); Valentyn75 (cra); Velikanpiter (fcra/2); Tententenn (cra/4); Yodke67 (fcla, cr/2); Xiao Zhou (cr/3, br); Swissmargrit (cr/4); Sara Fanciulli (fbr); Iamtkb (bl); Menno Van Der Haven (clb); Elena281 (clb/2); Jolanta Wojcicka (crb); Daboost (crb/2). **Getty Images / iStock:** jon841 (fclb). **Getty Images:** Ed Reschke (cla/4). **Science Photo Library:** Smithsonian Institution (tr, fbl, clb/5). **Shutterstock.com:** zaferkizilkaya (cla). **86 Alamy Stock Photo:** agefotostock (fcra/1); Nature Picture Library / Alex Hyde (tl/1); The Picture Art Collection (ca); Nature Picture Library / Wild Wonders of Europe / Benvie (fcla); Nature Picture Library / Kim Taylor (cla); Minden Pictures / Piotr Naskrecki (fcr); Nature Picture Library / MYN / Gil Wizen (cr); Nature Photographers Ltd / Paul R. Sterry (fcrb); Library Book Collection (cb). **Dreamstime.com:** Costasz (bc); Agustín Orduña Castillo (tl); Mattiaath (tc); Digitalimagined (ftr); Cosmin Manci (cra); Alexander Hasenkampf (fcl); Iamtkb (cl/1); Lawcain (c); Marcouliana (clb); Eivaisla (bc/1); Isselee (crb). **Getty Images:** vinisouza128 / 500px (ftl). **naturepl.com:** Nature Production (fcra); RSPB Handbook of Garden Wildlife Second Edition / Books / Collaborations (tr). **Science Photo Library:** Pascal Goetgheluck (cl); F. Martinez Clavel (fbl). **88 Alamy Stock Photo:** Archive PL (cra/1); Wirestock, Inc. (cl); Zdenk Mal (fcl); Cbstockfoto (cr); Denis Keith (fcr); Nature Picture Library / Alex Hyde (cra, fclb); Francisco Martinez-Clavel Martinez (fcra); Nature Picture Library / MYN / Javier Aznar (ftr); imageBROKER.com GmbH & Co. KG / Steve Trewhella (ca); Nature Picture Library / Kim Taylor (tc); Minden Pictures / Piotr Naskrecki (tl); Gibson Green (br). **© Lech Borowiec:** (cr/1). **Dreamstime.com:** EPhotocorp (br/1); Viter8 (ftl); Oleksandr Shpak (cb); Alexander Hasenkampf (clb); Cosmin Manci (fbr). **Centre for Biodiversity Genomics:** (tr). **Getty Images:** Designpics (crb/1); Darrell Gulin (c); Yuta Nakase (fcla). **Getty Images / iStock:** Wirawan Prabowo (fbl). **Guy Hanley, Northern Plains Entomology:** (cla/1). **Seig Kopinitz:** (bc). **Photo courtesy of the Spencer Entomological Collection, Beaty Biodiversity Museum, UBC:** Don Griffiths (crb). **Science Photo Library:** Pascal Goetgheluck (cl/1). **Shutterstock.com:** Alslutsky (fcrb); Anton Kozyrev (bl). **Udo Schmidt:** (cla, clb/1). **90 Alamy Stock Photo:** ephotocorp / Zeeshan Mirza (cra); Nature Picture Library / Robert Thompson (cla); Nature Picture Library / Alex Hyde (clb/1); Minden Pictures / Thomas Marent (br). **Dorling Kindersley:** Natural History Museum, London / Frank Greenaway (ftl, tl, ftr, ca, fcl, cl, c, cr, fcr, cl/1, cr/1, cb, crb, crb/1, bl). **Dreamstime.com:** Palex66 (clb). **naturepl.com:** Bernard Castelein (tc); Andy Sands (tr). **Shutterstock.com:** Margus Vilbas (bc). **93 Alamy Stock Photo:** agefotostock (cr); Christian Musat (tl); blickwinkel / AGAMI / W. Leurs (cla); Natural History Museum, London (cl/1); Bryan Reynolds (clb); Domiciano Pablo Romero Franco (bl). **Dorling Kindersley:** Thomas Marent (tr, crb/1); Natural History Museum, London / Frank Greenaway (tc, ftr/1, cra/1, fcra, cl, fclb, cb, fclb/1, crb/2, fcrb/1, bc/1, br); Natural History Museum, London / Colin Keates (fcl, fbr); Natural History Museum, London / Tim Parmenter (c). **Dreamstime.com:** Alslutsky (fbl); Elitravo (ftl); Feathercollector (ftr); Tobyphotos / Torbjrn Swenelius (fcla); Christian Weiß (ca); Ihar Balaikin (ca/1); Stuart Andrews (clb/1). **Getty Images:** Moment / Jasius (cra, bc). **naturepl.com:** Alex Hyde (cb/1); Andy Sands (cla/1); Thomas Marent (crb, fcrb, clb/2, clb/3). **94 Alamy Stock Photo:** Biosphoto / Stuart Wilson (cl); Minden Pictures / Heidi & Hans-Juergen Koch (ca); Nature Picture Library / MYN / Joris van Alphen (cr); Mark Newton (c/1); ephotocorp / Aamod Zambre (bc); blickwinkel / B. Trapp (fcr/1, br). **Depositphotos Inc:** Davpe (ftr). **Dreamstime.com:** Ernest Cooper (cl/2, fcl/1, cb); Digitalimagined (ftl); Grafvision (cla); Danut Vieru (ca/1); Spineback (fcra/1, fcr, fcl); Jsmcqueen (cl/1); Iamtkb (cr/1); Dwiputra18 (fcrb). **Shutterstock.com:** A BugMan's Life (fcla); Niney Azman (tl); Chase D'animulls (tc, clb); Nynke van Holten (tr); Chelnokov Vladimir (cla/1); Image Source Trading Ltd (fcra); Anton Kozyrev (cra, cra/1); Alen thien (fcra/2); Lukas Gojda (c); Usha Roy (fclb); Kurit afshen (clb/1); Gan Chaonan (bl). **95 Alamy Stock Photo:** blickwinkel / G. Kunz (bl); CDC / S.Dupuis (fclb); Minden Pictures / Piotr Naskrecki (tc); Nature Picture Library / MYN / Gil Wizen (fclb/2). **Avalon:** James Carmichael Jr (cb/2). **Dreamstime.com:** Amwu (fcl); Sergey Chumakov (tl); Jason Ondreicka (tc); Dean Pennala (ca); Spineback (cl); Conny Skogberg (cb); Willypd (cb/1). **naturepl.com:** Photo Ark / Joel Sartore (fclb/1). **Shutterstock.com:** aaltair (c); iSKYDANCER (ftl, fcla/1); Anan Suphap (tl/1); Pamela Au (fcla); devmograph (bc). **SuperStock:** Biosphoto / Adam Fletcher (cla). **96 Alamy Stock Photo:** Mark Conlin (cla/1); Ed Brown Wildlife (cr); Sibons photography (bc); Michael Durham / Nature Picture Library (c). **Dreamstime.com:** Isselee (clb/1, clb/2, crb/1); Johannesk (tc); Slowmotiongli (cla/2); Pnwnature (crb/2). **Getty Images / iStock:** wrangel (ca); **naturepl.com:** Piotr Naskrecki (cr). **97 Alamy Stock Photo:** Nicolas Fernandez (c/1); FLPA (cla/4); Nature Picture Library (cla/1); Chris Mattison (fcla/3); Michele and Tom Grimm (cra/5); Christopher Scott (cr). **Depositphotos Inc:** ImageSource (bl). **Dreamstime.com:** Philip Bird (cra/6); Spineback (ftl); Vasyl Helevachuk (tc); Stu Porter (tr); Brian Kushner (cra/1); Narupon Nimpaiboon (ftr); Henk Wallays (fcla); Chernetskaya (ca/2); Chanon Tamtad (ca); Chesampson (cra/4); Iakov Filimonov (cl/1); Rudmer Zwerver (crb/2); Eric Isselee / Isselee (fcrb); Duncan Noakes (br); Isselee (fcla/2, cla/2, cra/3, crb/1, fclb/1, clb/1). **Getty Images / iStock:** Leonello (clb/2). **Getty Images:** piet haaksma / 500px (bc); Paul Starosta (cl/2). **naturepl.com:** Daniel Heuclin (cla/3); Markus Varesvuo (cra/2). **99 123RF.com:** Andrea Izzotti (cb). **Alamy Stock Photo:** Helmut Corneli (cra); Nature Picture Library / Pascal Kobeh (ftl); Michael Patrick O'Neill (1); blickwinkel / A. Hartl (tc); Jeff Mondragon (ftr/1); blickwinkel / Teigler (fcra/1); Stephen Frink (cra/1); Nature Photographers Ltd / PAUL R. STERRY (cl, c/1); SeaTops (cr); WaterFrame_dpr (fcr); Brook Peterson / Stocktrek Images (fclb); Nick Polanszky (clb); Norbert Probst / imageBROKER.com GmbH & Co. KG (crb); PAUL R. STERRY / Nature Photographers Ltd (fbl). **Dorling Kindersley:** Terry Goss (fcl); David Harasti (ftr); Linda Pitkin (fcla/1). **Dreamstime.com:** Lukas Blazek (fcra/2); Serg_dibrova (tl); Johannesk (tl/2); Natalia Sidorova (tc/1); Ys7485 (fcla); Isselee (fcra, cla, cla/1); Lunamarina (fcra/3). **Getty Images / iStock:** atese (fcrb); irin717 (ftl/1); Christophe Sirabella (fbr). **naturepl.com:** Piotr Naskrecki (br). **Shutterstock.com:** Aaronejbull87 (c). **100 Alamy Stock Photo:** Dirk Funhoff / imageBROKER.com GmbH & Co. KG (fclb/1); imageBROKER / Fabio Pupin (tl); Nature Picture Library / MYN / Lily Kumpe (tc/1); All Canada Photos / Kitchin and Hurst (tc); BIOSPHOTO / Quentin Martinez (fcla); Piotr Naskrecki / Minden Pictures (cla); Ivan Kuzmin (c/2); Imago (cl); Chris Mattison (cl/1); Nature Picture Library / MYN / Andrew Snyder (cr/1); Nature Picture Library / Wild Wonders of Europe / Hodalic (fclb); blickwinkel / A. Hartl (fbl); Michael & Patricia Fogden / Minden Pictures (fbr); Nature Picture Library / MYN / JP Lawrence (c/1, cr, crb/1, cra). **Bridgeman Images:** Jaime Abecasis (bc). **Dorling Kindersley:** Thomas Marent (ftl); Twan Leenders (fcra). **Dreamstime.com:** Wirestock (br); Lana Langlois (tc/2); Maffeifabio (tr); Matthijs Kuijpers (fcla/1); Valeriy Kirsanov (cra/1); Nynke Van Holten (c); Isselee (cl/2); Amwu (cr/2); Melinda Fawver (clb); Brian Magnier (clb/1); Farinoza (ftr, clb/2). **naturepl.com:** Daniel Heuclin (fcrb/1); Bert Willaert (fcl); Joel Sartore / Photo Ark (crb, fcrb). **Shutterstock.com:** Craig Cordier (fcra/1); Lauren Suryanata (cla/1). **102-103 Dreamstime.com:** Isselee (c, cb); Spineback (ca). **102 Dreamstime.com:** Amattel (cra); Isselee (r, br). **103 123RF.com:** jackf / Iakov Filimonov (bl). **Alamy Stock Photo:** Arto Hakola (tc); Juniors Bildarchiv GmbH / F259 (cra/2); Nature Picture Library / Chris Mattison (fcl). **Depositphotos Inc:** REPTILES4ALL (cra/1). **Dorling Kindersley:** Andrew Beckett (Illustration Ltd) (ftl); Jerry Young (br). **Dreamstime.com:** Amwu (cl); Matthijs Kuijpers (tl, c/1); Steve Byland (tc/1); Andrei Shupilo (tr); Torsten Kuenzlen (ca); Isselee (cla, c); Dwiputra18 (cr); Verastuchelova (cl/1); Farinoza (cb); Mikhail Blajenov (cb/1, clb); Michelle Bridges (crb/1). **Shutterstock.com:** Ekaterina Gerasimchuk (crb); Danny Ye (ftr); Sista Vongjintanaruks (cra). **104 Alamy Stock Photo:** A.B.Sheldon / Dembinsky Photo Associates (br); Anton Sorokin (ca); Zeeshan Mirza / ephotocorp (b). **Depositphotos Inc:** REPTILES4ALL (crb). **Dreamstime.com:** Matthijs Kuijpers (clb/1). **naturepl.com:** Tony Phelps (cra). **Shutterstock.com:** J-Re (clb). **105 Alamy Stock Photo:** Axis Images (cla/1); Anthony Bannister / Avalon.red (fcl); Jared Hobbs / All Canada Photos (cl); Ashok Captain / ephotocorp (fbl); Zeeshan Mirza / ephotocorp (bl); Michael & Patricia Fogden / Minden Pictures (br); Chris Mattison (fbr); Dinodia Photos RM (ftr). **Avalon:** Mark O'Shea (ftl). **Chien C. Lee:** (clb/ tritaeniatus). **Dreamstime.com:** Dwiputra18 (fcla, cla, fcrb); Matthijs Kuijpers (cr). **S.R. Ganesh:** (clb/Gerrhopilus). **Dr. Vincenzo Mercurio:** (clb/malagasy). **naturepl.com:** Joel Sartore / Photo Ark (fclb/1); MYN / JP Lawrence (tr). **Shutterstock.com:** DSlight_photography (fclb). **107 123RF.com:** Eric Isselee / isselee (c/1); kajornyot (tl/6). **Alamy Stock Photo:** Ian Beattie (fbr); Ivan Kuzmin (tr/2); user685475 (bl/4); blickwinkel / Lammers (br/7). **Dorling Kindersley:** Andrew Beckett (Illustration Ltd) (br); David Cottridge (tc/1); E. J. Peiker (br/8); The Flag Institute (tr/3, clb). **Dreamstime.com:** Natalya Aksenova (br/1); Dndavis (cl/2); Pixworld (tl/4); Photographerlondon (tc/2); Kaye Oberstar (tc/3); Ondřej Prosick (tr/1); Jan Martin Will (bl/1); Rudolf Ernst (bl/3); Stu Porter (br/6); Isselee (tl/1, cr/2, cr/3, br/5, 1); The Flag Institute (bl/5). **Getty Images / iStock:** Film Studio Aves (cl); GlobalP (cr/1, br/3). **Getty Images:** Daniel Parent (ca). **naturepl.com:** Pete Oxford (bl/2). **Shutterstock.com:** Agami Photo Agency (bc). **109 Alamy Stock Photo:** Christian Hütter (fcrb); Stuart Morley (cr); Naturepix (ftr); Fabrizio Troiani (tc); Nature Picture Library / David Tipling (clb/1). **Dorling Kindersley:** Natural History Museum, London / Peter Chadwick (tl, tr, tl/1, cra/2, cla/1, fcla, bl, fbl, br/1, fbr); Natural History Museum, London / Philip Dowell (tc/1, fclb). **Dreamstime.com:** Melinda Fawver (tl/2); Evgeniya Moroz (fcl); Feathercollector (ftl); Jill Shepherd (bc/1); Picstudio (bc/4). **Featherbase scientific feather collection, www.featherbase.info, HAASE, SCHWENK, SCHLUSEN et. al. (2024):** (tr/1, cra, bl/1, bc/3). **Getty Images / iStock:** Harry Collins (bc); Gregory_DUBUS (cr/1). **Esha Munshi (Feather Library):** (br). **Michael Nahm:** (cla). **©2022 Usagi no Nedoko:** (c). **Marie Reznikova:** (fcr, tr/2). **Shutterstock.com:** Boonchuay Promjiam (cra/1); Tramont_ana (cl, clb). **110 Alamy Stock Photo:** Dorling Kindersley ltd (fbr); Panther Media GmbH / germanopoli (ftl); Nature Photographers Ltd / PAUL R. STERRY (tl/2, cla/1); Richard & Susan Day / DanitaDelimont.com; Natural History Museum, London (tr/3); Photo Researchers / Science History Images (ca/2); PAUL R. STERRY / Nature Photographers Ltd (fcra/2, cra/4, fcr, cl/2, c, fcrb, bl); Thomas Marent / Minden Pictures (cra/5); Life on white (cl/1); SBS Eclectic Images (cr/3); The Natural History Museum (fbl). **Dorling Kindersley:** Peter Chadwick / Natural History Museum, London (fcl, cr/2, bc, br). **Dreamstime.com:** Edmongin (cla/4); Isselee (ca/1, fclb); Fiskness (cra/2); Seadam (cl/3); Ivan Paunovic (cr/1); Vasiliy Vishnevskiy (clb). **Getty Images:** Paul Starosta / Corbis (tr/2, ftr); Paul Starosta (tl/1, fcla). **Getty Images / iStock:** THEPALMER (cla/5). **naturepl.com:** Klein & Hubert (cra/1, cla/3); Tui De Roy (cla/2). **Shutterstock.com:** Armchair Naturalist (cra/3); Jrs Jahangeer (tc/1); ShubhamZarwal (tc/2). **112 123RF.com:** javarman (c/1); Keith Levit. **Alamy Stock Photo:** Axis Images (ca); Signal Photos (tr); Jimlop collection (cra/1); Karol Kozlowski Premium RM Collection (cra/3); AGAMI Photo Agency / Jacob Garvelink (fcla); imageBROKER.com GmbH & Co. KG / Konrad Wothe (br); AGAMI Photo Agency / Pete Morris (fcl, cl); Ian Dagnall (clb). **Dreamstime.com:** Wirestock (ftl); Isselee (tl, fbl); Lukas Blazek (cla); Jaap Bleijenberg (fcr); Martin Pelanek (cr); Thiago Rocha Dos Santos (fclb); Dragoneye (bc). **Fotolia:** Olena Pantiukh (cra). **Getty Images / iStock:** Olha_stock (fcra). **naturepl.com:** Doug Gimesy (c); Pete Oxford (tc, bl); Michael Pitts (tc/1); Rod Williams (cra/2); Troels Jacobsen / Arcticphoto (cla/1); Brent Stephenson (cla/2); Tui De Roy (fcla/1). **Shutterstock.com:** Wright Out There (ftr). **SuperStock:** Dominique Halleux / Biosphoto (br/1). **115 Alamy Stock Photo:** Louise Heusinkveld (tc); simon margetson travel (ftr); Zoonar / Carsten Braun (cr). **Dorling Kindersley:** Blackpool Zoo (br); Cotswold Wildlife Park / Gary Ombler (cra). **Dreamstime.com:** Agami Photo Agency (fcla, fcra); Wrangel (tc); Martin Pelanek (bl). **Getty Images:** LightRocket / Wolfgang Kaehler (tr). **naturepl.com:** Stefan Christmann (cl); Klein & Hubert (ftl); Brent Stephenson (fcl); Nick Garbutt (fbr); Pete Oxford (fcr). **Shutterstock.com:** LouieLea (tc/1). **116 Alamy Stock Photo:** Album (tl); Nature Picture Library / Axel Gomille (tc); Oliver Thompson-Holmes (fcra); lifes all white (c); Nature Picture Library / Mark MacEwen (cra); The History Collection (cl); Universal Images Group North America LLC (cl/1, clb/1, bc/2); Ben McRae (crb); Volgi archive (bc/1); markku murto / art (bl, cb). **Dreamstime.com:** Nynke Van Holten (fcl); Matthijs Kuijpers (ca); Snyfer (fcr); Isselee (cr, bc); Irina Kozhemyakina (fbl). **Getty Images / iStock:** Enrico Pescantini (ftl). **Getty Images:** Universal Images Group / Florilegius (clb). **Science Photo Library:** Gerry Pearce (fbr). **Shutterstock.com:** Liliya Butenko (cla). **SuperStock:** Animals Animals (br). **119 Alamy Stock Photo:** Amazon-Images (ca); Universal Images Group North America LLC / Encyclopaedia Britannica (cra, cla, fcl, cl, br). **Bridgeman Images:** British Library archive (cr). **Depositphotos Inc:** Trek13 (bc). **Dorling Kindersley:** Andrew Beckett (Illustration Ltd) (ftr). **Dreamstime.com:** Farinoza (fcr); Janusz Piekowski (fcla); Vasyl Helevachuk (crb). **Getty Images / iStock:** E+ / holgs (c). **Getty Images:** Martin Harvey (tc). **naturepl.com:** Photo Ark / Joel Sartore (clb); Fiona Rogers (ftl). **120 Alamy Stock Photo:** dotted zebra (fbr); Nature Picture Library / Rebecca Robinson (cra). **Dorling Kindersley:** Natural History Museum, London / Frank Greenaway (br). **naturepl.com:** Carwardine / Martin Camm (cra/1); Yumiko Wakisaka (tr, fcra, fcra/1). **121 Alamy Stock Photo:** Nature Picture Library / SCOTLAND: The Big Picture (tc/1); Nature Picture Library / Rebecca Robinson (tc/2); WILDLIFE GmbH (fbl). **Dorling Kindersley:** Natural History Museum, London / Frank Greenaway (br). **Dreamstime.com:** Smgirly / Simone Gatterwe (tr). **naturepl.com:** Carwardine / Martin Camm (tl, ca, ca/2, fcl, c, cl, clb, crb, cb); Yumiko Wakisaka (ca/1, cla). **Science Photo Library:** Nature Picture Library / Carwardine / Martin Camm (ftl, tc, bl). **122 Depositphotos Inc:** mecan (crb). **Dorling Kindersley:** Dave King / Whipsnade Zoo, Bedfordshire (bc). **Dreamstime.com:** Parinya Feungchan (cl); Wrangel (c); Alexey Sedov (cr); Isselee (br); Sergey Uryadnikov (bl). **123 Alamy Stock Photo:** Vincenzo Iacovoni (fbl); Kyle Moore (cr); Tierfotoagentur / m.blue-shadow (fcl). **Dreamstime.com:** Frank Fichtmueller (br); Michal Ninger (fcr); Angel Luis Simon Martin (clb); Lianquan Yu (fbr). **Getty Images / iStock:** Laura Hedien (bl). **Getty Images:** Lea Scaddan (fclb). **naturepl.com:** Eric Dragesco (c). **Shutterstock.com:** JHVEPhoto (cl). **124 Getty Images / iStock:** bazzier (bc). **125 123RF.com:** Eric Isselee / isselee (fcrb/2). **Alamy Stock Photo:** Arco / G. Lacz / Imagebroker (fcrb/1); Jean-Francois Noblet / Biosphoto (fclb/1); Sebastian Kennerknecht / Minden Pictures (crb/4); Roland Seitre / Minden Pictures (br); Hemis (bc/2). **Depositphotos Inc:** sanc4u (ftl). **Dorling Kindersley:** Wildlife Heritage Foundation, Kent, UK (tr). **Dreamstime.com:** Anankkml (fcra); Isselee (tl, c/3, fcr, c); tpán Kápl (ca); Vasyl Helevachuk (cl); Broker / Rafael Angel Irusta Machin (c/2); Dkadra89 (fcl/2); Lianquan Yu (cb/2); Slowmotiongli (crb/1); Outdoorsman (crb/2); Dwiputra18 (bc/1). **Getty Images / iStock:** anankkml (cl/1); ugniz (fbl/3). **Getty Images:** Backpacking & hiking all over the planet. - www.panafoot.com (bl); Whitworth Images (fcla). **naturepl.com:** Jean-Francois Noblet / Biosphoto (fclb/2); Daniel Heuclin (c/1); Photo Ark / Joel Sartore (c/4, cr, fbl/1); Joel Sartore / Photo Ark (cr/1, crb/3, fbr/1). **Shutterstock.com:** Sanit Fuangnakhon (cb/1). **126 Alamy Stock Photo:** Blue British Shorthair Cat Standing Studio (fclb); Nevodka (fcra); Juniors Bildarchiv GmbH / Schanz, U. / juniors@wildlife (c/1); Juniors Bildarchiv / F215 (fcl, crb/1); Idamini (br); Hemis (fbr). **Dreamstime.com:** Wirestock (fcla/2); Vladyslav Starozhylov / Vladstar (tc); Axel Bueckert (tr); Kalinin Dmitrii (ftr); Dmitri Pravdjukov (cra); Isselee (fcr, fbl); Aleksandr Volchanskiy (fcl/1); Nousha (clb); Ievgeniia Miroshnichenko (crb/2). **naturepl.com:** Robert Pickett (bl). **Shutterstock.com:** Ken Griffiths (cr/1); Julia Remezova (ca); viatoslav_Shevchenko (cl). **127 Alamy Stock Photo:** Idamini (cra); PLANCHARD Eric / hemis.fr (c). **Dreamstime.com:** Chrispethick (cra/2); Nynke Van Holten (tr, ca/1); Pavlo Vakhrushev (cl); Isselee (clb/1, br); Kozzi2 (crb); Taniawild (bl). **128 Alamy Stock Photo:** Olena Danileiko (tr/3); Perky Pets (ftr). **Dreamstime.com:** Alexey Kuznetsov (br); Cynoclub (crb/2); Erik Lam (fcla); Otsphoto (tl, cla/2); Paul Ransome (clb); Jagodka (bc); Isselee (fbl, crb, fbr); Volodymyr Melnyk (cr/2); **Dorling Kindersley:** Tracy Morgan / A.G.C. Simmonds (cr/1); Tracy Morgan (cla); Mdorottya (tr/2). **Shutterstock.com:** TrapezaStudio; Xyo (ca). **129 Alamy Stock Photo:** Petra Wegner (tr/2, cl/1). **Dorling Kindersley:** Tracy Morgan (fcla). **Dreamstime.com:** Adogslifephoto (tl/2); Flydragonfly (bl); Natallia Yaumenenka (fcl); Monkey Business Images (ftl); Rohit Seth (tc); Vladimir Mucibabic (tr/1); Moori (ftr); Erik Lam (cla); Lisasvara (ca); Iakov Filimonov (cl/3); Gajus (cl/2); Farinoza (c); Isselee (fbr); Andrey Medvedev (bc); Vladimir Suponev (br/2). **Getty Images / iStock:** cynoclub (cr/1). **Getty**

Images: Hans Surfer / Moment Open (fbl). **Shutterstock.com:** Dmytro Lobodenko (cr/2); Sashulity (br/1); TrapezaStudio (tl). **130 Alamy Stock Photo:** CountryLife (cb). **Dreamstime.com:** Kseniya Abramova (ca); Isselee (br, fcrb, crb). **Getty Images:** De Agostini / DEA / B. LANGRISH (clb). **Shutterstock.com:** Dan Baillie (fclb). **132 123RF.com:** Andrei Samkov / satirus (cl). **Dorling Kindersley:** Royal Veterinary College, University of London / Tim Ridley (tl). **134 Alamy Stock Photo:** Nature Picture Library / MYN / JP Lawrence (fclb/1); Nature Picture Library / Xi Zhinong (cr); Marcos del Mazo (fbl); Nobuo Matsumura (bl). **Depositphotos Inc:** ronnarong (cb/2). **Dreamstime.com:** Anankkml (fclb); Cosmin Manci (clb); Jamen Percy (cb); Matthijs Kuijpers (clb/1); Torsten Kuenzlen (cb/1). **Getty Images / iStock:** GlobalP (cb/3). **Getty Images:** Moment / chuchart duangdaw (br). **Shutterstock.com:** Supriyo Ghoshal (c). **135 123RF.com:** Keith Levit (clb). **Alamy Stock Photo:** Zoltan Bagosi (crb/1); Janice and Nolan Braud (fcl); Iain Lowson Wildlife (cl/1); Minden Pictures / ZSSD (cr); blickwinkel / Hummel (fcr); RooM the Agency / kuritafsheen (cr/1); Nature Picture Library / MYN / Gil Wizen (fclb/1); Minden Pictures / NiS / Oliver Lucanus (clb/2); Nature and Science (cb/1); The History Collection (br/1); blickwinkel / B. Trapp (cb/3); Ger Bosma (cb/4); Yeriyan Nurramadhan (bc). **Dreamstime.com:** Kcmatt (cb/2); Vladvitek (bc/1). **Getty Images:** DE AGOSTINI PICTURE LIBRARY (cl). **Getty Images / iStock:** Asim Patel (clb/1); Wirestock (c); Vac1 (fclb); Stanislavs Vasilkovs (cb). **naturepl.com:** Carwardine / Martin Camm (bl); Photo Ark / Joel Sartore (br). **Science Photo Library:** Dante Fenolio (crb). **137 Alamy Stock Photo:** FLPA (c); SBS Eclectic Images (tc, cr/3); Nature Picture Library / David Tipling (tr); Bilwissedition Ltd. & Co. KG (cla); Mark Daffey (cla/1); Maidun Collection (ca); The History Collection (ca/2, cl, bc); Rapp Halour (cra); FLHC 22 (cr); The Natural History Museum (cl/2, bc/2); Antiquarian Images (cr/2); Minden Pictures / Michael & Patricia Fogden (c/1); Darling Archive (clb); PhotoStock-Israel / Historic Illustrations (cb); Historic Illustrations (cb/2, br); Art Collection 3 (bl); Library Book Collection (bc/1); Agefotostock (c/3). **Dreamstime.com:** Markusmayer1 (bl/1). **Getty Images:** Premium Archive / Field Museum Library (cl/1). **naturepl.com:** Bruce Thomson (tc/1). **Shutterstock.com:** Idealiz3d (c/2). **138 Alamy Stock Photo:** Mohamad Haghani (clb/3); Stocktrek Images, Inc. / Nobumichi Tamura (c); Stocktrek Images, Inc. / Sergey Krasovskiy (ftr, bl, cla/2, cb); Science Photo Library / Roger Harris (cla/3); National Geographic Image Collection / Raul Martin (cla/4). **Dorling Kindersley:** Jon Hughes (fcla). **Dreamstime.com:** Linda Bucklin (fcra, cra); Kitti Kahotong (fcl); Mr1805 (crb, cla, crb/2); Corey A Ford (fbr, cr, cra/3, crb/3); Mark Turner (clb). **Science Photo Library:** JA CHIRINOS (fcrb/2). **Shutterstock.com:** Herschel Hoffmeyer (cra/2); Sebastian Kaulitzki (ftl, br, tc, clb/2, clb/4, fcrb, fcrb/3); YuRi Photolife (ca). **141 123RF.com:** Corey A Ford (c). **Alamy Stock Photo:** Dinosaurs (tc); Stocktrek Images / Sergey Krasovskiy (fcla); Stocktrek Images / Mohamad Haghani (bl). **Dorling Kindersley:** Tim Ridley / Robert L. Braun (cra); James Kuether (fcra, fcl). **Dreamstime.com:** Kitti Kahotong (tr). **Getty Images / iStock:** Kitti Kahotong (br). **Getty Images:** Stocktrek Images / Nobumichi Tamara (cla); Stocktrek Images / Nobumichi Tamura (clb); **Shutterstock.com:** Sebastian Kaulitzki (tl). **142 Alamy Stock Photo:** Stocktrek Images, Inc. / Emily Willoughby (ca); Stocktrek Images / Paulo Leite da Silva (clb). **Dorling Kindersley:** James Kuether (tc). **143 123RF.com:** Elena Duvernay (tr); Mark Turner (br). **Dorling Kindersley:** James Kuether (tl). **Dreamstime.com:** Elena Duvernay (ca); Mark Turner (bl). **Getty Images / iStock:** Daniel Eskridge (bc). **Getty Images:** Stocktrek Images / Mohamad Haghani (c). **144 Dorling Kindersley:** Senckenberg Gesellschaft Fuer Naturforschung Museum / Gary Ombler. **144-145 Dorling Kindersley:** Senckenberg Gesellschaft Fuer Naturforschung Museum / Gary Ombler. **150 Dorling Kindersley:** Natural History Museum, London / Colin Keates (cla, cra, cra/1); Natural History Museum, London / Tim Parmenter (ca, ca/1); Oxford University Museum of Natural History / Gary Ombler (fcra); Natural History Museum / Tim Parmenter (fcra/1). **154 Dorling Kindersley:** RGB Research / Ruth Jenkinson (2:1); RGB Research Limited / Ruth Jenkinson (2:2, 3:1, 3:2, 4:1, 4:2, 4:3, 4:4, 4:5, 4:6, 4:7, 4:8, 4:9, 5:1, 5:2, 5:3, 5:4, 5:5, 5:6, 5:7, 5:8, 5:9, 6:1, 6:2, 6:4, 6:5, 6:6, 6:7, 6:8, 6:9, 7:1, 8:4, 8:5, 8:6, 8:7, 8:8, 8:9, 9:4, 9:5, 9:6, 9:7, 9:8, 9:9). **155 Dorling Kindersley:** RGB Research Limited / Ruth Jenkinson (2:4, 2:8, 3:4, 3:5, 3:6, 3:7, 3:8, 4:1, 4:2, 4:3, 4:4, 4:5, 4:6, 4:7, 4:8, 5:1, 5:2, 5:3, 5:4, 5:5, 5:6, 5:7, 5:8, 6:1, 6:2, 6:3, 6:4, 6:5, 6:6, 8:1, 8:2, 8:3, 8:4, 8:5, 8:6, 8:7, 8:8, 8:9). **Fotolia:** apttone (2:5). **156 Dreamstime.com:** Alexino (bl); Realchemyst (fclb); Maksim Loskutnikov (fbl); Phartisan (clb); Photka (cb); Brad Calkins (cb/1, fcrb/1); Mark Fairey (crb); Jasonjung (crb/1); Asmfoto (fcrb); Askoldsb (fbr). **157 Dreamstime.com:** Cammeraydave (bl/1); Stockeeco (fbl); Raychen (bl); Theclarkester (fbr); Tyler Olson (fcrb/1); Michalex (fcrb); Raja Rc (crb); Yobro10 (crb/1); Volodymyrkrasyuk (br/1); Siraphol (fclb); Daseaford (clb); Milosluz (clb/1). **158 Alamy Stock Photo:** Coroiu Octavian (bc/1). **Dreamstime.com:** Ayhan Altan (tc); Ridetheremuda (ftr); Eimantas Buzas (ca); Alexey Arama (c); Dmitry Panchenko (c/1); Laurenthive (cr). **Shutterstock.com:** Margrit Hirsch (bc); tengatt (tr); Roncsakj (cr/1). **159 Dreamstime.com:** Atman (cr); Danny Hooks (clb); Taigis (bl); Micha Klootwijk (bc); Dubovdaniilyu (tr); Tuja66 (ftr); Gulivermax (tr/1); Suljo (fcra); Gemenacom (cra); Georgii Dolgykh (cra/1); Aleksei Fefelov (fbr); Viachaslau Bondarau (fbr/1); Dmitry100 (br); Maxopphoto (bc/1); Revenaif (bc/2); Newlight (fcr); Rawf88 (cr/1); Gemphotography (c). **Shutterstock.com:** Cvetanovski (tc); Matee Nuserm (fclb). **160 Alamy Stock Photo:** David J. Green (fcrb); Stocktrek Images, Inc. / Terry Moore (br). **Dreamstime.com:** Baloncici (c); Mohamad Shafiq Shabri@sabri (fcl); Geargodz (fbl); Py2000 (clb/1); Yalcinsonat (cb); Nutthawit Wiangya (bc); Draftmode (bl); Birgit Reitz Hofmann (cr); Ivansmuk (fcr); Dmitrii Melnikov (crb); Brett Critchley (fbr). **Getty Images / iStock:** ZU_09 (clb/2). **Shutterstock.com:** Trong Nguyen (fclb). **161 123RF.com:** George Mdivanian (fcl). **Alamy Stock Photo:** BSIP SA / GILLES (fbr); Nataliia Mach (fcr); Marmaduke St. John (bl/2); JG Photography (br). **Dreamstime.com:** Chernetskaya (cb); Brett Critchley (fclb); Choneschones (fbl); Kropic (bl/1); Mardoz (clb). **Fotolia:** Natallia Yaumenenka / eAlisa (crb). **Getty Images / iStock:** sspopov (cr). **Science Photo Library:** (cl). **169 Alamy Stock Photo:** STEVE GSCHMEISSNER / SCIENCE PHOTO LIBRARY (fclb). **Dreamstime.com:** Puntasit Choksawatdikorn (br). **Getty Images / iStock:** enot-poloskun (cl). **Science Photo Library:** CLOUDS HILL IMAGING LTD (clb); PROF CINTI & V. GREMET (fbr); ZIAD M. EL-ZAATARI (bl); STEVE GSCHMEISSNER (fbl, fcrb, crb). **173 Dorling Kindersley:** The Natural History Museum, London / Philip Dowell (bc); Zygote / Arran Lewis (cl, cr). **174 Dorling Kindersley:** Zygote Media Group / (cl). **177 Alamy Stock Photo:** Gado Images / Smith Collection (tl); The Natural History Museum (tc); Image Source Limited / Callista Images (crb); Stanca Sanda (bc); Westend61 GmbH (br); Science Photo Library / Sciepro (fbr). **Dreamstime.com:** Ilexx (fclb); Kateryna Kon (fcla, cla, ca, cra, fcra). **Science Photo Library:** Juergen Berger (tr); David Mccarthy (ftl); Steve Gschmeissner (ftr, fcrb); Eye Of Science (fcl, fcr); Dr Tony Brain (cl); Dennis Kunkel Microscopy (c, cr, clb, cb); Tim Vernon (fbl). **Shutterstock.com:** Kateryna Kon (bl). **181 Alamy Stock Photo:** Richard Heyes (t, clb/1). **Dorling Kindersley:** Bicycle Museum Of America / Gerard Brown (c/1, cb/1, crb, bl); National Cycle Collection / Gary Ombler (cl); Llandrindod Wells National Cycle / Gerard Brown (c, cb/2); Gary Ombler / J.D Tandems (crb/1). **Dreamstime.com:** Wirestock (cr); Eshmadeva (cb); Ivan Ekushenko (bc); Maxim Sergeenkov (br). **Getty Images:** Velo / Tim de Waele (cb/3, bc/1). **Shutterstock.com:** Octographers (clb). **182 Alamy Stock Photo:** Universal Images Group North America LLC / Encyclopaedia Britannica. **183 Alamy Stock Photo:** Stuart Douglas (ca/2); Motoring Picture Library / National Motor Museum (ca); mauritius images GmbH / fact (fclb); imageBROKER.com GmbH & Co. KG / Thomas Schneider (fcla/2); Max Herman (cra/2); epo74 / Stockimo (fcra/2). **Dorling Kindersley:** Deepak Aggarwal / Harley-Davidson (br); Gary Ombler / National Motorcycle Museum (ftl, fcl); James Mann / National Motor Museum, Beaulieu (tr, cla); Gary Ombler / Phil Crosby and Peter Mather (fcla); Gary Ombler / Trevor Pope Motorcycles (c, fcrb/2); Simon Fielder / David Farnley (cb); Gary Ombler / Phil Davies (fbl); Gary Ombler / Neil Mort, Mott Motorcycles (crb). **Dreamstime.com:** Enriqueasalazar316 (fcrb); Sylvain Robin (cl); Mgallar (fclb/2); Vita Popova (fclb/3); Konstantinos Moraitis (fcr, cla/2); Tomislav Pinter (clb); Kamlesh Parate (fcra). **Getty Images:** Marc Pfitzenreuter (cr). **Shutterstock.com:** Guitar Studio (clb/2); Luxury Fred Sherman (cb/2). **184 Alamy Stock Photo:** Serguei Dratchev (br); Motoring Picture Library / National Motor Museum (crb); Ray Evans (bl). **Dorling Kindersley:** Haynes International Motor Museum / James Mann (ca); National Motor Museum Beaulieu / James Mann (cra/BMW). **Dreamstime.com:** Andrbk (cl); Dmitry Orlov (cla); Martin Hatch (cra); Maksim Ladouski (c); Konstantinos Moraitis (c/Citroen, crb/buggy); Ifeelstock (cb). **Getty Images:** National Motor Museum / Heritage Images (clb/1). **Shutterstock.com:** JasonRenfrow (clb). **185 Alamy Stock Photo:** PjrTransport (clb). **Dreamstime.com:** MMcreative House (cr); VanderWolfImages (ca); Teddyleung (cra); Ryhor Bruyeu (cl/ Nissan); Alex Zarubin (bl); Konstantinos Moraitis (bc). **Getty Images:** Heritage Images (crb); Martyn Lucy (br). **Shutterstock.com:** Debu Durllabh (cl). **187 123RF.com:** claudiodivizia (cla). **Alamy Stock Photo:** Arterra Picture Library / Arndt Sven-Erik (bc); Peter Moulton (tr). **Dreamstime.com:** Joy E Brown (cr); Rolandm (tl); Iandewarphotography (ca); Gestur Gislason (cl); MaleoPhotography (cl/Overland); Bjrn Wylezich (cr/OV); Wisconsinart (crb). **Shutterstock.com:** algre (c/minibus); LesPalenik (cra); PradeepGaurs (clb). **188 Alamy Stock Photo:** Robert Lloyd-Ashton (3:2); Norman Pogson (1:2); Gavin Zeigler (2:1). **Dreamstime.com:** Artzzz (6:2); Ilfede (1:1); Goce Risteski (1:3); Nerthuz (2:2); Debra Millet (3:1); Oliver Foerstner (3:3); Robwilson39 (3:4); Bjrn Wylezich (3:5); Zkruger (4:1); Zts (5:1); Eric Honeycutt (5:2); Maryia Kazlouskaya (5:3); Meunierd (7:1); Tom Dowd (7:2). **Getty Images / iStock:** Zorandimzr (6:3). **189 Alamy Stock Photo:** Derek Broussard (2:4); Radharc Images / JoeFoxBerlin (1:2); LGPL / Alan Barnes (4:3). **Dorling Kindersley:** Doubleday Swineshead Depot / Gary Ombler (4:2); Gary Ombler / David Bowman (3:2). **Dreamstime.com:** Eternalfeelings (1:1); Wisconsinart (2:2); Woodsy007 / Steve Woods (3:1); Lucapbl (3:3); Plmrue (4:1). **Getty Images / iStock:** CaoChunhai (b); ewg3D (1:3). **191 Alamy Stock Photo:** Archive PL (crb/1); dpa picture alliance archive (fcla); RWP Photography / Rick Pisio (c/1); Andrew Findlay (cb); Chronicle (fcrb); Hugh Williamson (bc/1); Imaginechina Limited (fbr). **Dorling Kindersley:** Gary Ombler / B&O Railroad Museum, Baltimore, Maryland, USA (ftr); Science Museum, London / Mike Dunning (tl); Railroad Museum of Pennsylvania / Gary Ombler (cla, ca/1); London Transport Museum / Mike Dunning (ca); National Railway Museum, New Dehli / Gary Ombler (clb); Eisenbahnfreunde Traditionsbahnbetriebswerk Stassfurt / Gary Ombler (cb/2). **Dreamstime.com:** Viktor Karasev (fbl). **Keith Fender:** (br, bc). **Getty Images:** Corbis Historical / Bettmann (crb); Science & Society Picture Library (ftl, tc, tr, cra, cra/1, cb/1); Universal Images Group / Universal History Archive (cr); Hulton Archive / Print Collector (fclb). **Alex Leroy:** (cla/1). **Danie van der Merwe:** (c). **193 Alamy Stock Photo:** Ben Barden (bc); Sam Rollinson (tl); Teila K. Day Photography (tc); Lars Hagberg (fcla); Uwe Deffner (cra); Ewing Galloway (cra/1); Military aircraft refuelling system (cra/2); Patrick Barron (cl/1); Peter Brogden (fcr); Stocktrek Images / HIGH-G Productions (cr); Niall Ferguson (c); imageBROKER.com GmbH & Co. KG / Dirk Enters (br); chris24 (fbl); Malcolm Haines (clb); Bayne Stanley (fclb). **Dorling Kindersley:** Real Aeroplane Company / Gary Ombler (bl); Norfolk and Suffolk Aviation Museum / Gary Ombler (fbr). **Dreamstime.com:** Dirk Daniel Mann (cl); Manifeesto (tr); Tonyv3112 (cla); VanderWolfImages (cla/2, fcl); Josefkubes (cr/2, fcrb); Wellsie82 (crb). **Shutterstock.com:** Angel DiBilio (clb/1). **194-195 Dorling Kindersley:** Virginia Museum of Transportation / Gary Ombler. **196 Alamy Stock Photo:** Imaginechina Limited (fcr). **Dreamstime.com:** Alexat25 (c); Typhoonski (cr); David Steele (cb, fbr); Cathy Locklear (fcrb); Orhan am (bc). **Getty Images:** Xiaodong Qiu (cl). **Getty Images / iStock:** Alex_Wang1 (crb). **Shutterstock.com:** Bunbok (br); Scott Mirror (clb); Mirelle (bl). **197 123RF.com:** Lopolo (fcr). **Alamy Stock Photo:** eye35.pix (clb); Wirestock, Inc. (cl); Angus McComiskey (cb); Lensmen Photographic Agency / Susan Kennedy (br). **Dreamstime.com:** Douglas Mackenzie (cr); Torsakarin (c); Olrat (bc); Natalia Volkova (bl). **Shutterstock.com:** Aydinsertbas (crb); Busan Oppa (fcrb); Leo Moitinho (fbr). **204 Dreamstime.com:** Nvard Akopyan. **205 © Walda Verbaenen / Braille meets emoticons** (crb). **211 Dorling Kindersley:** The Flag Institute (ftl, ftl/1, tl, tc, tr, ftr, fcla, c/1, cla, ca, ca/1, cra, cra/1, fcra, fcla/1, cla/1, cla/2, fcra/1, fcl, cl, c, cr, c/2, c/3, cr/1, fcr/1, clb, clb/1, cb, cb/1, clb/2, cb/2, fcrb, fclb, clb/3, fcrb/1, bc, bc/1, br, fbr). **Dreamstime.com:** Patiwit Hongsang / Patiwit (cra/2). **215 Alamy Stock Photo:** Sabena Jane Blackbird (cl, crb); Lanmas (c); MLouisphotography (clb). **Dorling Kindersley:** Philip Dowell / Natural History Museum, London (tr); Gary Ombler / Oxford Museum of Natural History (fbr, cr/1). **Dreamstime.com:** Markus Schieder (cla). **Getty Images:** UniversalImagesGroup (cr). **Science Photo Library:** PHILIPPE PSAILA (cra); JAVIER TRUEBA / MSF (fcra). **220 Alamy Stock Photo:** Album (bc, cb/2); Art Collection 2 (ftl); FORGET Patrick (tc/2); Science History Images (cla); funkyfood London - Paul Williams (fcla, cra/2, br/2); World History Archive (fcr); Ian Dagnall (fclb); Magica (clb); Alain Guilleux (crb/2); Zev Radovan (fbl); Zev Radovan / BibleLandPictures (bl); Peter Horree (br); History and Art Collection (fbr). **© Ashmolean Museum / Bridgeman Images:** © Ashmolean Museum (tl); Museum of Fine Arts, Boston. (tc/1); Brooklyn Museum / Charles Edwin Wilbour Fund (ftr). **Getty Images:** Werner Forman / Universal Images Group (fcrb). **The Metropolitan Museum of Art:** Gift of J. Pierpont Morgan, 1905 (ca); Gift of Theodore M. Davis, 1914 (cb); Purchase, Edward S. Harkness Gift, 1926 (cla/1). **221 Alamy Stock Photo:** Ian Dagnall (tl); The Print Collector (tr); Peter Horree (cla); Adam Eastland (cra); Tuul and Bruno Morandi (bl). **Bridgeman Images:** Israel Museum, Jerusalem / Gift of Abraham Guterman (clb). **Getty Images:** Werner Forman (br). **The Metropolitan Museum of Art:** Bequest of W. Gedney Beatty, 1941 (crb). **225 Alamy Stock Photo:** CPA Media Pte Ltd / Pictures From History (cl, bc); GRANGER - Historical Picture Archive / Granger, NYC. (tl); Ian Littlewood (fcra); The Print Collector / CM Dixon / Heritage Images (ftr); Xinhua (tr); MET / BOT (cr); Penta Springs Limited / Artokoloro (cb); Robert Kawka (fbl); Roger Parkes (br). **Bridgeman Images:** Christie's Images (ca). **© The Trustees of the British Museum. All rights reserved.:** (tc). **Dorling Kindersley:** Angela Coppola / University of Pennsylvania Museum of Archaeology and Anthropology (fcrb). **Getty Images:** Asian Art & Archaeology, Inc. / Corbis / Martha Avery (fclb); Fine Art (cra). **The Metropolitan Museum of Art:** Gift of Lisbet Holmes, 1989 (bl); Purchase, The Vincent Astor Foundation Gift, 2009 (ftl); Purchase, The Rosenkranz Foundation and Shelby White Gifts, 2004 (fcla); Gift of Mrs. Richard E. Linburn, 1979 (c); Rogers Fund, 1918 (crb); Gift of Florence and Herbert Irving, 2015 (clb); Robert Lehman Collection, 1975 (fbr). **Shutterstock.com:** cl2004lhy (cr); Shan_shan (fcl). **226 Alamy Stock Photo:** Asia Alan King (tc); Pictures From History / CPA Media Pte Ltd (c); Angelo Hornak (ftr, fbl); LMA / AW (tl); The History Collection (tr); Rajesh Avhad / ephotocorp (cr); Suzuki Kaku (ftl); MCLA Collection (br). **Dreamstime.com:** Shailen Photography (bc); Saiko3p (fcl); Satish Parashar (fbr). **Shutterstock.com:** Satish Parashar (cl). **227 Alamy Stock Photo:** Album (cr); LMA / AW (ftl); Logic Images (tl); Heritage Image Partnership Ltd (tc, c); Angelo Hornak (tr); Godong (ftr); Alfonso Vicente (fcl). **Dreamstime.com:** Michele Ricucci (br); Shariqkhan (fbr); Satish Parashar (cl). **The Metropolitan Museum of Art:** Gift of Barbara Stoller-Miller, 1990 (fcr). **229 Alamy Stock Photo:** agefotostock (fcla); Dinodia Photos RM (tc/1); Eraza Collection (cra); The History Collection (ca/1, c); Chronicle (ca, cla); incamerastock / ICP (fcl); ART Collection (cl); The Picture Art Collection (c/1); Art Collection 2 (fcra, cr); Historic Collection (bc); CPA Media Pte Ltd / Pictures From History (bc/1, bl). **Bridgeman Images:** British Library archive (br); Christie's Images (fbl). **Getty Images:** Dinodia Photo (ftr, tr, tl, ftl, tc); Pictures from History / Universal Images Group (fcr). **The Metropolitan Museum of Art:** Gift of Cynthia Hazen Polsky, 2011 (fbr). **234 Alamy Stock Photo:** Album (8:1); CPA Media Pte Ltd / Pictures From History (2:2, 3:5, 5:2); Robert Kawka (6:3, 6:7); Penta Springs Limited / Artokoloro (7:5); Hoberman Publishing / The Hoberman Collection (7:4, 2:7). **Bridgeman Images:** (7:2); Pictures from History (3:3, 5:6); Granger (7:6). **Getty Images:** De Agostini / DEA / J. E. BULLOZ (8:3). **Getty Images / iStock:** diane39 (1:1). **234-235 Nicholas Read (Westair Reproductions):** (x58). **235 Alamy Stock Photo:** CPA Media Pte Ltd / Pictures From History (4:2, 6:3); The History Collection (7:1); LMA / AW (8:2). **Bridgeman Images:** (5:3). **237 Alamy Stock Photo:** GL Archive (5:8); Chronicle (1:3, 1:6, 2:1, 2:2, 2:5, 8:4); The Print Collector (1:8); Falkensteinfoto (2:4, 2:6); IanDagnall Computing (4:1, 5:2); The Picture Art Collection (5:7); Classic Image (6:2); World History Archive (7:2); Pictorial Press Ltd (8:5). **Dreamstime.com:** Yujie Chen (4:2, 4:3, 5:1, 5:6); Georgios Kollidas (2:7, 2:8, 3:2, 3:5, 3:6, 3:8, 4:4, 4:5, 4:6, 4:7, 5:3, 5:4, 6:1, 6:3, 7:6, 8:1, 8:2, 8:3); Arthur C James (8:6). **Getty Images / iStock:** Bauhaus1000 (6:4); Duncan1890 (1:1, 1:2, 1:4, 1:5, 1:7, 2:3, 3:7); Benoitb (3:1, 3:3, 4:8); Illbusca (3:4); Hein Nouwens (5:5); ZU_09 (7:1); Nastasic (7:3); Grafissimo (7:5). **Getty Images:** Hulton Archive (6:5, 6:6). **Library of Congress, Washington, D.C.:** LC-DIG-ppmsca-15713 / Pether, William, 1731-approximately 1795, engraver / Frye, Thomas, 1710-1762, artist (7:4). **Shutterstock.com:** Muhammad Aamir Sumsum (br). **238 The Metropolitan Museum of Art:** Bashford Dean Memorial Collection, Bequest of Bashford Dean, 1928 (l); Helmet: Bequest Of George C. Stone, 1935; Body Armor: Gift Of Lai-Yuan And Co., 1916; Sword With Scabbard: The Collection Of Giovanni P. Morosini, Presented By His Daughter Giulia, 1932; Spear: Bequest Of George C. Stone, 1935 (r). **242 Alamy Stock Photo:** Antiquarian Images (fcrb); The Picture Art Collection (ftl); World History Archive (tl); IanDagnall Computing (tr, fcla, cla, fcra); The Artchives (ftr); Yogi Black (cra); Peter Horree (fclb); Heritage Image Partnership Ltd (clb); Niday Picture Library (fbl); Everett Collection Historical (bc); Penta Springs Limited / Artokoloro (br); Artgen (fbr). **The Metropolitan Museum of Art:** Gift of André and Clara Mertens, in memory of her mother, Jenny Pulitzer Steiner, 1964 (cb). **243 Alamy Stock Photo:** Active Museum / Active Art (fbl); Historic Images (tl); Peter Horree (cla); Zoonar GmbH / Vitalii Rud (fclb); Jan Fritz (clb); Todd Strand / © 2020 James Rosenquist Foundation / Licensed by Artists Rights Society (ARS), NY and DACS, London. Used by permission. All rights reserved. / © DACS 2024 (bl). **245 Alamy Stock Photo:** Hemis.fr / Garcia Julien (bc). **247 Alamy Stock Photo:** Artokoloro / Penta Springs Limited (tc); Oleksiy Maksymenko Photography (tl); Lebrecht Music & Arts (cla/1); ephotocorp / Perfect Images (cla); Keith Morris (cla/3). **Dorling Kindersley:** Bate Collection /